Italian Folk

CRITICAL STUDIES IN ITALIAN AMERICA

series editors: *Nancy C. Carnevale and Laura E. Ruberto*

This series publishes works on the history and culture of Italian Americans by emerging as well as established scholars in fields such as anthropology, cultural studies, folklore, history, and media studies. While focusing on the United States, it includes comparative studies with other areas of the Italian diaspora. The books in this series will engage with broader questions of identity pertinent to the fields of ethnic studies, gender studies, and migration studies, among others.

Italian Folk

VERNACULAR CULTURE
IN ITALIAN-AMERICAN LIVES

Edited by Joseph Sciorra

FORDHAM UNIVERSITY PRESS   NEW YORK   2011

Lara Pascali's essay, "The Italian Immigrant Basement Kitchen in North America," is a revision of her "Two Stoves, Two Refrigerators, *Due Cucine*: The Italian Immigrant Home with Two Kitchens" in *Gender Place & Culture* 13:6 (2006), pp. 685–95. Reprinted by permission of the publisher (Taylor & Francis Ltd., http://www.informaworld.com). All images in Pascali's essay: Design by numberbox.ca (N. Vairo).

Fordham University Press has no responsibility for the persistence or accuracy of URLs for external or third-party Internet websites referred to in this publication and does not guarantee that any content on such websites is, or will remain, accurate or appropriate.

Fordham University Press also publishes its books in a variety of electronic formats. Some content that appears in print may not be available in electronic books.

Library of Congress Cataloging-in-Publication Data

Italian folk : vernacular culture in Italian-American lives / edited by Joseph Sciorra.
    p.   cm.—(Critical studies in Italian America)
    Includes bibliographical references and index.
    ISBN 978-0-8232-3265-9 (cloth : alk. paper)—ISBN 978-0-8232-3266-6 (pbk. : alk. paper)—
    ISBN 978-0-8232-3267-3 (ebook)
    1. Italian Americans—Folklore.   2. Italian Americans—Social life and customs.   I. Sciorra, Joseph.
  GR111.I73I85   2010
  398.2089510 73—dc22   2010013607

Printed in the United States of America
13 12 11 5 4 3 2 1
First edition

To Felice Ceparano, Gaetano Giacchi, Francesco Pepe, and Mark Pezzano
Community scholars of folklore in Italy and throughout the Italian diaspora

Contents

Acknowledgments

This collection began as a special issue of the social science journal *Italian American Review*, and I would like to thank those at Queens College's John D. Calandra Italian American Institute who helped make that publication a reality at the time: the late Philip Cannistraro, Francisca Viera, Carmine Pizzirusso, David Aliano, and Rosaria Musco.

This current publication would not have been possible without the energizing leadership of the current director of the Calandra Institute, Dean Anthony Julian Tamburri, who has created the ideal conditions of academic rigor, collegiality, and intellectual freedom that helped bring this book to print. Rosangela Briscese, the Institute's coordinator of Academic and Cultural Programs, has provided invaluable support.

I am indebted to a community of artists and scholars working in folklore and Italian American studies who are contributing to an innovative, intellectually engaging, and gracious approach to documenting history and expressive culture. In this regard, I thank the contributors to this publication, as well as Stefano Albertini, B. Amore, Giorgio Bertellini, Nancy Carnevale, Clarrisa Clò, Paul D'Ambrosio, George De Stefano, Giovanna Del Negro, Teresa Fiore, Donna Gabaccia, Fred Gardaphé, John Gennari, Edvige Giunta, Jennifer Guglielmo, Joanna Clapps Herman, Annie Lanzillotto, Gina Miele, Rosina Miller, Jason Pine, Goffredo Plastino, Leonard Norman Primiano, Stephanie Romeo, Laura Ruberto, and Robert Viscusi.

I would be remiss not to acknowledge, if only anonymously, those Italian Americans who routinely undermine a healthy exchange of ideas and a general climate of amity. Their provincial dispositions and obstinate reactions are cautionary examples of how not to operate in the ambit of Italian Americana.

Thanks to Robert Oppedisano, the former director of Fordham University Press, who proclaimed spontaneously at a gathering of colleagues, "What we need is a book on Italian-American folklore" and then shepherded this book in its early stages. I'm grateful to the Press's new director, Fredric Nachbaur, and his assistant, Mary-Lou Peña, as well as managing editor Eric Newman and copy editor Teresa Artman for their help in making this book a reality. I offer a special thanks to the two anonymous reviewers whose close readings of the essays made this book a better one.

And finally I thank Zulma, Akela, and Lucca, with whom I lovingly share my everyday life.

Italian Folk

Listening with an Accent

Joseph Sciorra

Folklore must not be considered an eccentricity, an oddity or a picturesque element, but as something which is very serious and is to be taken seriously.
ANTONIO GRAMSCI, *"OBSERVATIONS ON FOLKLORE"*[1]

Their [the descendants of Italian immigrants] italianità—where it has persisted at all—resides in the humble details of everyday life, not in the glories of any nation or its state.
DONNA GABACCIA, *ITALY'S MANY DIASPORAS*[2]

In March 1985, a parish priest had introduced me to Vincenza after I contacted him about my research on yard shrines and domestic altars among New York City's Italian Americans. As a young "urban folklorist" at the onset of my career and new to the practice of fieldwork—ethnographic research with living people—Vincenza was everything I could have hoped for. A diminutive septuagenarian wearing a floral house dress and slippers graciously greeted me at the door of her finished basement kitchen in Bensonhurst, Brooklyn, where she spent most of her days. At first blush, I couldn't help but view her as "a little, old Italian lady." She was classic, I thought.

Vincenza was the perfect person to interview for my documentation on religious material culture.[3] She had assembled and maintained an altar in her bedroom, complete with embroidered cloth and photographs of her extended family tucked in the crooks of the multiple plaster statues of the Virgin Mary and the saints. She had told me on the telephone that she had "received the grace," a miraculous intervention that had saved her young son's life several decades ago.

It was too good to be true. I felt as if I had hit the jackpot by arranging this interview. I gloated. I knew exactly what to expect.

As I sat at the kitchen table and began setting up my tape recorder, Vincenza shuffled toward me, asking in her pronounced Brooklyn accent, "Do you want some coffee? I made these cookies this morning." Ah, I thought, I know the routine, the cultural script I had learned as a child: Say no to be polite, and then she'll ask again. The norm for this obligatory ritual was an exchange in triplicate: offer-decline, offer-decline, offer-accept. My God, I thought, this is like "Italian-American Folkways 101."

"No, thank you. I'm good," I answered.

And with that, Vincenza turned from me, quietly placing the dish of homemade cookies back on the counter top.

"So, what is it you want to know?" she asked.

I begin this collection of essays on Italian-American folklore with my encounter with Vincenza to draw attention to popular perceptions and representations of vernacular cultural expressions of Italian Americans. Elderly women dressed in black reciting prayers *sotto voce*, men ardently playing on a dirt-packed bocce court, Sunday dinners with cornucopic bowls of spaghetti and meatballs in red sauce, and saint statues festooned with dollar bills and paraded through urban streets are cultural referents resurrected in myriad cinematic renderings and journalistic accounts. These seemingly innocuous representations are emblematic types and scenarios that trigger immediate and ingrained assumptions about people's beliefs, politics, aesthetics, values, and behaviors that leave little room for nuance and elaboration. It was just this set of presuppositions that allowed me to categorize Vincenza as a known type—the little, old Italian lady—whose subjectivity and history I presumed to know. The estrangement of the ethnographic moment disrupted my normative notions, demanding reassessment and engaged listening. This collection offers a similar opportunity to re-examine and re-think what we know about Italian Americans.

Community-based knowledge and vernacular aesthetic practices are a rich source for creativity and meaning in everyday life. People's ability and willingness to create and reproduce certain cultural modes connect them to social entities such as the family, the neighborhood, and the amorphous and fleeting communities that emerge in large-scale festivals and now on the Internet. Creative forms that mark perceived differences based on class, race, gender, sexuality, and so on are some of the most entrenched and powerful expressions of group identity.[4] For example, Catholic devotional processions in heterogeneous urban neighborhoods are deeply felt religious celebrations mapping and reinforcing the physical and psychological boundaries between insider and outsider.[5] Expressive culture—including foodways, music, dance, material culture, architecture, religious practices, and verbal arts—is how people articulate, examine, critique, and reproduce deeply felt values and meanings. These forms emerge from and in dialogue with aspects of lived realty, be it migration, work, leisure time, family dynamics, or other aspects of people's daily lives.

The terms "everyday life," "expressive culture," and, in particular, "folklore" do not constitute bounded and distinct entities (i.e., this is folklore and that is not) but are useful yet problematic tools for interpreting observable behaviors and objects.[6] Consideration of seemingly imperceptible and often dismissed mundane activities offers opportunities for understanding how individuals and groups reproduce and contest identities and ideologies through expressive means. Many folklore and folklife scholars use performance theory to approach everyday expressive culture by locating those aesthetic forms of communication that are stylistically framed as distinct and involving the display and appreciation of competency.[7] Viewed from this perspective, vernacular expressivity can include established artistic genres such as theater, as well the less recognized or less privileged artistry of gesture or body movement. Performance is dynamic and constantly enacted, whether through the repetition of inherited forms or by the introduction of inventive elements.

A deeply felt attention to artistry in everyday life has historically been a discernible element in Italian and Italian-American cultures. Folklorist Alan Lomax observed this attention to and appreciation of artistic competency during his experience recording Italian folk music during the mid-1950s:

> Italians, no matter who they are or how they live, are concerned about aesthetic matters. They may have only a rocky hillside and their bare hands to work with, but on that hillside they will build a house or a whole village whose lines superbly fit its setting. So, too, a community may have a folk tradition confined to just one or two melodies, but there is passionate concern that these be sung in exactly the right way.[8]

This "expression of Italian everyday aesthetics" is most evident in the simple yet common declaration "*Che bello!*" or "How beautiful!" that is used to articulate an appreciation for the most common objects, such as freshly baked bread or a perfectly formed fruit.[9] Author Mario Puzo vividly captures this quintessential trait in a passage from his 1964 novel *The Fortunate Pilgrim*:

> "*Che bella insalata*"—what a beautiful salad—the words rose up to the sleeping children at their moment of awakening. They all sprang out of bed, and Gino looked out the window. Below was the hawker, standing on the seat of his wagon as he held up to the sky and the watching windows a pearly green lettuce in each outstretched hand. "*Che bella insalata*" he said again, not asking anyone to buy, only asking the world to look at beauty. Pride, not cajolement, in his voice, he repeated his cry each time his horse took a mincing step along the Avenue. In his wagon were boxes of onions dazzling white, great brown potatoes, bushels of apples, bouquets of scallions, leeks, and parsley sprigs. His voice rose rich with helpless admiration, disinterested, a call for lovers. "What beautiful salad."[10]

Pellegrino D'Acierno observes that Italians' and Italian Americans' appreciation for and expression of beauty in everyday life are characterized by the aestheticized display of self in social performances. Behavior for Italian Americans is informed by the notion of the spectacle—the "eye-intensive culture of scenes and the theatricalized individual"—that dramatizes aspects of public interaction, from private Sunday dinners to annual religious processions.[11] It is not merely the pleasure of beholding a simple head of lettuce that Puzo conveys, but also the need for a discerning and knowledgeable audience that is part of an enactment of values and aesthetics to be judged by others. Italian Americans have historically scrutinized such social interaction for a performer's ability to enact *una bella figura* (literally, a beautiful figure): that is, an adherence to proper comportment and the aesthetic dimensions of such performance. For Gloria Nardini, *bella figura* is a "central metaphor of Italian life . . . that as a cultural code is deeply embedded as one of the primary arbiters of Italian social mores."[12] Its antithesis is making *una brutta figura* (an ugly figure) that implies a lack of (class-based) refinement as well as a lack of morality.[13] The lack of style and finesse often bears the stigma of being labeled a *gavon* (from *cafone*, for an uncultured peasant, a boor). What constitutes a *gavon* is situational and historically grounded, but the adjudicating sentiment and power is pervasive.[14]

Given the puissant proclivities for an Italianate aesthetic ethics, it becomes particularly revealing to note that vernacular cultural productions of Italian Americans have long been ridiculed, denigrated, and grossly misrepresented. Their religious practices, rites of passage, food, speech, dress, and kinesics have been offered as exemplars of superficiality, prodigality, gaucheness, and kitsch: folklore as bad taste and the butt of jokes. Italian-American cultural practices are imbued by a historic conflict of hegemonic and counter-hegemonic forces at play originally in Italy and subsequently in the United States. The devaluation of folk expressions—vernacular knowledge and aesthetics— was perpetuated by dominant institutions, be it the state, the Catholic Church, political parties, social reformers, labor leaders, or university intellectuals.[15] As a result, Italian Americans are the inheritors of a negated culture (*una cultura negata*) that has produced a history of insecurities and tensions.[16] A diachronic approach to Italian-American expressivity demonstrates that identity is not a unilinear path of assimilation from Italian immigrant to American of Italian descent, but is instead fraught with conflict, negotiation, and creative solutions often involving hybridic cultural forms.

Given this history of disparity, it is no surprise that Italian Americans have had a problematical relationship to their own folklore and expressive culture. Historically, children of immigrant parents jettisoned a host of cultural practices deemed an embarrassment and impediment to what they perceived as modernization, Americanization, and a desired acceptance by the dominant society. Social aspirations and class sentiments continue to fuel an aversion to vernacular cultural production marked as *gauche* or vulgar, activities that ultimately pose a threat to the enterprise of "getting ahead." "Only a *gavon* would put a statue of a saint on the front lawn," is a statement I have heard on more than one occasion from suburban Italian Americans. The work of Barbara Grizzuti Harrison is telling for its explicit disgust with Italian-American folk and vernacular aesthetics. In her Italian travelogue, *Italian Days*, the New York–born author repeatedly references Italian-American cultural expressions as examples of unmitigated repulsiveness, from speech deemed "the Brooklyn *walyo* (vulgar)" pronunciation of a Pugliese dialect that "grates" her ears to "palates that have been corrupted by 'Italian-American' restaurant food," to the colors "rusty red and powdery blue" Italians paint their houses but that "my parents' generation tried to transplant to Newark and Brooklyn, with remarkably unhappy results."[17] In a gratuitous passage, Grizzuti Harrison recounts an object she finds so distasteful that she can only imagine it being the work of an Italian American despite the fact that she is on an island in Lake Maggiore that spans the Italian-Swiss border: "In a window of a shop I see a wooden box covered with lentils sunk in resin. It is so inventive in its ugliness I almost buy it. I have the feeling that the Italian who made this atrocity has been to America. In Little Italys all over America these things, or things of equal ugliness, are sold; what happens to people's aesthetics when they are uprooted?"[18] As she informs the reader in a later passage, Staten Island is where "ugly" Italians have been sent, banished from the true land of beauty and grace that is Grizzuti Harrison's imagined Italy.[19]

This intragroup repulsion and attraction illustrate the dialectic between vernacular and elite/institutional expressions as they have historically manifested themselves as tensions involving, on the one hand, the policing of Italian-American culture, in the forms of condemnation, reform, and co-optation; and, on the other hand, acquiescence, compliance, and also resistance. During the first half of the twentieth century, Italian-American radicals on the left ardently condemned Italian immigrants' public expressions of Catholic practice, while Italian-American adherents of Mussolini's Fascist government supported folk dance troupes and embroidery workshops for ideological motives. Representatives of mainstream culture and elite Italian Americans have historically devalued and dismissed the aesthetic creations and religious practices of working-class and lower-middle-class Italian Americans, characterizing them as lowbrow.[20] Ultimately, issues of power and representation are critical to understanding Italian-American expressive culture and identity.

Inquiries into the aesthetics of everyday Italian-American life prompt examination of elite notions of culture, how such ideas are reproduced and by which segments of the population, and under what social conditions they become prevalent.[21] Studies of the folklore of the *prominenti* (ethnic leaders) include Elizabeth Mathias' work on former *contadini* (peasants) living in south Philadelphia who borrowed prestigious funerary practices of *i signori* (the landowners) remembered from Italy in their attempts at social competition in America.[22] The historian Philip Cannistraro's examination of the self-serving association the *prominenti* had with Fascism during the 1920s and 1930s and their preferred performance modes of self-congratulatory award ceremonies, banquets, dinners, and receptions is a fruitful suggestion for further analysis.[23] Such a research project would call for Gramscian lines of inquiry into hegemonic discourse and cultural production: How are positions of power established and institutionalized? How are collective histories created and reproduced? How is group identity constructed as normative, traditionalized, and disseminated? What are the aesthetic components and cultural codes by which such identities and relationships are enacted? And how has the transnational flow of *italianità*, especially in its historical center–periphery trajectory with the nation state dispatching prized items to its "spontaneous colonies" abroad, influenced local Italian-American cultural practices?[24]

Since the "white ethnic revival" of the 1970s, Italian Americans increasingly invoke "tradition" (often in tandem with or in exchange for the terms "heritage" and "culture") in an attempt to reinterpret and (re)define what constitutes the group. Familial allegiance, hard work, and Catholic upbringing are touted in laudatory tones and celebratory prose as essentialist attributes of a bounded and homogenous group and framed as positive, core "values" in the establishment of a mainstream, middle-class identity coupled with overwhelmingly conservative politics. Mainly in opposition to the above forms of self-identification, other Italian Americans are turning to aspects of abandoned folk culture once practiced by their ancestors in a politically liberal project of cultural reclamation and religious revitalization. Interest in the *malocchio* (evil eye), the ritual music of *tarantismo* (tarantism), and images of the *Madonna Nera* (Black Madonna) is part of an ethnic revival predicated upon establishing legitimacy for the Italian-American presence within American multicultural discourse, with particularly feminist and environmentalist emphasis.[25] Together, these two seemingly dichotomous sets of examples illustrate that tradition is not a series of circumscribed elements, but instead "a process of interpretation, attributing meaning in the present through making reference to the past," and, as such, illustrates how folklore is evoked in the continuous process of identity re-evaluation and reformation.[26]

Regarding group identity, Italian nationals have a particularly troubled relationship to Italian-American expressive culture. D'Acierno notes, "Italian Americans stand to Italians as degraded copies, as simulacra that are poor imitations of the real thing."[27] It is not uncommon to hear Italian nationals working in New York City distinguish themselves from Italian Americans with the self-referential phrase "real Italians," as they critique Italian-American food, language, music, and so on. Just as Italian Americans measured their social and economic progress after World War II by comparing themselves with relatives living in Italy, so do current Italians gauge their own modernity by looking at Italian Americans. "They don't even do that in southern Italy anymore!" one aghast Italian assured me concerning the ongoing practice of pinning monetary donations to ribbons attached to statues of Catholic saints processed in various American cities and suburbs. Conversely, some Italians objectify Italian-American culture as a touchstone for authenticity linking them to a vanished Italian past, as did the twenty-something Italian (whom I have chosen not to identify) photographing Italian-American religious processions in Brooklyn who confided to me in 2007, "You don't see this anymore in Italy. I'm happy young people here are keeping the tradition alive for us, so it doesn't get lost." From this perspective, Italian Americans function for Italian nationals as religious and cultural surrogates of Italian folk tradition, displaced yet maintained in a living museum in the United States.

Italian Americans have also been participants in the development of emergent and new forms of folk arts and cultural practices. Tattoos, subway graffiti, rap music, and Christmas house displays are just some of the community-based, nonstudio-trained art forms that Italian Americans, at least on the East Coast, have contributed to in the second half of the twentieth century.[28] These community art forms are not coded as "Italian" per se (although journalists often point out the strong Italian-American presence in seasonal lighting in New York City), but instead speak to the ways in which an individual can ascribe to a multiplicity of identities. They are the result of cultural mixing, the hybrid products that constitute the great American minestrone. Italian-American culture is not a static museum piece but dynamic and open to transformation. This adaptive expression of ethnicity is exemplified by "Guido" youth culture, in which young Italian Americans in the northeast rely not on traditional Italian cultural elements to reproduce ethnic identity, but instead on commercial products (clothing, automobiles, and so on) and leisure activities (body-building, clubbing, and so on) that are re-signified in the performance of style.[29] In the end, the changing nature of Italian-American culture and identity reflects the elastic and highly porous boundaries that separate "us" and "them."

Folklorists maintain that ethnographic methods (participant observation and interviews) are critical for understanding aesthetic practices in everyday life.[30] It is through a sustained interaction with various individuals that we move toward a deeper understanding of how behaviors and objects are learned, conceptualized, implemented, and interpreted. The deterritorialized and virtual nature of current life increasingly makes traditional ethnographic methods a challenge at times. The hyperkinetic flow between the local and the global world engenders cultural forms with complex relations and associations, as when mediated images become the fodder for everyday expressivity. For example, many young Italian-American rappers base their musical personas and repertoires on the figure of the gangster. This artistic choice is not a simple relationship of artists emulating real-life *mafiosi* but is instead a mimetic house of mirrors in which Italian-American rappers are responding to African-American rappers imitating Italian-American actors playing the role of real-life mobsters.[31] Ultimately, listening is key to any ethnographic endeavor. In her study of Italian-American women authors, Edvige Giunta calls attention to what she terms "writing with an accent." "I use the word 'accent' to refer to a series of elements—narrative, thematic, and linguistic—that, collectively, articulate the experience of living between cultures."[32] In keeping with Giunta's conceptualization, I propose listening with an accent as a means for understanding the variety of Italian-American vernacular expressivity.

This collection grew out of a special issue of the *Italian American Review* devoted to Italian-American folklore that I guest-edited. The issue had a small run (300 copies) and is now out of print. This new publication includes five revised essays from that publication, one revised article from another journal, and five new essays. The scholars featured in this book work in different but related disciplines, including folklore, anthropology, cultural geography, history, ethnomusicology, and art history, all of whom add to a growing body of literature on Italian-American folklore.[33] The essays explore historical and contemporary subjects in locales from New York to California as well as communities and activities that are national and transnational in scope. Although not all contributions follow a strict ethnographic methodology, all rely upon local knowledge as a way of better understanding their subjects. Historical research of popular practices from the great wave of Italian immigration during the late nineteenth and early twentieth centuries is enhanced by the use of primary sources (diaries, memoirs, and recorded interviews) and oral histories. I have organized the book to highlight the interconnected themes of the individual essays so that the reader moves from food-ways to material culture to cultural landscapes to explicit art forms to large-scale ceremonial events to religious belief.

Food is the quintessential Italian-American folk subject. In his essay on Sunday family dinners in New York's East Harlem neighborhood, historian Simone Cinotto looks at how food became an arena for compromise between immigrant parents and their American-raised children. What we have come to know as a "traditional" event was not transported wholesale from Italian *paesi* (hometowns) but was, according to Cinotto, a negotiated settlement between generations in response to the changing socio-economic conditions of urban America. Outside forces involved not only the hegemonic social order of the American elite—in the guise of dietary reformers and health workers—but also Italian Americans' African-American and Puerto Rican neighbors in Harlem. Food became one of the ways by which Italian Americans created a collective identity that distinguished them from people marked as socially inferior even to Italian Americans by the dominant culture.

The dynamics of food and family are at the heart of John Cicala's investigation of a single meal prepared and consumed in a Detroit home in 1993. This in-depth study looks at the author's grandmother, Leonarda Cicala, as she prepares and serves the

Sicilian dish of *cuscuszu* in a specific ceremonial Sunday meal. Relying upon interviews and participant observation, Cicala reveals how biography and family history shape not only how food is prepared and eaten, but also conceptualized. This intimate essay moves us beyond the nostalgic trope of grandma's homey Sunday dinner and into the realm of real life.

The setting for food preparation and consumption is the subject of Lara Pascali's essay about the two-kitchen homes of Italian immigrants in the United States and Canada. Her essay is a significant contribution to vernacular architecture studies as it shows the creative ways in which home owners modified and adapted extant buildings to meet their cultural needs. Upstairs and downstairs kitchens are distinct realms serving different functions, with the former a marker of socioeconomic status and the latter as the center of everyday life. Offering alternative understandings to popular depictions of the Italian-American home, Pascali eloquently shows that the pristine upstairs cannot be reduced to the effectuations of the *nouveau riche* but can be understood as a "dream space" for events that may never happen. The basement kitchen, far from being a cloistered backwater of provincialism, is perceived by its female users as a vehicle for domestic liberation.

Literary scholar Kenneth Scambray's article looks at working class cultural expressions in the forms of two California vernacular environments: Baldassare Forestiere's Underground Gardens and Simon Rodia's Watts Towers. These two Southern Italian immigrant men single-handedly created site-specific wonders that were based upon their own aesthetic visions and architectural ingenuity. The author examines how memories of Italian cultural landscapes, building skills acquired in the United States, and the California environment itself contributed to the builders' monumental undertakings: one an underground abode, and the other a series of decorated spires. These gargantuan architectural works—one burrowing deep, and the other soaring skyward—are testaments to immigrant imagination, skill, and style that served as both elucidation of and resolution to cultural dislocation.

In contemporary New York, homeowners living in former Italian-American neighborhoods are the fortunate beneficiaries of heritage harvests, plucking figs from trees planted in backyard gardens by Italian immigrants decades ago. But what of the everyday gardens of today's Italian Americans? Joseph Inguanti maps the landscapes of residential gardeners in New York City and the larger metropolitan area. His approach is that of an art historian who examines the formal attributes and specific plantings of small, urban front yards and larger suburban plots. Symmetrical design, tidiness, and preponderance of hardscape and planters are some of the characteristics of what Inguanti calls "landscapes of order" of New York City domestic gardens. In the suburbs, where post–World War II Italian immigrants cultivate gardens in adherence to the American conventions regarding distinct planting realms (ornamental plants in the front yard and food crops in the backyard), they do so using horticultural skills learned in their respective Italian *paesi* to create "landscapes of memory."

Memory and place are central to the Sicilian language poetry of Vincenzo Ancona (1915–2000), who emigrated with his family from western Sicily to Brooklyn in 1956. As a *contadino* and fisherman, Ancona was schooled in the oral poetry tradition of his hometown. As an immigrant laborer, he composed poems to address and appease his nostalgic yearning for the cultural landscape of his *paese* and to eventually formulate a diasporic critique of the economic conditions that caused his departure. Ancona's verse, declaimed in formal and informal settings, was instrumental in giving voice to a collective memory for his Sicilian-American community. As a folklorist, my approach in this article is to situate the individual artist within the larger social world of cohorts in which he operated and thrived.

Immigrants not only brought various art forms with them from Italy, but they also created new styles in the United States. Ethnomusicologist Marion Jacobson's article looks at the artistic and commercial ventures of northern-Italian musicians who developed the new genre of accordion music known as *Valtaro musette*. Italian-American composers and musicians, such as brothers Guido and Pietro Deiro, Charles Magnante, and others were instrumental in raising the piano accordion to new levels of sophistication and national prominence. Jacobson reveals how John Brugnoli, Peter DelGrosso, Peter Spagnoli, and other musicians and entrepreneurs working in Manhattan nightclubs brought together a variety of musical styles and repertoires to create a specifically northern-Italian musical tradition in the period between the 1930s and the 1950s. Her musical analysis shows how style and sound have come to be associated with an Italian-American identity marked as distinctly "Northern Italian" that continues to be cultivated by performers in contemporary "ethnic feasts."

The public realm is a powerful staging ground for developing and exhibiting performance modes that articulate a seeming consensus about group identity. Religious *feste* (street feasts) and political parades are ambulatory narratives that community members recount about themselves, for themselves, and for others. Folklorist Joan Saverino writes about two events—the Columbus Day Parade and the "Italian Days" Festival—in Reading, Pennsylvania, during the 1920s and 1930s. Saverino's chapter provides a closer look at how the *prominenti* crafted public festivals in their attempt to serve as cultural brokers between working-class Italians and American elites, and to dictate how "Italian-American" culture and identity would be represented. She poignantly illustrates how Fascist ideology and Italian nationalism informed public display events among Italian Americans during that time.

The behind-the-scenes preparation for the large scale *festa* in honor of St. Gerard in Newark, New Jersey is perceptively unveiled in anthropologist Peter Savastano's contribution to the collection. Each year, a select group of devotees of the eighteenth-century Italian saint prepare the statue for its journey from the interior of St. Lucy's Church and through the city streets. The exclusive ritual of cleaning and dressing the statue is part of the larger process in which the inanimate object is spiritually activated and the intimate relationship with the saint is dramatically engaged. Some of the statue's handlers are gay; consequently, they provide alternative exegesis of hagiography and the cult of the saints that provides a congenial rereading of their place within Roman Catholicism.

Luisa Del Giudice provides a highly personal account of retrieval in her exploration of family memory, religious belief, and identity. She examines the circumstances surrounding the death of her brother-in-law Giuseppe Poldi in Italy to discover the cultural and religious forces at work in her family's history. Del Giudice, an Italian-Canadian folklorist living in Los Angeles who maintains intimate ties with her immigrant parents' hometown in the Lazio region, embarks on an "ethnographic voyage" that ultimately challenges the literary conventions of memoir and ethnography.

The revival of folk culture from the past is a historically situated attempt to infuse new meanings to older cultural forms at the service of contemporary priorities and perspectives. Folklorist Sabina Magliocco explores how Italian Americans have adapted past practices in recent years, specifically those surrounding *stregheria* (witchcraft). Magliocco first outlines how Italian immigrants' religious belief—a syncretism of sanctioned Catholic doctrine and popular magical practices—was stigmatized by both the dominant American society and class-conscious Italian Americans. She then goes on to describe and analyze Italian Americans' recent revival of *stregheria* and their claims of an uninterrupted tradition. Magliocco sees this revival as a reformulation of an ethnic political strategy and ultimately Italian-American identity.

These chapters deepen our understanding of the imaginative choices and artfulness that Italian Americans have brought to bear on their lives and American society. The authors' perspicacious and sensitive approaches demonstrate that listening with an accent offers prolific opportunities for understanding and appreciating the aesthetics and dynamics of everyday life.

"Sunday Dinner? You Had to Be There!"

THE SOCIAL SIGNIFICANCE OF FOOD IN ITALIAN HARLEM, 1920–40

Simone Cinotto

Many immigration historians have emphasized that the family has been socially and psychologically central to the Italian-American experience. Accordingly, different scholars and observers pointed out that the relevance of food habits and food rituals in Italian-American culture is related to a strong family *ethos*. The private ideal of a rich family life, symbolically represented by the familial consumption of food, is portrayed as lying at the core of the Italian-American ethnicity in scholarly works; Italian-American narratives; oral histories; community cookbooks; and popular culture, such as film and advertising. Scholars have traditionally interpreted the intimate connection between food and family culture, and the consequent comparably high persistence of distinctive food habits among Italian Americans, as a legacy of the traditional Southern Italian peasant culture that endured in America because it was successfully passed to the younger generations. In his classic study of an Italian-American working-class community in Boston, Herbert Gans noted that

> Generally speaking, the Italian and Sicilian cultures that the immigrants brought with them to America have not been maintained by the second generation. A number of Italian patterns, however, have survived, the most visible ones being food habits. The durability of the ethnic tradition with respect to food is probably due to the close connection of food with family and group life.[1]

Richard Gambino's *Blood of My Blood*, probably the most widely quoted catalog of the Italian-American ethnicity, the peculiar relationship between family life and traditional food is stressed at length as a major feature of Italian-American culture and likewise interpreted as a "transplanted" cultural trait.[2]

This chapter offers a different opinion: It suggests that the important role of food in family life and ethnic identity for different generations of Italian Americans is the result of a process that took place in modern America. The case study is that of the Italian-American community of East Harlem, New York, in the 1920s and 1930s, and it shows that the relevance of food habits resulted in a two-way interaction between the family and the changing socioeconomic context. The Italian-American family of the interwar years emerged, therefore, not as a place where a minority could preserve its ethnic traditions against, or in spite of, social workers, nutrition experts, and the lures of mass consumption; but, rather as a place where ethnic traditions have been created, drawing *selectively* upon and recasting old values and cultural features as a result of new economic and social pressures and needs. The notion of the family as an independent transmitter of ethnic traditions is further challenged by the fact that the family of Italian Harlem, as a producer of ideology and traditions, was conditioned by the interdependence of the Italian-American community with neighboring ethnic groups over time and developing ideas about race and morality.

The meaning of food culture in the Italian-American family cannot be separated from the Americanization of immigrants and their children: their political, social, and cultural integration into the host society. Food and food rituals played a leading role in the construction of a particular family ideology that functioned as the moral foundation upon which many Italian Americans structured a large part of their ethnic experience and identity. The idealized importance of the family—with its supposed devotion, solidarity, responsibility, and work ethic, but also with its suspicion of and impermeability to the outside world—not only influenced the private organization of generational and gender relations, roles, and identities but affected also the way in which the immigrant community negotiated its place as Italian Americans in the public realm.

As Italian immigrants of Harlem and their children developed their particular brands of Americanization, family ideology, ethnic identity, and food culture, they made use of and ultimately internalized a peculiar version of middle-class "American" concepts and values such as home, domesticity, respectability, privacy, and secrecy. They reexamined and redefined the boundaries between the public and the private in their lives because these concepts and values were often of little or no meaning in the rural, small-town societies that most immigrants came from. While building a family ideology—which became, in turn, a producer of an Italian-American ethnicity—Italian Americans of East Harlem abandoned the community primacy that in the old *paese* (hometown) partly blurred individual and family into the community to embrace the notion of the family as a distinct cell of social life: a notion characteristic of late-nineteenth-and early-twentieth-century's middle-class culture. The Italian-American domesticity that many contemporary observers saw as traditional was, in fact, largely an American invention and an important feature of Americanness.[3]

This chapter discusses the way in which food came to be a symbol of both domesticity and ethnicity for Italian Americans in East Harlem and stresses four issues in particular: first, the generational conflict over the continuity of distinctive food habits, largely caused by the influence of a public discourse linking immigrant food to sociocultural inferiority; second, the use of collective rituals centered on food consumption as spaces where a group ideology was produced; third, the symbolic and ideological use of food in the strategies immigrants adopted to socialize their children; and fourth, the symbolic and ideological use of food habits as a means of racial and ethnic differentiation and assertion of the American citizenship of the group.

Family Conflicts and Food Conflicts in Italian Harlem, circa 1919–29

Throughout the twentieth century, East Harlem (the northeastern section of Manhattan) received the most recent waves of immigrants, who replaced older ones, who in turn moved to better neighborhoods. In the first two decades of the century, the mass influx of Jews and Italians displaced the established Irish and German-American communities. At that time, Italians, who were mostly illiterate, unskilled laborers from southern Italy, were the most economically deprived and socially despised group of East Harlem. During the 1920s, Jews and other European ethnics began to leave the neighborhood in significant numbers, slowly replaced by poor migrants from Puerto Rico and the American South. By the 1930s, the 80,000 Italian Americans living in the area finally reached a position of relative political dominance over the neighborhood and were replaced at the bottom of the social ladder by Puerto Ricans and African Americans. The new relative security contrasted, however, with the poor conditions of the neighborhood, as younger and better-off Italian-American families left East Harlem in search of better housing and safer streets. By the late 1950s, the whole of East Harlem had eventually turned into Spanish Harlem.[4]

In the years after World War I, important social changes occurred also within the Italian enclave. An opportunity to understand the daily life and the culture of the people of Italian Harlem in that period of its history is provided by the interviews and life histories collected among immigrants and their children by Leonard Covello, a high school principal, public leader, and observer of the community. Born in Avigliano, Basilicata, in 1887, Covello arrived in New York in 1896 and lived in East Harlem almost uninterruptedly since. An immigrant himself, Covello experienced all the anxieties and contradictions of second-generation Italian Americans of East Harlem. This twofold experience had a deep impact on his subjectivity, life-long public commitment, and scholarly work. His early intellectual formation was affected by the Progressive Protestant thinking of Anna Ruddy, the founder of Harlem House, one of the first settlement houses in uptown Manhattan. Ruddy's help was also instrumental in providing Covello with a grant that allowed him to enroll at Columbia University, from which he was graduated in 1911. As a teacher, he devoted himself to help overcoming the low levels of educational success among Italian-American students. In 1934, he was appointed principal of the recently established Benjamin Franklin High School in Italian Harlem. His mission became that of transforming this school into a "community centered school," as he labeled it, which helped solving the many problems of a poor, heavily immigrant community. For Covello, this aim was to be accomplished through multicultural education; the participation of parents, associations, and public leaders in the life of the school; and the involvement of students and teachers in the life of the community. In 1944, Covello received his Ph.D. from New York University with a dissertation that dealt with the impact of the parental Italian culture on the school education of immigrants' children. Most of the sources utilized in this chapter are oral histories that Covello gathered from the immigrants and their children for his dissertation.[5] Covello's pioneering ethnographic effort adds much to the value of his work because it lets the voices of immigrants be heard in a time when they rarely were.

In the 1920s, as the immigration flow came to an end, the immigrants' bonds with Italy became weaker, and the American-born became numerically predominant. It was at this critical time that immigrant parents of Italian Harlem manifested an increasing distress about their family life, harshly criticizing what they called the "lack of respect" and the "departure from tradition" of their children, which they blamed upon the evil influence of Americanization. As Covello's interviews show, generational conflicts erupted—sometimes violently—on matters such as the destination of children's pay-checks, children's occupational and educational choices, the selection of spouses, the girls' demands to go out unsupervised, and so on. As a matter of fact, second-generation Italian Americans were likely to be attracted by values and lifestyles of urban America, or rather to be influenced by a class- and ethnically filtered version of the emerging youth subculture of the time.[6] As a result of the widespread stigma of inferiority attached to their parents' culture, many thought that they could become Americans—meaning, with that to achieve a new identity and belong to the larger white society defined by the official and popular culture[7]—only by discarding everything "Italian" in them. Covello noted that many Italian Harlem youths reasoned:

> The native-born Americans are American because they speak English; the foreign-born can only become good Americans by forgetting everything their parents brought along with them: language, habits, culture, dress, festivals, song, dance and even food.[8]

Food habits, in particular, were not spared by the second-generation's rejection of parental material culture. It has been pointed out that food is a powerful means for building and reinforcing ethnic bonds and identities because it is a cultural code learned in early years, like language, which leaves indelible marks on one's subjectivity and identity. But food culture can be interpreted in the opposite sense: Being a strong marker of difference, a food pattern may be promptly rejected in the presence of a minority's desire for conformity and integration. The writer Helen Barolini remembers her childhood in Syracuse, New York:

> Once in a while my mother would have me accompany her to get cheese in an import store which I hated to enter because of the smells—smells that were Italian and which intensified my own determination not to be. I hated the fish store because of the revolting un-American eels and squid that were displayed there. I even hated Josie's pastry shop because Josie, who made all those foreign-looking cookies, was fat and foreign looking herself, with black circles under her eyes—not at all the image of life I was seeing each Saturday afternoon at the movies.[9]

As will become clear in examining the narratives of immigrants and their children, the public world from which "American" messages reached the immigrant community and threatened the immigrant culture consisted of three main areas: the mass media, like film in Barolini's example; the youth culture of the peer group although the latter should more precisely be considered as straddling the public and the private, as a group whose accesses were relatively permeable; and the school. In Italian Harlem, school was an important agent for the development of critical attitudes among second-genera-tion Italian Americans. School provided the public arena in which immigrants' children were for the first time exposed to and confronted with cultural and class differences and hierarchies. At school, the sense of inferiority, the feelings of young Italian American children of fear and fascination toward the largely unknown outer "American" world were often expressed in the idiom of food. "Lunch at elementary school was a difficult problem for me," remembered one of Covello's students:

> To have a bite I either stole some money from home or took it from my shoe shining on Saturdays and Sundays. With this money I would buy the same stuff that non-Italian boys were eating. To be sure, my mother gave me each day an Italian sandwich, that is half a loaf of bread filled with fried peppers and onions, or with one half dipped into oil and some minced garlic on it. Such a sandwich would certainly ruin my reputation; I could not take it to school. My God, what a problem it was to dispose of it, for I was taught never to throw away bread.[10]

The prevalent dislike for day-to-day immigrant culture made this boy struggle to control his privacy as information and knowledge. Shamefully hiding and throwing away his sandwich, the boy defined and defended his privacy as the realm of the secret and the unknown. In the whole experience of second-generation Italian Americans in East Harlem, the conflict between the public and the private and the adjustment to the conflict through secrecy were recurring and important features.

The school's agenda labeled the diversity of ethnic food habits as un-American. Indeed, in the 1910s and the 1920s, reforming immigrant children's diet was by no means a secondary concern of New York schools. Nutrition and cooking classes were functional to an educational project aimed at assimilating and making loyal Americans out of a school population comprising more than 50 percent Southern and Eastern European immigrant children.[11] As New York's school historian Diane Ravitch put it, the basic assignments of the public school in the effort of Americanizing the children of the new immigration were "teaching them how to speak English; inspecting their heads for lice; lecturing them on cleanliness and hygiene; teaching them to salute the flag, to recite the Pledge of Allegiance, to sing the national anthem, and to revere American heroes," and each single part was functional to the whole task.[12] Teachers in East Harlem schools were mostly lower middle-class, second- and third-generation Irish and German Americans, and were often highly unsympathetic toward their difficult Italian-American pupils. The Italian-American student would hear daily criticism directed at his family habits, but which ultimately emphasized his own diversity, his own nonbelonging. In the classroom,

> . . . his father, whom . . . he has regarded as omnipotent and ideally self-reliant, is pointed out unfavorably for his speech, his dress, his wine drinking, and perhaps his wine making. His mother—for her methods of keeping house, her feeding of her children, and for the clothing she provides them. . . . The usual meals likewise, are preached against, since the breakfast is seldom likely to be exactly recommended by the pink faced cherub of the cereal advertisements. Hot cereals are a nuisance to prepare, while the beverage of the breakfast remains . . . coffee, for both young and old. As a substitute for the "balanced" hot lunch which is strongly recommended to him in the class, the boy brings instead a sandwich of Gargantuan proportions.[13]

Most second-generation Italian-American students were ready to accept the ideal connection between food habits and citizenship, as typical of the mainstream public discourse that they were fascinated by and that they were eager to identify with. When idealized American dietary imperatives were introduced into the domestic area, Italian-American students often faced their parents' lack of understanding or hostility. A student told Covello:

> At elementary school I was thrilled with everything that was taught about America: its history, geography, and what it stands for. It was very pleasant to hear about it. But when I came home in the afternoon, I felt a painful contrast between what I saw at home and what had been taught during the day. The teacher had say [sic], for instance, that clean hands, clean clothing, and a toothbrush are essentials. And that plenty of milk should be taken in the morning. I felt so ashamed, so inferior, when I realized that my parents do not exemplify such things at home. . . . My mother showed opposition to the teacher's recommendation about food. She began ridiculing all my teachers for their ideas, and this made me very sad, for she ruined my dreams of becoming a real American. I felt that I needed milk in the morning more than anything else. But my mother, and so my father, insisted that this was not according to the good customs; that American milk was poison. "These teachers of yours are driving us crazy," they told me.[14]

The resistance of Italian immigrants in Harlem can only partially be explained by their difficult relationship with American schools, extensively discussed by Covello and other scholars after him. There is no doubt that the diet of Italian immigrants changed considerably soon after their arrival in America. Their diet was affected by different market conditions, and the various regional and local patterns melded into many hybridizations and exchanges. Foods in Italy that were consumed on a regular basis only by the upper classes were frequently accessible in the United States also to the poorer families, so that a food historian could define the immigrants' dietary experience as a "carnival come true."[15] There simply was no such thing as a traditional Italian cuisine. Still, Southern Italian immigrants retained distinctive food habits. They brought with them a set of beliefs regarding foodstuffs and their relationship to health, which they thought was worthy of being transmitted to their children as part of their own experience. As the sociology of food has illustrated, the parental control over the children's diet is closely related to their control over the whole development, both subjective and physical, of the young person. For many mothers, in particular, regulating the children's diet means fully assuming the maternal function.[16] It is understandable that Italian immigrant parents in Harlem interpreted the publicizing of food, an area traditionally managed by the family, as a critical factor to be resolutely opposed. An immigrant mother clearly expressed such an adversary feeling when she unexpectedly showed up at school and confronted the teacher:

> I came to find out—she said—whether Tony eats his sandwich I give him each morning or whether he throws it away. You people in school have no interest in that. You will probably tell him that he does not have to listen to his mother. You have different customs here; and if I let Tony do as you tell him, I cannot control him.[17]

For immigrants, meals were important narrative spaces of verbal and symbolic communication with their children, which they used to emphasize and reinforce the role of the father as breadwinner and the mother as breadgiver. Immigrant parents struggled, therefore, to make their children participate in the daily meals. They used to call their children *Americani* to signify their opinion that the American-born generation lacked deference of parental authority and respect for "family values."[18] Immigrants also used the word *mangiacake*—cake-eaters—to reproach younger people about eating fast food in the streets, a common practice in contrast with the formal family meal and symbolically rebellious against familial demands.[19] For an eighteen-year-old girl, the sense of liberation after the death of her tyrannical father had the taste of the forbidden food. "Never shall I forget," she told Covello, "the enjoyment derived from the ambrosian taste of pancakes eaten at 2 A.M. and flavored with strange excitement and dare-devilness."[20]

The family dinner was frequently the stage where generational conflict was dramatized in a sort of theatrical *mise-en-scène* of the cleavages in the immigrant family caused by the pressures of the larger society. In New York, first compulsory school education and then wage-work separated both boys and girls from the household, which in Southern Italian rural society had once been a space of production, consumption, and socialization. Wage-work outside the home allowed daughters and sons to gain some independence because they could sometimes have access to better jobs than their parents had. After a few years in America, children came often to act as interpreters of American life to non–English-speaking parents, thus upsetting the hierarchies based on age and status.

The troubled transition of the Italian-American family of East Harlem was symbolically represented during meals. Social workers were shocked by the potential conflict they observed at the table of Italian-American households. "A family of Italian children seldom eats its meals in peace," noted one of them. "Someone is nagging, scolding, or, in their phraseology, someone is 'yelling' at them all the time."[21] One of Covello's witnesses recollected how her father's demonstration of authority over the family during meals was becoming increasingly symbolic and fictional over the years.

> [In the beginning] The supper table was fraught with ceremonious forms. The father
> would sit at the head of the table to the left of his wife. All the children sat around quietly
> and waited until served. No one made a grab for the food. Each child was served
> individually according to age. Only Italian could be used at the table and conversation
> had to be sparing and confined to the limits of necessity. The father acted as
> disciplinarian. [But,] Later when many of the children grew up, it was difficult for the
> parents to stop the use of English at the table. The children became more voluble and
> Yiddish, which was learned in the factories, developed into a useful tool to avoid the
> parent's knowledge of their social plans and activities. After a time Francesco [the father]
> stopped trying to insist upon quiet or the exclusive use of Italian at the supper table.[22]

As the evidence suggests, in the interaction between the public and private realms, the public called for a significant transformation of private life, affecting habits, language, symbolic communication forms, and authority structures. Daily, immigrant family life was significantly reshaped by domestic reverberations of social changes.

The New Parental Strategies of Socialization and the Food Rituals of the Italian-American Family, circa 1930–40

The crisis of the family meals as rituals and symbols of the traditional family structure was but one evidence of the breakdown of arbitrary patriarchal authority in the new American context. In Harlem, many Italian-immigrant parents became increasingly aware that imitative behavior and coercive discipline could no longer control and socialize their children. Historian Michael J. Eula has argued that between the 1920s and 1930s, Italian immigrants began to adopt new, more indirect strategies of control of their children's lives.[23] Immigrants stopped insisting on habits that were not viable in urban and industrial life, and seemingly refrained from interfering in the many new ways that their children had adopted at this time. Interviews made in Italian Harlem in the late 1930s show, for example, that 87 percent of immigrant parents declared that they would allow their children to choose their future spouses. According to the interviews, even girls were given an amount of freedom that was unheard-of a few years before.[24]

But, while youth were apparently granted a much greater autonomy, they were also called upon by the older generation to show their allegiance to the family through ritual and symbolic actions. In particular, they were requested to take part in the numerous gatherings that brought together families of close and distant relatives. The transition to home rituals that allowed for more independence in public is exemplified by the interview of a second-generation Italian-American adolescent. The young man told Covello that his family, which had immigrated from Sicily in 1924, showed a deep behavioral breakdown along generational lines, together with the emergence of a more democratic, companionate family pattern, after a few years in East Harlem. "All the social activities of the parents are pretty well confined to visits to relatives, Italian movies, Italian plays, and friends. The children prefer the American movies, the American newspapers, American dance steps, sports, and other activities."[25] Parents spoke mostly their Sicilian dialect, while children spoke only English. Both boys and girls enjoyed an increasing degree of freedom outside the home. After many fights, the use of make-up was eventually tolerated, and girls were allowed to go out with youth groups of both sexes. When Italian-American children were with their friends in the streets and at school, they enjoyed "American" food. At home,

> the children tend to break away from most of Italian patterns, except the foods. When the children were younger, the father was the supreme head of the family and his wishes were considered first. Now, there is no noticeable head of the family. Each member is fairly independent in many ways, and is not obliged to keep any of the rituals that are kept by the family, *except being present at the family gatherings*.[26] (Emphasis mine)

which amounted to a fundamental part of a new "generational contract."

Immigrants reacted to the crisis of a coherent community behavior among the American-born by themselves adopting a deeper separation between the public and the private. In historical circumstances that made the direct control of immigrant parents over the public behavior of their children impossible, the older generation granted the new one a much greater autonomy in the "American" public world. Immigrants actually had to grant that space of freedom in order to continue to control their children's behavior by subtler means. In the meantime, immigrants built a private arena of in-vented traditionalism within which, in exchange, they required coherent "Italian" be-havior of younger family members. Eventually, the internalization of the boundary between the public and the private, which was basically an "American" middle-class feature, went hand-in-hand with the invention of an ethnically branded domestic sphere, with its rituals and values, to answer to many of the dilemmas and generational conflicts produced by the influence of modern "American" values on Italian-American family and community life. Even the pattern of an emerging Italian-American domestic-ity, which involved extended families and kin networks, needs not be considered as in contrast with the appropriation of "American" middle-class values and behaviors by the immigrants because middle-class domesticity, with all its emphasis on the nuclear family, was often based upon larger and manifold family organizations. The assump-tion of a clear distinction between the public and the private, even though accom-plished in different ways and for different purposes, was a key step in Americanization (and ethnicization) for both immigrants and their children.

Amidst crisis and change, immigrants became convinced that they could control and shape their children's behavior and allegiance by means of ideological indoctrina-tion—to be performed during collective rituals—rather than by counterproductive forms of coercion. As a consequence, food and food rituals were mobilized by immi-grant parents as a major productive force in the ideological construction of the "Italian family," with its stress on continuity; suspicion of the new, strong gender roles; dedica-tion to hard work; appreciation of private ideals of happiness; responsibility for the common good; and renunciation to individual inclinations to meet group expectations. The convivial consumption of food, for which Italians in New York spent a budget share that vastly surpassed that of any other ethnic group,[27] was ultimately a strategy of investment in family and community ties, aimed at maintaining group solidarity as well as delaying the uncontrolled embrace of middle-class values on the part of its members, even when their income and social status rose. The ideology of the family was functional and related to a developing urban working-class culture that would prepare individuals to the proletarian life that most of them were bound to live. Con-vincing though the narrative was, it could however be unsuccessful if it were not grounded in the fact that family ties remained critical to survival for members of the urban working classes, as was even more evident during the Depression years. The ceremonies through which each individual was socialized into the group culture were centered on the ritual consumption of food. It was through the intergenerational negoti-ation that the "Italian" food, which the American-born generations had earlier rejected as a marker of social inferiority, became a central symbol of the cultural identity of the group.

The duty to "be present at ritual family gatherings" was an acceptable requirement for younger generations because taking part in convivial family rituals was not in con-flict with their lives outside. In the interwar years, many younger Italian Americans indicated that the public scene (the peer group, the school, and the street) and the family (with its often persistent bonds of affection) were sharply separate, a division that represented the key strategy of negotiation and adjustment for the American-born generations to keep the conflict between public and private to a minimum. The veil of secrecy that many Italian adolescents in Harlem drew over their family lives allowed an area of compromise with the older generations. Children could keep on disliking the esthetics of immigrant culture when they were in the company of their peers while, at the same time, be receptive to family moral norms. Covello remembered the plight of the second generation of Italian Harlem in these terms:

> We were highly critical if not disrespectful of the many traditions that the old folks wanted us to live up to and conform to. Many of my Italian friends would say, "They have lived their own lives in their own way. We want to live our lives in our own way and not to be tied down to fantastic customs that appear ridiculous not only to us but particularly to our 'American' friends." And I can assure you we were particularly keen about that ridicule. In fact, so much so that we never invited our "American" friends to our home. And while "American" boys took their parents to some of the school functions, we not only did not take our parents but never told them they were taking place. That was our life—exclusively ours and that of the other boys. The deadline was the threshold of the door of the house or the tenement in which we lived. Beyond that, the older folks went their way and we went ours.[28]

Being concealed by and confined to domesticity, family food rituals were accepted because they did not conflict with behaviors accepted by the peer group. Taking repeatedly part in family food rituals was consistent with a twofold allegiance to different social groups, both requiring cooperation and commitment. As another young man explained,

> I find the old custom of all relatives meeting together a very beautiful custom. It makes sense to me. So I accept it wholeheartedly. But there are other things which are a trifle old-fashioned; these I don't follow, especially if they make me look ridiculous in other people's eyes.[29]

Still, oral history frequently shows that participating in festive family meals was all but compulsory. A second-generation Italian American whom I interviewed in East Harlem told me that, "Sunday dinner was absolutely special. We would observe it religiously. Starting from early afternoon. Everyone would be at the table, not such a thing like going in, going there. We all had to be at the table."[30] Trying to summarize the core of living in Italian Harlem to his interviewer, another second-generation Italian American man explained: "We were taught religion and we were taught family life. That was it, that was it. We weren't taught family—we just picked it up. We were very close. Sunday meal was the meal you had to be there."[31]

Sunday dinners and the other formal meals helped the family ethics to be internalized without being "taught."

The formal meals of the extended family had additional social meanings for immigrants. First, the relative abundance of food that Italian immigrants had access to in New York was perhaps the promise that America kept most fully. The relatively abundant consumption of foodstuffs such as meat, pasta, white bread, coffee, and sugar was important to immigrants, both socially—as the breakdown of a long standing class barrier—and emotionally. Food rituals celebrated the victory over need—at the cost of daily hard, often exhausting, labor—and the display of food was a significant aspect of the ritual. Typically, festive meals had several courses, and foodstuffs with a high social status were central in the format of the meal. The absence of meat from the table of the Southern Italian peasant had had a strong implication of social inferiority. Its presence at the immigrants' festive meals was, therefore, perceived as vital. "For weekday suppers a soup course, some spaghetti and meat, followed by a salad, was an ample meal," Jerre Mangione recalls in *Mount'Allegro.* "But on Sundays and holidays, besides soup and salad, you were expected to stow away at least three different courses of meat, four or five vegetables, all topped off with pastry, fruits, and nuts."[32]

The cult of family feasts was also nurtured among Italian immigrants in Harlem by the Southern Italian culture of hospitality, in which the offer of food was a way to gain social dignity, reputation, and respect. The Southern Italian rural host was ashamed when he could offer only little food, and the same was true of the family that could not help showing neighbors its lack of food. Covello remembered that: "In Avigliano there were times when there was no food in the house. Then we bolted the door and rattled kitchen utensils and dishes to give the impression to our close neighbors that the noon-day meal was going on as usual."[33]

In *Mezzogiorno* (Southern Italian) society, the ostentation of food by the better-off and the shame of the hungry were two sides of the same coin, which suggests that the offer of food was closely related to the family's self-perception and to its status in the community. Italian immigrants in Harlem drew heavily upon their traditional understanding of food and hospitality to manage their social relations and adapted that tradition to the new purpose of respectability. For them, the newly gained possibility to organize gatherings centered around food consumption was a major accomplishment.[34]

Food rituals had the significant social function of determining inclusion and exclusion from the group, drawing boundaries between those who had to be invited and those who ought not, determining a clearly defined area of privacy. Strangers and acquaintances were not allowed in because private matters were not to be discussed in the presence of third parties. Younger Italian Americans remembered their embarrassment when their visiting friends were bluntly invited to leave by their parents and relatives. "'We do not want a stranger knowing the business of our family,' they would say."[35] Within the family and kin group, hospitality and food sharing were the most powerful and frequently used ways to express, manage, and pacify conflicts. Mangione noted that

> The impossibility of getting all the relatives together under one roof sometimes resulted in bitter family quarrels. Some relative would decide to take offense because he had not been invited to a family gathering and the quarrel would be on. The chances were that it would continue over a long period of months and get increasingly worse, eventually reaching the point where no one could recall the original cause of the quarrel and everyone would offer dozens of reasons to prove that it was entirely justified and should probably go on forever.[36]

The emphasis on ritual collective food consumption as a central domestic event also had important gendered implications. The framing of a private arena of family meals chiefly responded to male demands and dilemmas, but it also produced a considerable feminization of family life. Because of their domestic skills, women were in charge of supervising the emerging ethnic domesticity. In rural southern Italy, cooking and housework were easier and were secondary activities to other feminine responsibilities such as (on the one hand) working in the fields, tending animals, and growing vegetables, as well as (on the other) caring for the elderly, and giving birth to and raising children.[37] In Italian Harlem, even those wives and mothers who stayed home contributed to the family economy in various ways: managing family money, purchasing goods from the market, earning additional income through household labor, careful and extended childcare, and domestic chores performed under circumstances that called for more time and skill than in Italy. As a result of this unpaid work, while lacking public power, many Italian women in Harlem ruled at home through the routine of domestic life and rituals. They often decided who was to be invited to convivial occasions, thus regulating acceptance and exclusion and the social interaction within the kin and family circles. During formal meals, the role of the mother "as the family's center was celebrated by her culinary arts."[38] The cooking and serving of food during the ceremonies constituted not only rewarding expressions of care and togetherness, carried out with a creative personal effort, but was also a competitive assertion of status among women in the group.

In short, food rituals had the social function of celebrating, displaying, and sharing with a selected group the private rewards that American life offered to immigrants in exchange for their hard, consuming work: victory over food scarcity and a rich family life, which had been both longed for but left unaccomplished in the society that immigrants came from. The longstanding myth of prevailing cooperation within patriarchal extended families has been sharply rejected by recent historians and family sociologists of the *Mezzogiorno*, who have shown that unlike other areas of the country, the nuclear family and the neolocal pattern of residence were very prevalent in nineteenth- and early-twentieth-century southern Italy.[39] As Donna Gabaccia has pointed out, on both sides of the Atlantic, family relations became increasingly important and cared for during the process of migration and adjustment. Even in later years in America, especially because of the high level of residential mobility typical of working-class neighborhoods, immigrants continued to rely mainly upon family networks for cooperation and support. The "familism" of Italian immigrants, Gabaccia concludes, was mostly a product of immigration and life in the United States.[40] The continuing rituals of food sharing as symbol of family commonality had an important part in creating and reinforcing family bonds and family ideology. Finally, as immigrant parents struggled to suppress what they perceived as their children's individualism, these rituals worked as means of socialization of younger people into the ideology of the communal group.

Narratives of the Past, Food Memories, and the Ideology Building of the Italian-American Family

The mental focus on the "Italian family" in America, which was largely the result of migration and adjustment, could function as a means of communication, socialization, and definition of a distinctive group identity if it were instead perceived and narrated in terms of continuity, namely as a tradition. Accordingly, the uses of the Italian past were central in the strategies of (re)socialization of their children adopted by Italian-Harlem immigrants. Italian-American historian Robert Orsi has pointed out that the ideological power of memory in the narrative of tradition was enhanced by its asymmetry. Immigrants told their American-born children tales of a different land, an imaginary "other side" that their young ones had never known.[41] The needs and stresses of American life made immigrants redesign and narrate the old country as one where the family was an all-inclusive world in which parental authority went unchallenged; women knew their place; children took care of their elders; every relative dutifully cooperated for the common good; and, in summary, the family ate "as a family." "When you all grow up and are earning money and are married, we must buy or build a house which will hold our whole family together," an immigrant woman told her children:

> We should have a house like my grandfather had in Italy. He had four sons and there were four houses all joined together. Each son and his family had his own place but it was one household—grandfather, of course, was *il padrone* [the boss], and grandmother *comandava tutte le nuore* [ruled over all the daughters-in-law]. *La famiglia* ate together and in the cool autumn evenings or cold winter nights would gather around a tremendous fire-place and talk over the events of the day.[42]

The stories of the Italian past immigrants told their children often rehearsed the image of the family meal, table, and food as a symbol of cohesion and commonality. At the center of the immigrants' memory of the old country was the family gathered around the table, and older Italian Americans were most touched when they recalled themselves as young children being served dinner by mother in the stone house in the little village. The most vivid, sensual recollections were those of good food: fruit trees, vines, freshly pressed oil, the smell of homemade bread. In the memory of immigrants, Italy became a timeless narrative, filled with distant sounds, tastes, and smells. Mangione recalled:

> From the way my relatives usually talked about it, Sicily sounded like a beautiful park, with farmland around that produced figs, oranges, pomegranates, and many other kinds of fruit that refused to grow in Rochester. The air was perfect in Sicily, neither cold nor damp as it was in Rochester most of the time. The wine tasted better, and you could pick almonds and olives off the trees. In the summer the men strummed guitars and sang in rich tenor voices, and the women went on picnics in the country. Everyone was much happier there.[43]

For immigrants, the opposite of "Italy" was "America," the place where food was mass-produced and tasteless, meant only to fill one's belly, where people ate their meals alone and on the go; and the family was dominated by indulgence and indifference. The idiom of immigrants and their children drew the meanings of "America" and "American" from the limited segments of reality outside the boundaries of the community that they experienced or imagined. Italian Americans of East Harlem tended to limit the diversity and complexity of American society to a set of social values and behaviors—verbally labeled as "American"—whose appreciation varied, depending upon the discursive context. It was, for example, the case of the white, urban middle-class family—the post-Victorian, smaller, more affectionate, and egalitarian unit—

which granted some independence to women and children, and even tolerated dating behavior and freer sexual conduct.[44] Most Italian Americans in East Harlem knew only the outer appearance of such a family and the version popularized by the media, but they assumed it as the regular American family pattern, and thought it also included the other white ethnic families (Irish, Jewish, Slovaks, and so forth), those whom they came to know in most cases. In immigrants' tales, the "American family" was plainly the opposite of the "Italian family." In America, a 58-year-old immigrant said to Covello:

> Children run wild and are taught not to have any respect for their parents. They do exactly what they please. Young married women no longer attend to their household duties but run here and there all day long and at night too. They think that it's perfectly alright [sic] to be seen in public with men, other than their husbands, and to be alone with them. Here they get away with it. Such things were unheard of in Italy. Women stayed home and were only too happy to take care of their husbands and children.[45]

Indeed, to identify women, home, and family was central to the ideology of the "Italian family," of which immigrants spoke to their New York–born children and which they tried to play out in front of them. In particular, the notion that the respectability of the entire family depended upon the reputation of its women caused the special emphasis that immigrants placed on the moral education of their daughters. Girls had to be protected from temptations or situations dangerous to their virginity, and had to be prepared for marriage and maternity. However, they also had to be in a position to find a husband because for the family of Italian Harlem, a spinster daughter was both a social disgrace and a serious economic burden. For immigrants, no other acceptable way existed to prepare the daughters to fulfill these discordant aims than the "Italian way." Some of them still dismissed the love-based marriage as an "American" custom, and many believed that only an "Italian" education could instill in girls the gifts of decency, devotion, and modesty that would make of them good wives and good mothers. Because to a significant extent, a woman was considered a good housewife and mother because of her gift, competence, and commitment in food preparation, food preferences and cooking skills were strategic symbols in the definition of the good Italian girl. A man told Covello he believed that his daughter was a good housewife in the Italian tradition because of her preference for Italian cooking:

> She likes Italian cooking and knows herself how to cook. She is 18 years old now, and by now has made up her mind what her own home should look like. And I bet, she knows that it is safer to marry an Italian, because she knows in advance what to expect.[46]

Immigrant mothers praised the practical education in housekeeping and cooking that would make their daughters fit for the working-class family life for which they were intended. Mothers insisted that their sons should marry only Italian girls who "liked Italian cooking" because such girls had been raised in the proper way so as to make them turn out to be good wives in the traditional way.[47]

In the collective self-representation of Italians as the only people who could raise a family properly, food was a vital code in articulating a discourse of identity and differentiation. An old immigrant woman told Covello that she was "delighted at the sight of her children and grandchildren eating good and healthy Italian food, and being brought up in the good Italian tradition." "It is very good to be Americans, it is not even a great fault not to be able to speak Italian," concluded the woman. "But I know of only one way of bringing up a family in a decent manner, and that is the Italian way."[48] No matter how the apparent freedom had changed the esthetics of the immigrants' daughters, the indoctrination into the ideology of the "Italian family"—as suggested by the allegiance to Italian food—was regarded as reaching a deeper moral level. In the 1930s, a recent immigrant from southern Italy was pleased to see that Italian girls of East Harlem, while Americanized in their appearance, had kept "Italian family traditions." "I was proud to see families gather together on Sundays; their preference for the good old Italian cooking," the man told Covello. "And when I saw how industrious the Italian girls in the community were . . . I was willing to forgive their layers of lipstick and marry one of the American Italians."[49]

How deeply internalized the ideology of the "Italian family" was by the second-generation Italian Americans of East Harlem is effectively witnessed by their marriage pattern. By the 1930s, the practice of a family-arranged marriage had virtually vanished, and young people "freely chose" their spouses according to the "American custom." Nevertheless, they married other Italian Americans at a rate only slightly less then that of their parents.[50] What happened, then, to the longings for autonomy, integration in the larger society, and emancipation from parental culture that had made a large part of the second generation often come into conflict with their relatives? Had the American-born of Italian Harlem ultimately accepted the moral world that immigrants had articulated and passed on to them by means of symbolic strategies performed during family ceremonies—and, as a consequence, had sons and daughters made the ideology of the "Italian family" their own? The matrimonial pattern of the second generation suggests a positive answer. Tony, the son of Neapolitan immigrants in his late twenties, told Covello how some years earlier, the hostility of his parents toward the German-American girl he was in love with had wrecked his plans of marriage. But Tony now saw things differently. "How it came about I don't know, but somehow today I share my mother's viewpoint. I have nothing against American girls, but just the same I feel they carry things a little too far," confessed the man. He claimed that the ideal of romantic love that had guided him in the past was not important for him anymore. Now it was the stereotype of the "good Italian woman" that oriented him in his choice.

> My mother's sister is still in Italy, and has a large family of 12 daughters. As my mother tells me, they are very well brought up. They can cook, sew, help the husband to earn a living, and they are quite free from modern crazy ideas. My mother worked on me for several years, suggesting that I should marry any one of the girls. They don't look to me like great beauties, but I gave up long ago to be attracted by good looks. . . . As my mother says, any of the girls would make a good wife; besides my marriage would greatly help the family.[51]

Although they were granted apparent autonomy and freedom of choice, many children of immigrants made the ideology of the family their own through the internalization of its symbolic code.

The psychological process was dramatically helped by structural causes. Many second-generation Italian Americans had still limited occasions of social interaction with potential partners from other groups. The endogamic matrimonial pattern and the acceptance of the "Italian way" of choice were in part a result of such a narrow social condition. Furthermore, many class-related reasons suggested to younger Italian Americans, confronting the harsh reality of the marketplace after the school years, the enduring critical importance of the family and kin for survival and welfare. "As a kid, I was ashamed of everything Italian," an adolescent of Italian Harlem recalled:

> I would deny my own mother. I would hate to come home after school. But after several years at elementary school, I learned that home means something solid, a source of comfort, rich with the warmth of family friendship. It ceased to be a place to which I reluctantly returned to eat and sleep. I saw I was not born to be a president of the United States. And when my parents spoke of my approaching age—I was fourteen at the time—and recommended my going into the trucking business with a cousin, I counted the days 'til school would be over.[52]

Italian immigrants in Harlem apparently succeeded in making the ideology of the "Italian family" into a narrative that was able to respond to some of the numerous changes produced by the social and market conditions of American urban life, but that was especially capable of controlling the individualization and subjectivization of younger family members.

Also, after much negotiation, the younger generations eventually adopted and endorsed their own version of the distinctive food pattern they inherited from their parents. Familial moral norms and values were internalized together with the food culture that represented the strategic symbolic code in the building of the "Italian family." In the Tiano family, for example, the American-born young men openly poked fun at their parents' customs, but at the same time, they shared with them the beliefs in highly differentiated gender roles and in the consequent supremacy of the husband over the wife. Marco, the son who married a Protestant Scottish-American girl and therefore "almost broke his mother's heart," was determined, though, to raise his children Catholic and to teach them Italian. Marco "admits that as a child he resented Italian cooking, but now has come to like it and insists that his wife learn how to cook Italian dishes."[53]

Days of Hunger, Days of Anger: Food, Ethnic Identity, and Race in the Depression Years

The collective identity shaped by the widely shared ideology of the family came to be strengthened by its being instrumental in articulating a narrative of otherness of those non-whites whom Italian Americans encountered in the streets, at school, at work, and even in the houses of East Harlem in increasing numbers in the 1930s and 1940s. Racial tensions arose in those decades as Italian Americans started to perceive *their* neighborhood as threatened and doomed by the "invasion" of Puerto Ricans and African Americans. As Italian Americans felt the urge to distinguish themselves conceptually and publicly from "non-white" people with whom they now shared the same urban space, once again, their discourse of identity and differentiation was articulated in the language of the family and the food.

By the 1930s, both immigrants and their children had learned the importance of race as a fundamental category of American social discourse and experienced the need to negotiate their position in the social order rationalized by that notion.[54] For Italian-American schoolchildren, for example, "Americans" were no longer an undifferentiated group to fear and admire at a distance. A student told Covello:

> My most miserable days were the first two years at public school. I was scared even to talk to the other boys, not to mention chumming with them. In the sixth and seventh grades I could hold my ground. They didn't scare me any more. I knew I was just good as they were. Just a bunch of kikes, spiks, no real American among them. In high school it was the same thing. Why should I feel inferior when I know I am a better American than this bunch of Negroes, Puerto Ricans, Poles and Germans. My father came here fifty years ago, and he is anyway more American than those. I think East Harlem is a good place to live in. Without Puerto Ricans and Negroes it would be swell.[55]

Immigrants and their children learned also that the public discourse on food had racist implications and internalized the notion that racial inferiority and food inferiority were interdependent. In the newly unified Italy, both positivist anthropologists and northern public opinion cited the deficient nutrition of the southern population to explain their "moral and biological inferiority."[56] In turn-of-the-century America, where the racial identity of Southern Italians was correspondingly considered puzzling as it stood insecurely between whiteness and blackness,[57] experts and teachers condemned immigrant food habits, blaming the high rates of malnutrition, rickets, and tuberculosis among their children on their ignorance and their resistance to changing their poor and monotonous diet. The different terms of the debate on ethnic food habits in New York in the 1930s made first- and second-generation Italian Americans even more conscious of the direct relationship between the social conditions of an ethnic group and the public perception and evaluation of its food habits. In the 1930s, while one New Yorker in six was either Italian-born or born in America of Italian parents, and while an Italian-American mayor sat in City Hall, Italian restaurants and some Italian foodstuffs became very popular among non-Italians, and nutrition experts now approved the Italian-American diet as "balanced" and particularly efficient in terms of cost and benefit.[58] On the other hand, the diet of the new Puerto Rican migrants, monotonously based on starch and cheap cooking fats, with scarce supplements of meat, milk, and other nutrients, was held responsible for their physical "underdevelopment" that supposedly made them unfit for urban life and work. Their diet was considered a major reason for the critical health conditions of Puerto Ricans, whose costs had to be carried by taxpayers. In newspapers as well as in official reports, Puerto Ricans were also said to be carriers of dangerous tropical diseases.[59]

In the first place, Italian Americans of East Harlem used the same notions of domesticity they had mobilized to frame their own identity to define their undesired and threatening neighbors by contrast. The "Italian family" was used as an interpretive lens; and, therefore, the great number of single mothers, desertions, neglected children, and enlarged households containing lodgers, which were mostly the result of poverty and migration, were interpreted as cultural traits that revealed the innate tendency of Puerto Ricans and African Americans toward lack of morality as well as family failure.

Moreover, the living conditions of these poor newcomers did not allow them to conceal from strangers many behaviors and bodily functions that East Harlem's Italian Americans had come to regard as private.

The preconditions for the construction of the "Italian family" were three American achievements: a home able to provide rich convivial events; a space for privacy that had been equally denied to many Italian immigrants in their early years in America; and a clear boundary between what was to be shown in public and what was to remain hidden, which Italian Americans of East Harlem came to appreciate as a response to some of their peculiar needs and anxieties. In the early years of the Great Depression, in West (Black) and Spanish Harlem, men, women, and children could be seen rummaging through garbage bins for food.[60] In the Puerto Rican section, people "eat, drink, make love, and suckle their babes on the streets because there is no space for them to do so indoors."[61] Things were done differently in Italian Harlem, as a lifelong resident second-generation Italian American was anxious to tell his interviewer: "One thing about those days, we never said we were poor. We always had something to eat."[62] For the community that "ate as a family," and symbolically expressed respectability, status, affection, inclusion, and exclusion in terms of food, it was natural to use food habits to morally distinguish themselves from the hungry newcomers, who didn't "eat as a family."

Ironically, to frame their narrative of difference, Italian Americans of East Harlem made use of the same racist discourse linking food habits to social hierarchies and citizenship of which they had recently been themselves the victims. In 1938, after violent clashes between Italian American and Puerto Rican youth gangs, Covello toured the neighborhood trying to understand the sources of the fight. A group of young Italian Americans explained to him: "[Puerto Ricans] are not like us. We're American. We eat meat at least three times a week. What do they eat? Beans! So they work for beans. That's why we have trouble here."[63] The children of Italian immigrants in Harlem were taught in school that one could not be an American if she or he did not eat the food that an American is supposed to eat. While accepting and legitimizing this notion, as they had done even against their own families, young Italian Americans acknowledged the concept that becoming American meant struggling to fit in a racial hierarchy, defining themselves in opposition to others, who had to be kept at a distance. The ideology of the "Italian family" that they were not formally taught, but that they had just "picked up" around the table during family gatherings, provided them with a collective identity that albeit still conflicting and insecure, allowed them to fit into the American social order as Italian Americans.

Conclusion

In conclusion, the ethnic food culture became a major source of ideological strength for the mutually reinforcing ideas of domesticity and ethnicity. At home, second-generation Italian Americans of East Harlem were made to feel that the family, even when poor, could always feed and take care of its members. They learned that trustworthy people were the ones with whom food was shared. They were told that enjoying familiar food and company was the down-to-earth, solid reward for the working-class life that most of them were bound to live. By no means the inert legacy of the rural past, the ethnic food culture itself was continuously redefined and reinterpreted. Its relative stability across different generations did not come naturally but was a result of struggle and negotiation. Italian-American food culture was not a tradition of the past preserved inside the threatened boundaries of the family but was a tradition shaped and mobilized by a symbolic strategy of socialization in response to present social needs and changes occurring inside as well as outside the immigrant family.

In 1920s and 1930s East Harlem, domesticity was the terrain where the Italian-American ethnic identity, symbolically represented by food habits, was built. The invention of the Italian-American ethnicity was the result of the tension, often marked by conflict, between a private domesticity seen as the repository of an Italian identity and a public sphere perceived as a transmitter of Americanizing and modernizing messages. Nevertheless, the Italian-American identity built upon private performances eventually carved out a space for Italian-American values and behaviors in the public "American" world. How the private Italian-American identity reverberated in public behaviors is shown by the examples of youths who convinced themselves of the goodness of Italian food and Italian wives, and articulated their whiteness in an ethnic idiom of food and the family. The construction of an Italian-American identity grounded in domesticity affected the behaviors and convictions of those same youths who had been bearers of "American" ideals from the public into the private.

The fact that a peculiar Italian-American domesticity was created upon the assumption of the public/private distinction, which was less important in the community culture of the agrarian past, can be interpreted as a sign of an immigrants' early approach to urban middle-class cultural values. Also, the exporting of private values into the public terrain, which the Italian American family eventually accomplished through the socialization of younger generations into the domestic ideology of ethnic identity, was itself a significant, middle-class family cultural trait. On the one hand, then, domesticity was the foundation on which the Italian Americans of East Harlem built and strengthened their own ethnic identity. On the other hand, while accepting and internalizing the public/private dichotomy and building a family ideology whose private ideals inspired public actions and behaviors, Italian immigrants to Harlem and their children in some ways transformed their family world—and, as a consequence, framed their ethnic identity—according to American middle-class patterns.

Cuscuszu in Detroit, July 18, 1993

MEMORY, CONFLICT, AND *BELLA FIGURA*
DURING A SICILIAN-AMERICAN MEAL

John Allan Cicala

I have always known about *cuscuszu*. A unique and difficult-to-prepare ceremonial dish found on the coastal province of Trapani in northwest Sicily, *cuscuszu* is a version of the North African grain delicacy *couscous*. Brought to the island in the ninth century by the Saracens[1] who ruled for more than two hundred and fifty years, *couscous* became localized as *cuscuszu* in towns and villages following the Sicilian seacoast from the city of Sciacca to the inlet at Castellammare del Golfo. Maghreb *couscous* is made from worked grains of semolina steamed in either a large, flat perforated spoon or a double boiler; cured in a chicken, fish, or lamb broth; and served mixed with meat, fish, or vegetables. In contrast, Sicilian *cuscuszu* consists of formed semolina kernels that are steamed and then ripened in a fish soup, or in a meat or vegetable stock if fish is unavailable.

My grandmother Leonarda Cicala prepared *cuscuszu* in honor of my aunt Rose's annual visit to Detroit from her home in Louisiana and invited members of the family for the ceremonial meal. I never thought the dish was very special. One spring afternoon in 1990, a group of Sicilian-American women I was interviewing concerning their traditional ceremonial dishes responded with interest when I mentioned that I was going to my grandmother's house for *cuscuszu*. They told me that few women from Sicily even knew about *cuscuszu* and that those that did lacked the skill or patience to make it. One elderly lady said, "Homemade *cuscuszu* is not a recipe, it is a craft. The old-time women would devote their lives learning the *cuscuszu* technique and spend hours preparing something that nobody would appreciate now."[2] The idea that I participated in a "dying" ancient craft tradition piqued by my folkloristic interest, and so I decided to examine it further not really knowing what I was getting into.

The task would be difficult. I surveyed the *cuscuszu* tradition among the Sicilians and the North African immigrants living in the Detroit area (Moroccans, Berbers, Egyptians, Tunisians) and learned that it is a quintessential family dish. Accordingly, to understand the tradition, I would have to document the social interactions during the meal within my family circle. That intimate group consisted of my father; his sister,

Rose; his half-sister and half-brother, Katie (Caterina) and Joseph; and the cook, his stepmother, Leonarda.

On the Sunday, July 18, 1993 *cuscuszu* dinner, I assumed the role of a researcher working within my tiny extended family. My informants were blood relatives, I knew their behavior, and they knew mine through years of association. There was one main drawback: During the dinner, the senior family members behaved in an excessive formal way that seemed to suggest a repressed tension boiling underneath. Something was going on that I did not understand. I had noticed it before, but I did not think it was important enough to bring up the issue. I had lived with it all my life; and furthermore, I did not care because my grandmother did not like me and I did not like her. When I realized that I would be studying this ceremonial food tradition and asking questions concerning my grandmother, I felt that I would be studying the last person on Earth whom I wanted to know, and I was in no mood to deal with her coldness or possible rejection from her children.[3]

My grandmother had to be the focus of my research. The *cuscuszu* maker is a tradition-oriented cook who prepares a ceremonial dish that unifies the most intimate blood related group that exists in Sicilian folk culture: the family.[4] I wanted to investigate the following questions: What was my grandmother's *cuscuszu*-making technique? What degree did family history affected her preparation of the dish? How did she influence the behavior at the table? Did she unify the family? I could not see any unification, and that feeling led me to the question: Why did she make it at all? She was close to her daughter Katie and her family as well as her bachelor son, Joseph. She could have made it just for them. Why did she invite Rose and my father when it was clear that they were not comfortable at the table? What was it about *cuscuszu* that brought out these feelings? What principle was operating here?

This chapter will explore these questions by using the behavioral method to understand my grandmother's motive and role in shaping the events during one *cuscuszu* meal. The behavioral approach, developed by material culture specialists Simon Bronner, Michael Owen Jones, and John Vlach, focuses on the individual folk artist by collecting the artist's life history and documenting his or her creative activity and thought processes to better comprehend traditional behavior as it is communicated in the artifact.[5] Simon Bronner defines the behaviorist agenda and its implications for material culture studies in his dissertation on Indiana chain carvers:

> Examination of artifacts is not the end of research in this approach, but a means of understanding specific individual behavior. . . . Each individual is assumed to embody a unique complex of skills, beliefs, values and motivations that defy categorization into cultural or regional divisions. Rather than conformity, variation is emphasized; instead of tradition, motivation is stressed. One individual thus reflects one complex of behavior, or stated negatively one society does not equal one culture. . . .[6]

Bronner asserts that the artist's personal history, observed creative activity, and the resultant artifact are part of one process and together explain the distinctive meaning of the material object. He employs this method in his study of elderly, rural Indiana chain carvers to show that they perform a familiar pastime—whittling, learned from childhood—to keep their minds occupied from worrying about family troubles and their approaching deaths.[7] Michael Owen Jones relied on the behaviorist method in his work on the reclusive Kentucky Appalachian chair maker Chester Cornett to demonstrate that the distinctive chairs he constructed reflected his feelings about his life at the time of their creation.[8] John Vlach utilized this method in chronicling the life of a South Carolina blacksmith, Philip Simmons, and describing his Afro-American improvisational style when Simmons designed wrought iron motifs that fit within the Charlestown gate tradition.[9] These behavioral folklorists concluded that the meaning of the artifact through formal analysis is only partially realized unless the focus includes a discussion of the individual craftsperson's background, skills, knowledge, and the process that has resulted in the completed object.[10]

Applying the behavioral method to ceremonial cooking involves changes in perspective because the meal—not the artifact—is the subject of study. I have written elsewhere that because the preparation of food is a social act, the emphasis, especially for a family ceremonial dish like *cuscuszu*, must include the personal history of the cook and her relationship to her family as well as the social interactions that occur during the meal itself.[11] Only in this way is it possible to understand the motive of the cook and why she chooses to make *cuscuszu* at all.

The following discussion will employ the behavioral method to my grandmother's ceremonial *cuscuszu* by discussing

- Her life history before she married
- Her relationship to her family
- Her preparation and presentation of the dish
- An explanation of the family interaction that took place during the meal on July 18, 1993

Primary data for this study came from my own background as family member and participant in the *cuscuszu* tradition; the observations of my grandmother preparing and presenting the dish; journal entries concerning her behavior at the table on July 18, 1993; and tape-recorded interviews of my father, his sister Rose, his half-sister Katie, and half-brother Joseph.

Comparative information resulted from recorded discussions I had between 1989 and 1993 with 25 female *cuscuszu* makers in Detroit who emigrated from the villages surrounding the ancient mountaintop town of Erice (previously called Monte San Giuliano).[12] These villages have a regional cooking style that Detroiters refer to as *Montese* (short for Monte San Giuliano.) They include my grandmother's native village of San Marco, as well as Croce Via, Fulgatore, San Andrea, Argentaria, Xitta, Custonaci, Pizzalungo, Trentapiedi, Paceco, San Vido Lo Capo, and Buseto Palizzolo, all in the province of Trapani.

Leonarda's Life History Before Marriage

Leonarda Cicala possesses behavioral characteristics that I experienced when I talked to women from the *Montese* region: She has a self-effacing manner, does not say much (I have never heard her complete a sentence in my life), trusts only those whom she considers as intimates (namely, her children Katie and Joseph), is wary of intimates she does not feel close to (namely, my father and his sister, Rose), and keeps a formal distance toward strangers (such as her fellow townspeople—her *paesani*—neighbors, store clerks, policemen, and so on.) Her reticence would not make a good verbal informant.[13] Her daughter, Katie, was much more promising. Katie was a successful legal secretary, very talkative; she remembered her experiences within her family. What made her important was that she assisted her mother in the preparation of all the ceremonial dishes, including *cuscuszu*. Katie functioned as a surrogate for Leonarda and was the ideal person for my purposes.

When I asked Katie how she felt about her mother, she responded by saying that her mother was the only family she had:

> My mother and I were drawn together because of family circumstances. We had sympathy for each other. I knew what she was thinking even though she never talked. We were both alone. My father was much older, he was like a grandfather, and he favored your father, so he was not a father. Rose had an abusive personality. When your father was not fighting with my mother, he was fighting with Rose. Joe was too young to know what was going on. There was just Ma and me. When Joe got older, he became part of the family.[14]

The behavioral method requires open-ended questions that reveal how remembered events affect the individual artist's current behavior. Bronner stresses that behaviorism is intensely data driven and emphasizes that it is the task of the fieldworker to judge what is or what is not relevant.[15] One aspect of relevancy deals with historical accuracy that I confirmed through independent sources. Another, feelings and impressions, I validated through what I had experienced and the statements of other family members. After these aspects were on surer ground, a reasonable interpretation could then follow.

My first question dealt with what Katie knew about her mother's personality and how it affected her cooking style. Katie responded

> My mother is very fussy. She is a real perfectionist. I have thought about why she is like that. I concluded that an incident occurred before she was born that was responsible for the way she is. It led to a chain of events that affected her. I am not sure of all the facts.
>
> This is what I know: my mother's mother, or my grandmother, was married to an abusive husband. My grandmother decided not to put up with him anymore. She poisoned him and tried to commit suicide. The suicide did not succeed. All this happened around 1898. My grandmother had to carry the stigma of being a murderess, someone with bad blood, for the rest of her life even though she was not put in jail.[16]

My aunt continued. Her grandmother remarried in 1900; Leonarda was born in 1902; and ten years later, the young daughter was sent to a religious establishment— the San Carlo Institute—that took in orphans and others with "bad blood."

Mary Taylor Simeti, a popular writer knowledgeable about Sicilian culture and social life, explains in her oral history of a young girl who learned culinary artistic skills at the Institute during the 1960s that San Carlo was never really a proper convent.

> The actual management of the institute was placed in the hands of the Tertiary Order of Franciscans . . . lay sisters who had not completed their vows, and who were often

recruited from the ranks of the Sancarline, as the institute's charges became known. Local, almost personal tradition imposed the observance of certain rules proper to a cloistered-order hence the selling of pastries by wheel and grate rather than across the counter, but the so-called nuns had no formal obligation to observe these rules. . . .[17]

These "so-called nuns" had attended the Institute as children. Given the choice to stay or leave, they had decided to remain when they turned 21.[18] Katie stated that the reason why her parents sent her mother to the San Carlo Institute was to teach her obedience and humility and to become a properly brought-up, marriageable Sicilian woman. However, the nuns knowing Leonarda's past, focused on her "bad blood" that carried with it the stigma of mortal sin.

> They knew my grandmother was a murderess, so the sisters saw sin in everything my mother did. Their thinking was that the only way to get rid of the evil in my mother was to criticize her even if she committed the tiniest offence. For example, questioning authority or even asking a question was an offense. If my mother asked a question, the sisters would say: "Why are you asking that question? Who are you to open your mouth? Who are you to want to know anything? What right do you have to know anything? You do what you are told without any hesitation. You come from evil blood. Your mother's blood is your blood. Everything you do is bad and worthless and you are worthless. You have no right to ask any question."[19]

Katie believed that life in the convent was a prime factor that helped shape her mother's *ethos*.

> My mother had to submit to a vow of silence, and she did not complain. She had to follow a very rigid schedule: up early in the morning for mass, perform chores during the day like scrubbing the stone floors, or washing clothes by hand in stone tubs or kneading the marzipan, and learning how to make the sweets and pastries that would later be sold. Then it was dinner, mass, and lights out. She had no time to play with girls her age or do silly things girls do. She viewed her duties as tasks to be completed and did them as best she could.[20]

Kate surmised that her mother employed this focused discipline to work for her benefit in whatever she did.

> She did everything she was told to do because that was the rule, and she had to do it well or she would be criticized. She coped by handling everything with a stoic attitude and became a perfectionist and a workaholic with me and my kids and Joe. I have seen her form the *cuscuszu* kernels and then calmly throw them out because they were not "right." She makes these gorgeous Ericini sweaters. She spent two months knitting one for my daughter. She looked at it and said, "not look good," and took it apart and spent three months more knitting a new one. She always felt that she could never accomplish a task "the right way." She learned that lesson at the Institute.[21]

Later I will show that something "looking good" and "not looking good" is an Italian cultural value that formed an important aspect of Leonarda's motive for making her *cuscuszu* for her family.

Leonarda's Relationship to Her Family

The behavioral approach to ceremonial cooking requires documentation of the relationship of the cook to the people for whom she prepares her food. In this paper, the "people" are her family. The questions that are relevant in this section are: What is the history of the family? Who exactly are the members? What are their relationships and how did they develop, and which ones does the cook favor when she makes her *cuscuszu*?

I have summarized the Cicala family history by using information from interviews with my father, my aunts Rose and Katie, and my uncle Joseph.[22]

My grandfather Ignazio was born in the village of San Marco in the western Sicilian province of Trapani in 1870. After working as a customs officer and immigrating several times to Chatham, Ontario and Detroit, he returned, married, and left his native village with his wife in 1906 to work as a caretaker on the McCormick estate near San Francisco. They had two children in Redwood City, California: John and Rose. When my father, John, was eight years old in 1918, his mother died of the Spanish flu. Four years later, Ignazio took his son and daughter back to San Marco and married Leonarda, his deceased wife's half-sister. In 1924, they all went to Detroit where his brother-in-law got him a job as a gardener for the city.

Katie describes her mother's experiences after her marriage and explains why the family came to Detroit.

> My mother did not know what she was getting into when she married my father in San Marco. He was 47, and she was a naïve 20-year-old. She thought they were going to live out the rest of their lives in San Marco. But when his sister in Detroit told him her husband could get him a job, my father took it right way. So he was gone most of the time working, leaving my mother alone with her stepchildren in a foreign environment.
>
> She hated Detroit. She would look out the windows and see dreary industrial buildings, no mountains or sea. Then she had to put up with Rose and John's fighting and got migraines and eventually took to the bed whenever they went at it, which was anytime they were together. There was a lot of anger between them. Rose was jealous because my father got rid of her when her mother died by sending her to live with her aunt. "I was thrown to the wolves," she would say. She never got over that rejection.
>
> The only time John and Rose got along was when they would turn my father against my mother. I know when they were in Sicily, John and Rose wanted to come back to America. They did not like Sicily because it was so primitive. They convinced him to return. Oh, there were other reasons. My father was a Communist, and Mussolini's Fascist influence was being felt at the time. He became worried when his close friend, the Communist Mayor of Erice, was murdered by the Blackshirts. My mother did not know what was going on, and she could not do anything about this because she was politically naïve and did not know English.[23]

Katie explained that in Detroit, John graduated from high school in 1928, got his Bachelor's and Master's degrees from the University of Michigan, married in 1937, and worked for companies throughout the country. In the summer, he would visit Leonarda, Katie, and Joseph for a few hours. He never sent them money during the Depression. Rose left for Los Angeles in 1930 and rarely returned. With only three members of the family left, Katie describes the situation during the next two decades.

> My father was in poor health. He was bedridden until 1930 when he died. Fortunately, he bought a small grocery store in the late twenties and made my mother go to night school to learn English. We worked throughout the Depression and World War II—just my mother, Joe, and me—12 hours a day, seven days a week, 365 days a year.
>
> Things got better after the War. I married Ferris (a Syrian), and we all lived in the same house. Joe and my mother occupied the upstairs apartment, and my family stayed downstairs. After the War, we sold the store. With money my mother saved and a small pension coming in, she retired with my blessings; she had labored long enough, and I asked her whether she could take care of my children, Janet and David, while Ferris and I worked. We had no financial problems. We ate our meals together. We were finally a family. No more migraines, no more Rose and John shouting at each other.
>
> My mother had time on her hands and took an interest in making the old *Montese* dishes like *cuscuszu* and others. Joe and I told her we loved the *cuscuszu*. To please us, she took an interest in perfecting her *cuscuszu* style.[24]

Leonarda considered Katie, Ferris, and their children, and her son, Joseph, her inner family. Her stepchildren, John and Rose, occupied an outer intimate circle.[25]

Cuscuszu Preparation

I asked my aunt in late June whether I could photograph my grandmother preparing the *cuscuszu* she would serve on Sunday, July 18, 1993. It would involve two days of work. Leonarda would form the kernels on the first day, and on the second, she would steam and cure them. Katie was hesitant to give her permission and said that she would have to think about it. My aunt feared that if her mother allowed my presence in the kitchen on both days, Leonarda would dwell on it—she did not like people other than Katie in the kitchen—and she would get so nervous that "something" would happen. "Something" was a code word in our family that meant my grandmother might have a heart attack, stroke, or something equally as serious.

Although my grandmother did not suffer any tragic ailment as a result of my documentation, a problem arose. When I arrived on the first day, my aunt said that we would have to postpone the visit for another time because it was the "refined" thing to do. "Refined" meant that I was dealing with *bella figura*, the cultural code that Gloria Nardini states is so embedded in Italian social mores that Italians themselves are not always aware of it.[26] The definition would be particular to my grandmother, and it would be situational: that is, it would be her desire to act in what she considered appropriate behavior in special circumstances. I did not know what those circumstances were or the behavior appropriate to them, and I knew that my ignorance would bring shame and discredit to the woman herself. So I asked Katie what she meant by "refined."

Katie stated what her mother considered the term to mean. She said that Leonarda did not want to be photographed while she was making *cuscuszu*. She explained that her mother believed that whenever she had her picture taken, she should wear appropriate formal attire when she was at her husband's side or with family members. Whether married or widowed, she should be seen with her loved ones because that was the "refined" thing to do, yet I was asking her to be photographed alone wearing a worn apron over a house dress with her hair tied up "like a gypsy." The concern was that I would show them to relatives or friends, who would think she looked "unrefined" or that she did not know how to dress. Katie understood that Leonarda would be upset if she saw herself dressed the way she always dressed when she prepared a meal, and she was aware that her mother would think that I would show these pictures to relations even though I did not know who my relations were on my father's side and had never met any of them. I recalled at the time that I had never seen my grandmother photographed without a loved one such as Joseph, Katie, or several of her grandchildren, and she would always be tastefully dressed. If I took these photos of her making *cuscuszu* in her kitchen garb and showed them to other relatives, she would be portraying herself as uncouth and would be acting "unrefined" (that is, the opposite of *bella figura*: *brutta figura,* or making an ugly figure). Thus, these photographs would break two rules that my grandmother held concerning the sanctity of her body image. The first would be that her self-image would be violated—the way she wishes to be portrayed to the outside world—and that would be morally unacceptable. The second would be that her relations would see her as "unrefined," and that would shame her: She would not be able to show her face to them. Furthermore, if she experienced the feelings that accompanied these transgressions and acted on them—for example, not visiting her relatives to avoid being shamed—they would ask why she had her pictures taken in the first place. Why would she put herself in such a vulnerable position? Everyone would turn around and look at me because this situation would not have occurred if it had not been for my desire to take the photos in the first place; I, as a family member, would have to bear the guilt. I had to think quickly in this situation; otherwise, I would not have a project. I assured my aunt that these images would be private, and that if I wanted to show them, I would ask for my aunt's permission, and she would have to consult with her mother.

On Saturday, July 17, 1993, I stood on a chair in my grandmother's kitchen and photographed her for three hours forming and straining the kernels. She was so intent on what she was doing that she was oblivious to my presence and did not say a word to Katie, who stood nearby acting as a chaperone to reassure her mother in case "something" happened and she got upset.

The most important skill in the initial stage was the technique of forming the kernels. Afterward, Katie selected eight photos from those I had taken that day and put them in order. I asked why Leonarda was forming the kernels and then stopping to add water or more semolina. The technique seemed cumbersome. Why couldn't she form the kernels with one hand and add the water or semolina with the other? Katie explained the process:

If she were back in Sicily, she would get the right ground of semolina. We call it *semolina miscada*, or mixed semolina, which consists of large kernels and smaller ones. The maker binds the large ones with the small ones. The process is quick with a good cook.

Here we do not have this kind of semolina. My mother uses the Regular Cream of Wheat, which is too fine and can cause problems. What she does is to put in a few grains of the Cream of Wheat with her right hand. Then she moves it in quick circles over the semolina. It is her hand motion that helps shape the granules. At the same time, by doing a series of complex movements with her fingers, she forms them into kernels, which are all the same size. With her left hand, she is holding a spoon dipping it in water and dribbling it into the mixture if it gets too dry. If it gets too wet, she stops the forming, and uses her right hand to add more Cream of Wheat.

The idea is that dry kernels do not form, and wet ones will turn into paste during the steaming process. It is the American style of semolina that she has to contend with. She has not found a way to add the right proportions of semolina and water to make the kernels with one smooth action.[27]

The next day, Sunday, July 18, 1993, I arrived at noon and observed Leonarda and Katie working together to complete the preparation of the dish. They steamed the raw

Leonarda forming kernels with the water and the Regular Cream of Wheat. (Photograph by the author.)

cuscuszu, created the tomato-based cure, folded it into the cooked *cuscuszu* that was in a large pot, and covered it with a blanket so that the heat inside would do its job. Ninety minutes later, my grandmother ladled in hot chicken broth and let it stand in the pot covered with a white cloth for half an hour. The *cuscuszu* was then ready to be served.

Six months later, there was a Christmas get-together at my aunt's and grandmother's home. Katie asked me to come (only me: not my mother, father, or brother) and bring the pictures of her mother making *cuscuszu*. She had told her two first cousins of my project, and they were anxious to ask me questions concerning how my grandmother prepared the dish. I did not even know the cousins by name. When I got there, I asked my aunt whether it would be all right for me to show the pictures, and she said it would be fine. Just to be sure, I asked my grandmother, and she nodded her head. One cousin said, "This brings back so many memories when Ma made it. But Z'Narda [Aunt Leonarda], you are really an artist, all that work! It must taste wonderful."[28] Katie had subtly made her point with her mother: Her clothes and appearance were not as important as her skill as a cook. I received permission to show the photographs to other relatives and members of the Detroit *cuscuszu* community.[29]

The Detroit makers voiced approval of my grandmother's kernel formation style, but a few "purists" questioned her two-step tomato-based and chicken soup cures, one referring to them as a "sacrilege." "Chicken soup is chicken soup and fish is fish," she said. "Your grandmother mixed them up. It is a heresy."[30] *Cuscuszu* was defined by the cure, and this woman (along with the other makers) held to the belief that *cuscuszu* in Detroit was not *cuscuszu* without the fish-broth cure.[31] Katie had told me that she and her brother preferred the chicken and that her mother was aware that chicken soup alone would be too bland to make the kernels flavorful. After numerous attempts, she developed a two-cure method that suited her children:

> Joe and I did not like the fish version. It was too smelly and unappetizing. I asked her if she could do the chicken. We had it a few times, but she didn't make it. We liked that better even though it was flat. She continually worked on it to make it more flavorful.
>
> I remember the day she got inspired and found the new method. She took some tomatoes, tomato paste, almonds, and garlic and created a thick mixture like you do with the fish, only she left the fish out and folded the concoction into the steamed *cuscuszu* letting it stand for 90 minutes. Then she ladled in the chicken broth and let that cure for a half an hour. Joe and I had never tasted anything like that before. The *cuscuszu* had a peculiar taste. My mother found a way to make it uniquely her own. Later, she made many refinements, and her *cuscuszu* became more distinctive.[32]

In Sicily, both fish and chicken cures are acceptable along with turkey, fava beans, and a pig's head (usually served on Ash Wednesday.) Inhabitants from coastal villages relied on the fish, and those who lived in the interior would use the chicken or other kinds of meat and vegetables because of the difficulty of acquiring the fish and keeping it from spoiling. Leonarda had experience with both processes.[33] To please the tastes of her daughter and son, she perfected a style whereby she borrowed elements from the fish tradition and mixed them with the chicken preparation to create a two step cure innovation, rejecting the "fish-only" American proscription.

Leonarda ladling hot chicken broth into the steamed cuscuszu *for the second cure. (Photograph by the author.)*

The *Cuscuszu* Guests Gather

On Sunday, July 18, 1993, guests began arriving in the evening and waited in the family room for the meal to begin. They included Leonarda's son, Joseph Cicala, 63; Katie's husband, Ferris, 75; and their two children, Janet, 41, and David, 34; Leonarda's step-son, John Cicala, 83; his wife, Linda, 80; and the two children, Wayne, 36, and me, 42 (who was in the kitchen). The guest of honor, Rose, 80, sat alone amidst the guests. Katie asked everyone to stay in the family room until she invited them to sit at the table. She explained to me that she had made this request because *cuscuszu* during its final stages of preparation resulted in her mother creating a mess. According to Katie, Leonarda believed that the dirty pots and pans, and bits of food on the stove, floor, sink, and countertops would reflect on her and that the *cuscuszu* would appear unclean and inedible because she had made it with her own hands.

Leonarda's reluctance to have anyone come into the kitchen because of its messy appearance did not follow the usual pattern of Italian cooks who make specialty dishes. In my fieldwork, the difficulty documenting the last stages of the preparation had more to do with limited space, the main cook having to accomplish too many tasks in a short length of time, and my being in the way. Instead, Leonarda was employing her notion of refinement/*bella figura*. She was making the *cuscuszu* to display before the guests and hid herself while doing the messy preparation so that the *cuscuszu* would appear inviting in the dining room. Erving Goffman's notion of "back region"—where behavior not expected is acted out—and "front region"—where behavior that is expected is acted out—came to mind along with Mary Douglas' idea that individuals draw a line between "purity" or what is edible and "danger" or what is not edible or filthy.[34] When I questioned Katie why her mother was so insistent about keeping everyone out of the kitchen, her reply confirmed both Goffman's and Douglas' concepts.

> When she is in the kitchen making *cuscuszu*, she is so focused on what she is doing, food is flying all over the place, and I am picking up after her. There is *cuscuszu* on the floor, on the countertops, on the walls. Nobody ever sees her behave that way and nobody would eat the food if they saw it like that. It would appear unappetizing. My mother is very formal and meticulous in the dining room. I am telling you it is a real contrast. She is extremely clean, but in the kitchen she is so self absorbed that it is a mess.

Katie added a more personal reason why her mother does not want anyone around during this period.

> You see, for my mother, *cuscuszu* is a generational thing. She would make it for her family in the old days, you know, my father, John, Rose, Joseph, and me. She does not make it for you or your brother or my children. She does not make it for your mother or my husband. She knows that you all love it, but they are not her audience. Your father, Rose, my brother, and me are the ones she has in mind.
>
> Now John is very critical, he is always finding fault, especially with my mother, and Rose is far worse. If they see the messy kitchen, you can be sure that one of them will say something negative and ruin the dinner. It has never happened, John and Rose have never come into the kitchen, but my mother fears it will happen. She is extremely sensitive to criticism from your father and Rose, and the worst would be if the kitchen is messy or dirty. She would get upset if either one made a remark. So to put her mind at ease, I made this rule: No one comes in while we prepare *cuscuszu*.[35]

Katie protects her mother from the imagined criticisms my father and Rose would subject her to if they entered the kitchen. If that happened and "something" were said, she would be accused in the dining room—a "refined" area—of behaving in an "unrefined" manner; and in her mind, refinement/*bella figura* affects the acceptance of the dish. She would not be able to resolve the contradiction of being portrayed as an active cook on the one hand and a presenter on the other. In other words, her self-identity would be threatened.

Gloria Nardini states that *bella figura* is the "central metaphor of Italian life" and involves "self preservation and identity, performance and display" and has as many associations as people who practice it.[36] The one that I have chosen as relevant for Leonarda is "refinement" because that is the term that Katie and her mother use as a synonym for *bella figura*. "Refinement" and all its associations control Leonarda and her guests' behavior during the consumption of the dish. The associations include the serving tradition, seating arrangements, table presentation, making an entrance, lighting the candles, first tasting, the *dry rule* (which involves the judicious use of chicken broth to dampen the *cuscuszu* kernels), family conversation, and the signal for the ending of the meal.

Before dinner on that Sunday in July with the guests sitting in the living room, Leonarda spooned the *cuscuszu* into bowls in the kitchen, and Katie put each one at the place setting. This procedure is part of the *cuscuszu*-serving tradition and one followed by other Detroit women. Putting the kernels in a large bowl that would be passed around so guests could serve themselves was not done. I asked one lady about this practice, and she said, "The cook puts the *cuscuszu* in each bowl. Everyone has the same amount. No one has more than the other."[37] Another said, "It is just done that way. My mother did it, and so did my grandmother."[38] When I asked Katie, she said, "That is the way it has always been done. I think, though, my mother would like to see all the white bowls filled for each individual. A big bowl in the middle of the table looks crude; it does not look nice."[39]

The family members assembled at the dinner table and took their assigned places. Katie's children (David and Janet), my brother (Wayne), my mother (Linda Cicala), and Katie's husband (Ferris) sat on one side. Directly opposite were Rose, Joseph, me, and Katie. The seating arrangement was an ideal method of separating conflicting personalities. David, Janet, and Wayne were college educated, had professional jobs, and got along. My mother and Ferris always liked each other and engaged in conversation. On the other side, Rose and her half-brother Joseph were fellow travelers in their Christian Science beliefs. I sat next to Katie who, as my key informant, would answer my questions or make comments as to what was going on during the meal. John Cicala, the

Katie and Leonarda pose before spooning the cuscuszu *into the bowls. (Photograph by the author.)*

surrogate patriarch for the family, was at the head; and Leonarda, the matriarch, was at the foot near the kitchen entrance where she could make a quick exit if something was needed.

What I saw on that July Sunday in 1993 was an arrangement of guests, settings, and food set in an integrated symmetrical form. Each place setting consisted of a white bowl filled with *cuscuszu* on top of a large white plate to catch any of the grains that might fall and stain the embroidered cream-colored tablecloth. A large spoon over the hand-stitched napkins as well as water in crystal glasses were placed to the right. Near Katie and Leonarda was a tureen filled with chicken broth that could be used to moisten the kernels. Everyone waited until the matriarch arrived. She came in from the kitchen wearing a modest black dress with a tiny gold cross around her neck. She lit the two candles at the center of the table, signaling that the meal could begin.

Family Dynamics

As head, my father would announce that the guests had his permission to start eating by observing the custom of the first tasting.[40] Katie told me that when Ignazio was alive, he would sit at the head of the table, and no one would start consuming the *cuscuszu* until he had sampled a few of the grains, offered a look of satisfaction, and nodded to signify that the *cuscuszu* had "come good." She explained that this phrase meant that the steamed grains were light, fluffy, and flavorful, and were not soft and pasty. At this meal, my father tasted the spoonful of the *cuscuszu* and announced that it had "come good," thus emulating his father. When I asked Katie, who had decided to have my father act as a surrogate for his father, she told me that her mother had said that John should be there because he was the eldest and that it was only proper that he continue the family tradition. In this instance, she trusted him to pay Leonarda the traditional compliment. Ignazio had never said that the *cuscuszu* had not "come good." Katie added that my father was Ignazio's favorite and that it would be right to have him occupy the seat at the head of the table. If the seat were left empty, she added, "It would not look right."[41]

An important practice was eating the *cuscuszu* dry. This procedure was not followed by other Detroit makers who had given up trying to enforce the dry rule on their spouses and American-born children who would fill their bowls with broth. *Cuscuszu* makers believed that the kernels were the focus of the meal. Adding too much broth changed the dish from a ceremonial one into a mundane everyday soup. It was an insult to the cook who spent hours forming, steaming, and curing the *cuscuszu*. In our family, the dry tradition was rigidly enforced. Leonarda and Katie placed the tureen of chicken broth between them so that anyone who requested it would have to get their approval. The senior generation—my father, Rose, and Joseph—would only have to ask for the broth because they had been socialized in the family *cuscuszu* etiquette. The younger generation, however, had to learn, usually by criticism, and they were not to be trusted because their tastes ran along American lines, and the meal did not have the same significance for them as it did for their elders. On this day, Rose set the tone for this practice by asking Leonarda for some broth and then put only a teaspoon in her *cuscuszu*, saying, "See, Allan, just enough to wet the kernels." Twenty-two years before,

I had broken the dry rule, and it had not been forgotten. In response, Leonarda said, "Too much broth. I remember." I replied, "Now I know better. Before, I did not know how to eat it," and she nodded her head in approval that I had learned my lesson.

The table conversation continued on the dry topic and then changed to the *cuscuszu* itself and the difficulties that Leonarda had to surmount to adapt the dish when using American ingredients and implements. Katie stated that our relatives in Sicily could make their *cuscuszu* in a short length of time because they had the *maffaredda* (a *terra cotta* bowl with flared edges, which provided a smooth bonding surface) and a *pignota di cuscuszu* (the top implement of a double boiler whose *terra cotta* material allowed the heat to spread evenly and cook the raw *cuscuszu*). Leonarda had to contend with American-style semolina and find a suitable bonding surface and develop a technique using an aluminum tomato strainer for her *pignota* with its many "hot spots" to keep the kernels from turning into paste. Then she had to make her inventive cure to please Katie and Joseph. Rose looked at her stepmother and said, "Ma, this is the best *cuscuszu* I have ever eaten." Katie agreed and told a brief story about how she gave a small portion to a friend who was from Erice. After tasting it, the woman said that this *cuscuszu* had the most distinctive flavor she had ever experienced. Seeing that everyone had finished eating, Leonarda stood up, which was a signal that the dinner was over. The dinner had consisted of *cuscuszu* and water. There were no accompaniments and no dessert.

When I entered these observations in my journal, I noted that the individuals who spoke at the table were Rose and Katie and that Leonarda and Joseph made a few comments. Except for my apology for an indiscretion concerning the dry rule, I said nothing and neither did my brother and Katie's children, David and Janet. My mother and Katie's husband, Ferris, said a few words to each other. I was surprised at this conversational behavior because I had eaten many dinners at my grandmother's home, and there had always been lively conversation. In this case, only several members of the senior generation conversed.

Two weeks after the dinner, I discussed these questions with Katie, and I asked why there was so much formality. The phrase I used was, "Everyone seemed to be walking on eggshells." As an observer, I had felt it throughout the meal. Katie said that I did not really understand the situation. The reason why only a few people talked was that at the *cuscuszu* dinners, my father's temper would flare up if Rose said "something." The fact that John sat at the head of the table (assuming Ignazio's role) irked her. To avoid any problem, Katie kept the conversation going on the difficulties that her mother had experienced in adapting her *cuscuszu* to the American scene. The consequence was that my father did not say anything and that Rose praised her stepmother's *cuscuszu*. It was then I realized my role as researcher was that of the "naïve intimate": I did not belong nor understand the memories or conflicts that had occurred during the previous generation in the teens, '20s, and '30s, and that had continued to define the social interactions during the *cuscuszu* meal on July 18, 1993.

After going through this refined ordeal, I asked the basic behavioral question: Why did Leonarda have *cuscuszu* with these guests? Katie replied, "In my mother's mind, her real family is Joe, me, my husband, and children. We have always lived together, and we are blood related. Rose and your father's family are not close, but they are family because we are partially blood related. You do not reject family; otherwise, you have nothing."[42] To which I asked, "I have been to family Sunday dinners and holiday meals. There was no problem then. Everyone seemed happy and talkative. Why does *cuscuszu* bring out these bad memories?" Katie explained:

> *Cuscuszu* is a family dish. Most *Montese* I know do not invite strangers to *cuscuszu*. Just family, however you want to define it. For our family *cuscuszu* is associated with the past. When we have the dinner, memories of the old relationships return, and we may start behaving the way we did back then, and nobody wants that.
>
> Normally we never talk about those times. But *cuscuszu* brings everything out, especially when Rose sees your father sitting in Ignazio's seat. You can feel the tension. I think that is why nobody tries to say too much during the meal. If we do, I am in charge. I control the conversation, especially with my half-sister, because I don't want my mother getting upset.[43]

In other Detroit families I interviewed, *cuscuszu* provided a stage for people to bring up reminiscences related to family affairs that were joyous because they re-created the good feelings they had about the generation and individuals they had known as children and young adults. In the Cicala family, the stage was retained, but the associations with the past had to be repressed.

Refinement/*Bella Figura* and the Desire for Perfection

Refinement/*bella figura* was the guiding principle of my grandmother's behavior surrounding *cuscuszu*. It was refined, for example, to make the *cuscuszu* preparation as complex as possible: Every kernel had to be light and fluffy; and at the end of the steaming process, none could be seen sticking to the double-boiler pot. It was refined to set the table and have the *cuscuszu* in bowls with a large plate beneath to catch the loose grains that might fall from the spoon. It was refined for my grandmother to present herself at the table wearing a black mourning dress to signify allegiance to her dead husband and have a gold cross hanging from her neck to show her belief in Catholicism. It was refined to light the candles to tell everyone that the meal would formally begin. It was refined to have the eldest male—in this case, my father—to voice approval stating that the dish had "come good" in the manner of the deceased patriarch. It was refined to have Katie and Leonarda make sure that the dry rule would be observed by keeping the tureen of broth nearby so they could control access to the children who had not been socialized into the *cuscuszu* etiquette.

As a "naïve intimate" conducting ethnographic research in my family, I found myself acting in an unrefined/*brutta figura* manner. It was unrefined for me to take photographs of my grandmother in her old clothes making *cuscuszu* when her photo should have been taken formally with either her husband or family. It was unrefined for me as a grandson to show these pictures to my grandmother's relations who would have interpreted her as a woman lacking discriminating taste. It was unrefined for a grandson to study women's domestic labor because men were supposed to engage in masculine activities and not be concerned with women's work for fear of being perceived as homosexual (and that orientation would reflect negatively on the family). It was not refined for a grandson to be in the kitchen before dinner and see the dirty pots and pans and bits of food before consuming the dish. Although that rule was directed toward Rose and my father, my transgression was overlooked with the help of my aunt. Even so, it was mentioned to let me know that I had not acted appropriately and that I had made myself an exception to a proscription that was applied to all guests. Finally, it was unrefined for me to study the family because the newspapers and television could have publicized private family affairs and left members open to gossip, ridicule, and jealousy.[44]

Leonarda engages her sense of refinement/*bella figura* as the behavioral motive of the ceremonial meal to keep the only family she knows from disintegrating despite deep-seated tensions. Leonarda does so by adhering to a specific progression of the meal: She makes a dish that is ingrained in family history and tradition, prepares it with a distinctive flavor that is uniquely hers, serves the *cuscuszu* from the kitchen, seats the guests, creates the table presentation, makes an entrance, lights the candles, and then withdraws. My father continues the refined/*bella figura* behavior by observing the "first tasting" tradition; Katie and Leonarda preserve the dry rule; Katie monitors Rose's conversation to make sure it does not drift into past events, thereby preventing disruption of the meal and, by extension, a display of disrespect for the matriarch; and Leonarda gets up to signal that the meal is over. There is no lingering like there usually is after this particular meal. Members of my family put on their coats, praise my grandmother's *cuscuszu* again, and leave. No room is possible for negative comments or sarcastic remarks.

There is another aspect to this behavioral analysis with its unified motive of refinement/*bella figura*. I mentioned that during the dinner, Katie monitored the conversation praising her mother's cooking skills, especially the work she put into adapting the *cuscuszu* so it would taste the way it did in Sicily. I noticed that my grandmother did not seem to be affected by these compliments. Later, I wrote in my journal: "My grandmother was in another world after she lit the candles. I do not think she heard a thing anyone said." I asked Katie whether what I had seen was correct. She agreed and offered this interpretation of her mother's behavior:

> My mother was having a migraine because she thought she had made too many mistakes in the *cuscuszu*. This was the first time she was not able to get the Regular Cream of Wheat and had to use the Instant Cream of Wheat. The stores did not have the Regular anymore. The Instant is pre-cooked, and it is easy for the kernels to become pasty. They didn't, but she did not like the way they turned out.
>
> Now she had to create adjustments so the Instant would turn out as good as the Regular. They were experimental. She was trying them out, and she was not satisfied with the outcome. Also she found fault with the cure. I think she felt she did not use enough of the right kind of almonds, the hard-shelled instead of the soft-shelled. Her self-criticism after every meal is never ending. She always finds fault with her *cuscuszu*-making technique.[45]

This consciousness of failure was also expressed by other Detroit women I had interviewed and invited me to their respective *cuscuszu* dinners. These cooks believed they had erred in their *cuscuszu*-making technique and that the meal was not as good as it could have been. In these cases, the women stated that their mothers, grandmothers, or other female relatives prepared *cuscuszu* dinners that were superior to their own, but the cooks expected to be praised for their hard work. Leonarda did not use any one's individual version as a standard; indeed, she had learned how to make the dish on her own and had no one person as a model to emulate. Leonarda set an imagined standard which she could never attain. Unlike the other Sicilian-American women of Detroit, Leonarda was impervious to compliments: She had internalized her belief in her lack of skill in her *cuscuszu* preparation. All she could think of was improving the preparation of the dish down to the tiniest detail and know that she could never reach her goal of perfection. This behavior suggests that Leonarda's grueling and demeaning experience at the San Carlo Institute resulted in her seeing herself as incapable of doing anything well and that she should feel guilty because of her perceived shortcomings. This censorious sentiment and enacted behavior go beyond the self-criticism expressed by the Detroit women and the Italian concept of refinement/*bella figura*. Her outlook approaches the introspection and obsession of an artist.

Conclusion

The behavioral approach to a specific ceremonial meal that took place on Saturday, July 18, 1993, reveals critical issues of individual psychological motivation, small-group dynamics, innovation and change, and style. Focusing on an individual cook and her personal family history using the behavioral approach to ceremonial cooking suggests that it provides a holistic method of understanding social and aesthetic subtleties involved in the preparation, presentation, and consumption of a specific ceremonial dish. My grandmother was motivated to keep the family together by culinary means even though *cuscuszu* was not only laden with painful memories that threaten its unity but was, in fact, a ceremonial performance of those very raw associations. To prevent the family's dissolution, she engaged in the psychocultural resource of refinement to prepare the most perfect meal possible and present an elegant and controlled culinary ceremony that perpetuated her status as family matriarch. Beaten by religion, family, and immigrant experience, the taciturn Leonarda combined *bella figura*, her stoic personality, and artistic skills to assert and retain her authority.

The Italian Immigrant Basement Kitchen in North America

Lara Pascali

For many Italian North Americans, the basement kitchen is the social center of the home. Less formal and often more spacious than the rooms upstairs, this is where Italian women typically prepare food, families gather for dinner, entertain guests, and celebrate holidays. The basement is also where Italians make tomato sauce, preserves, and sausages: a workplace where no one worries about making a mess.[1] In contrast, Italians maintain the kitchen upstairs in pristine condition: a showroom that is virtually unused except for receiving the occasional special or unfamiliar guest. Although such a setup is pervasive in cities across North America, homes with two kitchens are uncommon in Italy.[2]

This chapter explores the significance of the basement kitchen as a feature characteristic of postwar Italian houses in and around Toronto, Montreal, and New York. As a subject of analysis, the basement kitchen is one that scholars have curiously overlooked despite its ubiquity as a cultural phenomenon and the frequent use of food as a lens through which to study Italian traditions and folklore. Italian homeowners and their children equally treat the custom as unremarkable: "Everybody has two kitchens" or "That's just the way it is" are common statements made in response to inquiries into the practice, suggesting that the basement kitchen has become naturalized within the community to the point that it is no longer visible. And yet, it is precisely by bringing into focus the ordinary places we do not "see" that we shed light on the values and beliefs that underlie all human interaction with the built environment, and gain insight into the ways in which these places hold meaning in our everyday lives.[3]

In broad terms, this study is concerned with the human experience of space, which encompasses both human behavior patterns as well as their sensory relationships to place. To investigate the latter, oral testimonies are revealing because as in the words of folklorist Michael Ann Williams, "They give form to the intangible, experiential aspects of architecture."[4] As I entered into the homes and kitchens of first-generation Italian immigrants, I was struck by the overwhelmingly emotional responses I received when asking Italian women about why they had two kitchens. Whether it was in Toronto, Montreal, or New York, intertwined with seemingly practical arguments for having a basement kitchen were shared notions of comfort and freedom associated with

Preparing food in the Puglisis' basement kitchen in Mississauga. (Photograph by the author.)

the quality of the basement space. As homeowner Livia Liberace states, "Upstairs I feel closed [in], in the basement I am free."[5]

The Italian immigrant home with two kitchens provides a unique source to explore the immigrant experience in North America, and in particular, the ways in which Italian immigrant women use their domestic environments as vehicles through which to perform and construct their identities. In this chapter, I analyze the dynamic relationship between Italian women and their kitchens, arguing that the basement kitchen is a liberating space, free from the constraints of formality and traditional room divisions. This sense of liberation is intricately linked to the physical qualities of the basement as well as the meanings attached to upstairs and downstairs spaces. Folklorist Gerald Pocius has written that "People create meaning in their lives through their conceptions of the proper ordering of their actions and surroundings."[6] By separating upstairs from downstairs, isolating "clean" from "messy" spaces, Italian women give meaning to domestic space and make their homes conform to a vision of propriety and order that is bound to self-identity. This conception of home is shaped by the social, cultural, and historical contexts of the Italian immigrant, who typically came to North America with dreams of a better life, and is particularly revealing of the values of Italian immigrant women, who are mostly responsible for cooking and cleaning the home.

Often, Italian postwar immigrants in Toronto, Montreal, and New York bought homes with unfinished basements, using the first-floor kitchen for all cooking and eating-related activities until they acquired enough funds to finish the basement, complete with a second kitchen, dining area, living room, and/or recreation room. The family would then "move downstairs": The basement became their primary living quarters, while the upstairs spaces were reserved for sleeping or hosting the rare, honored guest. Finished basements with kitchens were on many Italians' "to do" lists, and the amount of time needed to finish the basement was generally contingent upon economic resources. The Raccos, for example, added a basement kitchen to their two-story, single detached home located in the Italian community of Woodbridge (Vaughan, north of Toronto) within months of acquiring it in the early 1970s. In contrast, it took the Puglisis nine years to install a kitchen in the basement of their bungalow home in Mississauga (west of Toronto), which they bought in 1966. This indicates the importance of the basement kitchen: It was a goal that Italians eventually accomplished.

In Montreal, the practice of finishing the basement with a second kitchen became so common in the 1950s and 1960s that Italian contractors such as Ennio Di Fiore, noticing the trend among Italian immigrants, began to design homes with two kitchens to serve his Italian clientele. Between 1964 and the early 1990s, his company built more than 600 bungalows and multifamily "-plex" homes designed with two kitchens prior to occupancy. Duplex, triplex, four-plex and five-plex homes are widespread among Montreal Italians living in communities such as St. Leonard. Generally, Italian homeowners live in the main unit, comprising the first floor and basement, and rent out the other unit(s) located either above or to the side. Duplex homes are also common among New York Italians in Brooklyn (New York). In contrast, Toronto Italians often own bungalows or two-story, single detached homes.

One way how Italians justify the need for a basement kitchen is for the purpose of entertaining a large number of guests. Growing up in Montreal in the 1970s, Ennio Di Fiore's son, Gene, recalls that his parents would regularly host large parties with friends and family. He explained that it was more practical to receive guests downstairs: the basement "was a bigger area. . . . You could put a table and you could put a lot of people there. I remember, even with us. Every weekend they had parties. They used to party more than we did! And all the friends and all the families, so it was very convenient."[7] Many Italians entertained like the Di Fiores, particularly on major holidays such as Christmas or Easter, and on special occasions such as wedding engagements. For these events, the basement transformed into a banquet hall in which friends and relatives celebrated over a long, sit-down meal, sometimes followed by dancing.

Italian immigrants suggest that the trend to finish the basement with a kitchen developed from the need to accommodate these habitual, extended family gatherings because basements provided more space for big groups.[8] With fewer room divisions than upstairs, the plan of the basement creates the impression of a larger living space, particularly in bungalows or multifamily homes, since the first floor is divided into both living and sleeping quarters. The plans of the first floor and basement of the D'Aloisios' bungalow home in Etobicoke (Toronto west) indicate that the kitchen downstairs provides a more fluid, multipurpose space than any of the rooms because the dining room, kitchen, and living room on the main floor are neatly divided by walls;

Engagement party in the Navarra family's basement kitchen, Gravesend, Brooklyn, 1982.
(Photograph courtesy of Giuseppina and Tom Navarra.)

comparatively, these spaces merge in the basement, where the kitchen acts as a combined living and dining room. It is as a result of the open plan that many Italian families feel that the basement is the most practical space for hosting family functions, even when the basement remains in a semifinished state. When the Navarras, for example, celebrated the wedding engagement of their daughter, Fran, they chose to host guests in the basement of their two-story duplex home in Gravesend (Brooklyn, New York) despite the exposed electrical wiring on the unfinished ceiling.

The basement kitchen therefore serves a practical purpose because it enables food to be prepared immediately next to where it is consumed by guests on the occasion of large family gatherings. However, this explanation for having a basement kitchen does not account for the fact that many Italian families use it on a day-to-day basis now that family gatherings have become less frequent, nor is it always true that the basement spaces are larger than the rooms upstairs. In the Puglisi bungalow, for example, the kitchen and living rooms upstairs and downstairs are virtually the same in area. Furthermore, the basement kitchen is also characteristic of the 3,000-square-foot, two-story suburban villas in Woodbridge, where space is presumably not as limited. Writing about the houses of these affluent Italians living in the suburbs of Toronto, folklorist

SCALE: 1:10 $\overline{}$ 1 m

First-floor and basement plans of the D'Aloisio bungalow home in Etobicoke, Toronto. (Drawings by Natacha Vairo.)

Luisa Del Giudice suggests that interior living space is neither lacking nor limited: "The homes of these upwardly mobile Italians are enormous. . . . That much of the space in the new palatial homes is superfluous cannot be disputed. Scale is all: bigger and more is better, from the number of arches to the number of garages."[9] In these houses characterized by excess, it becomes more difficult to rationalize the basement kitchen in terms of its practicality. Clearly, a singularly functional argument cannot express the full meaning of the practice.

Indeed, the ways in which women speak about the basement reveal a more complex, emotional attachment to the basement space. Isabella Rotondi, who lives in Bensonhurst, had trouble explaining her preference for the basement, linking it only to a sensation of comfort. She suggested hesitantly, *"Non lo so. Mi sento più . . . comodo"* ["I don't know. I feel more . . . comfortable"].[10] What does it mean to feel comfortable, in material terms?

Many women, such as Livia Liberace, articulate this feeling of comfort in terms of the freedom that they associate with the quality of the basement space. A widow in her late 60s who lives alone in a duplex in Gravesend, Livia spends most of her time at home in the basement, which she can enter into directly from the outside through either a front or a back door. The kitchen is located in the center of the basement, behind the combined living and dining room at the front of the house. At the rear, there is a cold storage room and a workroom containing a sewing machine and ironing board, off of which a back door provides an exit to the garden. When I asked Livia why she preferred the basement to the spaces upstairs, she extended her arms across the living room and gestured to the front and back doors, indicating how easily she can move around. Upstairs, where the rooms are set in a row and neatly divided by walls, she feels "closed in," but in the basement, she is "free" to move as she pleases. From the centrally located kitchen, she can easily pick up a can of tomato sauce from the cellar, which is but steps away, or exit through the back door to pick basil from her garden. The sensation of liberation that she experiences is directly related to the open plan of the basement, which allows for greater facility of movement and control over space.

Locating the primary kitchen in the basement, therefore, simplifies housework for Italian women by reducing steps between work areas. In many Italian houses like Livia Liberace's, the basement kitchen provides more direct access to other food-related spaces such as the *cantina* (the cold storage room, generally located right beside the kitchen) and garden: Basements often lead directly to the outside through a back, side, or garage door. In addition, the basement kitchen is usually close to household appliances and objects such as washing machines, dryers, sewing machines, and ironing boards. As a result, Montreal homeowner Mary Pirro feels that it is more convenient to do housework in the basement: "I find I've got more stuff at my fingertips. . . . I'll cook and I'll wash and I'll hang it [the laundry] out."[11]

Like other women, Mary also found that it was easier to look after her children from the basement kitchen. "When the kids were small, it was heaven," she said, because the kitchen offered a direct view of her children's play area. The open basement allowed for more visual control over space, resembling the idealized, open, "command post" kitchens of the typical postwar home, which were designed to increase a woman's control over the domestic environment and her ability to perform simultaneous activities from one single point in the house.[12] The freedom and comfort that women associate with the basement are therefore linked to the possibilities of the space: the ways in which they make housework more efficient and allow women to feel more in control of their surroundings. In this respect, the basement in the Italian homes exemplifies the ideals extolled by domestic reformers of the turn of the century who advocated a "progressive" approach to house design and a radical simplification of the home. The new open-plan homes encouraged simplicity and utility. Kitchens were conceived as "rationalized workrooms."[13]

The freedom of the basement, however, is not simply defined by the open quality of the space nor the ways in which it simplifies housework. Notions of domestic cleanliness also inform the sensation of freedom and control. Many Italians engage in seasonal food production, such as making tomato sauce, sausages, or wine, all of which are labor-intensive, messy activities that require a lot of space. (In fact, wine making is often considered too messy even for the basement kitchen and is an activity generally relegated to the garage.) Rather than "mess up" the formal upstairs, Italians find it more practical to use the basement kitchen for this type of food production. They explain that in Italy, these activities would typically have occurred outside in the garden, suggesting that the basement kitchen derived, in part, from the incompatibility of Italian outdoor food practices with the North American climate.

The basement kitchen can therefore be seen as an attempt to make the North American home more conducive to practicing Italian food traditions. However, a purely essentialist argument for the setup does not explain the necessity for two separate kitchens. Presumably, if the basement kitchen were simply a more practical space for Italian living, builders such as Ennio Di Fiore would have designed homes with basement kitchens *only* rather than offer homes with two kitchens on separate floors. Moreover, this argument does not acknowledge the ideological nature of the separation of "clean" and "dirty" spaces. In many Italian homes, even regular, daily cooking is often perceived as a messy, smelly activity better confined to the basement. In the Racco home, for example, cooking is done in the basement kitchen, but food is brought upstairs to be consumed in the kitchen on the first floor. Robert Racco says that his mother "wanted to keep one kitchen pristine and neat, a place where she could easily receive guests and not worry about having to mop floors and clean grease stains off of the wall. . . . It was always because of the aesthetic aspect—keeping the upstairs neat and clean."[14] Similarly, Mary Pirro explains that she prefers not to use the newly renovated kitchen upstairs because she is afraid of spilling food and ruining the marble counter tops. In the basement kitchen, furnished with older, less-precious items and finished with lower-grade materials, she feels that "if it gets dirty, it doesn't matter."[15]

The desire to keep the upstairs clean, however, does not mean that the basement is dirty. Standards of cleanliness are high both upstairs and downstairs. Anthropologist Mary Douglas writes that cleaning "is not a negative movement, but a positive effort to organize the environment": a way of "placing boundaries, making visible statements about the home we are intending to create out of the material house."[16] Cleanliness is fundamentally linked to maintaining control over space; cleaning contributes to a personal sense of well-being and is bound up in notions of self-identity and social class.[17] For Italian women, separating upstairs from downstairs is, therefore, a way of subscribing to a particular vision of propriety and order, and of freeing oneself from the worries associated with maintaining formal appearances, potentially damaging higher quality items, and masking the intense labor of cooking.

The spatial segregation of conceptually dirty and clean spaces within the Italian immigrant home is reminiscent of nineteenth-century homes in which builders separated kitchen/food preparation/storage zones from social spaces in order to protect residents and guests from the noxious odors and germs associated with the preparation of food.[18] However, unlike in these homes, the separation between formal upstairs and informal downstairs does not adhere to a clear division between public and private. In Giuseppina Navarra's house in Gravesend, friends know to come in through the back door, which leads straight into the basement kitchen; men walk in, sometimes without knocking, to gather and chat with her husband, Tom. Everyone is received in the basement, regardless of who they are and what the occasion may be. Like the kitchen of the Newfoundland fishing cottage,[19] the Italian basement is a public space, open to the community at large. This is not the case at the Barones, where the use of upstairs versus downstairs is often contingent upon the guest. At the Barones' house in St. Leonard, non-Italians are received upstairs, while Italians go directly downstairs. In these cases, the social use of interior spaces follows codes based on familiarity. Going into the basement, with its low ceilings and small windows that provide for little natural light, is literally and figuratively, a way of accessing a deeper, hidden part of the home, reserved only for special people who have achieved a certain degree of intimacy—generally, family and close friends.

Separating upstairs from downstairs is, therefore, a way of creating internal boundaries between formal and informal zones, and of protecting one's privacy. It is an attempt to control who is allowed within certain areas of the home and what identity a homeowner wants to project to those who enter. Because of its limited visibility, the basement provides a space in which one has the freedom to go about one's daily activities without having to worry about maintaining appearances or negotiate one's culture. In the more intimate space of the underground, one is free to be oneself.

In contrast, the kitchen upstairs typically serves as more of a showroom than a space dedicated to socializing or preparing and consuming food. It is often finished with more modern and higher quality items, as in the case of the Racco home, where the upstairs kitchen is finished with marble counters, bleached oak cabinets, tile backsplashes, and ceramic floors. Even in homes where the upstairs kitchen has not been renovated, Italians generally take greater care in its design and decoration. In Giuseppina Navarra's kitchen, elegant espresso coffee cups and clay figurines stand on display on the kitchen counter. Her daughter, Fran Favaloro, says that no one ever uses the coffee cups, and laughingly admits that, "They're just for show."[20] Since they added a kitchen in the basement in 1980, the Navarras have never used their kitchen upstairs for cooking. They use the refrigerator only as an additional cold storage space for extra food. In many cases, kitchens upstairs do not contain cooking items, such as pots and pans, and are not even equipped for making coffee.

The upstairs kitchen is thus part of a constellation of presentation spaces on the first floor, including the dining room and the formal living room, which are often furnished with stiff and straight-backed finely upholstered furniture, mahogany chairs, and dining room tables, above which hang chandeliers. Italian women keep these rooms in immaculate condition: They display the contents of the dining and living rooms like museum artifacts, anticipating that few visitors will use these spaces or touch the furnishings, which are sometimes covered in plastic. Although this practice may seem extreme, showroom spaces have been a characteristic of houses throughout history. Even today, a relatively unused formal dining room is common in many households, regardless of ethnic background. Extra spaces for display purposes play an important role in many homes.

Historically, the possession of a well-furnished and carefully decorated dining room has been considered an important indicator of wealth, status, and good taste. Historian Clifford Clark writes that by the mid–nineteenth century in America, "ownership of a house with a separate dining room had become one of the prime symbols of the achievement of middle-class status."[21] In a similar manner, the nineteenth-century parlor, also known as the "front room," was an important room for showing a public face to outsiders, and a means of expressing a family's position, accomplishments, and social aspirations through the display of their finest objects. Historian Katherine Grier suggests that "furnishings exist as fact, but, particularly in the rooms where others see just

First-floor kitchen in the Racco home in Woodbridge, Vaughan. (Photograph by the author.)

'who we are,' they also make rhetorical statements, that is, statements meant to persuade others (and, it can be argued, also ourselves) that we actually are what our possessions claim us to be."[22] The marble finishes of the upstairs kitchen, like the fine upholstery and furniture of the upstairs spaces, express identity: They are indicators of wealth and state that a family has succeeded.

The more formal kitchen upstairs therefore functions as a socioeconomic marker in the way that the formal dining room and parlor did in the nineteenth century, and often still do in many houses today.[23] As Del Giudice notes, Italians "found the dream of becoming a master of one's own castle—a homeowner—to be one of the prime incentives for starting a new life,"[24] and they endured extreme hardship to achieve this goal. Like many immigrants, Italians came to North America with little money and worked hard to buy a home and furnish it with items of the highest quality possible: mahogany furniture, fine crystal glassware, tile, and marble floors.[25] Naturally, the purchase of such items required extreme savings and sacrifice, as did the addition of a second kitchen in the basement. Many Italian immigrants started their lives in North America by sharing housing with large, extended families, tolerating crowded living conditions to save money so that they could one day afford a home of their own.[26]

First-floor kitchen in the Navarra house in Gravesend, Brooklyn. (Photograph by the author.)

Achieving success was a direct result of a history of saving in which women played key roles in finding ways to cut living costs.[27] Consequently, although most first-generation Italian women express the need for the second kitchen in practical terms, many of their children feel that it is more directly linked to conspicuous consumption and socioeconomic status. Orlando Barone says that it was his mother's dream to have a home with two kitchens.[28] It was a symbol of his parents having made it in the New World. Similarly, Robert Racco links the practice to upward mobility among Italian immigrants who worked hard to accomplish the goal of home ownership; he believes that the underlying purpose of the nicer furnishing upstairs is to show a good appearance to outsiders and to impress guests.

The ways in which second-generation Italians speak about the dual-kitchen practice suggest that the need for a basement kitchen must be understood within the context of working-class immigrants striving for a better life and for whom the home represented a symbol of their success. It may thus be associated with the notion of *fare bella figura*, which refers to a behavioral style that advocates showing oneself and one's possessions to their greatest advantage. Gloria Nardini explains that

> *Bella figura* is a central metaphor of Italian life, admittedly an extremely complicated one. It is a construct that refers to face, looking good . . . in short, self-representation and

Formal living room on the first floor of the Racco home in Woodbridge, Vaughan. (Photograph by the author.)

identity, performance and display . . . as a cultural code it is deeply embedded as one of the primary arbiters of Italian social mores, so deeply embedded that natives are frequently unaware (consciously at least) of conforming to it. But understanding Italian life is impossible without understanding the intensity with which one must *fare bella figura.*[29]

Spaces are shaped by their inhabitants but also by a community's expectations. The social pressure to make a good impression by displaying our possessions—and by extension, ourselves—in the best possible manner is widespread across cultures, as the history of the formal dining room and parlor indicates. But it is perhaps the intensity that distinguishes its manifestation within the Italian community and which underlies the reason for maintaining a formal upstairs kitchen. Still, while it is true that some women will offer "the grand tour" of their home to impress their visitors, it is equally true that many guests will never see the spaces upstairs. In these cases, the seemingly public kitchen upstairs becomes the less-frequented, more private space.

Perhaps the spaces upstairs are dream spaces, spaces that Italians are saving for a special occasion that may never actually occur. Perhaps they are parts of a home that

Italians no longer consider useful but maintain out of personal pride and the enjoyment of beauty for its own sake. It is impossible to generalize, given the variations of the practice. But clearly, these upstairs rooms, often filled with the best furniture and fine objects on display, are symbolic spaces and therefore statements of identity, even if only for the homeowners themselves. They state that Italians have the means to beautify their homes and to carve out areas in which they can fulfill the dream, even if it is only a dream of possibility. And from this stems the importance of saving the more-precious items from potential use or damage. If the rooms upstairs are to be kept in pristine condition, then the rooms downstairs offer a more practical, convenient, and comfortable space for cooking, eating, and living.

The Italian North American home with two kitchens reflects a distinct way of ordering, experiencing, and understanding space: one governed by the inhabitants' aspirations and lifestyles, as well as their codes and rules for living and interacting. At times, this home is a site of cultural negotiation; at others, it is the embodiment of a dream of success. Many now accept this home as an essential aspect of a broader Italian immigrant tradition: a response to cultural expectations of how a home should be.[30]

One could argue that locating the primary kitchen in the basement is a more practical way of accommodating the lifestyle of Italian immigrants. However, the two-kitchen practice cannot simply be understood in terms of function or convenience. Although most Italian women defend the doubling of space in terms of the physical qualities of the basement, their feelings are not shared by all Italian immigrants. Montreal homeowner Assunta Alfieri expresses regret over having spent many years cooking in the basement. She explains that she built a home with two kitchens because she felt "there was no other way. . . . Everybody had two kitchens."[31] Over the years, she increasingly questioned the practice and determined that it didn't "make sense" to save her possessions and to have a beautiful kitchen upstairs which she never used. After spending 27 years cooking only in her basement kitchen, she decided to consciously break with convention and use her kitchen upstairs, a move that she describes enthusiastically as one that has allowed her to reclaim her house.[32] For comparable reasons, Montreal Italian Angela LoDico made a conscious effort not to adopt the practice because she finds the basement dark and never liked the idea of having two kitchens. Instead of saving their possessions, she feels that people should take pleasure in the things they own and that they should enjoy them. According to her:

> The house must be our slave, we shouldn't be slaves of the house. We should live upstairs
> and enjoy it, enjoy the beautiful living room, the great, big television, the beautiful
> kitchen. When the kids come, or the family, or the daughter-in-law, or our friends, we
> should show them, we should put the beautiful plates, the crystal glasses, and if one
> breaks, it doesn't matter.[33]

The dissenting voices of these Italian women bring into question the practicality of the basement kitchen and suggest that its popularity is linked to a social pressure to conform. Today, most second- and third-generation Italians do not have homes with two kitchens because they, too, question its rationale; they express a preference to use the "nice" kitchen upstairs and often poke fun at the practice.[34] Orlando Barone finds it "ridiculous. . . . If you have the space, why not use it? We have a brand new kitchen, and nobody uses it."[35] Similarly, Robert Racco says: "You're buying two sets of appliances. I think it's just a waste of space and money and not a very practical thing. Even though they [his parents] see it in practical terms."[36]

Use of space is a choice dependent upon a variety of factors. Discourses about choice explode any notion of objective practicality. Clearly, the basement kitchen serves a practical purpose, but the voices and experiences of Italians reveal that the motivations for having two kitchens are far more complex. As Angela LoDico states, "You have to read into the memories of people" to fully understand the practice: to the history of the working classes and the sacrifices that paved the road to success.[37] For many Italian women, who often not only took on menial jobs as seamstresses or factory workers to generate extra income for the family but were in charge of cooking and cleaning the home, the basement is a liberating space: a place in which women can move and cook as they please without having to feel constrained or worry about appearances, a way in which they can simplify their daily routines and exercise control over their surroundings. While the spaces upstairs fulfill the dream of success and stand as a testimony to their personal sacrifice, the spaces downstairs offer more freedom of movement, usage, and ultimately, more comfort and peace of mind.

Creative Responses to the Italian Immigrant Experience in California

BALDASSARE FORESTIERE'S UNDERGROUND GARDENS
AND SIMON RODIA'S WATTS TOWERS

Kenneth Scambray

Baldassare Forestiere's Underground Gardens and Simon Rodia's Watts Towers are two works of "grassroots art" that express the conflicted and often bifurcating experience of Italian immigration to America. Under a ten-acre parcel of land in rural north Fresno, California, Baldassare Forestiere (1879–1946) dug more than 100 underground grottoes where he lived from 1909 to 1946. Throughout his extensive site, Forestiere planted a variety of plants and trees. While living in suburban Watts near Los Angeles from 1921 to 1954, Simon Rodia (1879–1965) built three towers reaching more than 80 feet surrounded by numerous other forms, all enclosed by a six-foot wall. He decorated his towers, forms, and walls with broken glass, pottery, shells, and other artifacts that he scavenged from the neighborhood and landscape around him in southern California. As a teenager, Rodia emigrated from a small village in southern Italy. Forestiere, as a young man, came from a largely rural, agricultural area in northern Sicily. Rodia and Forestiere drew upon their dissimilar geographical environments in both Italy and California to create the iconography of two of the most significant sites of grassroots art in North America.

For more than 50 years, the Underground Gardens and Watts Towers have been unjustifiably viewed in isolation from their respective local environments, both in Italy and California, as well as from their place in the Italian immigrant experience. Further complicating the understanding of the two works, scholars have disagreed over the use of the term "folk art." Folk art historian Holly Metz used the term "grassroots art" to describe Rodia's Watts Towers in her December 2000 presentation at the John D. Calandra Italian American Institute.[1] In her notes to her article, "Where I Am Going: Kea's Ark, Newark, New Jersey," Metz explains that in the late 1960s, "term warfare" erupted over the names used to describe what has conventionally been called folk art. She prefers the term "grassroots art" because it is more descriptive: "self-taught artists' environments are located at the grassroots level, . . . rural, suburban, and urban areas."[2]

Metz' definition of grassroots art applies accurately to the suburban and rural sites of Forestiere's and Rodia's works, as well as to the two immigrants' lack of formal artistic or architectural education. As engineer Bud Goldstone and co-author Arloa Paquin Goldstone explain in *The Los Angeles Watts Towers*, "expert observers" have variously described Rodia's work as "outsider art," "nonacademic art," "assemblage construction," "folk art," "fine art," and "architecture," as well as "sculptures," "buildings," and an "above-ground, mini-archaeological dig."[3] Although Forestiere's and Rodia's two sites have been written about for years, no one has brought these two remarkable works together as illuminating expressions of the Italian immigrant experience. By referring to the corpus of Italian-American literature, this chapter will show how these works express in their individual forms their dual impulse between recollections of Italy and a hope for success and settlement in America. The works of Italian-American writers such as Pascal D'Angelo, Garibaldi Lapolla, Jerre Mangione, Jo Pagano, John Fante, and scores of others illustrate that Italian peasants' immigration provided an escape from their feudal conditions to what they hoped would be the opportunities of a new social order. As D'Angelo narrates in his autobiography, *Son of Italy*, assimilation into American culture was not a simple, uncomplicated process. Italian-American literature tells us that immigration has been a bifurcating experience, leaving not only the immigrant but even later generations lodged between two worlds: their idealized recollections of Italy and the reality of their daily struggle for survival and success in the New World.[4]

Adjustment for Italian immigrants became a complex process that included at the same time the adaptation of Old World culture in the new land and assimilation into New World society.[5] But recollections of the past and settlement in the New World were not often easily reconcilable for the immigrant or even later generations.[6] Together, the iconography of Rodia's towers and Forestiere's grottoes expresses the tension between memory and hope that is central to the bicultural, immigrant experience. As Mangione wrote about his relatives in *Mount Allegro*, they liked to tell stories about Italy, "a past they had long ago romanticized," in spite of the poverty they left behind.[7] Forestiere's life and Underground Gardens articulate in their form the conflict between the past and present, while Rodia's life and his Watts Towers more successfully merge the past with contemporary life in southern California. As they reach upward above the sun-drenched southern California landscape, the form of Rodia's towers suggests hope and aspiration, much like the towers of a Gothic cathedral. On the other hand, Forestiere's grottoes are shrouded in shadows and are framed by their heavy arches and ceilings. The form of Forestiere's grottoes is traditionally associated with catacombs, cloisters, and the underworld abodes of mythical gods and goddesses. Neither the Underground Gardens nor the Watts Towers can be fully appreciated without an understanding of the environments, both in Italy and California, that influenced the lives of Baldassare Forestiere and Simon Rodia.

Baldassare Forestiere's Underground Gardens

Baldassare Forestiere was born July 8, 1879 in Filari, a small village in the Peloritani Mountains in the province of Messina. Forestiere's father owned an olive factory and adjacent groves, which provided a reliable income for the Forestiere family. However, his tyrannical father Rosario was unwilling to share his economic resources with his four sons, Antonio, Baldassare, Giuseppe, and Vincenzo.[8] Unable to foresee any opportunity for himself within his father's business or elsewhere in Sicily, at the age of 21 (in 1902,) Baldassare emigrated along with his older brother, Antonio, to America.[9]

Having lived until adulthood in his native village, he traveled to America with vivid memories of Sicily. The familiar sites of his ancestral village were replaced in a fortnight by the industrial cityscape of urban America. His resentment toward his father would be softened by time and distance, but it would never be forgotten.[10] Upon their arrival in New York, Baldassare and Antonio worked as "sandhogs" on the Holland Tunnel and Crouton Aqueduct in New York and later on the Boston subways.[11] By 1906, he and his brother quit their jobs in the east and traveled to Fresno. For a time, Baldassare left Fresno and worked grafting fruit trees in a Sicilian community of farm laborers on the Ventura County coast.[12] After three years of living frugally and saving his money, Baldassare returned to the San Joaquin Valley and purchased a ten-acre plot of land in north Fresno. Although the dry, semi-arid climate of the valley contrasted with the mild climate of his native Filari, Fresno had one major resource that Sicily historically did not provide for its peasants: an abundance of cheap land. Soon after purchasing the parcel, Forestiere built a small, wooden house on the barren land in advance of planting an orchard. He would soon find that the valley heat during the summer in his new home (which he often referred to as his "little sweat house") made living intolerable. To support himself upon his arrival in Fresno, he worked as a leveler and a grafter for other valley farmers.[13] However, when Forestiere began planting his own orchard, he soon discovered that approximately 24 inches below the topsoil was a thick layer of impermeable hardpan: a concrete-like packed clay that underlies many sections of the valley floor. His land was not suitable for trees. Perhaps the low cost of the acreage should have raised the suspicions of this poor Sicilian immigrant. Forestiere never planted his orchard. Instead, after work each day, he returned to his small wooden house and began digging his caverns under his isolated ten-acre plot of land near the corner of Shaw and Cornelia Avenues. Forestiere would spend the next 40 years, until his death in 1946, living in and digging what would become known as the Underground Gardens.

The stories that circulated within Fresno's Italian community depicted Forestiere as an eccentric. During his lifetime, he became an embarrassment to some, but not all, members of his family. A few of his relatives urged him to stop digging his grottoes.[14] As word spread of his work on his caverns, local residents in the Italian community were quick to label him the "human mole," a term that has unfortunately come to characterize his life to a wider public.[15] But the reality is that Forestiere's life was in many respects similar to that of most Italian immigrants, both in what he accomplished in his more-than-40 years as a successful farmer in the San Joaquin Valley and what his remarkable Underground Gardens expresses to us today.

Reported, but not understood, is the fact that by the time of his death, Forestiere owned more than 1,000 acres of prime valley farmland.[16] Over the years, he bought and farmed two vineyards: one near the corner of Shaw and Polk Avenues; and the other farther east in the farming community of Clovis, where he had a small house, which he never permanently inhabited. He also purchased a 640-acre section of land in the foothills of Coalinga on the far west side of the valley.[17] To reach that land, he took flying lessons, which he never completed, at what was then known as Furlong Field on Shaw Avenue, not far from his Underground Gardens.[18] In other words, like nearly all hard-working Italian immigrants, as a young man, Forestiere intended, in the words of Gennaro Accuci in *The Grand Gennaro*, "to make America."[19] What has never been fully appreciated by Forestiere's critics is that he had indeed achieved the American Dream.

Forestiere lived a relatively isolated life.[20] Settling in the far-north end of Fresno, he was far removed from the Italian community located approximately ten miles southwest of him in the immigrant neighborhood known as the West Side. In addition to other ethnic groups, the community was composed of a variety of Italian dialect groups, including Maschitans, Calabrese, Marinese, Piedmontese, Barese, and Sicilians like himself. However, he did not share in that ethnic solidarity known as *campanilismo* (localism) or *regionalismo* (regionalism), which characterized the experiences of most Italian immigrants in America at the time.[21] Even so, he visited with his brothers, Antonio and Giuseppe, and their families. Throughout the 1930s and 1940s, he would interrupt his digging to take his nephews and nieces to films.[22] Although he did not regularly attend church with the other Italians at St. Alphonsus Church in Fresno's West Side neighborhood, he went to mass occasionally, and he was vigilant in paying his respects to the families of his friends who died over the years. His success as a farmer allowed him to purchase a car that enabled him to travel the long distance to his Coalinga property and to visit his brothers' homes.[23]

Isolated farmhouses punctuated the flat landscape surrounding his Underground Gardens, framed by the towering Sierra Nevada Mountains north and east of the valley. During Fresno's frigid winter months, a cloud layer and the valley's infamous low-lying tule fog shut out the sun, casting a pall over the landscape for days and even weeks on end. The summer months, on the other hand, brought a scorching heat with temperatures that often exceeded 100 degrees Fahrenheit. Accustomed to the coastal temperatures of his native Filari and the Ventura County coastline where he first settled, Forestiere complained that the valley heat "burned your ears off."[24] Nevertheless, he was intent upon "making America." As a farmer he did succeed, no doubt beyond his wildest dreams. At the same time, those memories of Sicily that he carried with him to America began to take shape in the form of his tunnels and grottoes.

After nearly 20 years' work in his vineyards and on his grottoes, Forestiere still harbored strong memories of his native Filari. In 1928, he made a return trip to his native village. To his friends and relatives, he had expressed some ambivalence about his life in America and had told them that he was considering moving back permanently to Sicily. Some of his relatives believed that he would never return.[25] But apparently he was disappointed in what he found in Filari. Perhaps his idealized recollections of his hometown did not measure up to a region that had been depopulated by mass immigration. Forestiere returned to Fresno.

By day, he worked hard in his vineyards. In the late afternoon, he returned by traveling west down Shaw Avenue, a narrow country road in those days, to his underground dwellings to relax and continue his digging.[26] His vineyards and his tunnels served as meaningful icons that expressed both his new social position in American society as a landowner and his recollections of his life in Filari. In the literature of the period, the conflict between the nostalgic recollections of the Old World and contemporary New World experiences in an immigrant character's life resulted sometimes in eccentric behavior, and even at times, in a tragic end. In *The Grand Gennaro*, Davido Monterano can never fully assimilate into life in America and goes mad. "He could never be an American," the Calabrian immigrant, Gennaro Accuci, says.[27] Gennaro, in spite of his great success in the real estate and junk businesses in Harlem, for many years had refused to remove his earrings, symbols for him of his peasant past.

Although Forestiere, too, like the Grand Gennaro, lived in the work-a-day world of his vineyards, he was often characterized by friends and others as eccentric. However, he was not unaware of the political and social events of the period. During World War II and the internment of Italians and Japanese on the west coast, Forestiere commented, "How can I become a citizen of a country that imprisons its own people?"[28] But his life in his Underground Gardens never allowed him to forget his past. After laboring in his vineyards each day, he returned to his grottoes and dug with his pick and shovel. Their muted scraping against the valley's loamy subsoil below the thick layer of hardpan was the only sound that accompanied him in his isolated life underground. He explained to his relatives that his project was his relaxation after a hard day in his vineyards.[29] In his imagination, he took the religious and secular forms, arches and grottoes, of his remembered Sicily and re-created them in his tunnels. Forestiere's grottoes became for him the private world of his past, which he would inhabit nearly exclusively until his death in 1946.

While Forestiere's life underground may appear eccentric to his observers, his grottoes have cultural and historical antecedents in Sicily. In ancient Greek myth, many gods and demi-gods lived underground and in grottoes. The fabled giant shepherds, the Cyclopes from Homer's *Odyssey*, lived in caves where Odysseus, in his efforts to return home, encountered Polyphemus. In other versions of the legend, Cyclopes lived in the bowels of Mt. Etna where they forged Zeus' thunderbolts.[30] In Sicily, these legends formed part of the general cultural *milieu* of peasants, as well as the *latifondisti* (owners of large agricultural estates), who learned these tales in school. The region that surrounds Forestiere's native village also contains many underground dwellings and structures. The hillsides near the village of Rometta Marea, for example, contain a vast number of Saracen caves in which he and his brothers played as children.[31] Dating from the ninth century, when the Arabs invaded and colonized Sicily, these caves, dug from limestone cliffs, served originally as storage depots for food and armaments as well as housing for Saracen soldiers. As late as the nineteenth century, these caves provided storage for grain and shelter for shepherds tending their flocks on the remote hillsides.[32] South of Messina, Syracuse contains a plethora of catacombs, grottoes, sepulchers, and mines. Over the centuries, these subterranean formations have been reused as prisons, garrisons, work places, and domestic dwellings.

Certain aspects of the Underground Gardens bear a resemblance to the catacombs of San Giovanni in Syracuse. The catacombs' "conic-tapered *venture*" constructed for light and to enhance airflow are remarkably similar to the skylight openings that Forestiere designed in his chambers.[33] Just as important, the asymmetrical pattern of Forestiere's tunnels and grottoes reflects as well the sometimes "confusing geometry" of the San Giovanni catacombs.[34] Further, in the late-nineteenth century, when Sicily's sulfur mining industry employed nearly 250,000 people, many miners and their families lived in "underground grotto[e]s."[35] In his youth, Forestiere was adventuresome. Sleeping wherever he could, he would disappear for days in his explorations of the surrounding hillsides and neighboring towns and villages.[36]

Although his relentless labor underground embarrassed some of his relatives, he did not always work alone. His younger brother, Giuseppe, helped him dig sections of his tunnels and even completed the roofing of the largest space after Baldassare's death.[37] Giuseppe and his son, "Ric," often visited "Badassu," as they called him in their dialect, in his caverns.[38] As an immigrant who shared his brother's recollections of their native Sicily, Giuseppe understood the significance of Baldassare's grottoes.

The religious iconography of Forestiere's grottoes is unmistakable. He dug a small, unadorned chapel with a diminutive altar carved into one wall. In addition, niches, plants, and decorations are often arranged in the religiously significant numbers of 3, 7, and 12. In other areas of the United States, there are Italian immigrant sites reminiscent of the Underground Gardens' iconography. However, what distinguishes other chapels and religious grottoes from Forestiere's is that they were communal efforts: architectural narratives that express the aspirations, ideas, and identity of an entire community. Joseph Sciorra writes, when describing an elaborate shrine to the Madonna built in the Italian immigrant community of Rosebank, Staten Island, in the late 1930s, "There is no single person or community of people that speaks authoritatively for the [Rosebank] site, but a polyphony of overlapping voices that contribute to the shrine's symbolic meaning(s)."[39] Although Forestiere's vernacular "shrine" may have been created by one man, it is also at the same time an expression of the Italian-immigrant experience in North America. Although settled permanently in America, Forestiere could never forget his heritage and the village that he left behind in Sicily.

One of Forestiere's major tasks, which he had to repeat countless times throughout his excavations, was to break through the valley hardpan with his pick and shovel. He opposed the use of dynamite, used by many valley farmers, as too destructive and uncontrollable for his purposes.[40] He could not afford to compromise both the weatherproofing and the structural support that the hardpan provided his grottoes. Impermeable to water, the hardpan served as a natural roof for his tunnels and grottoes. Reminiscent of his days working as a sandhog with his brother, after reaching below the hardpan, Forestiere used only a pick and shovel to remove the subterranean rocks and dirt. He then had the daunting, back-breaking task of removing the soil up a ramp to the surface in his wheel barrow to be dumped. The number of yards of soil that he single-handedly removed with his wheel barrow is incalculable. Given the size of the Gardens, as well as the weight and durability of the hardpan he had to break and remove, Forestiere's excavation was a monumental undertaking, all completed after long days in his vineyards.

For the entire project, Forestiere's expenses for building materials amounted to little more than $300, most of which was for cement.[41] He carved thousands of hardpan "bricks" into the appropriate sizes and shapes needed for his arches and for support in some of the tunnels. In the forms of his arches, niches, and dome-shaped rooms, Forestiere displayed his skills as a mason and imagination as an artist. He became more skilled with his tools as his work progressed. His style changed over the years as he decorated chambers and walls and shaped his arches with his handcrafted bricks.[42] To control the winter rains, he constructed a series of underground cisterns and sloped the floors of his tunnels to capture runoff.[43] Before he died, Forestiere excavated approximately 100 chambers.[44]

Forestiere's intuition was his only guide in designing his tunnels. He once said, "The visions in my mind almost overwhelm me."[45] His nephew, Ric Forestiere, reported that his uncle would scratch out the next phase of his work on the dirt floor of one of his chambers, study it for a moment, and then shout, "*Singulare come il mare!* [Unique like the sea!]"[46] As he said about his grottoes' organization, "It takes no genius to make a straight line. Tie a string to the nose of a jackass and let him walk away. You and the jackass have made a straight line. But to make something crooked and beautiful . . . that is a wonderful thing."[47] This is precisely what Forestiere's imagination accomplished in his Underground Gardens. His arches and vaulted ceilings must be interpreted as both structural elements and cultural expressions.

There are parallels to the form his tunnels took in other parts of North America. As Luisa Del Giudice writes in "The 'Archvilla': An Italian Canadian Architectural Archetype," the arch became a predominant motif throughout Toronto's Italian-Canadian community after World War II. Where there were arches, there were Italians. The arch became an iconographic representation of the past for this community. Among other points, Del Giudice examines "the sources and meaning of the arch as the archetypal architectural expression of Italian ethnicity [which] largely derive[s] from the collective wisdom of his folk patrimony."[48] Although the Underground Gardens occupies a physical space, Forestiere's chambers do not represent the *real* space of public architecture, designed simultaneously to serve a utilitarian function and to make a public statement.[49] His grottoes represent his personal recollections of his Sicilian past.

However, Forestiere's grottoes do have a practical as well as aesthetic dimension. He devoted the first ten years to excavating his living quarters. To escape the searing summer heat, he fashioned a kitchen with a properly vented wood-burning stove, a chamber with two beds, and finally a living room.[50] Adjacent to his living quarters, he constructed what he called the Sunrise Plaza, designed to capture the morning sun. The Sunrise Plaza also contains a small fishpond in which Forestiere placed fish that he had caught in the nearby rivers and lakes, until he was ready to eat them.[51] One bed was adjacent to a window that overlooks the Sunrise Plaza and was designed to let in the light and warmth of the spring and summer months. During the long valley winter months, when bright sunlight was less frequent and valley temperatures plummeted, he slept in his winter bed, which was located deep inside the bedchamber and closer to the stove. He also dug a room for the storage and production of wine and cheese and the curing of meat, important aspects of the Sicilian culture he had left behind in Filari. In the evenings, when he was not digging in the dark recesses of his caverns, he was able to rest comfortably in his living quarters and work on his English by reading an occasional newspaper next to a kerosene lantern.[52]

In addition to his living quarters, he continued for the next 30 years to dig approximately 90 more grottoes, none of which he needed for his living space. The ten barren acres under which he dug his Underground Gardens became a place of refuge. His underground home became "a place representing a simpler and more harmonious life."[53] Since the ninth century and the Arabic invasion of Sicily, the island has been idealized as the Mediterranean's "garden paradise." On the land surrounding Palermo, which became known as the *conca d'oro* (golden conch shell), the Arabs introduced the first lemon and citrus groves, as well as a variety of other fruits and nuts.[54] However, by the end of the nineteenth century, in both agricultural productivity and diversity of crops, the province of Messina had surpassed Palermo.[55] His father's property surrounding the family olive factory was planted with a large olive grove.[56] This is another aspect of the Sicilian landscape that Forestiere wished to recreate in his Underground Gardens.

At selected spots, Forestiere cut round holes in the hardpan to allow sunlight for the lemon, orange, tangerine, lime, and grapefruit trees he planted. The horticultural knowledge he acquired as a farmer served him well in the creation of his gardens. Forestiere grafted one tree with as many as eight different varieties of fruit. The conical shape of the skylights allowed for an increase flow of air and also controlled the entrance of rainwater.[57] Forestiere's clever engineering and design of the skylights and the planters constituted an efficient drainage and irrigation system. The skylights funneled rainwater into the planters, thus irrigating the trees and preventing flooding in the chambers and tunnels.[58] His plants also benefited from the grottoes' ambient temperature, which varied little more than ten degrees throughout the year.[59]

Forestiere dug an Aquarium Chamber and filled it with fish. At a level below the Aquarium Chamber, he dug an Aquarium Viewing Chamber, where observers could view the fish through the glass bottom of the aquarium. In the Boat Planter grotto, he constructed a planter in the shape of a boat to recall his own and millions of other immigrants' passage to America. The elaborate labyrinth of tunnels led also to an Auto Tunnel, which was actually an open-air space where Forestiere parked his car. To complement his Sunrise Patio, he created the Sunset Patio on the west end of the Gardens. The approximately 30-square-foot space, open to the sun, has a central planter that contained originally an orange tree that Forestiere had grafted with grapefruits, kumquats, and lemons. In the center of the planter, he planted three grape vines. At the far west end of the Gardens and below ground level, Forestiere excavated and planted another larger garden with an assortment of fruit trees, vines, and decorative plants.

Forestiere completed his tunnels and grottoes with a "room" 100 feet long and 35 feet wide. Some have called this an auditorium or a dance hall.[60] No one is certain what Forestiere intended. The "room" contrasts with the intimate nature of the rest of the chambers. But observers have failed to take into account that originally there was no roof on the space. After Forestiere's death, Giuseppe, who scavenged the trusses from an abandoned airplane hangar at a local airfield, added the roof, windows, and flooring.[61] Without the roof, it can be read as one more iconic representation of an important aspect of the life that Forestiere left behind him in Sicily: the communal life of Filari. In the Underground Gardens, it serves as the *piazza*, the place of communal gathering, inaccessible to Forestiere in America. Shortly after arriving in America, Forestiere and his brothers began working in the tunnels and subways of New York and Boston. Their social and cultural dislocation could not have been more extreme. They were thousands of miles from their former communities based on family, friends, and

Archway and planter, Underground Gardens, 2001. (Photograph by the author.)

ritual feast days. The large, open-air public space recalled a sense of family and community that he missed both in Sicily and Fresno. For Forestiere, like the underworld that he created, comradeship and community remained idealized notions. The real space of his *piazza* was never filled with the community that it represented.

The interplay between light and darkness is a central feature of the Underground Gardens. Between the hours of nine in the morning and three in the afternoon, sunlight shines through the skylights of the various grottoes and permeates the Sunrise Patio and the larger garden area on the west end of the site. From late spring to late autumn, before the shortened winter days and fog return to the valley, there is a contrasting display of sunlight and shadows throughout the grottoes. The Underground Gardens have a monastic-like atmosphere conducive to introspection. Yet they also capture, at least for part of the day and part of the year, the light of the countryside surrounding them. The contrast between light and darkness characterized Baldassare Forestiere's inner and outer life. At night, he dug his grottoes, recalling his past; and by day, as a successful valley farmer in Fresno, he labored in the full sun of his vineyards.

Isolated in the semi-arid valley at the extreme edge of the North American continent, Forestiere re-created that Sicily of his youth. But for the Italian immigrant, the past can also represent discord and hardship. The problematic nature of the past is a seminal theme that runs throughout Italian-American literature. While Forestiere dug, hauled, carved, and built to reconstruct his remembered Sicily in his grottoes, he was also expressing, paradoxically, that other impulse to escape from the bitter aspects of his past. As Gennaro's rebellious son, Emilio, says in *The Grand Gennaro*, what past should the Italian immigrant recall: "The Roman past and the past of the sixteenth century? Or the past of their miserable enslavement? Or the past of their recent history—the betrayal of Garibaldi and the republican hopes of Mazzini?"[62] Similarly, Jo Pagano writes in *Golden Wedding* that in Italy his Simone family had lived for centuries "in a condition that amounted to feudal serfdom."[63] Baldassare and his brother left Italy to escape the patriarchal order that his oppressive father represented. Had he remained in Filari, he would never have been able to build a home or independent life for himself. While his vineyards recalled the labor of his past and even created for Forestiere another kind of serfdom, his grottoes were his castle: "*In casa sua ciascuno è re*" ("Everyone is a king in his house").[64] His grottoes allowed him to live comfortably between two worlds: the world of his San Joaquin Valley vineyards, in which he successfully set out "to make America," and his memories of Sicily.

Simon Rodia's Watts Towers

The Watts Towers is as much a story about Italians in southern California as it is about Simon Rodia, the Italian immigrant who built them. Forestiere's solitary life and Underground Gardens in many respects contrasts with the communal lives of Fresno Italians at the time. Rodia's life and towers, on the other hand, more positively reflect the immigrant experience in southern California and ultimately the experiences of most Italian immigrants throughout America at mid-twentieth century. Although the immigrant assimilation process was often presented as problematic in the works of such

Passageway, Underground Gardens, 2001. (Photograph by the author.)

Italian-American writers as Pascal D'Angelo, Antonia Pola, and Pietro Di Donato, western Italian-American writers such as Angelo Pellegrini, Jo Pagano, John Fante, and Steve Varni generally expressed hope and optimism in their works. The dramatization of immigrants' and their offspring's pursuit of the American Dream in Italian-American literature was at odds with the theme of alienation expressed by those members of the Lost Generation who had exiled themselves to Europe in protest over what they perceived to be the parochialism of American culture. In fact, in *Golden Wedding*, Pagano parodied the "fatuous, over-indulged prima donnas" of the 1920s, including, presumably, their anti-democratic, caustic oracle, H. L. Mencken.[65] Looking back to the pre–World War II period, Angelo Pellegrini wrote that for many immigrants "economic gain is no more than marginal relevance" in their struggle for success. For him in Seattle, Washington, the American Dream was "the inalienable right to seek happiness in self-realization."[66] Similarly, writers such as Varni, Pagano, and Fante would depict the problems of assimilation but ultimately celebrate the personal freedom and democratization of life in California for Italian immigrants and their offspring.[67] For both Pagano and Fante, California was not the terminus, geographical or otherwise, of the American Dream.[68] In *Golden Wedding*, Pagano's characters are on a New World quest that takes them beyond the traditional concepts of family and gender roles. As a southern California writer, Pagano tells us that his characters' experiences were "a part of that glittering, reckless world of the future, a world whose history was a history of light."[69] Rodia's towers reflect this same optimistic spirit that is expressed by the writers of the period, including a very creative use of "light."

One of four children, Rodia was born in 1879 into a poor peasant family in Ribottoli, Campania, a village with few resources. Rodia followed an older brother in 1894 to Philadelphia, where he began his American odyssey. Over the next 15 years, he moved from northern California to the southwestern United States and back to California, where in 1917, he settled in Long Beach. In 1921, he relocated again when he bought a small house on 107th Street in the Watts section of Los Angeles, at the time a largely Mexican-immigrant neighborhood.[70] Impetuous and difficult to get along with, he divorced his third and last wife shortly after moving to Watts. Rodia worked for the next 34 years on his towers. While employed in a Santa Monica tile factory, he came home each night and worked on his towers. Then one day in 1955, inexplicably, he simply abandoned them. He gave the property to a neighbor and moved to Martinez, California.[71]

Like Forestiere's relatives and acquaintances, Rodia's neighbors thought that he was eccentric. People called him crazy, and children even tormented him as he worked over the years on what would ultimately become 17 structures. He named his site *Nuestro Pueblo* (Our Town). One day when asked what the Towers meant, Rodia's only answer was, "Lotsa things, lotsa things."[72] Once he was asked why he built the towers, and he answered whimsically that his wife was buried under the tallest tower.[73] His evasiveness is not surprising, any more than the evasiveness of nearly all artists or writers over the meaning of their creative productions. I would suggest that the meaning of the towers lies in the two environments that influenced Rodia: his village life in Italy and his new life in America, especially suburban Los Angeles.

His last two marriages were to Mexican women, which was typical of Italian immigrant men in Los Angeles and the Southwest where Italians were wont to embrace Mexican culture.[74] Therefore, it is not surprising that Rodia would apply a Spanish, not Italian, name to his site. Furthermore, Rodia's travels and experiences before he reached Los Angeles are important aspects of his life that influenced the creation of his towers. Emigrating from his Italian village at age 15, he stopped first in Pennsylvania where his brother had settled a few years before.[75] In 1902, he moved to Seattle, and by 1905, he and his first wife moved to the Italian-immigrant neighborhood in Oakland, California.[76] At some point during this period, Rodia worked on the railroad. This experience took him physically and intellectually outside the ghettoized boundaries of the neighborhood, so typical of that western Italian-American experience.[77] His work on the railroad introduced him to the expansiveness and diversity of the New World and suggested to him its limitless possibilities. He often spoke of the cities he visited, from Berkeley and Cheyenne to Chicago, Denver, and El Paso, while working on the railroad.[78] In the West, opportunity would find itself firmly buckled to the immigrant work ethic, and together, they would suggest possibilities never before dreamed of by Italian peasants.[79] As Pellegrini wrote of his family's experiences in the Northwest near Seattle, the undeveloped land and the abundant resources were theirs "at no cost other than the sweat of their brows."[80]

Although he lived among other Italian immigrants in towns such as Oakland for short periods of time, Rodia remained a free and independent individual. As nineteenth-century Italian immigrant Antonio Gallenga wrote in his autobiography, *Episodes in My Life*, the Italian immigrant in America should have "no repining or hankering after things he left behind in the old one. He must start with a stout determination to be a settler among settlers; to do in America as the Americans do."[81] Conversely, although Rodia's migratory pattern of life indicates that he certainly set out to succeed, he would not do it at the expense of his Italian identity.[82] For Italian immigrants and their offspring in America, social and economic mobility did not always override other cultural values.[83] As Pellegrini wrote, the immigrant "should forget about economic gain and concentrate on becoming something—the best that is latent in us."[84] Rodia would never become rich, but he would make the past present in a timeless work of grassroots art that would be a fitting tribute, in Pellegrini's words, to the "immigrant's quest" for that less tangible side of the American Dream.

When he finally settled in Los Angeles, Rodia found a landscape as limitless as the rest of the country he had visited. By the 1920s, Los Angeles and its extensive valleys to the east (San Gabriel, Pomona, Coachella, and Imperial) had become a diverse region settled by a variety of ethnic groups, Italians among them.[85] In the magazines of the period, southern California with its moderate climate was promoted as a Mediterranean paradise.[86] At the time of Rodia's settlement in Watts, demographically, the Los Angeles basin and its environs had "taken on the traits of the nation as a whole. . . ."[87] As Frank Lloyd Wright said, "It's as if you tipped the United States up so all the commonplace people slid down here into southern California."[88] Lincoln Heights was only one of the many Italian neighborhoods in Los Angeles. *La Società Garibaldina Di Mutua Benefi-cenza* (Garibaldian Mutual Benefit Society), among other groups, met in the Italian Hall on the corner of Cesar E. Chavez Avenue and North Main Street, where it now serves as the Italian Hall Museum.[89] Pagano wrote that Japanese immigrants dominated the fruit and vegetable trade in the Grand Terminal Market on Third Street, which also included Italian merchants. In his Los Angeles novels, Fante described the Mexican, Filipino, and Chinese businesses that dominated the Plaza, once the historic center of Los Angeles. By the 1930s, Pagano explained that Third and Broadway had become "the real beginning of the modern city of Los Angeles, which through the years had spread south and westward." Then the hub of the metropolis shifted again, and the corner of Seventh Street and Broadway became "the center of the city, and one of the busiest corners in the world."[90] At the time when Rodia settled in southern California, Los Angeles was a dynamic, bustling immigrant center.

Change and dispersal characterized the Los Angeles immigrant experience.[91] Unlike Italian-American families before and after World War II in northeastern urban neighborhoods, in southern California, they would not inhabit for more than a single generation the same houses and neighborhoods. Italian immigrants moved from the Plaza and Lincoln Heights to towns such as Hacienda Heights, Alhambra, Tustin, and farther east yet to the Pomona Valley to such towns as Upland, Ontario, and Cucamonga. In Los Angeles and the Cucamonga Valley, Italians planted the first vineyards and were among the originators of the southern California wine industry.[92] Before and after World War II, they provided part of the work force for Kaiser Steel in Fontana. Seizing the opportunity that the western experience offered, Italian Americans became involved in a lucrative real estate market in construction, land speculation, and development.

Rodia's suburban Watts, although remote from bustling downtown Los Angeles, was the transportation hub for the southern half of Los Angeles County. The Pacific Electric Red Car Line connected Rodia's neighborhood with the Watts Depot and Santa Ana. Japanese produce brokers and Japanese farmers who hawked vegetables at Grand Terminal Market also farmed the land around Watts. Watts was home to German, Jewish, Mexican, and Greek immigrants as well as African Americans migrating from the South. Rodia's immediate neighborhood was the site of Baptist and Methodist churches, including Macedonia Baptist and African Methodist churches.[93] In the 1930s, each day, Rodia, either by car or train, revisited the diverse southern California landscape as he traveled to Santa Monica where he worked as a laborer in a tile factory.[94] California's expansive landscape provided space and opportunity for newcomers to achieve that American Dream.

Southern California's omnipresent sunlight played a significant role in Rodia's selection of materials for his towers. He traveled daily through neighborhoods containing open spaces, single-story homes, and commercial sites.[95] Before World War I, the motion picture industry moved from the Northeast to Hollywood, mainly because of the reliability of sunlight in which to do location shooting.[96] In *Golden Wedding*, Pagano used the phrase "history of light" in reference to the reason why the motion picture industry moved from the East to Los Angeles.[97] Southern California's varied and sun-drenched landscape, from its beaches and mountains to its deserts, was alluring for an industry that placed all of its stock in the cinematic image.[98] Through its films, Hollywood and southern California became something of a metaphor for that universal myth of the American Dream.[99]

The mythology of success has deep roots in American culture. As one European observer said in the 1920s, "The idea of success is in the blood of the nation, for the nation itself is success—the most gigantic success history has ever recorded."[100] Likewise, the mythology of success is recorded in Italian-American literature, from the eastern works of D'Angelo and Lapolla to the Central California and Los Angeles novels of Varni, Fante, and Pagano. As the three main towers spiral upward above the single-story houses surrounding them, Rodia's towers express his dream of success in America. Less obvious to the observer, they are also a recollection of his past.

Light and the abundance of space were central to the form and content of the towers. In 1921, he purchased a house on a wedge-shaped lot with a spacious side yard, like most southern California residential homes. The capacity to reflect light would be an important aspect of the materials he selected to decorate his 17 different sculptures, including three towers standing between 55 and nearly 100 feet tall. He collected fragments of glass, pop bottles, pottery, cups, plates, automobile glass, window glass, mirrors, bottoms of bottles, teapots, and tiles, as well as seashells he gathered during his walks on southern California beaches. The tiles, whole and fragments, came from a variety of manufacturers in southern California.[101] He placed these in bins on the site and carefully selected the fragments for their placement. He kept a fire burning on the back of his property where he melted glass into free forms before he embedded them into the walls of his sculptures.[102] He used household and industrial objects to press designs into his drying mortar, from the backs of ice cream parlor chairs, wire rug beaters, and faucet handles to gears, iron gates, grills, baskets, and cooking utensils. He poured mortar into cast-iron corn-bread bakers, removed the dried mortar, and inserted the panels into his sculptures. On other surfaces, he inscribed freehand designs into his wet mortar.[103] Into sections of his exterior wall, he pressed images of his tools—hammers, pliers, and files—signs of his immigrant working-class values.

But Rodia's site is not just a random collection of junk. The Towers are, in Steve Varni's words, not a "junkshop of the past" but a recollection of a "sensible past," one that remains intrinsic to the present.[104] It is a controlled work created from the many carefully selected materials collected from his surroundings.[105] As the southern California sunlight passes over the multicolored surfaces of his sculptures, it creates a polyphonic luminosity. The combination of free-form glass and tile fragments reflects the southern California light in harmonic tones and shades. The elongated, arched buttresses that crisscross the site and that also form the round circles on the towers cast a network of changing shadows. Like southern California around it and like Rodia's own life, the sculptures are not static. They change with the movement and intensity of the sun. Although made of reinforced concrete, the giant towers appear light and airy, more celestial than earthbound.

Just as important, many of the soft drink bottles are placed with their labels showing. The colorful fragments of the cups, saucers, tiles, plates, vases, and utensils are a cross section of the consumer life of the 1920s and '30s.[106] The objects that Rodia pressed into his sculptures have their identifiable sources in the community and industries that surrounded him in southern California. Nevertheless, his sculptures transcend the period in which they were constructed and leave an indelible record of an immigrant mind that went beyond the parochial and the mundane. R. Buckminster Fuller

Interior sculpture, Watts Towers, 2001. (Photograph by the author.)

credited Rodia with making innovations in his structural engineering, but Fuller was quick to add that Rodia's innovations were "intuitive" and not just technical.[107] Nor can the observer ignore the back-breaking labor and great danger that Rodia risked carrying iron bars, mortar, and decorative items as he scaled his towers countless times over the years. The Watts Towers site is a masterpiece of grassroots art that has permanently captured a record of both the era and the immigrant experience.

Although the towers are the creation of one man, they also express the recollections and hopes of generations of Italian immigrants in the New World. They are the paean of an Italian immigrant to both his past and his life in southern California. Like Forestiere's Underground Gardens, the Watts Towers expresses the psychological dislocating experience of immigration. Unlike Forestiere's grottoes, though, Rodia's site provides a resolution to the problematic nature of the bicultural experience. Rodia collected the discards of modern America and organized them into a new form. At the same time, while the 17 sculptures represent the present in their accumulation of contemporary artifacts, they also recall the past.

Folklorists I. Sheldon Posen and Daniel Ward have suggested that Rodia's towers were based upon the ceremonial *gigli* (lilies) annually paraded around the town of Nola, not far from his native village, in honor of the local patron saint, St. Paulinus.[108] Each year around June 22, on the occasion of the feast honoring St. Paulinus, ceremonial *gigli*, more than six stories high, and a ship are paraded around the streets of the town. The ceremony is referred to as the "Dance of the *Gigli*." The bearers of the *gigli* "dance" through the streets to the accompaniment of a lively brass band. Since at least the sixteenth century, the Dance of the *Gigli* feast was organized by Nola's eight craft guilds. The *gigli* represent the guilds, and the ship symbolizes the return of St. Paulinus after his and other villagers' kidnapping, liberation, and return from captivity during the fifth century. The shape of Rodia's towers, especially the central tower, and the ship are nearly identical copies of the ones carried through the streets of Nola. Rodia named the ship the *Marco Polo* after the great explorer who opened Western culture to a world beyond its borders.

If we look at the immigrant literature of the period, what motivated him becomes as transparent as the iconography of his work. Like Forestiere's Underground Gardens, it is remarkable that one man built the towers without help from others or assistance from machinery. The Italian immigrants who flooded America at the turn of the twentieth century were little more than, in D'Angelo's words, "pick and shovel" laborers.[109] Even so, in spite of their hardships in the New World, like Pagano's immigrants in *Golden Wedding*, they set out on another kind of voyage. As Lapolla explains in *The Grand Gennaro*, once settled, immigrants worked with a vengeance to overcome their historical subaltern status in Italy and in America. Lapolla's main character, the Grand Gennaro, pounds his chest and boasts, "I, I made America, and made it quick." Lapolla writes, "if one said of himself that he had made America, he said it with an air of rough boasting, implying 'I told you so' or 'Look at me.'"[110] It is often reported that Rodia wanted people to know how hard he had labored. He never failed to point out that he built his towers alone. Rodia was quoted as saying, "I'm gonna do something. . . . This is a great country."[111] Once someone showed Rodia a picture of Antoni Gaudí's Church

The main spires, Watts Towers, 2001. (Photograph by the author.)

of the *Sagrada Família* in Barcelona. Rodia asked, "Did he have helpers?" When he was told a crew of workers had built it, unimpressed, Rodia said, "I did it myself."[112]

Rodia's site contrasts with Forestiere's in their light/dark and public/private dimensions. Although he owned considerable land in the San Joaquin Valley, Forestiere confined himself to a restricted space for his chambers. His 100 grottoes underlie acres of land. However, like those catacombs and caves in his native Sicily, spaciousness is not each individual room's major characteristic. The visitor must duck at times to pass through a tunnel, and the majority of the rooms are little more than 50 to 100 square feet. Forestiere remained isolated underground as he re-created that environment he recollected surrounding his Filari. His signature was the black smudges that his lantern left on the arches of his tunnels. Forestiere's grottoes are characterized by a combination of seasonal light and darkness, but by contrast, Rodia's towers are bathed daily in total sunlight, which is nearly constant in southern California. Just as the *gigli* were intended to be seen and to impress their viewers in Nola, Rodia's three towers are visible for miles around as they spire above the single-story bungalows that surround the site today. Rodia inscribed his work with a public sign, *Nuestro Pueblo*, an appropriate name considering the towers' visible location in the middle of his suburban, immigrant neighborhood.

Although influenced by their different geographical environments in Italy and California, Rodia and Forestiere created sites that represent "home" for the two immigrant wayfarers.[113] They came from and lived in different environments in Italy and California. In southern California, Rodia was surrounded by suburban and industrial America. In the San Joaquin Valley, Forestiere was surrounded by a rural landscape. Rodia merged the common images from his regional ceremonial spires with the found objects of modern industrial America to recall his Italian past. With his hand tools, a pick, shovel, and wheelbarrow, Forestiere used his hardpan bricks, the most abundant resource he had, to create the arches and gardens of his Sicilian memories. Both men engaged in what can only be termed without fear of hyperbole, a Herculean labor. Their extraordinary physical accomplishments are a testimony to what the prescient Henry James wrote on the cusp of the Great Immigration, "It takes a great deal to make a successful American. . . ."[114] Work was a primary value that immigrant Italians brought with them as peasants to the New World.

Forestiere's Underground Gardens narrates for us the interior, private aspect of separation that characterizes all immigrant experiences in America. There is something fundamentally sad about a man who spent the better part of his life underground, recalling a past he could only revisit in its derivative forms. But there is also something joyful in the gardens he planted and in his successful efforts to bring the sunlight, if only seasonally, into his underground grottoes and planters. Rodia's sculptures were, as well, expressions of his past. In each case, both men narrated in their respective "dialects" their inner turmoil, which resulted from their bifurcating immigrant experience. Rodia's Watts Towers site, in its unique decoration with the materials that he found around himself in Los Angeles, as well as the three towers' soaring heights, speaks more eloquently to that dream of success that most immigrants brought to the New World than do Forestiere's retrospective underground arches. Ultimately, both Simon Rodia and Baldassare Forestiere transcended their parochial, subaltern origins in Italy and inscribed a timeless message about the immigrant experience in their unique works.[115]

Landscapes of Order, Landscapes of Memory

ITALIAN-AMERICAN RESIDENTIAL LANDSCAPES
OF THE NEW YORK METROPOLITAN REGION

Joseph J. Inguanti

In June of 2004, *The New York Times* reported that the fig trees in the Carroll Gardens section of Brooklyn were dying.[1] Accompanying this horticultural death was another transition. Like the fig trees, the elderly Italian-American people who tended them were also gradually disappearing from the neighborhood. The article demonstrated what most residents of the New York tri-state area already knew: The ethnic make-up of a neighborhood often may be "read" through the residential landscape choices of its inhabitants. For people of Italian descent, the fig tree (*Ficus carica*) is one of many ethnically significant components of the landscape.

Throughout the New York City metropolitan region, the residential landscape plays a prominent role in the construction of Italian-American identity. With their symmetrical plans, sheared shrubs, religious statues, and fig trees, Italian-American landscapes proclaim the ethnicity of homeowners and knit neighborhoods together with a shared horticultural and design idiom. Despite the facility with which the denizens of the New York tri-state region discern and describe this "Italian look," no study concerned primarily with the visual analysis and historical precedents of these Italian-American residential landscapes yet exists.

State of the Literature

Interest in the Italian-American landscape has grown steadily since the 1980s. In one of the earliest scholarly treatments of the Italian-American landscape, Joseph Manzo correlated the presence of yard shrines with that of elderly Italian ethnics in Kansas and Pennsylvania.[2] Robert Orsi's examination of a major *festa* (street feast) in Italian East Harlem and Joseph Sciorra's work on yard shrines in Brooklyn were among the first serious assessments of how New York's Italian Americans have shaped their space and imbued it with ritual significance.[3] Jerome Krase has compared the formal characteristics of Polish-American and Italian-American landscapes in Brooklyn; he has also invoked semiotics in the reading of Italian-American urban space.[4] Noting the significant formal similarities between Italian-American residential landscapes and cemetery landscapes, I have explored in an earlier work the meaning of the "domesticated" Italian-American grave and the tradition of grave-tending.[5]

Typology and Method

This chapter identifies and defines two basic types of Italian-American residential landscape in the New York metro area: "landscapes of order" and "landscapes of memory." These somewhat flexible categories involve such variables as location in the overall landscape (front or rear of house), land available for cultivation, choice of plant materials, and the histories of their makers/users.[6] The purpose of this chapter is to describe the formal characteristics of these landscapes, to situate them historically, and to explore their meanings and the manner in which those meanings are conveyed. I bring to this task—and to the fields of Italian American studies and Vernacular Landscape studies—an art historian's impulse to interpret space, composition, and materials in dialogue with history: in this case, the phenomenon of Italian immigration. Thus, this chapter examines the superimposition of Italian ideas about space and horticulture upon the existing parameters of the American urban and suburban landscape.

I use the term "landscapes of order" here for the highly conventionalized, small front-yard plots that form the landscape design fabric of traditionally Italian-American neighborhoods in the boroughs of New York City, especially Brooklyn and Queens. Often featuring a religious statue, these landscapes echo an ecclesiastic organization of space, sharing much as we will see, with other forms of Italian-American religious material culture.

Formal analysis provides an appropriate method for the "Landscapes of Order" section of this chapter. Close visual reading is fitting because the quasi-public landscapes discussed in that passage function like signage without the explication of their makers. Subsequent work by scholars from other disciplines may treat more fully the social history of those landscapes and their makers.

I have coined the phrase "landscapes of memory" in response to several remarkable landscapes, each tended by an elderly Italian immigrant. Recollections of Italian land and water use, foodways, and landscape design play an essential role in landscapes of memory. Although ornamental horticulture is an important feature of these intensively cultivated landscapes, the raising of food crops is of primary importance. The landscapes of memory included in the present work are from Long Island and Connecticut. Therefore, they have the added distinction of being to a certain extent islands of Italian ethnicity in suburbs where the prevailing landscape aesthetic conforms to that of American dominant culture. My definition of landscapes of memory is certainly shaped by the suburban samples readily available for this study, but one must also acknowledge that the backyards and side yards of Long Island and Connecticut allow for a more expansive expression of horticultural memory than do the comparatively small lots of the boroughs of New York. Nonetheless, in instances where the backyards in Brooklyn and Queens have not been converted into parking lots, it is not uncommon to find in them thriving landscapes of memory.

In the "Landscapes of Memory" section, visual analysis and comparisons to historical antecedents complement site visits and interviews with the makers/owners of several landscapes. The landscapes considered in that section often occupy a place that is both spatially deep on the home grounds and psychically profound. Discussions with their creators about technique, meaning, and memory shed valuable light on the landscapes of memory.[7]

All but one of the landscapes discussed in the present work are in the boroughs of New York City, in Connecticut, or on Long Island. The sole exception, the Peace Garden of St. Leonard's Church in Boston, is included here because it makes clear the connection between Italian-American ecclesiastic and residential landscaping in the northeastern United States.

Landscapes of Order

The small, neat, and intensely managed front yards of Italian Americans in Brooklyn and Queens represent for most New Yorkers the "typical" Italian-American domestic landscape. Typically, these landscapes of order are tidy, fenced little spaces that face the sidewalk. A statue of the Virgin Mary, Christ, or a saint commonly serves as a central organizing feature and focal point. Like related landscapes at Italian-American graves, residential landscapes of order feature a heavy reliance upon basic geometrical forms and visual balance. This and their continuous—indeed, ritualistic—maintenance render them shrine-like even if no religious symbolism is present. In many of these landscapes, the penchant for control, axiality, and symmetry reaches an almost feverish pitch.

A Front Yard in Bensonhurst, Brooklyn

A front yard in Bensonhurst, Brooklyn helps to define this type. Running roughly nine feet parallel to the sidewalk and about six feet from the house foundation to the property line, this small rectangular space is delineated by a black metal fence and brick stairs. The level ground plane and poured concrete paving serve to extend the sidewalk visually toward the house while the fence emphasizes the limits of public and private space. Two potted arborvitaes (*Thuja occidentalis*) flank a statue of the Virgin Mary. On either side of the arborvitaes, positioned slightly toward the beholder's space, are two potted cordylines (*Cordyline indivisa*).

The sculptural and horticultural elements of the composition align with the fenestration of the house. The Virgin stands directly below the middle window of the first floor; the arborvitaes occupy the spaces between the left and right windows; the cordylines sit in front of the basement windows. Rectangular form, religious iconography, contained plant materials, rigorous bilateral symmetry, and neatness of space are all attributes this landscape shares with Catholic church altars and some home shrines.[8] Even the mat of artificial turf under the statue and the black railed fence call to mind the analogous structures of altar cloth and altar rail.

Like many front yards in Bensonhurst, this one is a carefully orchestrated transitional zone between the private and public spheres. Although situated on private property, the little landscape is nonetheless designed for the public eye. Backed up against the exterior wall of the house, the statue of the Virgin gazes humbly at her small patch of concrete. Unobstructed by other objects, the statue faces the sidewalk, affording

A landscape of order, Bensonhurst, Brooklyn. (Photograph by the author.)

passersby a clear view. With its emphasis on the arrangement of things—both living and manufactured—and its orientation toward the street, this landscape addresses the public by using the same design idiom as the "dressed windows" discussed by Dorothy Noyes in her work on the material culture of Italian Americans in Philadelphia. The creations of Italian-American women, these assemblages of knick-knacks and figures decorate the front windows of South Philly. Noyes notes the "bilateral tripartite symmetry" of the assemblages and relates it to Henry Glassie's observation that this format is a basic European folk aesthetic, one that she observes correctly is "strongly embodied in traditional Italian religious imagery."[9] Noyes relates Italian-American dressed windows to the *edicole* (outdoor shrines) of Southern Italy.[10] Joseph Sciorra traces the translation of Italian *edicole* into the outdoor altars of late-nineteenth-century tenement yards and ultimately into contemporary yard shrines and sidewalk altars of New York's Italian neighborhoods.[11] Often the landscape setting for religious statuary, landscapes of order share the convention of rigorous symmetry. Thus, this style, an extension of shrine and assemblage conventions to the landscape, asserts its aesthetic on the entire front yard. With its central statue and balanced composition, this Bensonhurst front yard is indeed altar-like in its conception of space.

Elsewhere, I have noted that altar-like symmetry and tidiness of the landscape are salient features of both Italian-American graves and residential landscapes in the New York metro region. Italian-American graves that feature a centrally positioned statue or stele flanked by evergreen shrubs recall a typical planting scheme for front yards. Annual flowers in front of the grave marker—and, in some cases, vegetable gardens behind—further emphasize the connection between the residential/familial realm and the sacred or otherworldly realm. "Domesticating" their graves by tending grave gardens, Italian Americans make clear an ongoing relationship between the living and the dead.[12]

THE PEACE GARDEN AT ST. LEONARD'S CHURCH IN BOSTON

The Peace Garden at St. Leonard's Church in Boston's historically Italian North End provides another instance of the porosity between the design of sacred space and residential space among Italian Americans. A direct and literal translation of the altar aesthetic to the landscape is clear in the Peace Garden. Although located outside the New York tri-state area, the landscape of St. Leonard's demonstrates the strong connections between Italian-American ecclesiastic and domestic landscapes. Moreover, the Peace Garden offers evidence of the reach of Italian-American landscapes of order throughout much of the northeastern United States.

Founded in 1873, St. Leonard's is one of the oldest Italian Catholic congregations in America. Parishioners enter the church by walking through the adjacent Peace Garden. The garden is made up of two fenced spaces bisected by a concrete path linking the church entrance with the street. A row of saucer magnolias (*Magnolia soulangea*) defines the garden's perimeter. Symmetrical arrangements of sheared yew (*Taxus* sp.) frame religious statuary, paths, and entrances. The balanced arrangement of plant materials used in home shrines, at graves, and at entrances to Italian-American homes appears at St. Leonard's as well. In all these landscapes, symmetrical arrangements of plants recall the placement of flowers, potted plants, candles, and other ecclesiastic items on altars.

St. Leonard's Peace Garden offers a literal example of this practice. A plaque announces that the two yews flanking the entrance to one of paths in the Peace Garden had adorned the altar in the late 1970s when the Pope celebrated Mass in the adjoining church. This translation, a literal transplanting from altar to church garden, makes abundantly clear the connection between the heavenly and the terrestrial in Italian-American landscapes of order. The permeability of boundaries among church, cemetery, shrine, and home—all denotatively or connotatively sacred spaces—is announced by similar horticultural designs and a high degree of human interaction with the landscape. Thus, by direct allusion to ecclesiastic treatment of space and plant materials, these landscapes of order underscore the sacredness of the home and family in Italian-American culture so clearly articulated by Robert Orsi in his work on Italian East Harlem.[13] The Peace Garden at St. Leonard's shares other design elements with New York's Italian-American landscapes of order. Hardscape—the inorganic, manmade features of the landscape—prevails here. Belgian block or brick edging emphasizes the boundary between paved surfaces and planting beds, planters contain shrubs, and religious statues stand at the center of balanced compositions.

The abundance of hardscape is a defining feature of New York's Italian-American landscapes of order. In a front yard in Bensonhurst, two evergreens pruned into vaselike forms stand in small raised beds bounded by scalloped edging material. The rest of the yard is paved and punctuated by several planters; wrought iron fencing surrounds the entire landscape. Another Bensonhurst landscape conforms to the altar-like model discussed earlier. In this case, a pair of concrete containers, decorated in a Renaissance style with swags and lions' heads, holds evergreens and flanks a statue of the Virgin. A low brick wall set with decorative concrete elements borders the small plot and echoes the façade of the house.

The hardscape in these landscapes of order keeps nature tidy, within bounds. Paving, edging, raised beds, and planters all serve to contain and confine the plant materials. Evergreens sheared or bred to have strongly geometrical silhouettes further attest to nature's containment and subordination to the hand of man. This expression of control is in keeping with the religious or quasi-religious symbolism of landscapes of order. Indeed, the regularized arranging and bounding of both space and plant materials subtly suggest adherence to divine order. This view is particularly appropriate to landscapes dedicated to the Virgin: the *hortus conclusus*, the garden of medieval Marian legend, was as its name attests, an *enclosed* precinct. Moreover, the Virgin's attributes, cleanliness and obedience to the will of God, receive full visual and spatial expression in Italian-American landscapes of order.

Seasonal Decorations

Bensonhurst's Italian-American homeowners further embellish their landscapes of order with seasonal ornaments. In winter, silver garlands transform the shrubs flanking

A landscape of order at Christmastime, Bensonhurst, Brooklyn. (Photograph by the author.)

the statue of the Virgin into Christmas trees (see the figure on page 88). The display in the front window communicates with the little landscape, thereby bridging the religious and secular. Figures of Santa Claus and Frosty the Snowman flank the centrally placed Nativity. An angel in a golden starburst floats above the entire composition. At Halloween, a garland of orange jack-o'-lanterns adorns the black metal fence of the landscape discussed at the beginning of this section (see the figure on page 86). Such seasonal decorations represent the faint echoes of an agricultural cycle and lifestyle that many urban dwellers have never known. As Roger Abrahams has noted, "Though we are predominantly a highly mobile city people, we have maintained innumerable occasions for celebration from our country past."[14] Italian Americans in New York enthusiastically embrace the seasonal decorations of American consumer culture and incorporate them at the appropriate times of the year into their landscapes. This is particularly apparent at Christmastime. As the films *The Kings of Christmas* (2005; directed by David Katz) and *Dyker Lights* (2001; directed by Paul Reitano and Terrence Sacchi) demonstrate, Italian-American men in the boroughs of New York adorn house façades and front yards with a profusion of Christmas decorations. In his work on folk art assemblages, Jack Santino notes, "The façade of the house is itself an aesthetic element in these assemblages. It is the house that is being decorated in such a way as to make a public statement."[15] Abundant Christmas decoration, then, has in itself become an ethnically identifying practice and proclamation among New York's Italian Americans, one that was parodied years ago by comedienne Cheri Oteri in a hilarious *Saturday Night Live* skit.[16]

THE ROLE OF THE LANDSCAPE IN THE CONSTRUCTION OF ITALIAN-AMERICAN ETHNIC IDENTITY: HISTORICAL PERSPECTIVES

Much of the fieldwork in Bensonhurst, Brooklyn, and in Astoria, Queens, was conducted in the fall and winter following the terrorist attacks of September 11, 2001. Although the landscapes of Bensonhurst and parts of Astoria demonstrate an affinity with Italian ones in spatial arrangement, preponderance of hardscape, and choice of plants, almost every one was decorated with at least one American flag. At a time of national crisis and solidarity, these landscapes made obvious both the Italian cultural identification and the American nationalism of their owners. Yet the creation of a distinctly Italian-American landscape involves much more than sticking the Stars and Stripes into a planter or flowerbed in Bensonhurst. Rather, the Italian-American landscape results from the grafting of Italian aesthetic and horticultural customs onto existing American residential models. The belief that the landscape per se is the product of the civilizing, controlling hand of mankind over wild nature underpins these practices. Although the landscape design of all cultures represents a civilizing of nature, the Italians historically have favored a style that makes human intervention obvious.

The ancient Romans validated the order, regularity, and decorum of a well-designed landscape. Cato wrote, "A city garden, especially of one who has no other, ought to be planted and ornamented with all possible care." Pliny the Younger spoke of "elegant regularity" in the landscape. Quintilian advised that "trees be planted in a regular order." He claimed, "Regularity and arrangement even improves the soil, because the juices rise more regularly to nourish what it bears."[17] Elements of this classical regularity have persisted for 2,000 years in European—especially Italian—design history.

The medieval *hortus conclusus*, the enclosed garden associated with the Virgin Mary and the precursor of the Marian landscapes of Brooklyn discussed earlier, was a rectangular space. Italian Renaissance gardens stressed the ordering of the forces of nature through elaborate waterworks, topiary, and the imposition of classicizing symmetry upon the landscape. In fact, the work of Le Nôtre—whose designs for Vaux-le-Vicomte and Versailles define the French formal garden aesthetic—would not have been possible without the legacy of Italian Renaissance gardens, themselves revivals of ancient Roman villa gardens. The gardens of the exuberant Italian Baroque era conformed to an underlying geometrical balance and order that also derive from antiquity. Thus, as in other areas of Italian cultural production, a classical vocabulary of form is constantly reinscribed in Italian landscape design.

From the ancient Roman Republic to the twentieth-century Fascist state, classicism has been deployed over the millennia in the service of every political ideology imaginable. Although Luisa Del Giudice has argued convincingly that the "archvilla" (a vernacular house style of Italian Canadians) is the North American translation of a classicizing, Fascist architectural style, specific ideological linkages prove elusive vis-à-vis the Italian-American landscape.[18] The work of Elizabeth Barlow Rogers is helpful in this regard. Rogers, one of the most authoritative voices in the field of landscape history, writes from an art historian's perspective. Mindful of the role of social and political factors in shaping the landscape, she nonetheless acknowledges the potency of form itself, at times unbridled from the constraints of direct or even correct historical antecedents. Rogers writes,

> In tracing patterns of influence, it is apparent that form follows culture, but, once developed, form often follows form. By example, the revival of the forms of Greek and Roman art and architecture during the Renaissance and later periods of Western history exemplifies the ways in which people of other eras and in other places have found in the forms forged in antiquity an expressive design vocabulary for their own particular societal aspirations.[19]

Rogers' claim makes clear that adaptations of pre-existing designs need not—and often do not—bear their original political or social associations. Rogers' example of classicism is particularly useful in the current context because *as a form*, classicism retains its potency in the landscape designs of Italians in America. As such, regularity in planting survives as a dominant design feature in Italian-American gardens. So, too, does a design idiom that stresses clearly demarcated spaces, symmetry, order, and abundant use of hardscape.

The persistence of these ancient pagan and later Catholic ideas about the organization of space and their subsequent toleration by mainstream American culture permit the survival in America of a set of Italian values concerning the landscape. So deeply rooted in the Italian aesthetic consciousness is this penchant for order, stone, and statuary that it endures even when the practitioners of the landscape arts are several generations removed from their immigrant forebears. Reinforced further by post–World War II immigrants, this aesthetic perseveres.

In essence, Italian Americans have adapted the basic tenets of Italian landscape design creatively to fit within American patterns of urban and suburban development.

Thus, small urban front yards—the dominant model in the boroughs of New York—are transformed, indeed "Italianized," into symmetrical shrines replete with statuary, paving materials, and scrupulously pruned shrubs. Undergirding these physical manifestations of order is the distaste for—even phobia of—untamed land. Throughout history, this has been one of the most deeply held convictions of the Italian people vis-à-vis the landscape. Discussing the ancient Romans, Simon Schama writes, "In the ancient polarization between culture and nature, it was clear (not least from the radically deforested Italian peninsula) where their allegiance lay. In fact it is not too much to say that classical civilization has always defined itself against the primeval woods."[20] I recall architectural historian Vincent Scully discussing this Italian trait many years ago in his lectures at Yale; more recently, he described it succinctly as "the terror of nature."[21]

For centuries, Italians have distinguished physically and linguistically that which lies *fuori le mure* (outside the walls) of the city from urban space proper. An abrupt separation between town and countryside persists to this day in much of Italy. Once past the cemetery of many Italian towns, the landscape opens up to agricultural fields. The notable exception to this sudden transition occurs at the fringes of Italian towns where railroad rights of way are transformed into corridors comprising little vegetable plots. In the towns and cities of Italy, plants are set out in containers. Groups of potted plants appear at doorways; even street trees are grown in planters. The material culture of Italy constantly reminds us that nature must respect the confines imposed on it by civilization.

Historically, American residential land use patterns differ from Italian ones. Certainly, Italian immigrants to America in the late nineteenth and early twentieth centuries encountered both cities and rural areas as they had in Italy. However, mid-nineteenth-century experiments with suburbanization, the model that would eventually dominate American residential planning, had already begun. Several influential "garden cities" were founded prior to the Great Migration of Italians to America. Although a far cry from the well-heeled suburbs such as Llewellyn Park in New Jersey or Garden City on Long Island, areas of Brooklyn and Queens offered Italian Americans alternatives to the overcrowded tenements of Manhattan. By the 1920s, the early suburban model had extended to areas of Bensonhurst, Brooklyn, and Astoria, Queens. Whether freestanding or "attached," the houses in these newly developed areas came with land in the front and back that could be cultivated and designed.

ASTORIA, QUEENS

The landscapes of the Italian-American enclave in Astoria, Queens, boast a wide range of ornamentals and Italian culinary plants.[22] Generally—but by no means exclusively—ornamental plants are planted in front of the house, and fruits and vegetables at the rear or sides. The type of plant materials, the intense level of cultivation, and the tidiness of the plots construct an Italian-American ethnic model already observed in Bensonhurst.

In Astoria, a homemade grotto containing a mass-produced statue of St. Joseph holding the Christ child and another of the Virgin attest to the permeability between the sacred spaces of the home and the cemetery. Each landscape and hardscape element is deployed exactly as it would be at a typical Italian-American grave at Calvary Cemetery, New York's largest Catholic cemetery, located in nearby Woodside, Queens. Set out in the lawn amidst a balanced composition of evergreens, the figures in this Holy Family group gaze at the floral tribute of petunias planted in the ground at their feet. As in the altar-like front yards of Bensonhurst, the composition serves as religious "signage" announcing the belief of the owners. It announces their devotion to the Holy Family at the home: the site of the most important institution of Italian-American life, the family. Moreover, the park-like setting and obvious upkeep under the protective gaze of religious figures create a sacred landscape out of a small front yard.

Virtually ubiquitous chain link fences deny physical access to Astoria's Italian-American landscapes to casual passersby but permit extensive ogling of the horticultural bounty within. Grape arbors in Astoria, like in other Italian-American enclaves in metro New York, generally occur between the chain link driveway gates and the garage. In a fascinating instance of cultural syncretism, these arbors often serve as fructiferous carports conflating in a practical way the grape (*Vitis* sp.) and the automobile, archetypes of the two cultures that meet on this ground.

Italian Americans often stray from the strictly ornamental conventions of the landscapes of order discussed earlier by cultivating culinary plants in the public eye. In Astoria, where front yards are small and many backyards have been converted to asphalt covered parking lots, such flexibility of design proves useful. As such, there are numerous instances where fruits and vegetables join or replace traditionally "ornamental" plants. Moreover, a corner lot is a great asset because it comes with a side yard that may be cultivated. It is not uncommon, therefore, to see a fig tree growing in a front or side yard. The limited space available to the gardeners is the ostensible or practical reason for such placement, but ethnic identity is another. Basil (*Ocimum basilicum*) in pots, tomato plants (*Lycopersicon lycopersicum*), and fig trees announce the Italian-American ethnicity of the inhabitants to the rest of the street. In this regard, Colleen Sheehy's reading of yard art as a proclamation of identity may be extended to plant materials. Sheehy points out, "Yard art tacitly functions as a means to evaluate others through their choices of imagery and materials on display." She also asserts, "The use and preference for certain artifacts also reflects and maintains distinctions between ethnic, religious, age, and other kinds of groups."[23] Quoted in *The New York Times* article cited earlier, Joseph Scelsa acknowledges that the fig tree is a type of horticultural signage for the presence of "old-timers," elderly Italian ethnics; Scelsa correlates their disappearance with the disappearance of the cultivation of the fig tree, citing it among "those folk traditions [that] are unfortunately waning."[24] In Astoria, however, the tradition—and the fig trees themselves—appears robust. Astoria's culinary plants and arbors join religious statuary, hardscape, and a rigorous respect for boundaries as essential components of the Italian-American landscape and a visual proclamation of ethnicity.

Landscapes of Memory

Another kind of landscape, one directly informed by their makers' personal recollections of Italian models, occurs at many Italian-American homes in the New York tri-state region. These landscapes emphasize horticulture in its strictest sense, eschewing

Grape Arbor, Astoria, Queens. (Photograph by the author.)

a ritualized care of statuary and altar-like space in favor of intense involvement with plant materials. Old World methods of placing and pruning trees and shrubs and the cultivation of Italian culinary crops figure prominently on these plots. These landscapes conform to the general dictates of American dominant culture in that ornamental plants are grown in front of the house, and food crops are grown in the backyard. And yet, these landscapes fully recapitulate the Italian landscapes their owners once tended. As such, I call these remarkable reconstructions "landscapes of memory."

The three landscapes of memory studied most closely for this chapter are each the work of post–World War II immigrants. Moreover, their locations, with two in Connecticut and one on Long Island, indicate the presence of highly elaborated Italian-American landscapes in the suburbs of the tri-state area.[25] Nonetheless, this form also occurs in urban areas. Because memory and personal history play such an important role in the conception of these landscapes, visual and historical analysis is here supplemented by interviews with their owners.

These Italian-American landscapes result from the physical realization of a remembered Italian countryside against the backdrop of the American suburb. Landscapes of memory emphasize the intensive nurturing of ornamental plant materials as well as the raising of food crops over the creation of an overtly sacred precinct. Nonetheless, they share with landscapes of order a clear demarcation of spaces and boundaries.[26] Landscapes of memory frequently occupy the interior areas of the property rather than the more public front yard. In these comparatively private spaces, the interior minds of their creators work out late in life the memories of their Italian homeland. Close analysis of three properties, each one tended by an elderly Italian immigrant, sheds light on these landscapes of memory.

FROM NATURE TO ART: CARMELO BUSCEMI'S LANDSCAPE, CROMWELL, CONNECTICUT

Carmelo Buscemi's large comfortable house in Cromwell, Connecticut, sits on about an acre of land. Buscemi, who learned to cultivate the land in his native province of Syracuse, built the house himself about four decades ago. He also designed the landscape that he continues to tend. Like the other men interviewed for this section, resourcefulness, thrift, hard work, and memory characterize Buscemi's interaction with the landscape. Pointing out a large yew at the entrance to his driveway on the day I interviewed him in March 2002, Buscemi mentioned that he took it with him as a small plant when he moved from Hartford's Little Italy. Here, even an intermediary step from Syracuse to suburbia is recalled horticulturally. An abundance of rigorously pruned evergreen shrubs links Buscemi's contemporary Connecticut property to the ancient landscape of Italy.

Topiary, the art of sculpting living plant material into geometrical shapes or representational forms, originated with the ancient Romans. The Italians of the Renaissance revived this classical practice; it remains a feature of formal gardens in the Occidental tradition. Buscemi keeps this cultural memory alive and announces it to the neighborhood with the severely pruned yews in his front yard. Buscemi's pristine front yard is to a degree analogous to the tidy landscapes of order in New York's boroughs. However, in this suburban landscape, control and order are expressed most clearly at the level of the plant materials themselves. The intense cultivation, pruning, and coaxing of evergreen plants in this immigrant's landscape proclaim a direct connection with Italian practices and attitudes toward horticulture.

Personal memory undoubtedly guides Buscemi's topiary practice. This typically Italian desire to extend geometry and abstraction to plant materials is not always lost to subsequent generations. Many Americans of Italian descent transform their yews (*Taxus* sp.), privet hedges (*Ligustrum obtusifolium*), white pines (*Pinus strobus*), Chinese junipers (*Juniperus chinensis*), and border forsythias (*Forsythia* x *intermedia*)—all common landscape plants of the northeastern United States—into cubes, spheres, cones, and more. These observations raise two important issues. The first, treated at some length earlier, is that unbridled, untamed nature must be kept at bay; the second is that nature needs the helping hand of humans to reveal its art. In spite of differences in culture and geography, nature for Italians on both sides of the Atlantic must be subjected to the civilizing hand of man.

Perhaps the most compelling example in the history of Italian art of this impulse to order, assist, and aestheticize nature comes from Cesare Ripa's *Iconologia*. As the title makes clear, this is a book of iconology: the assignation of symbols and personifications to various moods, fields of endeavor, and even regions of the world. Ripa's *Iconologia* was first published in 1593; the 1603 and subsequent editions include woodcut illustrations. These codified representations were of great use to artists, particularly in the Baroque era.[27]

The illustration of Arte, the personification of art, from the 1618 edition of Ripa is particularly revealing. With her left arm, Arte embraces a stake and the *arboscello* (sapling) that it supports. She holds a paintbrush and a chisel in her right hand: tools, according to the accompanying text, with which the artist imitates nature. However, Ripa asserts that art must transcend mere imitation. Rather, he maintains that art, as in the case of agriculture, must compensate for the "defects" of nature. Thus the stake provides the twisted *arboscello* with "the vigor of art" upon which to grow.[28] Ripa's text and the accompanying woodcut reveal subtle attitudes about agriculture as an art—that is to say, as an enterprise that is both aesthetic and practical. The image conveys the rigor and quasi-military pose of Arte's right side, the side of art that is imitative of nature. In contrast, Arte's left hand, relaxed like her left leg, caresses the stake upon which the little tree grows. This side of her figure emphasizes the gentle, nurturing aspect of art that *works with* nature. Not surprisingly, Arte's facial expression is one of both serenity and awe. She conveys to the beholder the quiet wonder of a gardener admiring the plant she has raised.

In the later Hertel edition of Ripa, Arte, now designated by the Latin "Ars," presents a statue but turns away from it to face a plant on a stake. Here, the *arboscello* is interpreted as a grape vine, that most typical of Italian plants whose climbing habit is artfully arranged by Italians wherever they settle. Furthermore, this edition of Ripa points out that agriculture "is actually one of the most important arts of man."[29]

To civilize nature—to "correct its defects," as Ripa puts it—is one of the two sides of art itself. Carmelo Buscemi and the other men I interviewed are not historians who sit around reading the art theory of the Baroque era. Nonetheless, their attitudes about aesthetic creation are rooted in traditions that existed in Italy since antiquity. Revived during the Renaissance, these ideas were in turn perpetuated and codified by Ripa and his engravers in the sixteenth and seventeenth centuries. It would be spurious to maintain that there exists a single and direct line of aesthetic transmission that one may trace from antiquity to the *contadini* (peasants) of the mid-twentieth-century *Mezzogiorno* (Southern Italy). Rather, a culture's "given" way of creating things or shaping space—what art historians describe as a "style" or "convention"—is at work here. Indeed, style is so bound up with the culture from which it springs as to be invisible, unremarkable, or normal to its practitioners.

Arte, from Ripa's Iconologia, *1618.*

Buscemi's emphasis on care and nurturing of plants is not limited to the ornamental landscape; rather, it is especially evident in the productive landscape at the rear of his property. Here, he grows vegetables and fruits in an extremely orderly plot. Criss-crossed with paths and entirely enclosed, Buscemi's garden takes its place in the tradition of the medieval European *hortus conclusus* and even the Roman atrium garden. Anxious to share his knowledge, Buscemi demonstrated with a stake and a handful of soil how he sets out tomato plants. Slowly but effortlessly, his well-trained hands and eyes measured the intervals at which to place the plants. He demonstrated the use of a dibble for making planting holes and for pressing the soil against the roots. There is no doubt this is a space where nature is controlled, where the gardener's "artful" hand (recalling Ripa) makes up for the defects of nature and creates something beautiful: beautiful in its control, its productivity, and its ability to nourish the body and soul.

Buscemi's vegetable garden and orchard are a world apart from his suburban lawn and his gated fence emphasizes this fact. Buscemi's placement of the American flag at the boundary between the enclosed Italian garden of zucchini (*Curcurbita pepo* 'Cylindrica'), garlic (*Allium sativum*), and peppers (*Capsicum annuum*), and the stereotypically American suburban lawn is telling, if perhaps unconscious. The flag and fence mark an international boundary of sorts. It is a boundary of cultures and landscapes: a personal boundary of past and present for a Siracusano in Connecticut. Opening his garden gate and stepping onto the paths he made with his own hands, Buscemi walks into a living memory of Italy. Safe in the enclosure of chain link fence, privet hedge, and yews and pines "limbed up" Italian style to reveal their trunks, Buscemi's garden brings to the fore not only order and practicality but a flood of emotions. It is a place to recall one's personal and cultural history. Bending to the ground with his dibble in hand, Buscemi's body moves with the confidence and poise of a dancer who has learned his steps so well they are now second nature. With plant materials and hardware available in the New World, the garden's shape recalls the Old World. Typical of Italian-American gardens, it makes clear that ingenuity and hard work lead to productivity. Thus, Buscemi's efforts provide good food for his family and an understated but obvious sense of satisfaction for himself.

After touring Carmelo Buscemi's Italian-style fruit orchard, we crossed his very American lawn and came in from the cold for a cup of piping hot espresso prepared by Mrs. Buscemi. She also served slices of hardened preserves made from the fruit of the quince tree (*Cydonia oblonga*) we had just seen dormant in the garden. A neighbor dropped by and joined us for coffee but refused the delightful quince confection. He explained that he had been taken prisoner during the Nazi occupation of the Abruzzi region. The Germans had given the prisoners little more than quinces to eat during those dark days 60-odd years ago. Once again, the garden yielded a harvest of memories some less pleasant than others.

Labor Made Visible: Valentino Leombruno's Landscape, Wethersfield, Connecticut

One might call the tidiness and symmetry of Valentino Leombruno's front yard in Wethersfield, Connecticut strict or severe. Two Dwarf Alberta spruces (*Picea glauca*

Carmelo Buscemi's "International Boundary," Cromwell, Connecticut. (Photograph by the author.)

'Conica') flank a yew in a small bed of foundation plants at Mr. Leombruno's front door. These plants have naturally strong geometrical qualities; in fact, Italian Americans favor the densely conical Dwarf Alberta spruce for flanking tombstones. Leombruno has exploited this almost perfect natural form even further: He has trained the spruces into standards. By trimming off the bottom branches—as Buscemi also has done—he has modified the conical or "Christmas tree" shape of the spruces to reveal their central stems. The green tops of the shrubs have been shaped into semicircular gumdrop or mushroom cap shapes. The yew between them has been transformed into a dense and closely sheared cone. On the other side of the path to his front door, Leombruno has added another layer of symmetry. A carefully pruned spruce stands at the end of the foundation planting thus balancing the entryway. It shares the planting scheme with several other rigorously pruned or sheared shrubs each standing apart from its neighbor.

Leombruno's intensive shaping of his shrubs exceeds that of many Italian Americans, but it is not an anomaly. Topiary, an element of formal Italian villa gardens, makes a statement about elevated social class. Moreover, Leombruno's topiary makes abundantly clear a trait that characterizes most Italian-American landscapes: the desire to make labor visible even when the laborer is the owner. This attribute, already noted in this chapter's section on the smaller, urban landscapes of order, is fully exploited in the larger suburban context.

Gray-white granite chips cover the earth of Leombruno's entire foundation planting scheme. Growing up on Long Island, I learned from my parents that stone chips—especially marble chips—in the landscape were associated with overtly Italian ethnicity and low socioeconomic status. These were the qualities of people my parents would call *cafoni* (boors), ironically using an Italian word to distance themselves from other presumably less-acculturated Italian Americans. I am now willing to revisit my adolescent prejudice against stone in light of history and the slippery territory of taste.

A material rich in symbolic associations, stone connects Italians and Italian Americans to Italy in memory and in imagination. Stone recalls the ancient classical sculptures and ruins. It recalls also the work of Renaissance and Baroque artists and architects. Assuming one could go to Italy and remain indifferent to stone, a staggering amount of Italian visual culture would not register. The Greek temples, the Colosseum, Michelangelo's David, and Bernini's fountains—to name but a few—would be overlooked. Stone and concrete, itself comprising stone-based media, are the quintessential Italian materials of choice. Stone products play an important role in Italian-American landscapes as well. Paving, masonry walls, statues, and even humble stone chips keep alive the memory of the texture, sound, and color of the land left behind. These materials also evoke associations with the masonry trades pursued by many Italian immigrant laborers.

Leombruno's use of stone and the severity of his topiary forms speak of the hardness and formality common in Italian-American landscapes. Further evidence of this strictness lies in the containment of plant materials in beds, planters, small outbuildings, and seasonal wrappings. Nonetheless, a paternal nurturing of the plants in one's care tempers this subjugation of nature.

As a child, I was struck by the anthropomorphic aspect of fig trees in Italian-American gardens in Queens, Brooklyn, and Lindenhurst, Long Island. Typically wrapped in black tarp and bound tight with rope, they became creepy figures in the winter garden. These "figures" were often topped off with an inverted bucket over their "heads." Although not seen by their owners as part of a Halloween or harvest assemblage, the covering of the fig tree was certainly an autumnal event. Like the fetishistic sheathing by Italian-American women of living room couches and chairs in clear plastic, or the dressing of a cult statue, this wrapping was not just a seasonal rite but one that had a practical function: in this case, the protection of tender Old World plants against the cold winters of the northeastern United States. Nonetheless, one cannot help being moved by the care with which Leombruno wraps his fig trees in old blankets and stores them in niches built outdoors against his chimney. The love for and nurturing of plants that provide food for his family reveals the emotional aspect of the Italian-American landscape. Here, Italian values are reinterpreted in light of the harsh Connecticut winter.

For his biggest fig tree, Leombruno has built a large shed with a glazed façade facing south for ample winter sun. In summer, sliding plywood panels on the roof of the fig house allow Leombruno to ventilate the space in which the 20-foot specimen grows. The floor of the fig house contains a raised bed in which to grow salad greens in winter. A space heater ensures that overnight temperatures remain above freezing so that lettuce (*Lactuca sativa*) sown in the fall survives the winter and is ready for an early spring harvest. What a pleasant surprise it is to see lettuce reaching maturity in March in central Connecticut. With amazing ingenuity, Leombruno nurtures his contained crops and is able to replicate the seasonal rhythms of growing, harvest, and foodways of his warm native land.

Winter-hardy fruit trees grow outdoors adjacent to the fig house. Thus, both tender and hardy fruits are organized in a mini-orchard. Here, as in the small, urban landscapes of order, the importance of order extends to the productive zones of larger Italian-American landscapes. The orchard lies at the rear edge of the property. This way, the shade of the fruit trees does not fall upon the lower growing vegetables and inhibit their vigor. Moreover, Leombruno's rigorous arrangement of crops according to type would make a horticultural taxonomist proud. Vegetables whose fruits are eaten (such as tomatoes and peppers) and those whose bulbs are eaten (garlic and onions [*Allium cepa*]) are grown in one bed. Leombruno raises his leaf vegetables in another bed. Herbs grow in other small beds; such is the case of a patch of oregano (*Origanum vulgare*) watched over by a statue of the Blessed Mother, a landscape enhancement that Leombruno pointed out somewhat sheepishly was his wife's doing. With its statue and plantings amidst a large greensward, Mrs. Leombruno's small patch on the home grounds recalls Italian-American cemetery landscaping, an art form in which women's work is common.

Female labor in the Italian-American landscape is not unusual, but clear gender divisions characterize domestic labor among the elderly Italian immigrants whom I interviewed. In these households, daily care of the interior space is women's work; maintenance of the landscape is primarily a masculine endeavor. The small sample of suburban landscapes surveyed here precludes any general pronouncement on gender roles. However, one might conjecture that the bulk of landscaping activity of these immigrants emulates that which is promoted by the values and marketing of the dominant American culture. The primary tasks of suburban landscaping—mowing lawns and trimming shrubs and trees—require machinery and are gendered as male jobs. In the photos of almost every garden center flyer, men operate lawn mowers and chain saws, while women model gardening gloves and hand trowels amidst beds and borders bursting with flowers. Perhaps pressure to conform to this male/power tool versus female/flower garden norm of American marketing is felt strongly by Italian Americans in suburban contexts. In any event, among these Italian-born, post–World War II immigrants, almost every landscaping endeavor from topiary to vegetable gardening is men's work.

The Aesthetic of Labor, Thrift, and Abundance

Landscapes of memory announce the hard work of the man of the Italian-American household. Vigilant attention to the pruning and shearing of shrubs, the construction and maintenance of hardscape, and the coaxing of tender food crops to perform in a hostile climate are among the activities of these men. Implicit in these practices is an aesthetic that transcends the ornamental horticulture of American dominant culture. Erminio Dimascio of Wethersfield, Connecticut, who arranged my visits with Mr. Buscemi and Mr. Leombruno, captured its essence when he told me that his father used to say, "You can't eat flowers." Beyond the topiary, perfectly edged beds, and sturdy outbuildings, beauty in the Italian-American landscape involves abundance. Beauty resides in a patch of ripening tomatoes or a fruit-laden fig tree. In Ripa's *Iconologia*, Arte, the bringer of beauty, presents a well-tended vine. When frugality and ingenuity join hard work and nurturing, this beauty is tinged with awe and mystery. From virtually nothing springs something of great sensory and practical value, good food.

Leombruno's thrift impresses the visitor to his landscape. His rough-hewn fig house and his smaller fig shelters are made of modest materials, some apparently salvaged. An old piece of string secures the large fig house door. This passion for economy of resources attests to the gardener's recollection of lean times in Italy. Leombruno's landscape of memory conveys to the visitor an appreciation of frugality, hard work, and resourcefulness.

Memories of Pratola Peligna

Echoing the pairing of shrubs on the exterior, a pair of citrus trees greets the visitor upon crossing the threshold of the Leombruno home. An orange tree (*Citrus sinensis*) and a lemon tree (*Citrus limon*), their glossy green leaves, intoxicatingly fragrant blossoms, and colorful fruits bring a bit of the Mediterranean to Wethersfield, Connecticut. The citrus pair brings indoors the containment, productivity, and memory so important in Leombruno's landscape. In part, practical considerations force the citrus plants indoors. Intolerant of prolonged exposure to freezing temperatures, they *must* be grown indoors in a Connecticut winter, or they will die. However, their presence here is undoubtedly more nuanced than this. The citrus trees delight the senses with the sights, smells, textures, and tastes of a southern Italian grove. They lift the spirits and bring back memories of the familiar plants of the owner's youth in Italy.

This observer senses that every time Leombruno enters his house, the vision and fragrance of the citrus plants suggest a "coming home" to Italy. And yet there is a reminder of Leombruno's new identity just beyond one's immediate field of vision. To the right of the citrus pair stands a stereotypically Yankee artifact: namely, a grandfather clock. One does not need a background in semiotic theory to see that the elements of this assemblage spell out "Italian American" as clearly as the two words do.

Leombruno does much to keep a memory of Italy alive horticulturally, and yet he concedes symbolically that his Abruzzese hometown of Pratola Peligna is far away geographically and temporally. He acknowledged that the horticultural traditions of the dominant culture would eventually win out despite his wonderful retention of the old landscaping ways. Toward the end of our interview, Leombruno told me that his children are not gardeners. Standing in his yard he said to me, "All this will end when I die."

An Italian Farm on the Gold Coast: Amato Spagnoletti's Landscape, Glen Cove, Long Island

By far, the most intact horticultural memory of Italy in this study is Amato Spagnoletti's landscape in Glen Cove, Long Island. Spagnoletti's property lies within the Orchard section of Glen Cove, an Italian stronghold for generations. Even in this neighborhood, Spagnoletti's landscape is remarkable. Walking past the stone walls and up the driveway of Spagnoletti's property, one leaves behind the familiar landscape of suburban Long Island and seems to arrive magically at a farm in the region of Spagnoletti's native Avellino. On a warm October day, picked figs lay out ripening in the sun; tomatoes and garlic were already in storage in one shed, and rabbits lived in another.

The sensation of crossing an international boundary here is even more intense than that experienced at the Buscemi property. Aside from a small front yard and a tiny paved area at the rear of the house, Spagnoletti, a self-described *contadino*, has transformed his entire property into a small farm. The main area, a vegetable garden about 16 x 60 feet alongside the house, is enclosed by a stone wall in front, chain link at the rear and side property boundaries, and chicken wire fencing along the driveway. Carefully placed and pruned fruit trees dot the vegetable beds. Ornamental plants— marigolds (*Tagetes erecta*), hollyhocks (*Alcea rosea*), and dahlias (*Dahlia* hybrids) —grow at the edges of the property, the largest concentration in a small strip bounded by the driveway, the garden fence, the stone wall, and the sidewalk. The ornamental elements of the garden are public; they delineate and cloak the productive zone within. Not only does the Italian-American aesthetic of self-containment prevail in the landscape design, but it is matched by a cloister-like hermeticism of economics and ethnicity.

Spagnoletti's landscape is bubble-like both in its recapitulation of the customs, language, and foodways of his native Avellino and in its sustainable operation. Speaking entirely in Italian, Spagnoletti described how rabbits play a role in the ecosystem of his mini-farm. Kept safe and healthy in a homemade hutch in the yard, the rabbits eat leftover bread and hay harvested in a vacant lot nearby. Their manure provides rich compost for the vegetable beds. When mature, the animals are slaughtered for meat. Even Spagnoletti's use of water is a model of sustainability. On the same Long Island of underground sprinkler systems and built-in swimming pools, Spagnoletti catches rainwater in barrels fed by the gutters and downspouts on his house. Raised in a land where access to water was not taken for granted, he remains respectful of this life-giving resource.

In the midst of suburbia, Spagnoletti works contentedly and purposefully in a living memory landscape that provides an amazing degree of self-sufficiency. With pride, he related that his family does not buy any produce: His garden supplies their needs. Spagnoletti lives out the rituals of the agricultural year that are reduced to seasonal decorations in the small, urban landscapes of order in Bensonhurst. For example, when October frosts threaten his tender crops, Spagnoletti unfurls tarps on a framework of stakes and bamboo beams to protect them, thereby extending the season.

In spite of Spagnoletti's amazing fidelity to the design and practices of the Italian landscape, his creation sits on a small residential Long Island plot. One notes certain concessions to his adopted land upon close inspection of the plants. On the day of my visit, a large American Hubbard squash (*Curcurbita maxima* 'Hubbard') sat ripening in the sun. It shared the garden with Italian squash, peppers, and tomatoes, all foods associated with Italy. (Ironically, all are native to the Americas, their early forms entering the European diet after 1492.) When asked about the differences between the food crops in Italy and America, Spagnoletti pointed to the big Hubbard squash and related

Amato Spagnoletti's landscape, Glen Cove, Long Island, New York. (Photograph by the author.)

that his daughter had given him the seeds for it. In this instance, the first fully accultu-rated generation already plays a role in modifying a traditional Italian landscape. More-over, his Glen Cove landscape contains flowering herbaceous plants that Spagnoletti did not grow in Avellino. From Spagnoletti's perspective, however, the biggest difference between growing food in Italy and in America is the abundant water supply in the latter. Nonetheless, this amazingly accurate memory garden exhibits the first small but significant steps in the transition from an Italian landscape to an Italian-American one.

For Amato Spagnoletti, however, the design, the tasks, and the cadences of the Italian landscape remain relatively intact. Spagnoletti and the other creators of land-scapes of memory share a quiet pride in their wizardry. They transform the most hum-ble of materials—salvaged construction debris, saved seeds, fireplace ashes, free manure, and captured rainwater—into delicious produce and robust flowers and shrubs. The tidy landscapes these men design and the plants they lovingly nurture make manifest in America the age-old Italian esteem for horticulture as Arte. These landscapes provide many functions. They announce Italian ethnicity to the public and reify that identity to their owners; they make visible the value of hard work and the care of property and family; they afford the health benefits of exercise and fresh, or-ganic produce. One senses however that these outcomes are secondary to the solace of remaining connected in memory to the land of one's birth. In these landscapes of memory, the bodies of the elderly men who tend them follow the same movements they did in youth. They feel the texture of familiar plant materials, recognize the charac-teristic aroma of their leaves, and savor the tastes of decades past. Just as these men nurture the plants in their care, landscapes of memory nurture the souls of the men who tend them.

FADING LANDSCAPES OF MEMORY: THE N TRAIN EMBANKMENT GARDENS OF BENSONHURST

As Valentino Lemobruno prophesied about his own property, landscapes of memory are destined to fade like the memories that called them into being in the first place. Old men die, their gardens are neglected or destroyed; their knowledge and their art are forgotten. Certainly the most poignant landscapes of this study are the abandoned gardens along the subway embankment in Brooklyn. These landscapes of memory once realized by Italian immigrants now deteriorate before our eyes to be lost forever.

Running underground in Manhattan and in parts of Brooklyn, the N line of the Metropolitan Transit Authority's subway system emerges from its tunnel and travels in a trench through the Bensonhurst section of Brooklyn. The tracks lie above ground but well below street level. As the steep railway cut rises to the pavement of the surround-ing neighborhood, the embankment flattens to a wide swath of land at the same grade as the sidewalk. In keeping with the Italian practice of cultivating railroad margins, Italian immigrant men carved out small plots in which they grew vegetables and erected small wooden buildings. Anthony Esposito, who grew up in Bensonhurst in the 1950s and 1960s, recalled old Italian men "in white shirts, black pants, and suit jackets smoking cigars while their tomatoes grew." He remembered that each man had his own little "shack" in which to keep his tools and to rest while in the garden.[30]

In the fall of 2001, a chain link fence and locked gate separated the street from the railroad embankment and the old gardens of the Italian immigrants. Their sheds were in ruin. Of course, the annuals—the tomatoes, peppers, and eggplants (*Solanum melongena*) that Esposito described—were long gone. However, like the old roses in Frances Hodgson Burnett's 1911 classic, *The Secret Garden*, some perennials thrived. Grape vines ran rampant over still sturdy arbors constructed of steel fence poles, copper plumbing pipe, and wooden stakes. Fig trees, no longer lovingly wrapped each fall, persevered and even flourished in spite of their neglect.

A visit to these abandoned Italian-American gardens has the power to evoke the nostalgia and melancholy that often accompany the study of the recent past. Perhaps we are moved by our own recollections of a bygone era or the memories of those we know. Our connection to the period is direct and personal, our feelings of loss and longing greater than our grief for a fallen ancient civilization. The subway embankment gardens are doubly poignant. Conceived at least in part to soothe the soul that longed for a far away landscape, a landscape of the past, the gardens themselves have become relics of the Italian-American experience in New York, yet they continue to evoke memory. They recall an era less concerned about liability than our own: a time when the benefit to a neighborhood outweighed the possibility of litigation. The embankment gardens reveal how a thriving horticultural tradition helped to create the very identity of an Italian-American community by contributing an aesthetic cohesion in design and plants, an opportunity for social exchange, the financial and health benefits of fresh food, and many sets of watchful eyes.

Final Thoughts: An Italian-American Iconology

Cesare Ripa would probably delight in the fact that the cultivated grape, the accompaniment to his personification of Arte, perseveres in the abandoned embankment gardens. If one were to publish a contemporary *Iconologia*, one could find few better symbols for Italian Americana than the grape arbor. (See the figure on page 93.) Formally and conceptually, the grape arbor expresses succinctly the themes of order and memory that characterize Italian-American residential landscapes in the New York metro area.

The grape arbor is the herald of Italian neighborhoods in the boroughs and beyond. Constructed of pipes and poles and positioned over typically American features of home—driveway, backyard, or garage—the grape arbor announces like a signboard the Italian heritage of the residents. The materials of the arbor demonstrate the thrift of the gardeners and the respect for manual labor. The coaxing hand of the gardeners, like the poles and latticework of the arbor, impose order upon the naturally unruly habit of the grape plant. In keeping with Italian values, nature is civilized. It is not pummeled into submission or destroyed; rather, it is coaxed, nurtured, made to do man's bidding while retaining its own qualities. Nature is thus improved: It is ordered and made vigorous and beautiful, made into art by the gentle hand of the gardener who is seen *as an artist* throughout much of Italian history.

The arbor speaks of hard work, thrift, utility, and productivity. It provides a support for delicious grapes, themselves a reminder of Italy. Moreover, the broad leaves of the vine on the arbor shade a piece of the property in the heat of the summer. Admiring the arbor over his driveway, I asked an elderly man in Astoria what variety of grapes he was growing. Matter-of-factly he responded, *"Uve bianche, uve italiane"* ("White grapes, Italian grapes"). An economical landscape feature, the grape arbor feeds, cools, recalls sacred rites, and evokes "the old country"; in short, it helps to create Italian-American ethnicity. At harvest time, the grape arbor speaks of a stereotypical Italian joy of abundance expressed by the bounty of nature. It signifies the pleasure of being out in fresh air and sunshine in a structure partially open to the sky. And it speaks of the seasons and the cycle of life. With its times for flowering, growth, setting fruit, harvest, and wine making, the grape arbor vividly punctuates the seasonal cycle so important to the Italian-American psyche, one fascinated by decorations for major holidays and various saints' days.

The arbor speaks also of memory, of the old ways, of the land of ancestors or the land immigrant gardeners themselves left behind. It makes one wonder about the future of Italian-American culture. Will customs be abandoned like the forgotten fig trees and untended grape vines of the N train embankment, or will future generations harvest the bounty of Italian-American culture? Does what Richard Alba called the "twilight of ethnicity" mean the forgetting of authentic material culture, practice, and symbolism and the adoption of a corporate fiction of Italian-American ethnicity along the lines of an Olive Garden (Italian restaurant chain) television commercial or HBO's *The Sopranos*?

Italian-American landscapes of order and landscapes of memory are not the outward expressions of a preconceived ethnic identity; they are not illustrations of an abstract concept. Rather, these landscapes play a crucial role in constructing Italian-American ethnic identity. Their plans recapitulate historical models, some ornamental and prestigious, others agrarian and humble. Their care recalls both agricultural and religious seasonal practices. These landscapes give an ethnic face to the property and show pride in productivity through economy. Tidy and clearly delineated in conception, they provide spaces where visual and olfactory rapture, joy in abundance, religious ritual, and memories of pleasure and pain find fertile ground.

Postscript

In August 2009, two days before I submitted my revisions on this chapter, Joseph Sciorra, the editor of the present volume, alerted me to the fact that the N train embankment gardens in Bensonhurst, Brooklyn—landscapes I had consigned to history—were, as he put it, "resplendent." In the years that have elapsed since my first visit to the embankment gardens, several trends have gained considerable momentum in this country. Increased environmental awareness has translated into a desire for "green" living. At the same time a culture—some might say a "cult"—of food has grown in leaps and bounds in the United States. The terms "foodie" and "locavore" have entered everyday parlance. A third trend, the celebration of the racial and ethnic diversity of this country, has fueled in many Americans a search for their family's origins, traditions, and perhaps most compelling, foodways. Ecological consciousness and the desire for tasty, locally grown and "heirloom" fruits and vegetables of our ancestors intersect at the site of the home garden, community garden, or small farm. The perfectly round, translucent pink, mealy supermarket tomatoes trucked across the country in a cellophane-covered plastic caddie do not make the mark when the consumer demands flavor, seeks the variety his grandparents may have eaten, and rejects excessive use of fossil fuels. The values kept alive in the Italian-American landscape, the connection to the land, the preservation of traditional varieties of crops, sustainable horticultural practices, and the desire to bring beauty and bounty into the spaces around our homes, now align with the attitudes of the dominant culture.

Locating Memory

LONGING, PLACE, AND AUTOBIOGRAPHY IN VINCENZO ANCONA'S SICILIAN POETRY

Joseph Sciorra

It may be that writers in my position, exiles or emigrants or expatriates, are haunted by some sense of loss, some urge to reclaim, to look back, even at the risk of being mutated into pillars of salt. But if we do look back, we must also do so in the knowledge—which gives us profound uncertainties— that our physical alienation from India almost inevitably means that we will not be capable of reclaiming precisely the thing that was lost; that we will, in short, create fictions, not actual cities or villages, but invisible ones, imaginary homelands, Indias of the mind.
SALMAN RUSHDIE, *IMAGINARY HOMELANDS*[1]

Memory and dream are intermixed in this mad universe.
JACK KEROUAC, *DR. SAX*[2]

In his Sicilian language poem *"Chi vita fazzu"* ("The Life I Lead"), the late Vincenzo Ancona contemplated his retirement in Brooklyn, New York after two decades of working in America. In particular, he reflected on the miniature tableaux he had created by weaving multicolored telephone wires into representational figures depicting his former life as an agricultural laborer in Castellammare del Golfo (Trapani province).[3] "The Old Well" and "The Grape Harvest" were two of the "evanescent things" he had crafted "with patience and some ingenuity/and unconventional materials" (*e cu 'na gran pacenza, modi e versu/fabricu cosi pi diri a lu ventu/cu matiriali di tuttu riversu*). These hand-crafted objects, along with so many of Ancona's poems, were born of haunting memories and his longing for a time and place he understood to be irrevocably transformed:

Ora sunnannu sempri lu passatu	Now I'm always dreaming about my past life
di la me vita e di quantu ncuntravi,	and all that I've encountered,
e chi tegnu a la menti siggillatu	which I keep engraved in my mind
puntu pi puntu e chiddu chi passavi,	in detail and all I've experienced,
mi veni in menti un quatru stimatu	I recall a treasured scene of
di la vinnigna chi tantu aduravi . . .	the grape harvest, which I adored so much . . .[4]

Ancona's reminiscences were part of a painful expression of loss he struggled to reconcile. He concluded his poem by imagining himself as one of the tiny woven figures in his diorama:

Criditimi! Mi sentu un picciutteddu,	Believe me! I feel like a kid.
Mi sentu 'na figura di sunnari	I feel like a figure in a dream,
comu fussi a cavaddu a un muliceddu	as though I were astride a mule
'nn 'a un tempu chi nun pò chiù riturnari.	in a time that will never return.
Quantu ricordi vivi, chi smaceddu:	What vivid memories, and yet what shambles.
mi vinissi di chianciri macari.	Sometimes I feel like crying.
Tuttu lu me pasatu è na firita,	All my past is a wound,
si ci reflettu; ma chi è sta vita?	If I think about it; what is life?

Although Ancona left the larger existential question unanswered in this poem, musings on his life as an immigrant were at the heart of his creative works.

Ancona was a gifted and articulate individual versed in the cultural practices of the Sicilian agricultural working poor, which he adapted and transformed in urban America. He was a poet beloved by many who worked in the Sicilian tradition of *ottava rima* (eight 11-syllable lines with the rhyming scheme *ababab cc*), tackling topics such as culture shock, space travel, divorce, environmental pollution, and nuclear war.[5] He performed work songs associated with harvesting and fishing at folk music concerts and festivals in the United States. Ancona was also a talented storyteller who turned personal narratives into riveting accounts of everyday life. His wire dioramas chronicling a past way of life were based upon innovations he made to traditional basket weaving techniques. Ancona was, in a sense, a folk Renaissance man who reinvented his art and himself in America by mining the past.

My approach to Ancona's creative work is not a literary reading but rather an ethnographic one. As such, I am concerned with the aesthetic dimensions, including process, final product, and performance of his poetry as well as the social world in which he created and interpreted his art. By exploring the intertextual web of what Howard Becker calls an "art world"—that is, the "established network of cooperative links among participants . . . that radiates out from the work in question"—I hope to situate Ancona's poetry in the cultural and social world in which he lived and created.[6]

What we remember and what we forget is shaped to a large degree by our immediate concerns and circumstances. Memory is historically constituted, grounded in the needs and desires of present day affairs. As Maurice Halbwachs notes, "at the movement of reproducing the past our imagination remains under the influence of the present social milieu."[7] Ancona turned, in part, to autobiography and the remembered past to face immigration's "challenge of discontinuity" and to comprehend the radical changes that he was experiencing in America.[8] By calling into relief the distance separating "then" and "now" as well as "there" and "here," he was able to measure and subsequently bridge the psychological and cultural riffs that emigration engenders. Yet Ancona's expressive work articulated his changing relationship to the past and its contextualy derived meanings at different stages of his life in the United States. Neither Ancona's memories nor the meanings he associated with his past remained static. Shifting social contexts and new events—such as return visits to Italy, family crises, his encounters with scholars interested in his creative work, and retirement—influenced what he remembered and how he narrated and interpreted those memories. Ancona's expressive practices involving language, song, and material objects were acts of "self authoring" that assisted the continual process of integrating the past and the present into a coherent sense of self.[9]

Ancona's memory work and cultural production were not isolating enterprises, but instead were part and parcel of the social environment in which he operated and thrived, that of his immediate family and the diasporic community of working class Castellammarese *paesani* (townspeople) and Sicilian co-nationals. An individual's memory "relies upon, relocates itself within, momentarily merges with, the collective memory," reproducing itself through interaction with others.[10] Exchanges with members of these groups shaped Ancona's autobiographical memory. It is the social aspect of memory that charged Ancona's poetry with power and resonance for his audience of compatriots. Ancona's work constituted what historian Pierre Nora identifies as "*lieux de mémoire*" (realms of memory), crafted objects where "memory crystallizes and secretes itself" at a time when "consciousness of a break with the past is bound up with the sense that memory has been torn."[11] Ancona was a key cultural player in helping to stimulate, formulate, and sustain a collective memory—and, by extension, group identity—through his interaction with and performances for his cohorts, who were versed in the aesthetic practices of Sicilian vernacular culture and shared similar experiences in Sicily and New York. It was through informal and formal presentations of declaimed poetry at Ancona's social club and other venues that individual reminiscences were collectively grounded, constituted, and reproduced in "social frameworks of memory."[12]

Ancona's poetic creations were representations of a specific cultural landscape: that of his agricultural and fishing town in western Sicily. This landscape was inextricably associated with farming techniques, religious celebrations, and daily life that Ancona vividly evoked in his art. The immigrant Ancona and his nostalgic *paesani* imbued this remembered place with new and shifting meanings as they were making their lives in America. In fact, Castellammare was imagined in contrast to their Brooklyn homes and neighborhoods. In turn, Ancona crafted and revised images of "Brooklyn" and "America" as part of his and his compatriots' repertoire of topographical references and spatial memories. "Castellammare" and "Brucculinu" were defined, in part, through their differences but in the process were also brought closer together. These linked "imagined worlds" of affliction, aspiration, triumph, disenchantment, and toil were collective loci of memories and dreams that situated a diasporic group of individuals in their respective journeys.[13]

Castellammare del Golfo: Portrait of a Sicilian Town

Vincenzo Ancona was born on April 14, 1915, in the coastal town of Castellammare del Golfo, into what he humbly described as *una famiglia povera, dalla classe operaia* ("a poor working class family").[14] His father, Vincenzo, was a farmer; and his mother, Rosa Asaro, came from a fishing family. Ancona was the oldest of five sons and three daughters.

Western Sicily was historically one of the poorest and most neglected regions of Italy. Widespread poverty, unemployment, and illiteracy, as well as the repressive and violent *mafia*, were rampant well until the 1960s. Scottish author Gavin Maxwell lived in the area of Castellammare during the 1950s when Ancona was working the land and fishing the Gulf of Trapani, and wrote sympathetically of the Sicilian working poor in his book *The Ten Pains of Death*. Maxell's reportage of Castellammarese social conditions is relevant in our understanding of Ancona's life prior to emigration. Maxwell made use of unnamed "official statistics" to highlight the extraordinary number of townspeople who were considered destitute among the town's approximately 19,000 individuals, roughly 4,500 families,[15] as shown in the accompanying table.

YEAR	DESTITUTE FAMILIES	MALE	FEMALE	TOTAL PERSONS
1954	615	856	1,170	2,026
1955	736	1,066	1,415	2,481
1956	853	1,318	1,691	3,009
1957	960	1,473	1,842	3,315
1958	1,018	1,488	1,935	3,423

As one can imagine, poverty severely impacted people's diet. Breakfast simply did not exist for the majority of people in Castellammare. A piece of bread was usually the first meal, consumed during the early afternoon while in the fields. At night, the poor, if not completely destitute, ate some form of pasta. Foraging for herbs, snails, shellfish, and other items helped thems survive.[16]

One-quarter of the town's inhabitants lived in homes with a single communal room, while another quarter shared a room with an alcove. Running water was obtained from local fountains, which operated for three hours per day.

More than one-third of the population was illiterate, and an additional fifteen percent were considered "semi-literate"—that is, they were able to write or "draw" their names. Italian was a foreign language for illiterate individuals who spoke only a local version of Sicilian. Although schooling was mandatory for children up to age 14, children of the working poor labored alongside their parents or did errands, some as young as six years old.[17]

One-half of the town's inhabitants were agricultural workers, with 35 percent owning small parcels of land. The major crops were grapes, olives, tomatoes, and grain.[18] Maxwell observed that the harvests of small landowning *contadini* (peasants) were taxed to the extent that they were barely able to make ends meet even though they were not classified as destitute. *Braccianti* (day laborers) who "congregate in the small hours of the morning at an open air-market that irresistibly suggests a slave market," were able to work only approximately 120 days of the year, at a daily salary of approximately 700 lire ($1 US).[19]

Fifteen percent of the remaining 9,500 inhabitants were involved in mainly subsistence seasonal fishing because for half the year the Mediterranean was too rough for the small boats used by Sicilian fishermen. The *tonnara* (tuna fishing) operated out of the neighboring town of Scopello and involved a crew of approximately 50 men in boats, which encircled the school of fish with a system of nets, some several kilometers long. The men slowly entrapped the tuna in the ever-shrinking *camera della morte* (chamber of death), harpooning and hauling in the huge fish in a dramatic finale to the *mattanza* (tuna fishing killing).[20]

The town was infamously known as a stronghold of the violent *mafia*. "Castellammare has an evil reputation in Sicily; it vies successfully with Montelepre . . . as a place of blood and violence," Maxwell wrote, claiming that 80 percent of all adult males in the town had served prison terms, and, without citing a specific source for his information, that "nearly one in three have committed murder—many of them when they were little more than children."[21] It was because of dire poverty and destitution—*la miseria*—that the town's working poor turned to brigandage, the *mafia*, or emigration.[22]

It was under these conditions that Ancona and his family struggled to survive. Unable to feed her first child, Ancona's mother sent the two-year-old Vincenzo to live with her childless sister-in-law until he was old enough to work, according to his daughter Giuseppina Navarra.[23] By the time he was 13, after completing the compulsory fifth grade, Ancona had joined his parents in the local wheat fields, olive groves, and vineyards. Plowing, sowing, harvesting, transporting, and refining the raw produce were the cyclical tasks that shaped his early life. In alternation with the agricultural season, Ancona worked on the tuna crews sailing from Scopello.

From childhood, Ancona was immersed in the various oral art forms practiced in western Sicily that were part of the cultural life of peasants and laborers. His grandmother was an artful storyteller of terrifying tales, and Vincenzo's mother taught him to memorize poems. Ancona learned and sung the work songs associated with threshing, tuna fishing, and the carters' trade. His repertoire included the Sicilian *canzuna* (song), the competitive, often-improvised verse sung in *ottava rima*. Ancona also took in the itinerant street performances of noted *cantastorie* (singer-storytellers) Orazio Strano and Turiddu Bella, as well as the marionette theatrical productions known as *la opera dei pupi* that dramatized epic tales of the paladins. In addition, Ancona became familiar with Italian writers such as Edmondo de Amicis and Giacomo Leopardi when he was made to memorize their verse in school.

The profound admiration for poetry in Sicilian culture at all levels of society—and, in particular, declaimed and improvised verse—held pride of place. Folklorist Salvatore Salomone-Marino observed in the late nineteenth century that "no entertainment is so pleasing to our peasants as that which gives exercise in composing and reciting poetry, especially the improvised kind."[24] In Castellammare, a wide range of social groups practiced the art of poetic recitation in Sicilian, including near-illiterate peasants; artisans, such as blacksmiths, cobblers, and barbers; and professionals, such as photographers and physicians. People, mostly men, recited and listened to verse and engaged in competitive poetic *gare* battles) in such venues as barber shops, cafes, *piazze*, public gardens, workers' circles; and during religious *feste*.[25]

Vincenzo's first poetic composition was a song of social protest that voiced concern for the lack of food in the years following World War II, when he was in his thirties.[26] Using the melody of the Neapolitan love song, "*Senza rose*," Ancona composed a biting parody he called "*Senza pane*" ("Without Bread"), articulating a subaltern discourse of opposition to the *signori* (the rich; literally, gentlemen) who controlled food distribution. Here is a version of the song as Ancona sang it in 1989:

Avi quattr 'anni ca finìu la guerra,	The war ended four years ago,
e ancora di pitittu cca spi parra.	but the talk is still of hunger.
L'America cu tutta l'Inghitterra	Together America and England
vapura di furmentu veni e sbarra.	are coming to unload ships full of wheat.

CORO	CHORUS
Ma semu senza pani.	But we are without bread.
'Un si pò cchiù campari!	We can't continue living!
Senza pani,	Without bread,
'un si pò campari cchiù.	we can't go on.
Mi pozzu rassignari c'ai sta' senza manciari,	I can resign myself to living without eating.
Senza pani, 'Un si pò campari cchiù.	Without bread, we can't go on living.

E stu furmentu portanu all'ammassu	And this wheat is taken to the warehouse
ci sunu 100 cani 'ncapu un ossu.	there are 100 dogs on the bone.
Certi signori c'apperu lu spassu	Some gentleman thought it was fun
e ppi niautri lu pitittu è grossu	but for us hunger is overwhelming.

Senza pani	Without bread
e' grossu lu pitittu.	hunger is overwhelming.
C'è cu mori	There are those who die
e c'è cu campa afflittu.	and those who survive, but afflicted.
Non si po' stari drittu,	We can't even stand
Mancannuni lu vittu.	if we're lacking food.
Senza pani	Without bread
'un si pò campari cchiù	we can't go on living

E li carrubbi vanno a 20 liri,	Now the carobs cost 20 lire
nun si ponnu mancu capita'.	and they're even difficult to find.
'Na sigaretta venticincu liri.	A cigarette is 25 lire.
Me passa pura a voglia de fuma'.	It even kills your desire to smoke.

Senza pani	Without bread
e senza sigaretti,	and without cigarettes
manco u fumo,	you can't even fill up
'nda panza si ci metti.	your belly with smoke.

E' meglio stari inetti	It's better to do nothing
Cantannu sempre arietti.	and spend time singing ditties.
Senza pane,	Without bread
'un si pò campari cchiù.	we can't go on living.

The unrecorded song soon achieved popular success, with people singing it first in Castellammare, then the surrounding area, and eventually across the island. After emigrating, Ancona eventually heard a man singing a version in the United States.

Encouraged by this development, Ancona set out to master the poetic conventions of *ottonari* (eight syllable lines) or hendecasyllabic verse by consulting his nephew,

Francesco Leone, a grade school teacher who tutored him about precise meter. Ancona developed a preference for the *sestina* rhyming scheme, in which the first six lines are in alternating or uniform rhyme, and the last two "kiss" (rhyme together) in *rima baciata* (kissing rhyme). To keep track of longer compositions, Ancona wrote with chalk or charcoal on the concrete floor of his house, where chickens would scratch at his text. In this way, Ancona moved into that sizable domain that exists between the exclusively oral tradition and the standardized literary canon.

His first successful poem was in honor of Castellammare's patroness, the *Madonna del Soccorso* (Our Lady of Succor), and he followed it with poetic homages to Our Lady of Fatima and the saints. He became so well known that the town's priests called upon him to recite his devotional poems from the balconies as the passing processions paused during religious *feste*. A local artist used Ancona's verse commemorating the disappearance of a tuna boat and its crew in 1952 as the caption for a painting of the tragedy.

EMIGRATION, LONGING, AND THE NARRATED LANDSCAPE

Vincenzo was 41 when he arrived in America and took up residence in Brooklyn in 1956. He came with his wife, Vincenza (known as Virginia; b. 1918, d. 2000), *nèe* Como, whom he had married on October 27, 1937; and their two daughters, Giuseppina (b. 1938) and Maria (b. 1940); and two sons, Stefano (b. 1944) and Giuseppe (b. 1952). He worked in a broom factory in Canarsie, Brooklyn for 17 years, and when the company went bankrupt, Ancona was hired at a jewelry workshop in Queens, where he remained until he retired in 1979 at the age of 64. He lived in Brooklyn's predominantly

Ancona (center, with hat) and family the day they emigrated, surrounded by relatives, Palermo, January 27, 1956. (Courtesy of Fran Favaloro.)

Italian—and, more specifically, Sicilian—neighborhoods first at 88 Havemeyer Street in Williamsburg from 1956–1961, and then in an apartment on Wilson Avenue in Bushwick. In 1965, nine years after emigrating, the Anconas purchased a modest two-family house at 1979 West 7th Street in Gravesend, where he lived until his death on February 20, 2000. The Anconas' extended family of brothers and sisters, nephews and nieces, children and grandchildren lived within walking distance of their home.

Soon after arriving in the United States, Ancona turned increasingly to poetry to help assess and assuage his feelings of loss, confusion, and culture shock:

> Il 9 febbraio del 1956, sbarcai in America dalla montonave Saturnia. Naturalmente, come tanti, ero pieno di nostalgia per la mia patria lontana. Cominciai a scrivere poesie, quasi tutte nostalgiche. Venne poi Natale e ricordando il mio paese e la mia mamma lontana, l'ambiente che lasciai, ho scritto questi versi cui ho voluto dare il titolo di un vecchio proverbi, "E batti lingua dunni denti doli, ossia il primo Natale in America." (Interview, May 21, 1987).

> On February 9, 1956, I landed in America with the ship Saturnia. Naturally, like many others, I was filled with nostalgia for my distant hometown. I began writing poems, almost all of them nostalgic. And then Christmas came and, remembering my town and my mother so far away, the environment I left behind, I wrote these verses with the desire to title it with the old proverb, "The Tongue is Ever Turning to the Aching Tooth, or First Christmas in America."

The trauma that is emigration with its feelings of dislocation and loss was what drove Ancona's compositions during his first years in the United States. In "The Tongue is Ever Turning to the Aching Tooth," Ancona describes his longing as a constant source of pain that fires his imagination. His fantasies of flying like a bird to Castellammare to surprise relatives caught off-guard in their pajamas "transport me there/burning, tormenting me at every moment/with a deep yearning I can hardly bear" (*mi ci porta lu pinseri/chi brama, chi smania, chi nun riseri*). The first two verses establish the sorrowful tone of the immigrant's lament, in contrast with the joyful scene of imagined return:

E batti lingua dunni denti doli!	The tongue is ever turning to the aching tooth!
Pensu chi semu a lu Santu Natali,	I'm thinking Christmas is already here,
sentu stu cori battiri; e chi voli?	and I feel my heart pound; What's wrong?
Vulissi aviri li pinnuzzi e l'ali,	I wish I had feathers and wings
quantu varcassi sti mari, sti poli,	so I could cross the seas, the distant poles,
e comu aceddu spuntassi a ddi scali	and like a bird alight upon those steps
di lu paisi miu dda patria amata	of my hometown in my beloved land,
macari puru pi 'na mezz'urata.	if only for a half an hour.
Spuntari comu acceddu all'impruvvisa	Appearing suddenly like a bird
dda nni me Matri, davanti dda casa,	before my Mother's house,
faricci 'na terribbuli supprisa.	would be such a wonderful surprise.
Parisi un sonnu cuntari na frasa	It would be like a dream to say a few words
a cui currissi scavusu ncammisa;	to someone running barefoot in night clothes;

issi a finiri nta lu vasa vasa	It would result in kisses left and right
e nta un momentu, ntempu chi si dici,	and in the time it takes to say hello,
fussi abbrazzatu di tutti l'amici.	I'd be embraced by everyone I know.

As with Ancona's other post-immigration poems, this one stands in marked contrast to the traditional stories he heard and recounted as well as to the poetry he composed in Sicily. The first-person account differs from the collective voice found in his comic critique of post–World War II starvation, and from here on, it assumes increasing importance. Emigration brings forth its own cultural products, which take the form of epic accounts of the journey across the ocean and first encounters with the new.[27]

Autobiography, either as oral narratives or written literature, takes center stage in an emerging repertoire that bears witness to the dramatic changes in immigrant life.[28] The act of reminiscing "serves to create a coherent narrative past and to make meaning out of inevitable changes and transition into present circumstances, as well as hopes and dreams of the future."[29] The creative act of "self-authoring," those "modes of transforming experience, of retrospection, and of self-integration," become useful ways of addressing the disparities between past and present lives and creating a more holistic sense of self.[30] Such self-fashioning exemplifies the ways in which "the past is not preserved but is reconstructed on the basis of the present."[31]

The landscape of hunger and despair found in his post–World War II parody is missing in "The Tongue is Ever Turning to the Aching Tooth," as well as in Ancona's other early American poems. In its place, is a bountiful and celebratory geography, populated by archetypical scenes and characters from the Christmas season: a shepherd playing bagpipes in a church; families making holiday sweets; a butcher preparing sausages; street vendors selling various produce; and the teaming marketplace of a holiday *piazza*. Personages from the classic tableau of the *presepio* (Nativity scene) populate what the poet calls his narrated "dream."[32] Although Ancona's imagined vignettes are based on personal reminiscences, their characterizations are generic and archetypical. In this way, Ancona began to take a paradigmatic approach in his poetic and visual work, focusing "on the enduring, recurrent, and collective aspects . . . rather than on unique events that shaped or changed the direction" of his life.[33] This "summation of an entire period—the idea of a type of life" becomes increasingly pronounced in Ancona's work at this time.[34]

At the end of the Christmas poem, the narrator returns from his flight of imagination to his ever-present sorrow, silenced by his inability to fulfill his desires, concluding with the proverbial line that began the poem:

Tuttu mi veni in menti a macinari,	All these things are spinning in my head,
tuttu è prisenti nta na vampa ardita	everything is visible like a searing flame
e soffru. Nun mi pozzu rassignari	and I suffer. I can't resign myself
e soccu pensu è tutta la me vita.	as I think of my whole life.
Mi staiu mutu, nun pozzu parrari,	I keep quiet, I'm unable to speak,
ma sentu ca brucia comu 'na firita:	but I can feel it burning like a wound.
veni NATALI e tu munnu cunsoli,	CHRISTMAS is here and the world is consoled,
ma lingua batti dunni denti doli!	but the tongue is ever turning to the aching tooth!

Yet silence is a false literary trope, given the author's prodigious opus addressing themes of homesickness in other compositions including *"Paisi luntanu"* ("Distant Hometown"), *"Un ritrattu di lu me paisi"* ("A Portrait of My Hometown"), *"Peri d'alivu"* ("Olive Tree"), and a parody of the Neapolitan standard *"'O surdato 'nnammurato"* ("A Soldier in Love") which he rechristened *"Italia! Italia Mia!"* Ancona's compositions are in a keeping with the "pastoral allegory of cultural loss and textual rescue" found in ethnographic writing.[35]

Ancona's depictions of a Sicilian cultural landscape demonstrate "the experiential and expressive ways places are known, imagined, yearned for, held, remembered, voiced, lived, contested, and struggled over."[36] In "The Tongue is Ever Turning to the Aching Tooth," Ancona punctuates his lines with specific remembered sensations: the morning dew on his eyes; the smell of freshly baked biscuits; and the sound of church bells, vendors' cries, and quoted dialogue. *"L'arba spunta e chista è la vita"* ("The Dawn is Breaking and This is Life") begins with a string of remembered auditory cues as the town comes to life: a rooster's crow; a lark's chirping; a sheep's baahing; a carter singing over the wagon's wooden wheels and his horse's jingling bells; the voices of peasants leaving for the fields. As Robert Orsi observes, "The recreation of a place in memory is subject to all the pressures and forces that shape any exercise of memory: the distortions and displacement of desire, repression, fear, and denial."[37] It was Ancona's diasporic movement in search of work that engendered his longing that, in turn, imbued "Castellammare" and "Sicily" with a reconfigured and charged significance. Memory was inextricably linked to Ancona's perceptions and sentiments for those "geographies of disruption,"[38] with the bonds to the "physical locale gaining greater clarity in the very moment of their destruction."[39] A line from his poem *"La storia d'un briganti"* ("A Brigand's Story") states, "I would like to write, if my memory/allows me to walk this old street . . . ," best articulates this established connection between memory, art, and landscape.[40] His remembered and imagined homeland was closely linked with a particular way of life, a sense of belonging, and ultimately a sense of identity formulated in the diasporic voice that, as we will see, was shared and created with the members of his group.[41] By juxtaposing and measuring the differences between a remembered, reconstituted Sicily and his daily experiences in contemporary Brooklyn, Ancona mapped the psychological and cultural distance that he was traveling and created a sense of continuity despite a dramatic disruption in his life.

Redemptive Nostaglia

As Ancona noted, a deep-seated nostalgia permeated his creative output. First diagnosed as an illness in 1688 by Swiss physician Johnnes Hofer, nostalgia has been portrayed as a debilitating affliction of melancholy and despondency, an emotional slothfulness.[42] David Gross notes that remembering began to take on increasingly negative connotations with the onset of modernity. The initial devaluation of memory made the claims that memory was unreliable, it inhibited the imagination, it undermined the will, and it prevented people from being an active agent in the world.[43] By the late nineteenth century, the "disturbances of memory" were said to plague the "pathological rememberer" who was lost in a clinical melancholia of unrequited longing.[44] By the late twentieth century, late capitalist consumption, political ideologies, and the veneer of technologically induced style transmuted nostalgic longing into post-modernity's "social disease."[45]

A growing body of scholarly literature has emerged recently to reevaluate nostalgia and its post-modern critique.[46] Anthropologist Kathleen Stewart has written persuasively about the need to be attentive to the contextual positioning of nostalgic sentiment. Nostalgia "is a cultural practice, not a given content; its forms, meanings, and effects shift with the context—it depends on where the speaker stands in the landscape of the present."[47] Different nostalgias exist in public and scholarly discourses: "hegemonic and resistant," "middle-class and working-class," that of "'mass culture,'" and about "local, nameable places."[48] Stewart develops the idea of a nostalgia that is a "painful homesickness that generates desire and not, in itself, 'seductive' or debased" ... with "its own 'sophisticated,' or self-conscious, sense of its cultural constructions."[49] A contextual approach serves to better understand the local nuance of nostalgic longing. For Ancona, nostalgia was not merely an end product, a symptom of the immigrant's plight, but a source for comprehending the new conditions that he encountered, a way of dealing with pain. "In the age of forced mobility, uprootedness, discontinuity and rupture, nostalgia seeks to mend the torn fabric of the fragile psyche."[50] Stewart elaborates on the possibility of a "redemptive nostalgia": a set of practices with "the power to 'talk back' to an overcoded order that depends on unnaming and distanced speechlessness."[51] Thus, nostalgia can be seen as a strategy, a "rebellion, a movement of transgression against the limitations imposed physically by time and space; it is an attempt to push the parameters of possibility and impossibility."[52] It is this "talking back" that we find in Ancona's other poetic work, especially that which he created after settling into his new life.

For Sicilians in Italy and throughout the diaspora, "talking back" has historically been a devalued and, all too often, suppressed act. Instead, *omertà* (a practice of self-imposed silence) serves both to protect themselves against the *mafia*'s retributive violence and as a debilitating silencing against injustice.[53] The unsaid has also served to erase the history of emigration and southern-Italian cultural practices from national discourse in Italy and to create a false portrait of an ahistorical peasantry pathologically crippled by inarticulateness and violence in the United States.[54] In addition, there is a long history of silencing and demeaning Italian dialects in everyday use and as a legitimate expression in "art" and Italian-American literature.[55] The redemptive nostalgia of Ancona's artistic production bears witness to the exploitation and hunger of *la miseria*, as well as the tribulations of the immigrant's encounter with the host society, and acts as a countervalence to debilitating silence and erasure.

In *"Lu pani di furmentu"* ("Bread from Wheat"), Ancona creates an epic (35 stanzas) account of seasonal wheat production, from tilling the earth after the first spring rains to harvesting the grain under June's blazing sun. The poem is framed as a first-hand account—"I know it and I can tell you"—of one of the oldest agricultural practices in the West, depicted with ethnographic detail:

Lu beddu pani santu chi manciamu	The holy bread that we consume each day
a nui lu detti Diu. Nni lu gudemu,	was given to us by God. We enjoy it,
ma chi suduri amari chi jittamu,	but at what price?

e sulu dopo stenti nui l'avemu!	With sweat and bitter toil.
Si di stu pani li tempi pinsamu,	If we trace the steps it took to make it,
chiddi chi semu granni lu sapemu	we who are old know
comu vinia lu pani di furmentu,	how bread was made from wheat,
la gran fatica e lu granni turmentu.	the great fatigue and torment.
Ora nun è di tutti lu capiri	Not everyone understands
comu s'avia a ddi tempi siminari;	the way we used to sow the seeds back then.
nun è di tutti mancu lu sapiri	Also, not everyone knows
comu s'avia la terra a cultivari.	How the land needed to be cultivated.
Iu lu sacciu e vi lu pozzu diri,	I know it and I can tell you
e speru di putiri raccuntari	and hope I can tell you
tutta la longa storia di na vota,	the whole long story of a day long ago,
di la simenza fina a la ricota.	from when the seed was sown to harvest time.

While using the paradigmatic conceit, Ancona relies on first-hand knowledge to personalize and localize his account, as when he cites Castellammare's Tosti and Maranzano families who labored for hire on the large tracts of land. Embedded in the poem is a *canto dell'aia*, the work song used on the threshing floor.[56]

Sti versi 'un foru scritti né stampati	These verses were neither written or printed,
e mancu si canusci l'auturi.	and we have no idea who is the author.
Foru di vucca in vucca scatasciati.	They were randomly passed from mouth to mouth
a la finfusa tra stenti e suduri,	amidst the privation and toil,
e certu foru sempri arrubbacchiati.	and it's certain that they were always raided
di chiddi poi chi vinniru futuri,	by those who came afterwards,
ma nuddu sapi di comu nasciu	but no one knows how this beautiful,
sta bedda tradizioni chi muriu.	though now dead tradition, was born.

The song, which Ancona sang when he recited the poem, evokes and praises the Holy Family and the saints Rosalia, Anastasia, Benedict, and Nicholas. The workers, "*stanchi ed avviliti*" ("exhausted and debased"), Ancona noted, were helped by "*la forza umana, i santi e la natura*" ("human strength, the saints, and nature"). In a sense, Ancona was a "salvage ethnographer," and his poem was an anthropological document in verse retrieving a cultural way of life now gone.[57]

Again and again, Ancona bears witness to the labor's physicality and its impact on the workers:

A cavaddu a lu mulu lu azzuni	A farmhand on a mule used to bring bread
purtava postu allantu vinu e pani	and wine to the workers
pi risturari ddi carni vinnuti	in order to restore their sold bodies,
Stanchi quasi iunti addibuluti.	weary to the point of being weak.
Durava circa un misi sta pinura,	This painful work would last about a month,
ma cuminciava 'na sicunna ancora;	but then a second stage would begin;
a 'na vita faticusa la cchiù dura	Nowadays, no one thinks any more
Chi nun si pensa cchiù a li tempi d'ora.	About such a difficult and hard life.

The peasants' "unendurable life" (*Vita di nun putiri suppurtari!*) is masterfully contrasted with that of the landowners who kept a watchful eye on the proceedings in these two lines: "*A lu bagghiu ci stava lu baruni,/nta li loggi 'nfutavanu li cani*" ("The Baron would remain inside his courtyard,/riling the dogs on the balcony"). The closing verses speak eloquently to the exploitation suffered by Sicilian peasants, a poetic and personal account augmenting Maxwell's statistics:

E finalmenti arrivamu a la nsaccata.	And finally they bagged the grain in sacks.
Lu camperi mittia a misurari	And then the field guard started measuring.
prima di lu patruni la pigghiata	The owner's share of wheat was counted first,
e poi di lu burgisi. Si macari	and then the peasant's part would be doled out.
nun era chi vinta 'na mala annata	But sometimes when the harvest had been bad,
mancu sulami ci putia tuccari.	the peasant would not get a grain of wheat.
E doppu aviri lu sangu ittatu,	After he'd sweated blood for a whole year,
ristava friddu, a diunu e dispiratu.	he was left cold and starving in despair.
E chista fu la vita di 'na vota,	And that is how life was in days gone by,
chi si luttava p'un tozzu di pani:	when people fought for every scrap of bread,
priari santi fina e la ricota	praying to saints until the harvest came;
e tanti voti nun saziava un cani.	and many times we could not feed a dog.
Ora lu munnu si cancia e si sbota	And now the earth has turned and times have changed,
tempi chi chiù non tornanu domaini,	and those harsh days will not come back tomorrow,
vita di stenti d'un tempu chi fu,	that life of suffering of times gone by.
ed auguriamu c'un turnassi chiù!	Let's hope to God it never will return!

Wistful longing in a sentiment that finds no place in this tale.

This poem was created, in part, as a result of Ancona's collaboration with anthropologist Anna Lomax Chairetakis (today, Lomax Wood). They met in 1975 while she was researching Italian-immigrant folk music. She recorded Ancona singing Sicilian agricultural and fishing work songs, such as the *canto dell'aia*, and interviewed him about the music's historic context. She arranged to have Ancona perform these songs on stage in Philadelphia and most notably at the 1976 Smithsonian Museum's Folklife Festival on the Mall in Washington, DC. It was at Chairetakis' suggestion that Ancona took on the subject of the wheat harvest and other related subjects. The scholar's interest and Ancona's meeting with other Sicilian immigrants knowledgeable about various cultural practices created a stimulus for recalling aspects of the past with a new immediacy and a new agenda of recovery. The positive response of audiences consisting of people who did not share his experiences was an additional impetus to document in poetry (as well as song, speech, and visual art) a fading world. It was through these encounters that Ancona was developing an archive of creative work where memory and history were conjoined.

Memory, history, and talking back are called into play in a different way with Ancona's *"La storia d'un briganti"* ("A Brigand's Story"), an epic of 58 octaves about Pasquale Torregiani (1842–1870), a 20-year-old Castellammarese who led a revolt against military conscription in the nineteenth century until he died at the hands of the authorities in March 1870.[58] Descendants of the bandit leader approached Ancona during one of his return visits to Castellammare beginning in 1967 and requested that he set the story to verse, in part because Torregiani's exploits were fading from popular memory.[59] In this work, Ancona uses his artistry to capture a historical event that he did not experience by relying both on stories he heard and the evidence of "some yellowed documents in a neglected archive."

Nenti e' la vita, puru di cent'anni	Life is worthless, even if you reach a hundred years old,
quannu c'un omu nun lassa 'na storia	if you don't leave a story.
e nenti e' la figura d'unu granni	A great man is not worth a thing
quannu a la morti non passa a la gloria	if after death he achieves no glory.
di chiddu chi cuntavanu li nanni	The story of the brigand Turricianu
rinnova a cui la senti la mimoria	will refresh the memories
doppu di tantu tempu ormai luntanu	of those who hear this story, even after so much time has passed
la storia d'un banditu, Turricianu.	since the elders used to recount it.
Ora chi chiu' d'un secula e passatu	Now that more than a century has passed
di quannu fu sta banda e stu banditu	since this band and bandit existed
e forsi nuddu mai s'a 'ntirissatu	and maybe no one was interested in finding
truvari qualchi scrittu sculuritu	some yellowed documents
macari nta' n'archiviu ittatu	in a neglected archive
chi raccuntassi di chist' omu arditu	that told the story of this brave man
ma finalmenti qualcunu circau	but finally someone searched
e qualchi indiziu veru si truvau	and found some real clues.
Sacciu pi vucca e ni sintia parrari	I know by word of mouth, hearing
ci fu pueta di la razza mia	that there was a poet, a relative,
certu Caiozzu ed a quantu pari	a certain Caiozzu and it seems that
scrissi sta storia dici a puisia	he wrote this story in verse or so they say.
fussi curiusu putiri truvari	I would be curious to find
sti versi scritti dunni sia sia	those written verses, where ever they are,
parola mia ni fussi cuntentu	I give you my word, I would be happy
si ni gustassi st'anticu talentu	If I could savor his ancient talent.
Caiozzu era un frati di me nanna	Caiozzu was my grandmother's brother
e fu un pueta antinatu a mia	and a poet, my ancestor.
finominu ch' esisti e chi si ncarna	Poetry is a phenomenon that exists and comes to life
di rera in rera e forsi a fantasia	from generation to generation, perhaps by chance;
e sangu duci, na bava di manna	it is a joyous sweetness
chi' nnesta nta la menti sta malia	that casts a spell upon the mind.
ma pi sfurtuna chistu miu antinatu	But unfortunately my ancestor
fu puru nta sta banda affiliatu	was also part of this gang.

Epuchi tristi di tempi passati	It was a sad time,
doppu di Garibaldi, tempi addetri	after Garibaldi, long ago.
la genti certu mali organizzati	People were poorly organized,
privi di scoli e tanti anaffabeti	uneducated, and illiterate.
li ricchi signurotti sturiati	The rich and well-educated *signori*
si davanu fra d'iddi li sigreti	shared their secrets among themselves.
lu poviru chiamatu lu gnuranti	The poor were called ignorant
stava a suggettu di lu benistanti	and were subjugated by those who were well-off.

Scriviri voghiu, si la menti aiuta	I would like to write, if my memory
a caminari 'nta 'sta vecchia strata	allows me to walk this old street,
liggennu sta scrittura sculuruta	reading these discolored,
stravecchia ed ora mai diminticata	ancient, and forgotten documents
anchi s'a li prisenti scanusciuta	even if today people are unaware of them.
speru putissi essiri accittata	I hope this story will be accepted,
oggi com'oggi chi l'antichitati	now that ancient things are
su gemmi e su tisoru ricircati	sought after like gems and treasures.

The poem belongs to a well-established Sicilian popular tradition that heralded the exploits of bandits, brigands, and *mafiosi*. Ancona lays claim to this legacy by citing his great-uncle Caiozzu who, as a poet and member of Torregiani's group, composed a now-lost poem about his experiences as a brigand, and imagines being able to locate his relative's poem so as to "savor his ancient talent."[60]

Ancona proceeds to flesh out the social context for the narrated exploits. After Italian Unification, old landowners and the newly rich subjugated and maltreated the "illiterate" poor, who Ancona noted "were poorly organized." Torregiani had displayed leadership qualities that allowed him to rally disgruntled peasants into a fighting force that attacked representatives of state power. For Ancona, Torregiani was a "brave man" and a "heroic brigand" who exhibited "*l'arduri, lu curaggiu e lu gran cori*" ("ardor, courage, and a big heart"), a quote attributed to the anti-*mafia* Fascist prefect Cesare Mori. Completed in 1974, Ancona's "*La storia d'un briganti*" was an indictment of the historic exploitation of the Sicilian peasantry and an expression of hope for a just society.[61] With this poem and "*Lu pani di furmentu*," Ancona gives voice to a diasporic critique of the very economic and political conditions that led to his own emigration.

Amerisicula

The clash between the narrative constructs of the past and the experiences of the present creates a syncretic or creole perspective. These emotional and intellectual tensions create a bifocality that encompasses "two cultures differentiated through a lived experience of loss."[62] This interaction of divergent and often contentious voices at the crossroads of social discourse are heteroglossic sites of polyvalence, which Mikhail Bakhtin identifies as being "born on the confines of languages and cultures, which not only were in direct contact but in a sense interwoven."[63] The mingling of different languages is also "the collision between differing points of views on the world that are embedded in these forms."[64] Hybridization results in the struggle to invest words with one's own intentions and subjectivity in the continuous fashioning of distinctiveness and identity. It is this kind of hybridic tension and playfulness that gives Ancona's work its resiliency and cultural resonance.

The greenhorn's frustration with linguistic incompetence is the subject of the comic tour de force "*Malidittu la lingua!*" ("Damned Language!"). The opening verse addresses the aggravation of the poet struggling with the English language:

S'un mi la 'nsignu sugnu ruvinatu,	I'll be ruined if I don't learn it soon,
sta lingua 'nglisi c'un sacciu parrari	this English language that I can't speak.
Quantu malifiguri c'aiu pruvatu,	How many embarrassing moments I've endured,
sparti di chiddi ancora ch'è pruvari.	Without counting those yet to come.
Pi la me lingua sugnu un avvucatu,	I'm like a lawyer in my own language,
ma cu li mura pozzu ragiunari	but I feel like I'm talking to the walls
picchí sta maliditta lingua 'nglisi	because this damn English consists
è fatta di papocchi e mali 'ntisi.	of confusion and misunderstandings.

The poem goes on to recount an exchange between a factory worker (the narrator) who has had an accident, a co-worker who serves as a translator, and an insurance representative. The comic punch line turns on the literal translation of "feet" as a form of measurement. The tale is set at a time soon after immigration—"*Quant'avi ca sta terra fici sosta*" ("When I alighted on this land")—which Ancona and his Sicilian audience remembered as being particularly uncomfortable because of their lack of English. Actually, however, the poem requires that the Sicilian audience have a certain proficiency in English to understand the linguistic joke. The poem's specificity to Sicilian-American (and Italian-American) audiences is evident in the numerous Italianized English words: for example, "*giobba*" (*lavoro*, job), "fatturia" (*fabbrica*, factory), "mascina" (*macchina*, machine), and so on.[65] This is a work composed by and for those whose position is between two cultures and can creatively exploit the hybrid character of immigrant life.

Ancona expressed hybridity as a lived experience in "*Amerisicula,*" a work that examines the local ways in which Brooklyn's Sicilian diasporic community blurs, extends, and defines notions of the national boundaries, in Ancona's case, "America" and "Sicily."[66] According to Ancona, post–World War II Sicilian immigrants transformed the Brooklyn neighborhood Bensonhurst into their "empire." It is a place where not only a *lingua impastarduta* (bastardized *mélange* of Italian, Sicilian, and English) is spoken, but also where neighborhood institutions such as the bank or doctor's office accommodate immigrants' linguistic needs. According to Ancona, Sicilian has such an impact on New York City that it can be heard beyond the Italian community, especially at work sites. African Americans' use of Sicilian vulgarities represents the extent to which the language has infiltrated the city's everyday parlance:

La chiamu Amerisicula, ed è veru!	I call this land Amerisicula! It's true!
Ci stamu quasi tutti siciliani,	We're almost all Sicilians here.
Stu Brucculinu addivintau l'imperu	Brooklyn has become the empire of

d'i Siculi emigranti Amiricani.	Sicilian emigrants in America.
Ma si l'è diri cu cori sinceru,	But speaking from my heart,
ccà nni criamu la casa e lu pani,	it's here we've made our homes and earned our bread,
nta chista granni America ospitali	in this great and hospitable America
chi nta stu munnu nun ci nn'è uguali!	which has no equal in the world!
[. . .]	[. . .]
Parramu cu 'na lingua impastarduta,	We speak a bastardized language,
a comu megghiu si po' spitturari,	the things we say come as best as they can.
S'incontra qualchi amicu e si saluta,	When we meet a friend and greet him
"Bonciornu!" oppuru "Alò", comu nni pari.	We say either " *Bonciornu*" or "Hello," what ever we feel.
Poi di capiri, o a gesti o a la muta,	So when communicating with others,
quannu chi nenti si pò spiccicari.	and our English is not good enough, we'll use our hands.
Ma basta chi fai gesti cu li mani	But as soon as you start gesticulating,
chi si canuscinu li Siciliani.	they know we are Sicilians.
A Bensinosti, nta stu Brucculinu	In Bensonhurst, here in Brooklyn,
dunni riseru, e cui allatu a mia,	where I and others live,
nun c'è problema di nuddu caminu:	there's no problem what so ever
vai nta un ufficiu, nta 'na farmacia,	You walk into an office or a pharmacy,
puru a 'na banca d'unni è chiù vicinu,	or even in a bank in the neighborhood,
o d'un dutturi, nta 'na mirciria	or in a doctor's office or a store,
s'un sai lu 'ngrisi, ci poi dumannari:	and if you don't know English, you can ask,
"Sampari spicchi Italia?" e poi parrari.	"*Sampari spicchi Italia?*" and just start talking.
La nostra lingua poi si fa truvari	You find our language spoken
nta tutti li travagghi e ci nn'è tanti	at every job and spoken by every race.
di tutti i razzi, e nivuri macari,	and even blacks let rip with our coarsest words;
chi sbrogghianu palori ributtanti;	Embarrassing to hear them toss about
pari virgogna sentilli sbuffari	certain vulgar expressions!
cu ceri frasi macari pisanti!	Sicilians can indeed be gruff
Lu sicilianu è rozzu e 'nsigna a tutti	and they teach everyone uncouth
lingua balorda, parra e si nni futti.	language; they speak without giving a damn.
[. . .]	[. . .]

In Ancona's poetry, the boundaries between Sicily and America became increasingly blurred in the process of comparison. What emerged for Ancona and his *paesani* was a new, conflated entity—"Amerisicula"—that effectively transformed one into a *frazione* (neighborhood) of the other.

Despite having a house and raising a family in Brooklyn, the desire to maintain contact with and possibly return to Castellammare remained constant for Ancona. Immediately upon arriving in America, Ancona began submitting his poems to contests and publications in Sicily, engaging the transnational ethnoscape of Sicilian deterritorialed cultural practices.[67] He participated in a transatlantic poetic debate published in the Sicilian literary magazine *Po' t' u' cuntu* on the appropriateness of Castellammarese immigrants importing a replica of the town's spiritual patroness, the Madonna del Soccorso, for their annual feast in Brooklyn. In 1967, Vincenzo returned home for the first time to see his ailing mother and examine the damages sustained to her house during an earthquake. After retiring in 1978 and up until his first stroke in December 1995, Ancona and his wife spent close to half of each year in their house in Castellammare, in sight of the sea he once fished. In his hometown, he was known simply as *"Il poeta,"* and a collection of his work, *Casteddammari meu,* was published in 1984.[68]

Ancona addressed the domestic repercussions of his desire to repatriate in *"Contrastu tra maritu e mogghi"* ("Quarrel Between a Husband and a Wife"). Taking on the voice of both the husband and the wife, the poet's composition is a "double accented, double styled *hybrid construction* [italized in original]" that "contains mixed within it two utterances, two speech manners, two styles, two 'languages,' two semantic and axiological belief systems."[69] It is with this poem that the importance of the family as a social arena where memory is forged is most evident.

MARITU	HUSBAND
Ci dissi un jornu a me muggheri, "Sai,	One day I said to my wife, "You know,
quasi chi semu vecchi tutti e dui	we're both old
e nna sta terra nun si campa assai.	and people don't live long in this country.
Biatu cu ni scappa e si nni fui.	Blessed are those who escape from here.
E s'iddu tu la me' pinsata fai,	So if you think like I do,
cu' è chi sfari ni putissi a nui?	nobody can stop us.
Ni ricugghiemu sti du sordi spisi	Let's pull together the few things we own,
e riturnamu a lu nostru paisi".	and let's return to our hometown."
MOGGHI	WIFE
"Turnari a lu paisi!? Tu sì pazzu!	"Go back to the old town? You're crazy!
Sì sulu bonu pi parrari a mazzu.	You're only good at talking nonsense.
Doppu chi mi nni vaiu ddà, chi fazzu?	Once I got there, what would I do?
Sugnu na petra ittata 'nto 'mpuzzu!	I'd be like a stone dropped in a well!
Beni chi ccà travagghiu e mi strapazzu,	Ok, here I work hard and dash about,
ma vuscu grana e si mancia panuzzu;	but I make good money and eat well;
e poi, comu cci stassi dui minuti	What's more, how could I bear to be away
senza di li me' figghi e li niputi?"	from my children and grandchildren for even
	two minutes?"

The husband argues for returning to his hometown before retiring so that he can die where he was born in *"cu dda terra di suli e di misteri"* ("that land of mystery and sunlight" where there is clean air and fresh food. The wife, on the other hand, maintains a far more pragmatic approach: "I make good money and eat well" in America. Besides, the wife has adapted to the new life style, and she, like others who have returned, would be bored and dissatisfied "shooing flies" (*disfiziati di cacciari muschi*) in the old town. *"Cancia la vita e cancia li maneri"* ("Life changes, ways of living change as well"), she pronounces. Interestingly, Ancona told me his wife and children contested his representations of the past as depicted in his verse, and ultimately, the usefulness of his poetry.

In Sicily, and indeed in south-central Italy as a whole, tensions surrounding diverse opinions were voiced in the *contrasto* or *dialogo*, a form with roots in antiquity that is well suited to the "dialogic imagination." The *contrasto* provides the poetic space for differing positions to be articulated, with a pair of poets taking turns arguing their point of view.[70] Historically, these debates in verse were part of *sfide* (challenges) or *gare* (contests) that took place publicly in barbershops and *piazze*, often characterized by scathing attacks. In Italy, published chapbooks of *dialoghi* often pitted protagonists from different social strata, with the poor and marginalized triumphing with the last word, such as *"Contrasto tra una nobile ed una contadina"* ("Quarrel between a Noble-woman and Peasant Woman").[71] A descendant of the ancient Greek *agon* (contest), the poetic debate was often concerned with "change and renewal," located "between winter and spring, old age and youth, fasting and abundance, old times and new, parents and children."[72] For Ancona and his immigrant audience, the *contrasto* was a means of publicly airing the conflicts that arose as new alternatives. Divorce, male authority versus women's emancipation, and abortion, to name a few, were topics being considered, and traditional beliefs were being challenged. Written alone or in partnership, Ancona's *contrasti* open a space within his verse for alternative and even contradictory voices and opinions from his own, bringing together "the forces and phenomena of different times, of two poles of becoming, of the beginning and the end of a metamorphosis."[73] Ancona's nostalgic positions within these poetic dialogues provide opportunities for using "the backward glance as an instrument of critical evaluation and of efforts to (re)rebuild community."[74] They were creative ways for Ancona and his rapidly changing community to weigh the pros and cons of such issues as they engaged in the dynamic process of becoming.[75]

As the poet began visiting Sicily after 1967, he came to realize that the world had changed even in his beloved and somewhat romanticized Castellammare.[76] He photographed aspects of a fading lifestyle, such as a traditional fishing boat, as souvenirs from his past and as possible source material for future art work. The activities and way of life that he remembered were being transformed as immigrants returned with their hard-earned money from northern Italy, other European countries, North America, and Australia. In *"Contrastu tra maritu e mogghi,"* the husband proclaims that his townspeople have become dependent on the welfare state: *"Picchì travagghiu nun nni voli nuddu!/Vonnu campari a spaddi di lu statu"* ("Because nobody wants to work, that's why!/They want to be supported by the state"). For Ancona, his family, and his *paesani*, each return visit and reassessment augmented and changed memories of Castellammare, undermining their ability to sustain the same metaphorical power they had right after emigration.

Around 1980, as his youngest son was going through a divorce, Ancona addressed the issue in two incisive *dialoghi*; *"Na sciarra tra soggira e nora"* ("A Fight Between a Mother-in-Law and a Daughter-in-Law") and *"Dialogu supra lu divoriziu"* ("Dialogue on Divorce"). The first was a humorous yet vicious *repartee* that turns on a serious of hurled insults and curses, and threats of violence.[77] Ancona's protagonists quarrel about money, cleanliness, jurisdiction within a shared household, privacy, and respect. The daughter-in-law blames the impending divorce on the meddling of her mother-in-law, while the latter maintains that it is the younger woman's inappropriate behavior that is the cause. The family as a source of conflict, especially along generational lines, is most pronounced in this work and points to the immigrant family's difficulty in reproducing itself.

The topic of divorce was given more serious attention in *"Dialogu supra lu divoriziu."* Ancona used the telephone to collaborate with *paesano* and fellow immigrant poet Antonino Provenzano, creating their poetic dialogue long distance between their respective Brooklyn and Long Island homes. Ancona phoned Provenzano to read his two verses contesting divorce; after an interval, Provenzano responded with his two octaves supporting it. This exchange went on until the poets completed 16 verses. *"Divorziu"* ("Divorce"), for Ancona, *"è lu prublema chiù scuttanti/chi pisa 'nta lu cori e 'nta la menti"* ("is the most worrisome of problems/that weights upon the hearts and minds of all"). Our *"munnu pazzu"* ("crazy world") is populated with *"La casa e la famigghia 'unn'è curretta"* ("rudderless families"), *"Li figghi nun si ponnu cuntrullari"* ("Children can no longer be controlled") and sons and daughters who are overwhelmed with consumer goods, engaged in casual sex "on street corners," and seek independence from the family. The much younger Provenzano took a combative stance against the charges: *"Epuca e giuvintù su' sutta accusa/ed iu mi sbrazzu e pigghiu la difesa"* ("Our time and our young people stand indicted/and I roll up my sleeves in their defense"). He argued that Ancona's position derives from "envy": *"Chistu discursu to' a mia m'invita/a diri ch'è pi 'nvidia chi parrati,/chi 'nta ddi tempi scuri antichi e brutti/eravu schiavi di l'usanzi tutti"* ("because in those obscure and ancient times/of your youth, everyone lived as a slave/to custom and inflexible tradition"). Provenzano challenged Ancona's recollections by raising the issue of domestic violence.

Forsi ti criri tu chi anticamenti	Perhaps you believe in this regard
in quantu a chistu la munnu era sanu?	the world was better in the past?
Ni canuscemu mariti 'ncuscenti,	We all know irresponsible husbands,
Mugghieri schiavi e nirvati a la manu!	wives enslaved and battered!
O fimminazzi tinti e puzzulenti	Or dissolute and filthy women
Di ruvinari o' cchi bonu cristianu.	who ruined the most decent and good men.
Senza divoriziu chissa mali sorti	Without divorce this awful destiny
Accumpagnava 'ssi genti a la morti.	accompanied such people to their deaths.

The themes of this poetic teamwork were expanded in a second telephonic collaboration, *"Lu patri anticu e lu figghiu modernu"* ("The Old Fashioned Father and The Modern Son"). Again, Ancona opens with a stark pronouncement, *"chi munnu persu!"* ("the world is lost!"), pointing to the failures of *"Vita muderna"* ("Modern life"), where *"Tuttu canciatu, tuttu a lu riversu/ . . . mancu nta li famigghi cc'è chiù versu"* ("Things are all upside down . . . and there is even chaos in our homes"). He then tackles familial ethics and responsibility, parental respect, the protocol of courtship, sexuality, and gender roles. It is in these opening verses that Ancona begins to develop a "moral topography" of southern Italian village life where the *"l'ordine della famiglia"* ("the order of the family") reigned supreme.[78] Ancona recounts that he always showed respect for his elders and for parents who inflicted corporal punishment: *"e tanti voti di santa ragiuni/ tastava nta li spaddi lu furcuni"* ("and many times, and with good reason, too,/I was smacked on the shoulders with a pitchfork"). Courtship was a strictly monitored affair, with an engaged couple physically segregated:

Dui anni stesi zitu, tu à sapiri!	You ought to know I was betrothed two years
Nun parru pi vuliri esagerari,	and I am not prone to exaggerate,
E nta dui anni nun appi lu piaciri,	but in two years I never had the pleasure
na vota di putiricci abballari. . . .	of dancing with your mother even once. . . .
Picchì a ddi tempi c'era affruntu,	We were reserved back then and yet
Amuri veru cu russura e puntu.	we felt true love and blushed when our eyes met.

This remembered lifestyle, although at times morally severe, was recalled with fondness: *"i duci sirinati"* ("the sweet serenades") and *"li tempi di lu sciccareddu"* ("the time of the donkey"). For Ancona, part of the problem lies with a lack of faith: *"La riligioni 'un cunta e nun cunveni"* ("Religion is insignificant and inconvenient") for the young and the old. As a result, *"Però la libertà è un grossu mali"* ("liberty" becomes an "awful curse"). Provenzano's trenchant rebuke gives voice to the younger generation of immigrants who were better educated than their predecessors and had divergent opinions on various topics.

Su' megghiu assai sti tempi, si si penza	Our own times are much better, when you think
Ch'è libiru ogni adunu a diri e fari,	That everyone is free to be himself,
Esprimiri li idei di li pinseri,	Expressing every thought quite openly,
Cu arma aperta e cu cori sinceri.	With a free spirit and sincerity.

Ancona moves from the familial to other urgent problems of the late twentieth century: environmental pollution; affordable health care; disillusionment with democratic politics; education and unemployment; the wastefulness of the space program; the threat of nuclear annihilation; and, ultimately, humankind's predilection for violence and evil. *"E di d'unni pò veniri stu beni/si l'omu è l'animali chiù feroci?"* ("How then can all these benefits arise/if man's the most ferocious beast of all?"). Ancona's arguments illustrate how he straddles two worlds—that of the provincial Sicily he conjures from memory and contemporary life with its clamorous problems. His poetry creates the artistic space where he often serves as a foil to contrasting ideas that help usher in change and renewal. Ancona shared this subjectivity with many members of his Sicilian working-class community experiencing similar conflicts with changing notions of self.

Enacting Memory

Ancona's art was not a solitary endeavor. As we have seen, his poems were crafted within the interactions of the family, and, at times, in concert with another poet. In addition, Ancona's creativity was coupled with a very public and social performance component. As Ancona noted, *"La bellezza della poesia è nella declamazione, nell'essere in grado di esprimere la musicalità della poesia"* ("The beauty of poetry is in its recitation, in being able to express its musicality").[79] Ancona recited informally at home, during encounters with friends on sidewalks and in local stores, and in other mundane venues. As a recognized and esteemed poet, Ancona was often called upon to recite his compositions at formal gatherings such as dinner dances. Ancona participated in community-based Sicilian recitals where he offered his poetic voice and was the nominal artist-in-residence of the voluntary association Castel del Golfo Social Club, which sponsored an annual *serata culturale* (cultural evening) of its members' paintings, sculptures, and craft work. Ancona's recitations were always the highlight, with people howling in laughter at his humorous verse and chocking back tears at his nostalgic poems. His *contrasti* were performed with poet Provenzano and with schoolteacher Maria Portuesi, who recited the female voices in Ancona's poetic debates. Club members recorded his performances with audio and video recorders and made copies available to fans who lived out of state, as well as Italy and Canada, as part of a Sicilian diasporic mediascape.[80] It was especially during these group performances, with Ancona's poetry and wire sculpture at the center, that a "collective memory" was enacted, shaped, evaluated, scrutinized, and reproduced.[81]

With these formal events, Ancona and his audience developed a collective voice to commemorate the past and forge ways of moving forward. In his unique voice, Ancona married his own history with that of his fellow immigrants producing what Halbwachs notes is, "the collective framework of memory . . . the result or sum, or combination of individual recollections of many members of the same society."[82] As Halbwachs observes, "We can understand each memory as it occurs in individual thought only if we

Ancona reciting at the Castel del Golfo Social Club's 1987 "Serata culturale" (cultural evening). Maria Portuesi is seated at the table. (Photograph by Martha Cooper.)

locate each within the thought of the corresponding group. We cannot properly under-stand their relative strength and the ways in which they combine within individual thought unless we connect the individual to the various groups of which he is simulta-neously a member."[83] Ancona was able to couple his individual creativity with group identity by tapping into and contributing to collective language, the shared knowledge of lived experience, and ceremonial performances. He became a leading voice, artisti-cally shaping community identity.

First and foremost, recollection was articulated through the social life of language. In particular, Ancona composed and conducted his daily routine in Sicilian and Italian, languages he shared with his family and compatriots. Ancona's Sicilian was filled with words, phases, and ideas unique to the community of people who shared his experi-ences in Castellammarese agricultural life. As we have seen, that Sicilian was also fused with American English as spoken in New York City during the last half of the twentieth century. This hybrid language, encoded with memories of the past and the exigencies of the present, spoke to and for the emerging community of Sicilian immigrants. It was this "social language" that Ancona was able to articulate in a highly distilled and devel-oped manner that at once drew upon and fed back into the group.[84]

Ancona's work derived much of its resonance during performances because of what Barbara Kirshenblatt-Gimblett has labeled "cohort awareness, the point where the indi-vidual life and the historical moment converge."[85] As Ancona observed in April 1987, "When I tell my poetry to old people like me, from the first word to the last word they nod their heads, saying, 'Yes, yes.' They know—they have lived it too."[86] Historian Tamara Hareven notes, "Members of a cohort derive a sense of enlarged time and significance through forging links between their individual lives and a larger whole, in this case, a lost way of life."[87] In 1995, club president Filippo Navarra articulated this idea succinctly: "His poetry keeps us close together. It has become more important here than it was even in the old town. It makes us see what we left behind and gives us a mirror of ourselves."[88] As we have seen, group awareness was based on the memories of a Castellammarese past and a constantly emerging immigrant present in America. It was reformulated with each performance in the quintessential cohort space of the social club, the home away from home.[89]

It is at this nexus of shared experience between artist and audience that Ancona's personal creations were transformed into "realms of memory": that is, "any significant entity, whether material or non-material in nature, which by dint of human will or the work of time has become a symbolic element of the memorial heritage of any community."[90] Nora situates the current fascination with memory and the past—an "age of ardent, embattled, almost fetishistic 'memorialism'"—with the ending of the predominant agrarian culture in Western society, specifically France.[91] Gone are the "real environments of memory," what he refers to as "*millieux de mémoire*," that engen-dered "an integrated, dictatorial memory—unselfconscious, commanding, all-powerful, spontaneously actualizing, a memory without a past that ceaselessly reinvents tradition, linking the history of ancestors to the undifferentiated time of heroes, origins, and myth."[92] This definition of memory in oral and peasant societies is compared with the current state of affairs, where memory consists of vestiges, "the ultimate embodiments of a commemorative consciousness that survives in a history which, having renounced memory, cries out for it."[93] According to Nora, our current championing of memory implies that we no longer live by memory and that it is a marker of rupture and what has been lost. As a result, "we must create archives, mark anniversaries, organize celebrations, pronounce eulogies, and authenticate documents because such things no longer happen as a matter of course."[94] Yet, because the old symbols are not without their affective powers—"no longer quite alive but not yet entirely dead"—we are in a position to manipulate them to our needs.[95]

Ancona and his audience maintained a "visceral attachment"[96] to their individual memories and symbolic language of the past, but they were able to do so with a more critical distance than was available to them in Sicily. Their rupture from agrarian Sicily provided them with a set of references from the past which they used to create an image of themselves both in Sicily and New York. Ancona created realms of memory that were archives of the past and locations where group identity coalesced. Ancona also cultivated a distinctly "Italian-American" voice (albeit Sicilian-accented) and identity that moved beyond a specific Castellammarese. The self-crafted "Sicilian," "Italian," and "Italian-American" identities became increasingly pronounced as his work began to be presented at folk concerts and exhibitions beyond his principal Sicilian immigrant audience.[97]

Un dialogo tra la memoria e la storia

As the great rememberer, Ancona drew upon his lived experiences to address a host of topics using a variety of art forms. He sang, he wove, and he wrote his past into the present with a searing urgency. He committed the past to paper as a salve against disorientating and disrupting experiences. He tapped the aesthetic principals and performance modes of his Sicilian immigrant community as he crafted a public voice for their fears, desires, and hopes. The past served as a compass as he and his compatriots made their way through a strange and estranging environment. Together, they developed an understanding of the past and created a self-portrait that unfolded through time in response to shifting circumstances.[98] Ancona's work and its reception were testament to not only a remembered Castellammare, but also to their new and changing lives in the United States.

Halbwachs and Nora go to great lengths to distinguish between "autobiographical memory" and "historical memory" as well as between "memory" and "history."[99] Yet, the "tension and outright conflict between history and memory . . . seem necessary and productive" as a source of alternative readings of the past.[100] The documents that Ancona created and left behind opened up a space where dialogue, debate, and the possibility of anti-hegemonic narratives challenging dominant discourses could flourish.[101] These counter narratives spoke to the histories and "common sense" perceptions of an Italian national language, the exploitation of the Sicilian agricultural poor, the "voiceless" immigrant in America, and white working class understandings of gender and race. These artistic works, forged within the myriad social worlds Ancona inhabited, aided the understanding of the past while sorting through the possibilities for the future.

With Ancona's death and the dispersal of the aging immigrants (through return migration, the move to suburban homes, and, ultimately, death), the original urgency and purpose of his work are waning. Now, his printed and recorded poetry (as well as his recorded songs and wire tableaux) have entered into the realm of the historical, artistically crafted works that speak to a time when Sicilian immigrants faced the challenges in post–World War II New York with trepidation and hopefulness. They are the artful creations of a former peasant and fisherman, a factory worker, who crafted memory and meaning into verse, song, narration, and sculpture, enriching and empowering himself and his *paesani* audience with enlightenment as they moved into the future.

Valtaro Musette

CROSS-CULTURAL MUSICAL PERFORMANCE AND REPERTOIRE
AMONG NORTHERN ITALIANS IN NEW YORK

Marion S. Jacobson

In 1936, an immigrant from the town of Borgotaro in Italy's Emilia region opened the Val-Taro Restaurant and Bar at 869 Second Avenue, between 46th and 47th Streets, New York.[1] The club was located in the heart of a tight-knit Northern-Italian community in Manhattan's Turtle Bay neighborhood. The club was to feature dancing to live accordion music and an orchestra four nights a week. Surely the owner, John Brugnoli, must have been anxious with anticipation. The club would bring to fruition years of hard work, saving, self-sacrifice—and, in traditional New York City fashion, a lengthy wait for a liquor license. Finally, when the required document arrived, the restaurant opened its doors for the first time, on Christmas Eve. The new establishment was jammed—"an instant success."[2]

This account echoes thousands upon thousands of stories of other working people who left Italy in the early twentieth century to carry out various business ventures. It was less dramatic than many other "immigrant success" stories in that Brugnoli was already a noted and successful musician in Europe before he opened his Italian cabaret in New York City. But Brugnoli was also part of a long tradition of Northern-Italian musicians and musical entrepreneurs whose contributions to American culture have been little explored and understood by scholars.[3] This article explores the evolution of the *Valtaro musette* tradition (also referred by its practitioners as simply "Valtaro")—a song repertoire and style of Italian accordion music with roots in nineteenth-century Europe. Created in Manhattan's Italian nightclubs in the 1930s and 1940s by a tight-knit small group of musicians and composers with roots in Northern-Italian towns and villages who performed and composed in New York City, Valtaro has become part of the memory culture of Italians and Italian Americans today. As Valtaro musicians claimed ties to a region in Italy that was directly influenced by Austrian and French occupation and a variety of central-European cultural influences, it is difficult to discuss "Northern Italian" music as a singular repertoire or phenomenon. Therefore, I will also examine more generally the spread of the accordion and its repertoire from Italy through Europe and to America, and I will place the musicians in this context. I will evaluate the responses of their public—the Italian community, in particular—to their music and to the accordion phenomenon in general.

I first encountered Valtaro music when in search of repertoire to play at my accordion band Squeezeplay's "community service" gigs in upstate New York, where I lived at the time. We performed at nursing homes operated by Catholic charities. Our audience seemed to respond well to Italian songs. When we performed "Tutti Mi Chiamano Bionda,"[4] an energetic contingent of people often sang along in Italian. One year later, at a concert sponsored by the American Accordionists Association in New York City, a pair of accordionists announced a piece in "Valtaro style." I again heard the same tune, "Tutti Mi Chiamano Bionda," but performed in a dynamic, highly ornamented style. In their duet performance, the lead player performed the melody "straight" (but in much livelier fashion than did our band); the second player added florid ornamentation: trills, fills, and *arpeggios* (broken chords)—all improvised seemingly effortlessly. Their performance made our band's version sound austere by comparison: If our performance was a whitewashed Protestant church, the Valtaro version was a magnificent Gothic cathedral. My inquiries about what Valtaro style was led me to accordionist Dominic Karcic in New York City; and ultimately to his teacher, 88-year-old accordionist Peter Spagnoli, a contemporary of John Brugnoli's and his one-time business partner. Spagnoli especially was eager to discuss this repertoire, which he had not performed in public for some decades, and these discussions led to the present chapter.

Although I was first attracted to this music's lighthearted charms, I soon discovered many complexities behind its composition and performance. As I observed in my interviews of Valtaro musicians, and documenting their performances from 2006–2008, their music and song was not only the object of enjoyment and pleasure but were given careful attention and respect by the virtuoso musicians who meticulously recomposed and embellished them with intricate musical variations. How and why do these kinds of expressions motivate people to "feel connected" to the idea of Italian heritage? What are their modes of production and what processes of transmission and circulation are at work? In this chapter, I am concerned with the ways in which people construct a relationship to music, and the multiplicity of angles that motivate people to identify with and relate to their music.

In Valtaro music, I observed four types of musical activities that assert different types of relationships, each with specific status and power dynamics:

- Instrumental performance, and specifically the accordion—an instrument associated with Italy—is used to convey "respect" and forge alliances and affiliations with different ethnic groups in America.
- Nightclub performances defined shared roots and heritage among Northern Italian Americans and often connoted "high-class" sophistication in contrast with perceived crude or uncultured *meridonali* (Southern Italian Americans), from whom musicians wished to disassociate and distance themselves.
- The use of central-European music and dance forms: particularly, the Viennese waltz.
- The extensive study, practice, and efforts to disseminate the Valtaro tradition that expressed deep personal connections born of individual experiences.

In this chapter, I demonstrate how these four transnational musical activities realize perceived binary oppositions (hierarchical or egalitarian, intimate or distinct, contemporary or historical) between Italians and Americans, Northerners and Southerners, minorities and immigrants, the commercial music scene, and their musical subculture. I begin by contextualizing the shifting cultural associations of the accordion, an instrument featured in Italian-American and other ethnic dance styles, within the context of the Italian-American diasporic experience in the United States.

The Accordion in Cultural Context

New types of free-reed instruments known as *akkordeons* (in Germany and Austria) and concertinas (in the United Kingdom) had been invented in 1829.[5] Accordions are bellows-driven wind instruments, or aerophones, that produce sound as air passes through vibrating reeds in an enclosed frame or box (free-reed instruments). Expressive, rich in tone, and portable, these hand-crafted instruments spread along the pilgrimage routes of Europe, appearing in many different designs and tuning systems to suit local tastes and musical traditions. Generally speaking, the strong upward surge of the Italian accordion in the late nineteenth century converged with the rise of industrialization in the north, the agricultural crises in the Old World, and the strong, continuous interest in music-making at home and in local dance halls. Some scholars have noted that the accordion—an accessible, affordable instrument—seemed to define the new nation's emerging strains of nationalism and populism. Writes one scholar, "The accordion, with its uncomplicated and cheerful sound, its ease of use and transportation, was the ideal instrument to adopt in opposition to the elitist and costly music of previous years.[6] Travelers moving across the pilgrimage routes of Europe liked to carry accordions with them, and it was for their convenience and enjoyment that Cyril Demian was said to invented the "Demian," a portable free-reed instrument that became the prototype for the modern concertinas and accordions.[7]

According to various accounts, which are likely to be apocryphal, an Austrian pilgrim introduced the accordion to Italy by giving one to a Castelfidardo farmer's family in exchange for their hospitality. That family, the Sopranis, opened the first accordion factory in Italy. In first half of the 1900s, growing demand for the accordion pushed the Soprani family from making handmade instruments into starting a fully integrated production line powered by electricity. The Sopranis helped to transform Castelfidardo (and Italy) into an industrial powerhouse. The Soprani factory employed as many as 400 workers, and 100 additional accordion factories followed in their footsteps.[8] Soprani's brothers branched out to their own workshops—Settimo's in Via Cavour, Castelfidardo; and Paschal's in Recanati, which also became a center for accordion manufacture. According to a later account, "The intuitive Signor Soprani managed to revolutionize life in the Marche region, creating a new industry which in a short period of time succeeded in transforming the local economy from one based on agriculture, to an industrial one open to the international market."[9] While other nations—Germany, France, Russia, and Czechoslovakia—launched accordion industries of their own during the same period,[10] Italy's accordion industry had unparalleled access to the global market: In the 1940s and 1950s, it produced 90 percent of the accordions played in the United States.[11]

Indeed, the accordion industry developed at an ideal moment in which the accordion might reach a global market. Between 1840 and 1940, one of the most significant population movements occurred between Europe and the Americas. Estimates of the number of Italians who crossed the Atlantic hover around 16 million.[12] Among the pioneers of this movement in the early nineteenth century were artisans and craftsmen who perceived the demand for their products and services far afield of Italy. Many were agricultural workers or peasants settled in new homelands in Argentina and the United States. Others, however, sought other possibilities by practicing a trade or task that might be exportable. This was the path taken by, among others, Italian accordionists and composers. They were hopeful not only of marketing the accordion not only to fellow Italians but also to immigrants from Eastern Europe, Poland, Ireland, Czechoslovakia, and other nations that had experienced the accordion craze in Europe. In the age of emigration, the accordion traveled with Italian immigrants throughout the Americas, becoming the defining instrument in a variety of folk and popular musics.

The accordion had practical advantages for Italian immigrants (as it did for other immigrant communities). First, accordions were more affordable than pianos. The instrument is sturdy, portable, and relatively easy to learn to play at least on a basic level; the sound carries very well, and it could be adapted to play a wide range of musical repertoires. With the ease of playing chords in the left hand, the accordion was readily adaptable to a variety of dance rhythms played at social dance events. One account by an Italian historian suggests how the accordion may have been perceived within the Italian diasporan community: "The large Italian populations who had emigrated to the Americas eased their homesickness with the sounds of accordion music. For those forced to leave their place of birth to earn a living in a foreign land, the accordion became a standard part of their luggage, a piece of home that they brought with them."[13]

Bugiolacchi's account of accordion-playing immigrants implies that the instrument's appeal was instantaneous and automatic, yet the Italians' dominance in the field was carefully calculated. Along with other tradesmen and traders—ink-vendors from Parma, child street musicians from Genoa, and *figurinai* sellers from Lucca—the musicians and entrepreneurs from Italy were active participants in the mass migrations of the late nineteenth and early twentieth centuries.[14] When accordion craftsmen journeyed from Castelfidardo to America to sell their wares, they tested the market, following the routes and methods of other diasporic tradesmen. Accordion factories and retail businesses focused their efforts on in cities with large immigrant populations, locating their factories and shops in Italian neighborhoods. San Francisco's North Beach district (settled by Italians after the 1849 Gold Rush) and New York's Little Italy were two American cities that were home to "accordion districts," or clusters of shops and factories catering to accordionists.[15] These entrepreneurs carefully researched the musical tastes of their potential audiences and evaluated economic opportunities that might develop from them.

In 1938, with the accordion's popularity burgeoning in many different regional styles of music from country-western to polka, as well as in the mainstream of American life, Italian entrepreneurs sensed the possibilities of marketing their own regional and national music to a wider public. The name they chose for their repertoire and style, Valtaro musette, shows the careful considerations given to regional identity and specificity, while "branding" their music for much broader audience. According to discussions with musicians and practitioners of the style, "Valtaro" refers to a specific place in Italy: namely, Val di Taro, the valley of the Taro River running through the Parma province; and the town of Borgotaro (the place of origin, real or mythical, for Brugnoli and other musicians). "Musette" refers to French bagpipe (musette) music that was popularized in Europe by Italians, who recomposed and played this repertoire for the accordion.[16] By examining the this newly created genre—a unique musical genre created by Italians in New York—and the musical practices of Valtaro accordionists, we can see how, through their cultural connections, they were able to exert an influence on other immigrants from their own towns and regions and beyond.

The accordionists who invented a new playing style and repertoire they called Valtaro provide important insights into the sociocultural transition to American life. In their "multicultural performances," the accordion and the songs of his region and town served Brugnoli well. His inclusion and zesty reinterpretations of Northern-Italian (among other Italian) songs reveal a genius for the use of music, performance, and the nightclub stage as a means of bringing people together through sonic spectacle and participatory dancing. They often encouraged sing-alongs (especially when performing "Tutti Mi Chiamano Bionda") of Italian songs, while including their own arrangements of Irish, French, Spanish, and American tunes. Brugnoli and his fellow exponents of the Valtaro repertoire understood that the Italian songs they performed in these purely instrumental performances, absent the lyrics and the language/dialect barrier, would appeal to American audiences. He would draw his Irish, Irish-American, Polish, and Anglo audiences in closer under the universal ethnic "sign of the accordion" by encouraging them to dance to the relentless rhythms of the polka, mazurka, and foxtrot; the musicians gave others (of different ethnic origins and nationalities) a way to participate more fully in the American multicultural scene of the 1940s and 1950s than they ever had in the days of vaudeville and ribald ethnic comedy.

In the New York City that Brugnoli encountered when he arrived in the 1920s, Italian Americans often fell into marginal lives for which they were not prepared. Sometimes viewed by Anglo Americans as black, or "not quite white," Italian Americans frequently competed for unskilled jobs and tenement housing with African Americans.[17] They often suffered discrimination on the basis of perceived essential cultural differences from Anglo-American society. In this climate, when all Italians were seen as inferior, many Northern Italians—who represented about 15 percent of the Italian immigrant population—clung to the idea of cultural superiority: that they were better-educated, lighter-skinned, or less superstitious than their *meridionali* (Southern Italian) counterparts. Many Northern Italians even sought to distance themselves geographically from the *meridionali* by moving to specific neighborhoods where, as they imagined, they would not be plagued by overcrowding, noise, or threats from the *Cosa Nostra*.[18]

From his *Valtarese* upbringing and early interactions with French, German, and other American musicians, Brugnoli learned to use music as both powerful means of individual and collective ethnic expression and a reliable source of income. He followed the lead of fellow Italian Americans who were first to play piano accordion in

America—such as Guido Deiro, an immigrant from Turin, the only accordionist to become a vaudeville headline act; and Guido's brother Pietro Deiro, who had made the first-ever recordings of accordion music. Like the Deiro brothers, Brugnoli had both formal musical training and informal exposures to the rich musical influences of the north. As a young man, Brugnoli played the accordion at *ballo liscio* (literally, smooth dance) dance halls, which featured the popular waltzes, polkas, and mazurkas that had circulated to Italy from the Alps; like Guido Deiro, he had achieved the status of a minor celebrity in Europe.[19] When migrating to France, Brugnoli could not help but absorb the musette music he heard (and played) on the streets of Paris. In addition to this informal training, Brugnoli incoporated jazz and the new forms of popular dance music that were circulating in the hotels and nightclubs of midtown Manhattan. Indeed, story of the accordionists from northern Italy demonstrates different stages or levels of cultural interaction; their choices set them apart from the Old World immigrants who journeyed to New York and other American cities. They were not only immigrants from Italy, but from Europe; they had to come to grips with changing American tastes (e.g., the jazz craze of the 1920s and 1930s), which they did by becoming students of American music.[20]

The relationship that the migrants developed with cities and towns in America has an important bearing on another issue that has attracted ethnomusicologists and social historians: the accordion as a distinctively European and global contribution to the world of music (as opposed to its much celebrated role in national folk musics). An issue of the ethnomusicological journal *World of Music* devoted to Accordion Culture reveals the rich, varied, and multiple meanings of the accordion in Western culture.[21] As new styles of accordion performance emerge, it becomes clear that the accordion is not only one of the world's most unique instruments but a unique musical phenomenon as well. Socio-economic and technological developments in the modern world have engendered the proliferation of cheap, affordable instruments that have circulated beyond the accordion's place of origin in Italy and Austria, as far as China and Africa. In short, the accordion is seen as an instrument with a larger following and collective audience than any in previous music history. The materiality of the accordion (visible in the colorfully customized button accordions played by Tejano [*conjunto*, and *norteño*] musicians in the Texas-Mexico borderlands), makes it a powerful witness to the existence of realities outside people's immediate experience.[22] The accordion has special importance not just because of its traditional popularity and ease of playing, but as a multifaceted cultural experience for it has embodied and expressed new musical discourses and social identities emerging as a product of globalization.

The accordion's unique role in Italian-American culture, its capacity to engage issues of class, and ethnicity were the subjects of a recent symposium on the accordion as an "Italian-American icon."[23] The accordion, for a time, formed part of the vibrant, lively culture of urban and suburban first- and second-generation immigrants who saw the playing the accordion as a key part of maintaining their Old World cultural connections. According to William Schimmel, many saw the accordion as a more affordable version of the piano and the musical upward mobility it promised. "If you were Polish, Czech, German, or Italian, you played the accordion," he noted, recalling his choice of instrument as a child growing up in a Catholic family in inner-city Philadelphia. "Anglos and Jews tended to gravitate toward the piano."[24]

As European immigrants worked their way up the economic ladder in the first decades of the twentieth century, playing the accordion could become a particularly risky practice, particularly among the second- and third-generation of immigrants who wanted to conform to the suburban order. James Periconi, who learned the accordion as a child growing up in the Bronx during the 1950s but abandoned it in his teens, noted in a memoir article, that "The accordion and my skill with the instrument have been . . . a stigma for me, not unlike my frizzy hair, emblematic of a certain rejection by straight-hair American culture, a denial of my *Italianità* (or 'Italianness')"[25]

Another level of complication, also witnessed by Periconi as a member of the Baby Boomer generation, was the advent of rock 'n' roll and the "British Invasion," resulting in dramatic changes in American musical tastes and instrument preferences. As Maria Sonevytski observes, any ethnic stereotype revolving around accordion playing was negative.[26] For teenagers in the 1960s, no other musical instrument was as coded with as toxic a combination of bourgeois cultural aspirations and old-country ethnicity as the accordion.

In the public mind, at least during the period when the instrument was at the peak of its popularity in the 1940s and 1950s, the accordion is seen as an accepted part of American popular culture. Accordions were not too "other"—they were not the instrument of street musicians or underclass immigrants who needed to be watched with suspicion.[27] They were sold in respectable shops (like the ones on Mulberry Street in New York City), and taught by artists and teachers who sported tuxedoes in their publicity photos. Music critics writing for the mainstream press and the music trades presented evidence that the accordion was becoming the instrument of choice for middle-class Americans to play at home. Relatively easy to learn, it was particularly well suited for communal musical pursuits, such as accordion bands and clubs. The prime evidence of the accordion's suitability for mainstream America that the critics cited was the repertoire. Numerous works by the classical masters—Bach, Rossini, Mozart, and Beethoven—were arranged for the accordion by composers such as Guido and Pietro Deiro, Charles Magnante, Charles Nunzio; these same composers also created original works in the "classical style." Two new publishing companies were devoted to accordion music: O. Paganini and Pietro Deiro publishing. Accordion sales reaching 250,000 in 1953 (at its peak) created a stir in the music industry.[28]

How was it that in the climate of postwar America, Italian Americans made use of the accordion to symbolize their ethnic identity to themselves and others? During the post–World War II era, immigrants from the northern and central regions of Italy recontextualized a broad repertoire of Alpine, pan-Italian, and European folk songs, as well as film music and jazz standards by arranging it for accordion ensembles and performing it in handful of Manhattan nightclubs. This newly created subgenre of accordion music—an original Italian-American musical repertoire and style created in New York City and performed at Italian-American cabarets—reveals how a remarkably talented and diverse set of Italian and American-born artists gave a distinct voice to these familiar and widely circulated popular songs and marketed their creations as "authentic Northern Italian music."

Secondly, they created new spaces where the music could be heard and enjoyed by their compatriots in Valtaro nightclubs in the Upper East Side of Manhattan and later on recordings. By appropriating well-known popular songs, creating new versions, canonizing ideas about style, and collaborating with musicians from different backgrounds, Valtaro musicians worked out their transnational identities and translated them into sounds and lived musical activities. This process is akin to the affirmation of and celebrations of relationships and values expressed in music, as described by Christopher Small:

> By bringing into existence relationships that are thought of as desirable, a musical
> performance not only reflects those relationships but also shapes them. It teaches and
> inculcates the concept of those ideal relationships, or values. In articulating those values
> it allows those taking part to say, to themselves, to one another and to anyone else who
> may be paying attention: these are our values, they are our concepts of ideal relationships,
> and consequently, this is who we are . . . after taking part in a good and satisfying musical
> performance, one is able to feel that this is how the world really is, and "this is how I
> really relate to it."[29]

In the case of Valtaro, transnational relationships are not just brought into existence as if they were self-evident truths. Rather, at least for the musicians taking part, they are ideas transformed into tangible experiences and sound products in which Italian-American musicians directly interact with and relate to music and musicians from various cultures and eras, as well as their own past.

Performances at Nightclubs Defined Shared Roots

New York City in the early twentieth century was not only one of the world's most thriving industrial and trade cities, but it had also built a popular entertainment industry of worldwide significance. Since the nineteenth century, the city's musical life experienced waves of influence from African Americans and immigrants: most notably, the prolific Jewish, German, and Irish songwriters, composers, and musicians who helped to build the commercial song industry, Tin Pan Alley. Although New York City attracted Italians from all over Italy, Southern Italians were the most numerous. The "Neapolitan song" emerged as the Italian musical genre that drew the widest immigrant and American-born audience as it helped to fuel the popular American representations of Italians as innately musically talented, particularly in the field of singing.[30] The music of southern Italy had greater visibility vis-à-vis the Neapolitan song and the *tarantella*, musicians from northern Italy made up a large number of those living in the city. They distinguished themselves not as singers but as virtuoso instrumentalists—and as players of the accordion, an instrument with deep Italian and European associations.

Shortly after the advent of vaudeville theaters in the late nineteenth century, an elite group of accordionists—many of them immigrants from Italy—found their niche in a medium that prized novelty. Critical accounts speak to the appeal of the piano keyboard as a one-man band instrument. In 1911, an admiring reviewer from the *Pittsburgh Post* marvels that the accordion combined the tonal qualities of five distinct instruments: the violin, the flute, the cello, the bass, and the piano. "In the hands of a master, it is a wonderful instrument capable of playing the most involved symphonies and at the same time, the simplest harmonies."[31] In contrast to vaudeville's familiar low-life or buffoonish ethnic stereotypes, performers of the accordion (and other solo instruments) sought to present themselves as elegant and high class, both in their self-presentations and choice of repertoire. By 1916, Guido Deiro had established a glamorous *persona* as an accordion virtuoso. Guido was not only the first to play piano accordion in America, but the first to enjoy a full-time career playing the instrument. For the Italian community, his career pointed to the potential of an accordion career as a tool for upward mobility. Whenever Guido traveled on the vaudeville circuit, the local paper would run a story about his rise from impoverished mine worker to vaudeville headliner making $600 per week.[32] Musicians who played for the "community" (as Deiro did for the Italian war veterans: events that were chronicled in the Italian language newspapers) and nightclubs could maintain their public profiles as well as supplement their incomes.

Italian involvement in the American entertainment world did not come about automatically, but within the context of a multiethnic musical scene in which they often played a shadowy part. Many Italians enthusiastically supported their own performers, particularly in the field of *bel canto* opera, a medium that had a particular appeal among the *prominenti* (self-appointed leaders) Italians.[33] Neapolitan song was featured in operatic performances (Tito Schipa and Enrico Caruso) as well as Italian theater and vaudeville venues. The tango craze reached its peak in the 1920s and 1930s, a type of music cultivated by Italian immigrants to Argentina in the late nineteenth century. Italian musicians participated in white jazz orchestras, and Louis Prima—a brilliant synthesizer of blues, jazz, and Italian popular song—enjoyed a brief movie career. Italian participation in American musical life was conditioned in part by what they heard and saw around them. At the same time, Italian accordionists had never operated exclusively within an "Italian" or "mainstream" field. Like other musicians, they took the opportunities they could and carved some out for themselves. Following the collapse of vaudeville, Pietro Deiro assured his financial success by opening a chain of accordion studios in the 1930s and 1950s, capitalizing upon the accordion craze and the appeal of the instrument in mainstream suburbia. He also founded his own publishing company (Deiro Publishing, in New York City), which provided accordionists with arrangements of classical repertoire.

These polished arrangements and his performance of them on recordings and radio sought to bring elegance and dignity to an instrument that was tied to stereotypical assumptions about folk music.[34] The accordion's image—and the self-representation of its performers—was significant to these musicians. Indeed, one of the most notable of accordion performers, Anthony Galla-Rini, spent his youth playing accordion (in clown costume and makeup) as part of his father's duet act, "Pallo and Pallet." Becoming a solo accordion artist at the age of 21, he vowed to abandon both humiliating representations of Italians and the lowbrow image of the accordion. In breaking off from his father to launch a solo career as a virtuoso accordionist and performing classical repertoire for that instrument, Galla-Rini becomes one of the most phenomenally successful and highly paid accordion artists of his day, and his polished elegance is still imitated by concert accordionists.[35]

After the collapse of vaudeville in the early 1930s, the hotels and nightclubs of Chicago and New York became important sources of employment, at least for those who could master the "sweet" style of jazz becoming popular with white, upper-class patrons.[36] But only a few of the most elite performers could aspire to break into the profitable Manhattan dance band circuit. Fortunately, around this time, Manhattan's entertainment district began to spread east and below Times Square. This neighborhood, known as Turtle Bay, also had the distinction of being a popular destination for immigrants from the northern and central Italy—namely, from Genoa, Parma, Tuscany, and Emilia—as were the seven blocks of Manhattan's West Side in the 1920s (Chelsea).[37] These "Northern Italian" neighborhoods consisted only of a few city blocks: essentially 61st, 62nd, and 63rd Streets between First and Second Avenues, with some immigrants from the north on First Avenue between 61st and 63rd Streets.[38] The spatial divisions sought by some of the residents of these neighborhoods reflected a long-standing system of social stratification ranking northerners as alt'Italiani (high Italians) and southerners as bass'Italiani (low Italians).[39] According to some scholars—and my informants—perceived differences in status and economic standing posed serious barriers between these two groups. Northerners shunned southerners for being poorly educated, superstitious, and too easily drawn to organized crime. Southerners accused northerners of standoffishness and snobbery. Studies of clubs and fraternal organizations have indicated that Italians tended to socialize—and marry—almost exclusively within their own regional groups at least until the post–World War II era.[40]

According to my interviews with former residents of this area, who preferred to remain anonymous,[41] networks of immigrants in the Turtle Bay neighborhood sustained an informal social life within their tiny enclave—a world within a world, apart from Sicilians and Southern Italians. They tended to rent apartments in the same buildings. Most Northern Italians I have spoken to defined themselves as "not religious" in contrast to their Sicilian counterparts, whom they regarded as superstitious and religiously fanatic. However, some Parmigiani worshiped at their own church in Manhattan—Our Lady of Peace, at 237 East 63nd Street—with a Sicilian pastor, Father Leone.[42] Some scholars have noted the northerners' desire to suppress "characteristic religious practices" that would mark them as "foreign" and the relatively faster pace of their acculturation into American life and their move to "better" neighborhoods in Queens, Long Island, and beyond.[43] As friends and neighbors in Turtle Bay, they did favors for one another, and their informal employment network provided their husbands, sons, cousins, and nephews with employment in the building trades. Italians from Tuscany supported each other in starting small shops and businesses; immigrants from Genoa, Parma, and Lombardy followed one another into stonecutting, tile masonry, and the construction trades.

The idea for an "Italian cabaret" that would be open to the public began with John (Gianod "Scud'lein") Brugnoli (1901–1992).[44] John's nickname was inherited from his grandfather, who loved wine and drank it from a scud'lein (soup bowl).[45] The region had long sustained a vibrant ballo liscio tradition in which local and regional bands circulated through a network of public dances in local towns and villages, and John's brother and father played at these events.[46] His older brother Luigi was known on the dance hall circuit as an outstanding accordionist, and eventually migrated to Paris, where he is said to have pioneered the use of the piano accordion. Under Luigi's tutelage, John established himself in Paris as a virtuoso accordionist and band leader, playing and conducting bands in public dance halls throughout Borgotaro. Aiming higher as a professional musician, he first emigrated to France and, following a short stint in the clubs of Paris, John Brugnoli emigrated to the United States in 1928, earning a livelihood as a mushroom merchant. Because he was an illegal alien, Brugnoli had to exit the United States and reenter via Canada. He eventually became a naturalized citizen, and his wife and children joined him in New York in 1935. After playing accordion in cabarets such as the Francino, Brugnoli realized that his ambition was to open one of his own that would feature the popular Valtaro musette repertoire as well as music of his own region, but he needed a business partner. In Borgotaro, John had met fellow accordionist Pietro (later Peter) DelGrosso, and heard that Peter had emigrated and was well established as a musician in New York City. They did eventually meet, where DelGrosso was performing at a West Side nightclub called Bel Tabarin. They agreed to go into business together, and friends provided capital to support their vision. The opening of their club, The Val-Taro, as it was commonly known by its patrons, became a significant moment in the memory of New York's Northern Italians:

> Val-Taro became a mecca for people who loved good dance music, good times, and above all, the accordion. It was a place where notable accordionists . . . all worked . . . over the years . . . .[47]

The Val-Taro's success also was an incentive for other entrepreneurs to establish similar types of cabarets featuring Northern Italian accordion music. Many eventually flourished in the New York midtown area but "not one quite equaled the Val-Taro."[48] Selling his share of the business in 1939, Brugnoli left the Val-Taro and entered into another partnership with his long-time friend and landlord, Emilio Spagnoli. The new cabaret was known as the Terrace (Second Avenue and 59th Street). Spagnoli's son Pete, tutored by Brugnoli in exchange for room and board, was emerging as an accomplished accordionist, and in time joined the roster of notable, regularly featured Italian accordionists who had appeared at the Val-Taro and the Terrace. These notables included Mindie Cere, Addie Cere, Emilio Chiesa, Hugo Nati, and Aldo Bruschi. The Terrace's two house musicians—pianist Norma McFeeters, an Afro-Caribbean woman from Dominica; and Jewish drummer Willy Wohlman—joined with the immediately aforementioned accordionists in arranging and performing Valtaro music. Spagnoli later claimed that McFeeters and Wohlman learned to play Valtaro repertoire "as if it were in their DNA."[49] To Spagnoli and other musicians, the presence of musicians and listeners from many backgrounds seemed to validate the broader appeal and significance of their work, as well as the viability of the clubs themselves. The opportunity to play four or five weeks gave Brugnoli, DelGrosso, and eventually, Spagnoli, the opportunity to polish Valtaro as a distinctive repertoire and unique style, continuing to build on its foundation of familiar, traditional Northern-Italian and European popular songs by adding jazz, popular tunes, and Irish favorites such as "Danny Boy."[50]

Reinventing European and Italian Musical Forms in a New Context

It is evident through their prolific work as arrangers and composers that Valtaro musicians intended for their music to circulate beyond their community. Peter DelGrosso's work appears as volumes 1 and 3 of *Let's Waltz and Polka*, the ethnic dance folios mentioned earlier in this chapter. While performing four or five nights a week as well as teaching accordion at Elsie Bennett's Accordion Studio in Brooklyn (and eventually his own), Spagnoli managed to arrange most of the songs that are considered part of the Valtaro repertoire. Until I interviewed Peter Spagnoli recently, I had assumed (incorrectly) that the Valtaro repertoire consisted of the dozen or so pieces published in Deffner's folios, and the few numbers I had heard performed at accordion club gatherings.

> Marion: What is "Valtaro"?
>
> Pete: It's music from those mountains. Mountains don't make music, but the people that are from there . . . it's hard to explain . . . it's Italian and French music, with a likable, animated style. When they heard it, people would get off their chairs, run for the girls, ask them to dance, and that was it.
>
> Marion: How many songs can you play in that style?
>
> Pete: Oh, I dunno. Maybe 1,000.[51]

Although this repertoire is no doubt a testament to Spagnoli's genius and memory, it also provides an important window into the significance of the Italian cabarets and the culture of the Northern Italian–American community.[52] As promoters of a repertoire of Northern-Italian music in New York, the Valtaro clubs and their promoters had an important (but little recognized) role in shaping the future of this emerging New World tradition: the choice of songs, their instrumentation, and decisions about style.

Regional and national stereotypes played and continue to play a pivotal role in determining what music gets embraced by a particular community. Among the assertions I have heard from my informants was that Northern Italians invented the accordion, produced the world's greatest accordionists, invented opera, and have produced music that is better appreciated by outsiders than the folk music of *meridonali*. Some believe that talent for playing the accordion and a love for the music is innate for Northern Italians: "You have to grow up with it."[53] Indeed, some have pointed out that Americans have depended upon the cultural products of Northern Italians whose expertise in everything from maritime exploration to stonemasonry was a legacy more pivotal to American culture than the Southern-Italian tradition. However, although Northern Italians feel they have made an enormous contribution, they have not been recognized for their distinctiveness.

An analysis of the Valtaro repertoire can help to demonstrate the wide spectrum of songs and musical influences that it has absorbed from France, central Europe, Italian, and American popular culture—a dramatic collision of old and new, local and global. Spagnoli's comment references "music from those mountains." In their discourse about the origins of the music, the players tend to privilege native folk influences while glossing over its hybrid commercial, high-cultural, and cross-cultural musical influences. Some songs in the repertoire, such as "Mazzolin del fior," hail from the Italian film industry. Medleys like one conjoining snippets of Robert Schumann's "Carnival of Venice," the traditional Italian song "Vieni sul mar" (popularized by Tito Schipa and Enrico Caruso), and the ballad of "Il Sirio" may seem like haphazard pastiche. However, such productions can be seen as strategic as well. I would argue that Spagnoli and DelGrosso engaged in what anthropologists and ethnographers have referred to as the process of "folklorization."[54] Folkorization of Italian culture appropriates local music for the pleasure of its listeners, but at the same time creates spaces in which the community (Northern Italians) can assert their own claims to be true custodians of a national cultural patrimony (the accordion). The proponents of this music succeed in producing a collective identity based upon their mastery of their local folksongs in order to enhance the visibility and legitimacy of their community as well as foster integration into American culture. With his arsenal of 1,000 songs, Spagnoli was armed for any occasion. He aimed to satisfy not only listeners from his own region but all audiences: Northern Italian, Southern Italian, American, Irish, and German, and others. He learned that the greater his flexibility, the greater the demand for his services (as accordion teacher and bandleader), and the greater his financial success.

The Valtaro repertoire celebrates breathtaking mountain landscapes, the country lifestyle ("Il Mio Galletto"), and the brave, sure-footed Alpini soldiers fighting for their nation ("Il Bersaglieri"). These songs concern departure, nostalgia, and heroic acts; like their Southern-Italian counterparts, they avoid "heavy" or "serious" subjects. A key manifestation of regional identity in the repertoire is what Del Giudice has dubbed the *bella campagnola* (pretty country lass) subgenre of Italian song with idealized rustic portrayals. "Such songs are full of nostalgia and longing for reunion, and appear to ignore the impossibility of a return to a reality that no longer exists—if ever it did exist."[55] In other regional repertoires, this idealized female may appear as "La bella Romanina," or "Calabrisella," but in the Valtaro repertoire, she is the "*La* Signorinella Alpina" that we encounter in the song "Tutti Mi Chiamano Bionda." Among the most appealing female attributes celebrated in such songs are blue eyes and blond hair—perhaps symbolizing an important identity marker for some Northern Italian-Americans whose physical resemblance to white Anglo-Saxon Protestants could help distance them from the darker-skinned *meridonali*.[56] One of the best-known songs of this repertoire is the well-known "Tutti Mi Chiamano Bionda," popularized in the Italian nightclub scene and sung at many Italian-American gatherings today. It has also circulated the mainstream popular musical world.[57] Notes Peter Spagnoli's daughter Carol Schiavi, "To this day no Northern Italian social event can be considered complete without 'Tutti Mi Chiamano Bionda' being played.[58] The light-hearted sentiments expressed in the lyrics are right at home with the normative Italian popular song subjects: love, pretty girls, and longing.

Tutti mi chiamano "bionda"	They all call me "blonde"
ma bionda io non sono:	but I am not blonde:
porto i capelli neri,	I have black hair,
neri come il carbon.	black as coal.
Perché non m'ami più?	Why don't you love me anymore?[59]

The song's vignette about a young woman who dyes her hair gets to the heart of another important theme in Italian-American culture: self-transformation. The heroine of

"Tutti Mi Chiamano Bionda" is born dark-haired, but adopting a fair look from a bottle of dye, she is a hybrid goddess. Alpine ice queen and earthy Italian brunette, she is the uncertain and shifting object of admiration: idol of seductive femininity and Euro-American blond beauty. Like other stories and narratives of Italian-American life, the song speaks of the desire to "pass," imposing spatial and psychic distance from one's old-country "roots." Perhaps this vignette about a girl dying her hair puts forth a moral argument, or speaks to the need for authenticity—for no matter what lengths one goes through to "pass," one's folk "essence" will eventually show through. Indeed, Valtaro repertoire became a means of interacting with of small-town and country life. Images of women, especially, are predominant in this emotional landscape, as subjects of humorous, romantic, and inspiring lyrics. The range of content was a response to the market-driven demand for vividly familiar emotional experiences.

It is impossible to overrate the significance of regional songs as well as how these became associated (at least in the minds of Northern Italian-Americans) with the idea of Europe, per se. Dance sets played in Valtaro clubs invariably included waltzes, tangos, mazurkas, and polkas, which have been part of the regional repertoire. Polkas have been part of the regional repertoire of Italians from the Emilia region since the eighteenth century.[60] Traditional polkas were usually performed by musicians during *maggio delle ragazze* ("young girls'" May Day celebrations) at a ball in the village squares and in the homes of prominent families. Linked historically to the Emilian *ballo liscio* tradition, they also became part of New York City's nightclub and cabaret scene.

How does the idea of "Central European" and "Alpine" operate as cultural forces in this repertoire? In folk musical practice, a single song can circulate in multiple versions and multiple dialects. "Tutti Mi Chiamano Bionda"shares the same lilting waltz melody as the Croatian language song "La Mula di Parenzo," Parenzo referring to a region, bordering the Adriatic Sea, divided between Italy and Croatia. "La Mula di Parenzo" and "Tutti Mi Chiamano Bionda" have merged as a medley circulating through the repertoire of Italian Alpini and Istrian Croatian singers.[61] The transnationalism of this music helps to explain why Dominic Karcic, who is of Croatian descent, can present himself as a leading Valtaro tradition bearer without being perceived as an outsider.[62] The songs display to their listeners the significance of an Italian heritage as part of a much broader entity within the shifting landscape of European-ness.

A striking departure from the overwhelmingly cheerful and nostalgic cast of most Valtaro songs is "Il Sirio," a song that we encountered earlier in the "Sunny Italy" accordion medley arranged by DelGrosso for the *Let's Waltz and Polka* folios. This song touches upon historical references that are quite poignant for insiders. The ballad narrates the tragic events that surround the sinking of the ocean liner *Sirio* on August 4, 1906. The ship, leaving from the port of Genoa, struck a rocky ledge and sunk stern first. As the victims battled for places on the few lifeboats, the captain realized that he was powerless to control the panic, and consequently committed suicide by shooting himself.[63] Most of the 300 fatalities of this accident were Italians and Spaniards. This song gives voice to feelings of fear and loss engendered by travel and migration, as well as presenting the Italian experience as globally significant and accessible to others (through the obvious associations between the *Sirio* and the *Titanic*).[64]

Although many songs in the repertoire are valued as expressions of identity, or even documents of historical experience, Valtaro musicians typically create with little concern for "purity" and "authenticity." In Valtaro, like in other instrumental perform-ances of genres such as polka or klezmer, there is no vocalist and lyrics; the songs themselves are simply raw material to be carved and chiseled by the accordionist. As we have seen from Spagnoli's comment, the skill of the accordionist provided a point of connection with the musical traditions and with his audience, who would frequently sing along. Folk songs and traditional ballads provided an important sense of cultural continuity, but the draw for the audience was the accordion, and the name "Val-Taro" was synonymous with "good accordion music."[65] No doubt proud of and attuned to the potential to capitalize on the "cult of the virtuoso" phenomenon in the accordion world, Val-Taro players aimed to develop their own local following in Manhattan. They aimed to do this through the resignification of the music through a unique instrumental per-formance style and sound.

Valtaro Style and Sound

Seen on paper, most songs from the Valtaro repertoire appear indistinguishable from other Italian and Central European dance tunes. They share the same rhythms, har-monic progressions, and in many cases, the same melodies. In spite of generalized, nonregional, and Central European characteristics of much of this repertoire, the play-ers aimed to construct a distinct style. By employing an instrument with a sense of an artistically rich past (the Italian accordion), and simple, unadorned folk and popular songs, Valtaro musicians forged what might otherwise be heard as simple or "generic" material into a unique style. One way to understand this process would be to compare two performances of the polka "Tic Tic Ta." I first encountered this tune as a Polish polka in my accordion band Squeezeplay's repertoire. When I compared the Valtaro version of "Tic Tic Ta" (performed on the Taccas' *Nostalgia* album[66]) with the pounding and hard-driving renditions performed by my band, I detected a more lighthearted and easygoing quality, with distinct operatic influences present in the Italian polka. The instrumentation of a polka band most familiar to American Midwestern practitioners of the Slovenian or "Dutchman" styles features a piano and/or a diatonic accordion, guitar, bass, and a drum set, and it is similar to that used by Valtaro bands.[67] The accordion often plays lead (melody), using a single reed or a pair of reeds, high and middle, tuned at the same pitch, which enables the accordion to "cut" through the band texture.[68] For this purpose, many Polish-American accordionists choose instruments with so-called "dry tuning" or "polka tuning."[69] Most Italian-made piano accordions, however, unless the player specifically requests that they be "dry-tuned," are equipped with a "musette" switch, which comprises a pair of reeds that are tuned higher and lower than the desired pitch. This, the *musette* sound—or "wet" sound—is the one desired by Valtaro accordionists.[70] The ever-present vibrato of Valtaro—the singing accordion—evokes the resonant operatic voices of *bel canto* tradition and the historical significance of the Italian opera casting its shadow over this popular folk tradition.[71] The importance of singing, and the ever-present vocal soloists and choruses at Valtaro events, may explain why players value the "wet" *musette* sound, and strive for a lighter sound (easier to blend with the voices) than their Eastern European colleagues in the polka field.

Because Valtaro is an "accordion-centered" tradition, a performance of "Tic Tic Ta" witnessed at a 2006 "Reunion" of Valtaro musicians in Walkill, New York not only showcased the vocal soloist Mary Mancini but two accordionists presenting the "B" section of the song as a mini-composition/improvisation for accordion duet. The lead accordionist, Karcic, played the "Tic Tic Ta" melody in fairly straightforward fashion, with a harmony in thirds unfolding in the right hand (keyboard). The second part, improvised by Ray Oreggia, embellished the melody with triplet runs and arpeggios, creating a rich and varied texture. The tempo of the Valtaro version of "Tic Tic Ta" was slower and more elastic than my band's driving Polish polka version. As presented by the pair of accordionists, the tempo was much more relaxed, with plenty of *rubato*, which was much appreciated by the dancers who exploited the slow ends of phrases to add turns, dips, and other embellishments as they moved across the dance floor.

Although many players believe that Valtaro music is "innate" or absorbed in the womb,[72] Karcic has taken on the mission of teaching Valtaro workshops at accordion conventions. Karcic is concerned with perfecting "duet style" of accordion playing, developed by Brugnoli, in which the players take turns performing the lyrical melodic line and playing rhythmic chords, adding arpeggios, dynamic shifts (through the bellows), and ornaments.

> When you have two accordions, one guy is laying out the line, playing the straight melody, while the other guy improvises around the chord structure, I-V-IV.[73] But if you've got one accordion, usually the first time through you play it straight, the second time you add little flourishes. There is a trend in Valtaro music to use some passing diminished chords in the appropriate places. And the touch in playing is very light, *leggiero*. They use *leggiero*, but in many of the passages, especially fast passages, it's played almost with a *staccato* [notes detached and heavily accented]. I always tell people, think staccato when you're playing some of the intricate passages, think staccato. Think detached. Lighten up![74]

Indeed, the style that Karcic is describing also reflects many styles of music such as classical, jazz, and the scores of lighthearted popular songs (Italian and American) that Valtaro musicians played at their audience's requests. Karcic also offered a lengthy discussion of the French musette tradition, a parallel repertoire and style developed by Italian accordionists in Paris, and its boundary-crossing influences on Valtaro musicians.

Given that this music and the accordion itself has surfaced in so many areas of Central Europe, how does the sound and style of Valtaro mirror the musical identity of its core constituency, and how did listeners interpret this music's significance to their community? In this study, I sought to discover not only the songs and their patterns of use, but the ways in which they were constructed in the organization of social events. It was through the dance that Valtaro music actively engaged their participants (not just notable performers) in public display and bolstered their sense of respectability.

The creators of the Valtaro tradition were as eager to provide a space for social dancing as they were to present accordion music. Northern Italian Americans share

with both Southern Italian and Central European cultures a folk culture in which dancing, whether at social clubs or family gatherings, forms an important component of
their cultural identity. As Joan Saverino has noted in her discussion of folkloric dance
events at Columbus Day celebrations, the *tarantella* was seen as a key marker of *italianità* that would be nonthreatening, charming, and engaging to non-Italians.[75] For Northern Italian Americans, their primary cultural reference point is not the *tarantella* but
the elevated Viennese waltz. When the "Valtaro reunion band" played a waltz at a
recent gathering, dozens of couples followed the Viennese (and International Ballroom
Dance) tradition of moving around the floor counterclockwise in formal line of dance.
Their upper bodies erect, they exhibited a formality and elegance that my Northern-
Italians informants seem to emphasize in their memories of going out to the Val-Taro
or the Terrace wanting to meet a mate, or simply put on their best.

Karcic's commentary on the "correct" way of dancing speaks to familiar cultural
stereotypes about Northern and Southern Italian Americans:

> The Viennese style of dancing—you look at someone dancing a nice Strauss waltz, they're
> spinning man, they're spinning. They're making those turns, you know, and different
> movements, and that's the way you dance to the Northern Italian style. Southern
> Italians—you look at their feet, they can't negotiate the steps—no, it's true! I don't mean
> to be derogatory or negative but they're not used to it.

What the Northern Italian American community valued about their dancing, as Karcic's
comment reveals, was that it provided a space in which they could demonstrate to
themselves and to others that they were more socially advanced, more cultivated, and
more "European" than their *meridionali* compatriots. A summary of some of the main
features of musicians' perception of Valtaro is useful at this point:

- The Valtaro playing style has a special "lilt" (Karcic, personal communication, February 13, 2007). The accompaniments improvised for the melodies are full of *arpeggios*, up-and-down melodic runs with dramatic dips, peaks and valleys, like the
  mountainous terrain of Borgotaro.
- Northern Italians have a geographical and cultural affinity to the Austrian-Hungar-
  ian Empire. The Viennese waltz is in their blood.
- Northern Italians are better dancers than Southern Italians. They are more graceful
  and sure-footed, and they can negotiate the footwork of the waltz more skillfully
  than the Southern Italians.
- Suitable playing technique for Valtaro is innate: "You have to be born with it." "You
  have to grow up with it." "It's part of your DNA."[76]

What members of the Northern Italian American community valued about their dancing, then, was that it provided a space in which they could demonstrate their educated
and cultivated style, showing themselves and others that they were more modern and
socially advanced than their *meridonalin* compatriots, with their perceived coarse, crude
italianità.

Through discourse about music and song, as well as the music itself, the Valtaro
phenomenon touches upon attitudes and issues centering on the immigrant experience:

regional tensions; private and public behavior; and, self-presentation to outsiders. That Valtaro music survives at all is a measure of its ability to evoke and preserve ethnicity.

Epilogue: Efforts to Disseminate the Valtaro Tradition

A pivotal moment in the history of Italian Americans was the decline of Old Country identity that had been ongoing since the 1920s, as Italian Americans (and other southern European immigrants) left Little Italys for the suburbs. Whether one chooses to view this as the "twilight" or "dawn" of ethnicity for Italian Americans, there is evidence of major shifts in the group's entertainment choices and musical tastes.[77] The Valtaro, the Terrace, and all the Italian cabarets closed down between 1961 and 1974. There were the Beatles, the decline and fall of the accordion craze in America, and a turn toward electronic keyboard instruments—and, ultimately, the guitar. In addition, there was a general decline in live music at social functions and clubs, replaced by less costly dee-jays and the rise of the discotheque, largely catering to a younger crowd. These general trends were felt particularly strongly by many Italian-American performers, who faced the fragmentation of their audiences.[78] Brugnoli and DelGrosso were savvy businessmen who were aware of these trends and their erosive effects on their income.

After their nightclubs had to close, they ensured that their music to continue reaching a paying audience. They continued to perform, compose, and arrange Valtaro music. They played it at club dates, church functions, casinos, and summer resorts; they taught it to their accordion students.[79] The demand for ethnic recordings in the languages spoken by immigrant Americans allowed more stable future for this music took shape in the recording studio. In 1961, the Colonial record label, which published sing-along albums for the Italian-American market, gave Brugnoli the opportunity to release a series of albums called *Sing-Along In Italian*.[80] These consisted primarily of songs from the Valtaro repertoire and featured Brugnoli's work along with the Norwegian-American accordionist Walter Ericksson. In addition, the Fiesta label released a series of Valtaro LP records for accordion solo and ensemble, which reduced this originally forceful music to a pretty background sound.[81] It is my contention that the sing-along albums capture the spirit and energy of the Valtaro style through the ardent singing and the virtuosic yet spontaneous stylings of the accordionists. Conversations with fans of Valtaro attest to the sense of recognition and the awakening of cultural memories which hearing these albums stirs. A few songs have been "canonized." Indeed, contributing to the visibility of these songs are the many mainstream Italian American musicians and groups that have performed this repertoire.[82]

Could these songs and the accordion performances with which they are tied be resurfacing for the second- and third-generation Northern Italian Americans? An inkling of such a resurgence may be detected in the Valtaro Accordionists Reunion at the Magnanini Winery in Walkill, New York. The location for this event was significant, as the winery was located in the Catskills region, a one-time vacation mecca for Italian Americans (as well as other white ethnic groups), and where many Valtaro musicians once worked.[83]

Since the early 1990s, the Valtaro Accordionists Reunions at the Magnanini Winery have the spontaneous, celebratory flavor of resorts and clubs and the feel of the earlier sing-along albums. Valtaro accordionist Gelso Pellegrini organized these events for 15 years until his death in 2001; since 2002; they have been organized by Dominic Karcic. When I attended the 2006 event, a sold-out audience of more than 200 paid $75 per ticket for a sit-down banquet of Northern Italian specialties (such as polenta and risotto and wine), music, and dancing. Karcic had assembled an accordion band, vocal soloists Mario Nicolich and Maria Mancini, and a chorus of singers made up of students and graduates from a nearby music conservatory. Karcic alternated, and overlapped, sets of vocal and dance music—"Jolly Caballero" (a pasodoble), "Tic Tic Ta" (a polka), and "Tutti Mi Chiamano Bionda"—as well as operatic selections sung by Mancini. The audience, mainly couples in their 50s, 60s, and 70s, had brought their children and their grandchildren to the event. The older women were attired in elegant dresses and high heels, and the men wore suits, ties, and boater hats. A dozen or so couples commanded the dance floor, as they expertly performed tangos, pasodobles, and a number of up-tempo Viennese waltzes. Some members of the second- and third-generation also danced. Between the many courses of food, dozens of these elder Valtaro dancers and enthusiasts, noting my microphone and video camera, introduced themselves to me as lifetime fans of the accordion and Valtaro music, and a few claimed to have complete collections of all the Valtaro LP recordings. Outside on the patio, Joe Farda, host of an English-language Italian-American radio broadcast (WVIP, 93.5 FM, broadcasting from New Rochelle, New York) was interviewing the musicians and beaming observations of the event to his listeners in the Hudson Valley. A film crew documenting the history of Italian-American Catskills resorts recorded the day's proceedings.[84]

From the nightclub stage in the 1950s to the recordings of today, Valtaro songs, performed an ineluctable American truth: that music, particularly regional folksong and its hybrid offspring—influenced by jazz and pop—provide a powerful and positive medium of cultural exchange. Brugnoli's, Spagnoli's, and their audience's synthesis of Italian and American ethnic cultures have set an example that countless other artists have followed. The Gaylords, a popular song and comedy team, adapted "Tutti Mi Chiamano Bionda" for mainstream audiences; Geraldine Farrar, for the opera crowd.[85] Although Valtaro musicians could hardly have predicted it, one possible route to greater visibility for the music is the "ethnic feast" phenomenon. These summer festivals have become a significant part of the revival culture of Italian Americans as well as profitable ventures for the entrepreneurs that sponsor them.[86] These *festas*, presented by city tourism boards in collaboration with local Italian-American organizations, are in the business of "Italian family FUN."[87] The San Jose (California) *festa* Web site advertises their event as a celebration with "the Italian family you never had."[88] Although the musical entertainment at such event usually features a headline act that has been proven to draw large audiences outside the Italian-American community, pan-Italian and Italian regional musics are sometimes part of the mix as well. Valtaro accordionist Mario Tacca and vocalist Maria Mancini appeared at Milwaukee's "ethnic feast" in the summer of 2008. San Jose's *festa* promises "ample accordion entertainment," along with a grape-stomping contest and folkloric dance companies performing the tarantella. In the context of an event that promotes Italian "heritage tourism" and the exotic and familiar appeal of participant-friendly Italian "traditions," audience reception of these events, and their music, and how musical performances figure in the perception of *italianità*, is a topic worthy of further exploration. As Joseph Sciorra, the editor of this volume, has argued, these songs have become part of the memory culture of all Italians, Northerners and Southerners.[89]

For the artists who created Valtaro, and their audiences—past and future—Valtaro music demonstrates that popular entertainment built on folk-based music and on the drama of cross-cultural identification is a central market for cultural exchange, a light-hearted rehearsal of multiethnic community, open to the American public.

Italians in Public Memory

PAGEANTRY, POWER, AND IMAGINING THE "ITALIAN
AMERICAN" IN READING, PENNSYLVANIA

Joan L. Saverino

"Two-Ton Tony Likes Berks Spaghetti" headlines a photograph of national boxing cham-
pion Tony Galento in a 1939 issue of the *Reading Times* (Berks County, Pennsylvania)
newspaper. A local girl, holding a banner advertising "Holy Rosary Greater Italian Day"
stands beside him, while Galento stuffs a huge forkful of pasta into his mouth.[1] How
was it that 50 years after the mass immigration of Italians to the United States, Italians
had come to use a constellation of symbols like spaghetti to express a newly developed
ethnic identity? During the period between the two World Wars, in the industrial city
of Reading, Pennsylvania, Italians appropriated and recontextualized a *bricolage* of
American and Italian folk and popular images and rhetoric in ritual public events of
ceremony and celebration that they planned and staged. Through the lens of the two
most significant ones—namely, the Columbus Day and the Italian Days festivals—we
will see how Italians used these displays to create a public ethnic memory, shaping a
unique past distinct from the mainstream cultural consensus.[2] Although Italians, along
with other recent immigrants, took active parts in other public events, most significantly the six days of festivities for the 175th anniversary of the founding of Reading
in 1923, a key event in the city's history, these were orchestrated by the non-ethnic
majority and the Italians had limited freedom of cultural expression.[3]

Public memory is constituted in physical spaces. Italians staged celebrations in public locations historically infused with symbolic meaning for the majority population. By
using and sometimes permanently altering spaces (City Park, for instance) that were
sacred in a civic sense, Italians reinscribed these material places, creating ethnic sites
of memory in their adopted city. Even as Italians developed their own public memory,
through the process, they also changed the trajectory of the city's memory from one
that was primarily Pennsylvania German to a more ethnically diverse landscape. Geog-
rapher Allan Pred has written that our sense of present-day place as a "visible scene"
does not emerge from what was once a natural landscape and stop evolving. "Whether
place refers to a rural village or a metropolis, an agricultural area or urban-industrial
complex or some other observational entity, it always represents a human product.
Place, in other words, always involves an appropriation and transformation of space
and nature that is inseparable from the reproduction and transformation of society in
time and space."[4]

The role of performance and public display in the creation of ethnic identity has only recently caught the attention of scholars of immigration and ethnicity.[5] This paper contributes to that growing body of scholarship. By virtue of the nature of cultural performances as "intensified expressions of high affect and indirect, implicative reference that stand out from routine communicative passages because of their self-referencing style . . . performances help keep social, psychological, and epistemic systems openended and transformative in potential."[6] Sites of memory are created in the popular imagination through the transformative potential of performance and the places associated with their production. The dynamics of culture change are often most evident through performative display.

Public ritual events such as parades and festivals, meant to celebrate or commemorate and usually open to a general populace, may appear simplistic in their intent. Yet a close analysis of the orchestration of such events reveals how the events themselves and larger societal patterns also help change existing beliefs and social relations. These occasions convey key ideas through symbolic language and imagery. Symbols that carry the most emotional power are those that rely on ambiguity because individuals can ascribe their own meaning to them while simultaneously serving to bring people together. Symbols, then, can consolidate alliances even when the participants (both Italians and non-Italians) who rally together have different, even conflicting, values, meanings, and motives for joining together.[7]

Before I begin an analysis of public display, I will turn briefly to an explanation of the historical and cultural context into which Italians entered. Berks County is regarded as one of the nine counties in the Pennsylvania-German heartland. Three features distinguish Italian immigration here from other areas of Italian settlement in Pennsylvania. First, Italians came in smaller numbers compared with other parts of Pennsylvania. Second, Italians entered a region of little ethnic diversity, one dominated by the Pennsylvania Germans. Finally, while the city of Reading was industrializing and factories were sprouting in some of the boroughs as well, the majority of the county remained agricultural.

The city of Reading, 54 miles northwest of Philadelphia, was the most Germanic of the large towns in this regional area. Thomas Penn (William Penn's son) and his agents established Reading as the county seat in 1752 because of its central location in the county and its easy accessibility to Philadelphia, both on the Schuylkill River and along a main road to the city.[8] Reading was a prime location for attracting industries developing as a result of the Industrial Revolution.

By 1890, attracted by the growth of the iron ore industry, the new immigrants, primarily Italians and Poles, noticeably began to alter the Germanic face of Reading and boroughs surrounding it.[9] Unlike the Pennsylvania Germans, who had emigrated largely from a single region, the Rhineland Palatinate, and who could trace ancestors back to the early eighteenth century,[10] the Italians, coming from different regions and speaking different regional languages, had no uniform, shared past. In effect, they were a people without history, cut off from the lives and histories of villages left behind.[11] Italy was unified in 1861 but remained characterized by regional differences. Immigrants arrived with no real allegiance to an Italian national identity and none yet to the United States. Although some chain migration and settlement pattern clustering did occur in Reading, it was minimal compared with the colony formations that occurred in larger cities.[12] Because of the small numbers of family or fellow villagers who also immigrated, Italians in Reading were forced to expand their social networks to include the mixed regional composition of the neighborhoods, mutual aid and fraternal societies, and business partnerships.[13]

By the 1920s, the Italian population in the city itself was sizeable with a well-established social and economic infrastructure.[14] Mutual aid societies and fraternal orders were numerous and popular. A few, such as the lodges of the Order of the Sons of Italy, were affiliated with national organizations and wielded considerable influence among Italians. These groups became actively engaged in public display and bolstered their numbers at events by inviting organizational branches from surrounding towns to participate in ceremonies and parades.

The leaders of the fraternal orders were usually members of the Italian middle class or *prominenti*: that is, professionals or small businessmen who had gained respectability in the Italian community. These middle-class Italians, usually better educated or more Americanized than the majority of working-class Italians, often acted as ethnic brokers between Italians and the dominant society.[15] Those who emerged as leaders in the ethnic community became spokespersons for the rest who had no public voice.

The *prominenti* also sought recognition from the non-Italian, middle-class elite of Reading, while attempting to retain their influence in the Italian population. In public displays, the goals of the *prominenti* and those of civic officials and other city elite often appeared to be linked together in the concept of Americanization.[16] Nationally, popular sentiment also emphasized that new immigrants should assimilate as quickly as possible into the American mainstream. For the immigrants in Berks County, the distinctly Pennsylvania-German character of the social environment there was the American norm. Neither the *prominenti* nor working-class Italians, however, equated Americanization with assimilation. From their perspective, maintaining identification with Italian culture and adhering to its values and customs did not in any way conflict with being a good American. These differences in expectations were cultural misunderstandings that sometimes resulted in tension between the *prominenti* and the city leaders, signaling deeper divisions between the Italians and the general populace.

As we shall see in the example of the dedication of the Columbus Monument celebration, tensions also existed between the *prominenti* and working-class Italians. This will serve as an example of intra-ethnic tension, an area of investigation still under explored in ethnic studies. The image of a singular and unified Italian community, displayed during public events, fractures if we look behind the scenes, where a different social reality prevailed. Working-class Italians did not always identify with the middle-class goals of the *prominenti*, and many never attended the elaborate celebrations. Others, while proud that Italians could carry off such pageantry, harbored resentment toward the *prominenti* for their achievements. The Catholic clergy, often at odds with a large number of Italians, formed a third source of contention. Despite the cacophony of voices representing diverse interests, values, and expectations, usually one group's agenda prevailed, providing an illusion of unity to the non-Italian majority. With careful analysis of the orchestration of the event, the existing social and political fissures become evident. The Columbus Day celebrations were key events illustrative of the how the *prominenti* introduced and promoted the new role of American ethnic.

Columbus Holiday Celebrations

On October 11, 1992, rededication ceremonies of the newly restored statue of Christopher Columbus in City Park in downtown Reading marked the 500th anniversary of Columbus' voyage. The ceremonies also commemorated the 67th anniversary of the donation of the statue to the city by the Italians in 1925. Columbus Day and Italians have been synonymous in Reading since 1908 when Italians revived the celebration of their hero's holiday after a 15-year hiatus.[17] The celebration of Columbus Day is the most significant illustration of the development and maturation of an Italian-American identity in Berks County.

Columbus Day events were unique in that the Italian community itself organized them, and thus they provide a window to view the purposeful construction of a public ethnic identity.[18] Because Columbus was an American national symbol, these celebrations had widespread appeal for the entire local population. Nativistic feelings, echoing a prevalent national sentiment, were fervent in Reading during the decades prior to World War II. Columbus Day events provided at least one opportunity per year when Italians could capitalize on positive media coverage.

Americans had fully embraced Columbus as a national idol from the time of the Revolutionary War, giving him the status of a mythological hero. After the Civil War, Irish and French Catholics had been the first immigrants to promote him as an ethnic hero. Irish Catholics founded the Knights of Columbus in 1882, and the French contemporaneously mounted an appeal to Rome to grant Columbus sainthood.[19] In the late nineteenth century, the popular view held that "material progress" was a positive ideal, and geographical and industrial expansion seemed limitless. It was in this atmosphere that Americans further embellished the Columbus image, ascribing all the most admired human virtues to him.[20] With the yearlong commemoration at the World's Columbian Exposition in Chicago in 1893, Columbus became the symbol of American success.

Since the late nineteenth century, Italian *prominenti* in New York and Philadelphia had promoted Columbus as the ideal symbol to represent Italians in the United States. As early as 1882, the Italian-American organizations invited to march in the bicentennial of Philadelphia carried a float with a representation of Columbus. The dedication of a statue of Columbus in Central Park, New York in 1892, with the epigraph, "From the Italians of America," may have most influenced the acceptance of the symbolic imagery of Columbus. Following the example of Philadelphia's Italians, floats decorated with Columbus themes were part of the New York festivities and would be a mainstay for future parades held by Italians in towns and cities throughout the United States.[21] Thus the groundwork was laid for the reinvention of Columbus as a hero used to promote pan-Italian Americanism and to fight anti-immigrant sentiment.

Invoking the Columbus imagery in the city of Reading linked the Italians to an idealized prestigious past recognized by all Americans. From that first celebration in 1908, the Italian *prominenti* in Reading successfully (re)appropriated Columbus Day as

Nineteen-foot bronze statue of Christopher Columbus donated by the Italians to the city of Reading, Pennsylvania, on October 12, 1925. (Photograph by the author.)

their holiday. They carefully cultivated an air of inclusivity by portraying the celebrations as public events in which all Reading citizens were welcome to participate, even though few did, except for invited civic officials. Two organizations, *Società Italiana Colombo* (Colombo Italian Society) and *Società Italiana Spartaco di Mutuo Soccorso* (Spartaco Italian Mutual Benefit Society), sponsored separate Columbus Day celebrations in 1908. It is unknown whether the two societies attempted to coordinate festivities. In ensuing Columbus Day celebrations, the events, as well as the themes and symbolism employed, mirrored the pomp and circumstance of 1908, with many of the same men taking active roles through the 1930s.[22] When groups could rally around a local or national cause, it seems they often did coordinate efforts. Disagreements some-times marred the celebrations and probably account for separate parades that were held on many occasions. What seem like petty arguments often represented power struggles among mutual aid and fraternal societies, some of which were gaining in membership, and thus revenue and prestige, while others were declining. For instance, disputes oc-curred over which society should march at the head of the parade or who should bless the flags at the dedication ceremony of the Columbus monument in 1925.[23]

In spite of the internal arguments, the Italians managed to construct a distinct ethnic identity, separate from that of mainstream Reading, and linked with other immi-grant Italians nationally, while simultaneously endorsing the official message of Ameri-canization. For instance, by employing images on parade floats that evoked a sense of an artistically rich classical past (ancient Rome and Renaissance Italy), a simple and pure folk culture (dressing in peasant costume), all presided over by the universal he-roic figure of Christopher Columbus, Reading Italians forged the appearance of unity, adopting American values and behaviors, and reflecting national and local ideas about the benefits of assimilation. By engaging in sanctioned American-style public events, the Italians began replacing the prevalent stereotypes of themselves as swarthy, illit-erate criminals with images of civilized ethnic Americans, not so different from the Pennsylvania-German majority. Over time, this transformation in perception alleviated exaggerated fears in the majority population about the influx of the Italians. The gen-eral populace began thinking of Italians as an Americanizing community, thus allowing the process of legitimization to begin.

Dedication of the Columbus Monument in 1925

The Italians had participated in the 175th Anniversary of the Founding of Reading in 1923.[24] Consistent with a national trend for commemorating local history, Reading civic leaders invited the Italians, along with other southern- (Greeks) and eastern-European immigrant groups, to participate in this historic celebration. By incorporating such new Americans into community pageantry, officials promoted a vision of unity. The ethnic groups, on the other hand, viewed these celebrations as opportunities to display their distinctive cultural identities.[25]

The *prominenti* were pleased with the Italians' visibility in the 175th Anniversary of the Founding of Reading. Afterward, they continued to hold meetings at the home of Dr. Ferdinando Colletti to determine other ways that Italians could "demonstrate their devotion to Reading."[26] In her biography of her husband, Italo DeFrancesco, Ruth B. DeFrancesco remarks that it was Colletti and DeFrancesco who were "among the small group who were openly proud of their background as Italians in contrast to a large number who were self-conscious in their many limitations in a strange society."[27] It was Colletti, the only Italian physician in Reading during this early period and recog-nized by the Italians as a leader, who initiated a proposal to erect a monument to Columbus. In 1924, Colletti and DeFrancesco, along with eight other Italian business-men and professionals, formed the Columbus Monument Committee to place a perma-nent memorial of Columbus in Penn's Common (City Park).

Internal squabbling as well as fund-raising problems plagued the Monument Committee from the project's inception. Although the precise details of the disagreements are unknown, DeFrancesco alludes to them in the official pamphlet of the statue's dedication.[28] They are also mentioned in the DeFrancesco's biography: "Certain rivalries existed among individuals, organizations, even the churches, in the planning committee."[29] In spite of these setbacks, the Committee was ultimately successful in its goal.

On January 27, 1925, the Monument Committee signed a contract with Vincenzo Miserendino, a well-known Italian sculptor from New York. Before the statue was completed, a total of three contracts would be signed because of changes in the original dimensions and costs of the statue. Initially, the bronze statue was to be eight feet tall with a six-foot base of pink granite standing atop a four-foot stone foundation. The total cost was set at $5,000.

On August 4, 1925, a second contract was signed enlarging the statue's dimensions from 14 to 19 feet. The statue itself was to be eight-and-one-half feet high, and the pedestal's height grew from six to ten-and-one-half feet. Bronze tablets, depicting episodes of Columbus landing in America, were to be added to each side of the pedestal. The Monument Committee agreed to compensate Miserendino an extra $3,000 within one year of the statue's erection at the site for these alterations to the original design.

On August 17, 1925, yet another contract was signed. It stated that the committee would pay an additional $600 for six more inches to the statue's height, resulting from Miserendino's own error when he made the cast. The phrasing of the contract indicates that Miserendino's successful negotiation for the extra payment caused some bitter feelings. To protect themselves from any further indebtedness, the Committee stipulated in the contract that the $600 was considered a "voluntary contribution" to the sculptor and that they would not be held "responsible for any other expenses that Mr. Miserendino may have or may incur."[30] The total cost of the project had risen to $8,600.[31]

The cost of the statue was an extremely large sum for the time. Although working-class Italians were proud that a monument in their name would be erected in City Park, a prestigious location, they could not afford to donate much, if any, money to the project. The primary source of funds was pledges solicited from members of the fraternal societies, a majority of whom could afford to give only one dollar, and many of those who pledged never paid. The Columbus Committee also orchestrated fund-raisers, such as a raffle, held during the statue dedication.[32] The Committee was unable to raise the last few thousand dollars to pay off the debt. According to the original agreement, the Monument Committee members were held personally liable for the unpaid loan. Within the next few years and the onset of the Depression, several of them went bankrupt, and a few simply reneged. In 1940, 15 years after the statue was erected, Cologero Chiarelli, vice president of the Monument Committee and a successful businessman, paid off the bank note in order to clear his name.

The success of the dedication ceremony on October 12, 1925, overshadowed the issues over the cost of the statue. The statue rallied the emotional, if not the financial, support of the Italian population. Three thousand people, most of them Italians, attended the ceremony.

A statement in the *Reading Times* quoted Dr. Ferdinando Colletti:

I wish it clearly understood . . . that the statue presentation of tomorrow is not merely an Italian affair, but one affecting the entire city. In giving Columbus' statue to the city, the Italians not only wish to show their love for Reading, but also to honor a great man who belongs to the American people as a whole. . . . Of course the Italians are proud of Columbus . . . but they believe that Columbus, Washington, and Lincoln belong to the entire world, because their deeds benefited all humanity.[33]

Colletti's words clearly depict how the *prominenti* viewed the intertwining of heritages as a way for Italians to achieve legitimization and enhance their status in the community. By following the prescribed American format for such programs and by including non-Italians in the schedule of festivities, the Italians reinforced their message that Columbus was a hero for all the city's residents.

The celebration officially began at two o'clock with a parade that wound its way from the Italian neighborhood south of Penn Street to City Park. The parade marshal, Edward Damario, the first Italian police officer in Reading, led the marchers, comprising Italian groups as well as other local organizations. All Italians not affiliated with any society were also invited to march in the parade.

Committee members carefully blended Italian and American traditions. At the unveiling ceremony, after featured speeches by public officials, clergymen, teachers, and several officials from New York City, Ferdinando Colletti presented the statue to the mayor. Italo DeFrancesco, a prominent member of the Monument Committee, introduced Vincenzo Miserendino and presented an honorary cup to the model who, ironically, was not an Italian but a Pennsylvania-German weightlifter.[34] Anna Chiarelli, daughter of Cologero, unveiled the statue, draped in Italian and American flags, while the Ringold Band, a local Pennsylvania-German group, played "America." The speeches, as well as the accompanying music, were infused with patriotic themes. Festivities continued into the evening with the Ringold Band accompanying the folk dance performance by the Tarantella Dancers from the International Institute of the YWCA.[35]

The official pamphlet from the event states that the statue was as a "gift" of the "Italo-Americans" for the "hospitality" shown by the city. In fact, the treatment of Italians until 1925 had not been particularly welcoming. Although discrimination never escalated to the level of violence that occurred in other places in the United States, anti-immigrant fervor was prevalent in Reading and was keenly felt by the Italians.[36] So why did the Italians express a sentiment obviously not supported by the events of the times?

One explanation lies in the use of the word "gift." Marcel Mauss' classic work demonstrates that gift-giving is neither a simple exchange of material objects nor a disinterested action. The act of giving itself increases the value of the object because it initiates a social exchange process, obliging the receiver both to acknowledge the gift and eventually to reciprocate in kind.[37] Many scholars, including Marshall Sahlins, Annette Weiner, and Lewis Hyde further refine Mauss' early ideas about the role of gifts in the larger cultural economy and in the process of social exchange. If we consider the Columbus monument in the context of a gift, we can see implications for issues of reciprocity, power, and for the (re)negotiation of social relationships. This donation, whose

Tarantella Dancers, Italian folk dancing group from the International Institute, YWCA, in front of the old School Administration Building on Eighth and Washington streets, Reading, July, 1925. (Courtesy of Maria Prioriello Battisti. Original photograph by Joe Ricciardi.)

import had such immense symbolic importance to both the American and the immigrant Italian psyches, initiated the potential for a reshuffling of social relationships between the two groups.

Weiner argues that Mauss and others have oversimplified theories of exchange. Weiner suggests that reciprocity does not neutralize power as Mauss claims, but that "What motivates reciprocity is its reverse—the desire to keep something back from the pressures of give and take. This something is a possession that speaks to and for an individual's or a group's social identity and, in so doing, affirms the difference between one person or group and another." Weiner calls this "the paradox of keeping while giving."[38] Hyde suggests that a gift can be "the actual agent of change, the bearer of new life. In the simplest examples, gifts carry an identity with them, and to accept the gift amounts to incorporating the new identity."[39] Both Weiner's and Hyde's discussions around issues of social identity illuminate our understanding of the gifting of the Columbus statue.

The social context of the gift of the statue is complicated further by the difference in enculturation between the Italians and the city leaders. The *prominenti*, all recent immigrants, were operating under a southern-Italian cultural code that bound families, friends, and business associates in complex webs of reciprocal obligation.[40] The city fathers would be ignorant of the expectations around gifting (as well as many other issues). We could expect, then, that intercultural blunders might easily occur between the two groups.

The City Council initially opposed the idea of the statue being placed in City Park near monuments of war heroes.[41] Although permission was finally granted, I propose that this was not an instance of cultural disconnect, but the reluctance of the city fathers to allow placement of the statue in the park points to fundamental issues of identity that were at stake for both groups.

The role of city parks in nineteenth-century social ideology underscores the City Park's symbolic importance for Reading citizens. Historian Mary Ryan notes that by 1870, public places such as city parks were used as a method of ordering (according to gender and class) and sanitizing (prohibiting various forms of indecency) public space. Such spaces with specialized functions allowed a somewhat "controlled and unthreatening environment" of interaction among strangers.[42] The Italians threatened the hierarchy of this "ordered space," however, by sponsoring the introduction of a permanent statue of Columbus, the hero who Italians nationally had embraced and who would symbolically represent their presence in the city. By placing the Columbus statue in the park, the city's central green space, the Pennsylvania-German identity of the city was at stake. The city's social identity, already threatened by the sheer physical numbers of immigrants, was symbolically attacked. In a letter to C. R. Scholl, the president of the Historical Society of Berks County, Italo DeFrancesco invites him to be a member of the Honorary Columbus Monument Committee. DeFrancesco appears to reassure Scholl concerning fears about the Italians' intentions. "Our work has no religious or political scope; it is eminently a patriotic movement among the Italian Citizens and is motivated by the highest American ideals."[43]

The erection of the statue was truly a cause for celebration in the viewpoint of many in the Italian community. Its placement in City Park memorialized the Italians for present and future generations in a spot central to the public life of all residents at the time. Furthermore, it played the dual role of confirming the Italians' ethnic identity while reinforcing the difference between the Italians and the majority population. The location of the statue within the park itself cannot be overlooked. Columbus stands at the hill's crest, overlooking and pointing out over the city below. The statue visually linked the Italians' and the city's interests. The last line of the epigraph on the base of the 19-foot statue reads "by the Italian residents of Reading Pennsylvania, October 12 1925." By choosing a granite statue, a symbol of great physical permanence, the Italians portrayed themselves as a legitimate social group possessing a memorialized past who would be a fixture in the city's future. The Columbus statue, situated amidst other statues of both local and national historical significance, was a bid for official acknowledgement, identifying the Italians as stable and permanent participants in the civic life of the city. The transformation of the City Park site both reflected and constituted the transformation of society itself.

An article appearing in the *Reading Times* the day after the dedication of the statue noted that the ceremonies had transformed what had been in past years "merely a holiday" marked by bank and public office closings, to what was now "a day that will be given a full page in the city's history. For Reading Italo-American citizens made it a day of history when they joined together to present to their adopted city a bronze statue of the discoverer of America, Christopher Columbus."[44] The Italians were successful in projecting a public image of a unified ethnic front. Although Italians staged celebrations for the holiday annually after 1925, the monument dedication was the high point in the history of the Italian community's celebration of Columbus Day. After the erection of the Columbus monument, the parade route always ended at City Park, where Italians laid a wreath at the foot of the statue. Probably the most significant change in the Columbus Day celebrations from the late 1920s to 1940, however, was the increasingly adamant expression of *italianità*, or nationalistic sentiment, that sprang from pride in the new Italy under Mussolini.

Fascism's Role in Imagining the Italian American

The climate that existed in the Italian communities in the decades prior to World War II is a key element in the evolution of a unique Italian-American identity. After World War I, Italians in the United States expanded their concept of community and their ethnic identity from a local to a national and even international focus. This reorientation was attributable to a constellation of successive social, economic, and political factors, including post–World War I anti-immigrant sentiment with forced Americanization as its theme; the economic depression; New Deal politics; the conflict of Fascist and anti-Fascist struggle; and finally, World War II. Italians, feeling isolated and discriminated against in the United States, turned their sights toward their homeland and the new Fascist Italy. Capitalizing on their vulnerability, Mussolini's propaganda campaign promoted the idea that those Italians who emigrated constituted an international colony of united Italians who could all take pride in and work for a new Italy.[45] Cannistraro points out that while Italian Fascists encouraged support among Italian Americans, immigrant Fascism played an important role in the development of Italian-American communities.[46] Goodman's demonstration that ethnic leaders, ethnic institutions, and ideas about ethnic identity were linked as well as her claim that Fascism actually aided in both the construction and reinforcement of ethnic identity follows through locally for Reading.[47]

Italian-American organizations used newspapers as well as new and expanding media such as radio, photographs, and film to sell the concept of a local, national, and international Italian ethnic identity. For instance, film was used to promote this idea within the Italian community as well as project a positive image of Italians to the rest of Reading as early as the 1925 dedication of the Columbus monument. The Columbus Monument Committee paid for the production of a 16mm film of the parade and monument dedication, which was subsequently shown as a "short" before the regular features in the local movie theater.[48]

During these years, the maturing second generation was caught between two cultural identities: their Italian ethnicity and their emergent sense of being an American. Whatever their generation, however, Italians could not escape being influenced by the contemporary rhetoric: that of a unified Italian-American ethnic pride.[49]

From the 1920s, until the United States entered World War II, support for Mussolini swelled among Italian Americans, including those in Berks County. The earliest indication of Fascist sympathies in Reading was a *fascio* (local branch) organized about 1923 by Oreste Brunicardi, a prominent artist and inventor. In 1925, the *Fasci all'Estero* gathered for a conference in Rome. Delegates from Reading attended apparently because when the North-American *fasci* gathered for a group photograph taken on the *piazza del Campidoglio,* an unidentified person held a placard on which is printed "Reading." In 1928, the *Lega Fascista del Nord America* listed another *fascio* in Reading called *Fascio Nello Degli Innocenti.*[50]

With state-supported folk revivals and festivals, Mussolini's intense nationalistic focus romanticized and idealized Italy's folk past. At the same time during the 1920s, for philosophical reasons, the International Institute of the YWCA encouraged folk music and dancing among the immigrants.[51] In parades and commemorations, Italians, seeing no clash between the two, combined symbols of American patriotism with those of Italian nationalism (e.g., flags of both nations, Italian folk costumes, and costumes of Columbus and native Americans). By the 1930s, speechmakers used phrases such as *la Patria lontana* (the faraway Fatherland) to instill a sense of unity with a national homeland.[52]

Much of the encouragement to develop Italian nationalistic fervor emanated from national fraternal order headquarters and was spread via the Italian-American press. Giovanni DiSilvestro, the national leader of the Order of the Sons of Italy, endorsed Mussolini in 1922, and the Order became an unofficial vehicle for transmission of Fascist ideology.[53] In Reading, the Massimo D'Azeglio lodge of the Sons of Italy planned a huge celebration for 1932 in honor of the national Order's plans to unveil a statue of George Washington in Rome. City alderman Anthony Zaffiro, who was the assistant grand venerable of the national Order, assisted in the preparation for the event in Rome.[54]

In March 1934, a commemoration of the Birthday of Fascism was held in New York, promoted by the Fascist newspaper, *Il Grido della Stirpe* (The Cry of the Race). The *fascio* from Reading sent a telegram signed by Oreste Brunicardi greeting "'In a Fascist fashion' the consular authorities and the old leaders, especially Thaon di Revel," the former leader of the Fascist League of North America. It concluded: "'We swear loyalty to *Il Duce.*'"[55]

In the 1930s, the local council of the lodges of the Order Italian Sons and Daughters of America formed a group called the *Amici dell'Italia* (Friends of Italy). Propaganda from the Fascist government, supported by Italian-American organizations, helped build mass enthusiasm for Mussolini's occupation of Ethiopia. In 1935, *Amici dell'Italia* held a meeting to boost support for Mussolini's Ethiopian campaign and to begin an assistance drive for the Italian Red Cross. Representatives of the Central Committee of *Amici dell'Italia* in Philadelphia came to Reading to speak. A Reading resident and former soldier in the Italian army offered his insurance policy from the Italian government on the spot to signify his loyalty to Italy. Raising money for the Italian Red Cross was a popular cause in Reading, as it was elsewhere in the United States during the Ethiopian War. Women donated their gold jewelry, and people bought stamps printed with a picture of Mussolini and bearing the inscription, "November 18, 1935, Friends of Italy."[56]

Italian Days Celebrations

The "Italian Days" festivals that emerged in the mid-1930s also grew out of this fervent *italianità*. While Italians successfully merged the themes *italianità* and American patriotism in the Columbus Day celebrations, they cleverly exploited certain pan–Italian-American stereotypical symbols for specific money-making endeavors in Italian Days festivals.

The idea for an Italian Days celebration began on August 18, 1935, when the seven lodges of the Order Italian Sons and Daughters of America held an Italian-American Day festival and picnic at Socialist Park in nearby Sinking Spring. The Italian Sons and Daughters invited all the other Italian associations in Reading and the area as well as the public to participate.[57] By 1938, "Italian-American Day" had grown into a large annual fund raising endeavor for the Order's coffers. That year, the event—publicized as a program for people of all ages—was held on July 31 and drew about 4,000 people to Carsonia Park, a popular local amusement park. A free concert, featuring the newly reorganized Reading Royal Italian Band, was announced widely in order to attract people into the park.[58]

In 1938, Father Leonard Miconi assumed the pastorship of Holy Rosary Church, the Italian national parish in downtown Reading. Upon his arrival, Miconi immediately set his sights upon constructing a new church and recognized the potential of the festival format to raise revenue for a building fund. He convinced (some said coerced) the Italian-American organizations to allow Holy Rosary to take over the sponsorship of the event, renaming it "Greater Italian Day" in 1939. Representatives from 26 local Italian organizations and two assistant pastors from the parish expanded the event that year to cover an entire weekend in August, making it the largest Italian festival ever held in Reading.

The events began at Holy Rosary Church on Franklin Street in the heart of the largest Italian neighborhood in the city. On Saturday evening, the Royal Italian Band, featuring a soloist from Philadelphia, performed two concerts in front of the church. On Sunday morning, the band led a religious procession celebrating the Feast of San Rocco from Holy Rosary to the small chapel at Schuylkill Avenue and Green Street, where priests celebrated a mass. By orchestrating the merging of the sacred with what had formerly been a secular celebration, Miconi successfully redirected the Italians to the parish as the center of their community.

The festival continued at the Reading Fairground with afternoon and evening entertainment programs, including Joseph Campo's song-and-comedy routine from Philadelphia. The Italian General Consul and an Italian-American judge from Philadelphia were invited to address the crowd. Although the celebration was intended "to unite all the Italian families of the community and suburbs," the general public was invited to attend.[59] Emidio Cianci, the general chairman, stated:

> The purpose of Greater Italian Day is not to promote an exaggerated nationalistic spirit, nor to divide the Italian people from their fellow Americans. Indeed a hearty invitation was extended to all nationalities to participate in the celebration. . . . The supreme desire of the Italian people of Reading is to erect a new church worthy of their glorious history

and tradition. Greater Italian Day will prove ideal and serve to realize this aspiration if it enkindles a wider enthusiasm and forges a stronger bond of unity in the Italian community. It will be difficult, if not impossible to build a new Italian church, unless each Italian displays a personal interest, and strangles in his heart all ill feeling and bitterness toward his fellow Italians.[60]

This combination of a disclaimer and a call to Italians to unify indicates a heightened sensitivity on the part of ethnic leaders in appearing overly pro-Fascist in public. Recent investigations into Fascist activities in the United States by anti-Fascists, newspapers, and Congress had caused concern that Fascist propaganda was creating divided loyalties among Italian Americans.[61] Cianci wanted to urge the diverse Italian populace to unite for the Holy Rosary building campaign (a far from unanimous goal), while he simultaneously averted any public apprehension that might arise from a call to unify. In contrast to Cianci's statement, and appearing on the opposite page of the pamphlet, was a note of welcome to the Italian General Consul written by Giuseppe Battisti, a local Italian-American leader. It is worth noting that these remarks appeared only in Italian (obviously directed at the Italian readership), but Cianci's appeared in both languages. Battisti began by hailing the *Patria lontana* (faraway Fatherland) and greeting the Consul as

> . . . the representative of the supreme Mussolini who has given Italy new life, new
> enthusiasm, new valour, new strength and who will carry her to the highest destiny . . . .
> Your presence in the Patriotic Colony is symbol of the spiritual ties that unite the
> emigrant Italians to great and strong Italy. To you . . . the most cordial greeting from all
> the Italians of Reading and the assurance of their everlasting gratitude and faith.[62]

Whereas Cianci's statement shows that Italians were well aware of the need to preserve an American patriotic image, Battisti's warm greeting to the Consul illustrates the overwhelming popularity Mussolini still enjoyed among Italians in Berks County, sentiments consistent with national feeling. Although some Italians had grown concerned by the negative reports of recent Italian expatriates arriving in the United States, most continued to express loyalty to both their adopted country and their ancestral homeland until the United States declared war in December, 1941.

In 1940, Greater Italian Day underwent another change. Although community leaders who organized the event in 1939 still participated in the planning, Holy Rosary sponsored it alone, not jointly with the Italian societies. By 1941, only the clergy formed the planning committee. With what many described as an abrasive personal style and bullish tactics, Father Miconi had usurped the yearly event from the fraternal organizations for his own fund-raising aspirations; and in the process, he had alienated many parishioners.

It is likely that national and international political events (Italy invaded France in June, 1940) also contributed to the change in the 1940 festival. The emphasis on the event as a church-sponsored one rather than a secular expression of *italianità* could be read as a creative diversionary tactic in inter-ethnic relations. At this point, Italians were careful to separate ethnic identity from Fascism. In 1941, when the United States was at war, this trend continued with the festival renamed "Holy Rosary Day" under the pretext that it promoted parish unity. A history of Holy Rosary stated: "The purpose of the celebration was to strengthen the bonds of unity among the parishioners, to interest our youth in the parish movement and to draw more enthusiastic cooperation for the Church campaign."[63]

Fund raising was the primary goal from the inception of the Italian Days celebrations in 1935. For the first few years, however, the flavor was more local, using talent from the local community. Beginning in 1938, the planning committee incorporated and combined pan–Italian-American symbols of spaghetti and national celebrities in an American-style carnivalesque atmosphere to attract large crowds to the fairground, thus enhancing fund-raising potential. In 1938, Tony Galento, the heavyweight prize-fighter from New Jersey, refereed an amateur boxing match. For the 1939 event, the *Reading Times* identified the women's committee as serving "real Italian spaghetti dinners," with Tony Galento photographed eating one.[64]

Joe DiMaggio, baseball player for the New York Yankees, was the star attraction for Holy Rosary Day at Carsonia Park, August 11, 1941. Pat DeAngelis sitting in DiMaggio's lap, Samuel Damiano (behind), *Elio Biagianti* (standing at right). *(Photo courtesy of Catherine DeAngelis Potteiger.)*

In 1941, popular hero Joe DiMaggio of the New York Yankees was invited as the star attraction. He was quoted as saying: "I'm very glad to be in Reading and it was nice to get a good Italian meal here." By 1940, given the tumultuous political scene, food—in addition to being a fundraising method—became a benign, noncontroversial way of expressing Italian-American identity. By 1940, ethnic dishes such as spaghetti had become more widely known and accepted by Americans in general.[65] For Italians, food-sharing represents the ultimate expression of generosity and hospitality. Increasing the emphasis on food at the event and inviting non-Italians to the "table" could be interpreted as a symbolic gesture to the larger population for improved inter-ethnic understanding.

The orchestration of the Italian Days events and the changes that transpired must be viewed in light of the repositioning of groups and their influence in the Italian community during these years. The rapid rise in membership and influence of fraternal organizations such as the Order Italian Sons and Daughters of America represents a change in the interests of Americanizing immigrants and second-generation children. In addition, the transformation from mutual aid societies based on the membership of *paesani* (townspeople) to pan–Italian-American organizations can be explained, at least partially, by the unifying appeal of Italian nationalism that increasingly drew Italian Americans under one umbrella during the 1920s and 1930s.

From the *Tarantella* to Two-Ton Tony

The transition from peasant folk dancing the *tarantella*—as Italians had done in public performances and on parade floats in the 1920s—to Tony Galento eating spaghetti as ubiquitous symbols of Italian ethnicity, visually represents the movement from an immigrant identity to a pan–Italian-American one.

Italians recontextualized traditions to fit their new social situation, and in the process, invented an Italian-American identity that in theory fits neatly in the city fathers' plans for a model city: a city where, in theory, all lived in peaceful coexistence. The reality of the situation, however, was still that Italians were often victims of discrimination, and they remained separate from the majority population. World War I brought a sense of identification with Italy as a nation, but with the restriction in the new immigration laws of 1924, Italians could not travel back and forth to Italy as easily. They faced the reality that their future would be in America, and in response, imagined a uniquely Italian-American identity with the appearance of a "community" of Italians adopting "American" values.

The 1920s and 1930s were a time of maturation for the Italians of Reading and Berks County. By latching onto the Fascist symbols of unity and strength, bolstered by the rapidly expanding national Italian-American organizations, Italians gained confidence in their public image as ethnic Americans. The invasion of France by Italy in June, 1940, and the subsequent declaration of war by the United States in December, 1941, could have instigated a crisis in national loyalties among Italian Americans. Following the lead of national Italian-American leaders, Italians in Berks County quickly renounced Mussolini and declared faithfulness to American democratic principles, softening their rhetoric of *italianità*. Although we may chart such a gross chronology, the movement from an immigrant to an ethnic identity was neither linear nor smooth.

During the period between the two World Wars, specifically through events of public display, Italians developed a public ethnic memory transforming the social landscape. The public expression of a unified ethnic identity through performance was a key factor for Italians in the metamorphosis from immigrant to ethnic American. The peak of white ethnic pride that occurred in the United States in the 1960s and 1970s had a history. The expressions of Italian ethnicity as they exist today began with the immigrants' roots in Italy and the communities that they created after their arrival in the United States.

Changing St. Gerard's Clothes

AN EXERCISE IN ITALIAN-AMERICAN CATHOLIC DEVOTION
AND MATERIAL CULTURE

Peter Savastano

Devotion to St. Gerard Maiella in Newark, New Jersey is more than 100 years old. It was first brought to Newark during the great migration of 1880–1924[1] when large numbers of Southern Italians, my own ancestors among them, came to Newark from the regions and provinces in which St. Gerard lived his life. Places such as Potenza province in the region of Basilicata, where St. Gerard was born and grew up, as well as from the small town of Caposele located in Avellino Province in the region of Campania, in which St. Gerard died.[2]

In Newark, devotion to the saint takes many different forms and has evolved over the years since 1899. Many of these local forms of devotion to St. Gerard are rooted in the vernacular religious practices of Southern Italians in general. However, in Newark, they have become much more elaborate than what was originally practiced or, in fact, is practiced at present at *Materdomini*, the Redemptorist monastery, where the saint's tomb is housed; or in the small town of Caposele, where the monastery is located. In general, such Southern-Italian devotional practices include

- Making vows to the Madonna and the saints in exchange for supernatural assistance
- Carrying an image of the Madonna or the saints (in this case, St. Gerard) in procession through the streets of one's village, town or city
- Having a *festa* (street feast) in honor of the Madonna or the saints (A *festa* usually takes place simultaneously with a procession)
- Pinning money to the image or statue (in the case of St. Gerard, specifically, this practice has evolved to include the weaving of elaborate capes, blankets, and/or long ribbons of money which are then wrapped around the statue of the saint)
- Dressing oneself or one's children as the saint and walking in the procession dressed as such
- Walking barefoot in the procession or enduring some other ordeal to demonstrate the severity of one's need or the intensity of one's devotion or gratitude to the saint for answered prayers[3]

In addition to these practices and as part of the annual observance of St. Gerard's feast day on October 16, and approximately for over 88 years now, a small group of devotees of St. Gerard Maiella[4] gather at his National Shrine located at St. Lucy's Roman Catholic

Church in Newark, New Jersey to change the clothes in which the statue of the saint is dressed.[5]

Who Is St. Gerard Maiella?

St. Gerard Maiella was a lay brother in the Congregation of the Most Holy Redeemer (Redemptorists), founded by St. Alphonsus de Liguori in the Kingdom of Naples in 1732. Official approval for the order's existence was given by Rome in 1749.[6] Born on April 6, 1726, in the small town of Muro Lucano in Potenza province, in the region of Basilicata, St. Gerard is as much a local saint as he is a global one. He lived most of his adult religious life primarily in Avellino province in the region of Campania. While still alive, Brother Gerard Maiella was a wonderworker, ascetic, and reader of human hearts.[7] He died at the age of 29 from tuberculosis just a few minutes before the stroke of midnight on October 16, 1755, (technically, the last few minutes of October 15) at the Redemptorist monastery of *Materdomini* located on a hill overlooking the small town of Caposele. He was beatified by Pope Leo XIII on January 29, 1893, and subsequently canonized a saint on December 11, 1904, by Pope Pius X.[8]

The National Shrine of St. Gerard at St. Lucy's Church in Newark

The statue of St. Gerard is housed at the saint's National Shrine in what was once the heart of Newark's Little Italy. Established in 1891, St. Lucy's Church was historically an "ethnic" parish whose mission was to serve Italian immigrants and their descendants. As is the case with many ethnic communities, even though most of the Italians, and now Italian Americans, that St. Lucy's originally served no longer live in the neighborhood, St. Lucy's still maintains its Italian and Italian-American identity. As such, St. Lucy's also continues to serve the descendants of the original Italian immigrants who settled in the Old First Ward of Newark, the small number of Italian Americans who still live in the now predominantly Latino neighborhood where the church is located, and the small Italian-American community still living in Newark's North Ward.

On most Sundays, these Italians and Italian Americans come from the surrounding cities and towns where they now live to attend Mass at St. Lucy's. They do so in greater numbers on Christmas and Easter, two of the most important Holy Days of the Catholic liturgical year. Likewise, they come in droves to attend the annual *festa* and procession in honor of St. Gerard in October, along with many other Italians and Italian Americans from various parts of the East Coast, from other parts of the United States, from Canada and, occasionally, from Avellino Province in Italy.

Changing St. Gerard's Clothes: A Brief Overview

Along with changing the saint's clothes, devotees also come together specifically to clean the saint's shrine and St. Lucy's Church in preparation for the annual *festa* and procession in honor of St. Gerard. The preparations begin in the first few days of October, usually between the 1st and 5th, so that all will be ready for the public Novena[9] that takes place during the nine days prior to the *festa* and procession. The Novena, *festa*, and procession are solemn yet joyful occasions. They commemorate St. Gerard's holy life, and celebrate the many miracles that he has performed both during his earthly life and posthumously. These observances offer opportunities for the saint's contemporary devotees to express gratitude for the many blessings that have been bestowed upon them as a result of the saint's intercession, and in answer to the prayers of those who have turned to St. Gerard for help throughout the years, especially with problems related to motherhood, fertility, and childbirth.

Among Roman Catholics the world over, St. Gerard Maiella is known as the patron saint of expectant mothers although originally he was known as the patron saint of a good confession and the working-man's saint.[10] However, these areas of life are not his only domains. St. Gerard is also called upon for all sorts of other life problems, as the hagiographies written about him attest.[11] Problems such as sickness, emotional difficulties, family and legal disputes, finances, and unemployment are also addressed to the saint. Some of the areas of life for which his contemporary devotees call St. Gerard to assist them with are considered illicit according to the official teachings of the Catholic Church. For example, assistance in obtaining a divorce or the appeal for the saint's help in finding a boyfriend by Italian-American gay male devotees, both of which contradict the teachings of the Catholic Church on divorce and active homosexuality.[12] Despite these deviations from the norm, which in general are not unusual when it comes to the everyday practice of Catholic devotions, some of the miracles accomplished through St. Gerard's wonderworking powers have been performed on behalf of those devotees who still gather annually at St. Gerard's National Shrine to change the clothes of their patron saint.

In addition to the annual ritual of changing of the statue of St. Gerard's clothes, there are many aspects of the annual *festa* and procession in honor of St. Gerard that offer insights into the nature of contemporary urban religious life in a culturally, racially, ethnically, and sexually cosmopolitan setting, as are most cities in the rapidly globalizing world. However, focusing on the annual changing of his clothes, this unofficial "mini-ritual," as one devotee puts it,[13] also offers an intimate glimpse of what medical anthropologist Andrew J. Strathern refers to as "historical consciousness."[14] Within the context of changing St. Gerard's clothes, "historical consciousness" is the means whereby pieces of the past are brought into the present through a variety of mediums such as touch, bodily postures and gestures of affection, vocal prayer, parody, travesty, and the public recitation of communal stories. Through the process of changing St. Gerard's clothes, contemporary devotees of the saint who participate in this private and very intimate ritual connect with various aspects of their past and with their history as descendants of the Southern Italians who came to Newark, as one-time residents of an Italian enclave that is no more, and as Catholics with a specific set of devotional practices that in most cases have been passed on to them from great grandparents to grandparents and then to parents. This "historical consciousness" is then subject to interrogation, renegotiation, and reformulation with the complex present, most of time unconsciously but sometimes very consciously, by those who participate. There are also many instances during the course of the ritual when participants are both performers and audience simultaneously, thus providing additional opportunities for the reflexive consciousness, which, according to Barbara Babcock ". . . refers to any kind of doubling back or self reference . . .".[15]

In the changing of St. Gerard's clothes, devotees of the saint ritualize powerful emotions such as love and devotion, sadness and joy, despair and hope, anger and frustration, doubt and uncertainty. Likewise, they "work out" or "perform"[16] the some-times-conflicted relationships that they have with the authorities of the Catholic Church and its teachings on certain moral issues (divorce and homosexuality, for example) and with each other. Within this ritual context, contemporary concerns such as the tensions and contradictions that exist between collective and individual ethnic, sexual, and gender identities; the power relations between the church hierarchy and the "people in the pews"; the technological advancements; and the rapid cultural and social change brought about by globalization and the spiritual and communal values of the past inter-sect and clash with each other in both creative and unsettling ways. This mini-ritual also reveals a playful or "ludic,"[17] carnivalesque quality[18] to the religious worldview of many of St. Gerard's lay devotees as well as the tensions that sometimes (although not always) exist between their practice of Catholicism and the Catholicism of the local clergy who, as clergy, are obligated to give voice to the official teachings of the Church as they come down to the local level through the American Bishops via the Vatican. The latter is true despite the fact that in many instances, the Catholicism of St. Gerard's lay devotees and that of the local clergy are not very different when lived at the level of everyday life.

THE ETHNOGRAPHER AS INSIDER/OUTSIDER

I do not come to the devotion or to the ritual changing of St. Gerard's clothes as a stranger. Rather, I am an insider to the devotion to St. Gerard because I come from a Southern Italian, Catholic family who immigrated to Newark from Avellino Province and other parts of southern Italy in the early twentieth century.[19] Both my mother's and father's families eventually settled in the Old First Ward of Newark. Although I am Catholic by heritage (and culture), I confess to being very ambivalent about my Catholic heritage. This is partly because I am a religion scholar and an ethnographer, both of which require some degree of ironic distance, but probably more because I find the teachings of the Catholic Church on human sexuality to be out of step with a contempo-rary understanding of human sexuality based on the findings of social sciences—such as psychology, anthropology, sociology, history—and also by medicine. For both of these reasons, I am in many ways an outsider to the world in which I was both raised and educated for most of my childhood and adolescence. Yet, paradoxically, as much as I often feel like an outsider to both being Catholic and the devotion to St. Gerard, I am in many ways still an insider. This is so because having grown up Catholic and with the devotion to St. Gerard, the cultural impact of both are lodged deep within my physical body, my emotions, and my soul. And this is so despite my ability to intellectu-ally analyze and critique both the Catholic tradition and the devotion to St. Gerard.

Devotion to St. Gerard Maiella stems from my mother's side of the family.[20] As it was told to me, her maternal grandmother, Anunciata Mignelli, was devoted to Blessed Gerard before she came to the United States, and before Blessed Gerard was officially canonized a saint in 1904. Although I have never been able to get all the details straight about the history of the devotion in my family, St. Gerard was a very familiar presence during my childhood and well into my adolescence.

In 1924, my mother was born with an allegedly life-threatening illness.[21] She was not expected to live. With just about all hope gone, my great-grandmother prayed to St. Gerard Maiella, who at that time had been canonized a saint for only 20 years. She vowed that if my mother recovered from her illness, she (my great-grandmother) would walk barefoot every year in the procession that honors St. Gerard. She also vowed to dress my mother as St. Gerard and to carry her in the procession until my mother could walk on her own. At that point, my mother assumed the vow along with my great-grandmother. My mother continued to observe the vow until she was 14 years old. From then on, she stopped dressing as St. Gerard.

As a young child, I accompanied my mother and father to the *festa* and procession every year. When I was older, I collected money to offer to the saint in gratitude for his wonderworking powers on my mother's behalf. Eventually, the observance of my mother's vow to the saint was greatly altered because she came into conflict with the Catholic Church's teachings on divorce and homosexuality. My father had been married and divorced before he met my mother, and because of this, my parents could not be married in the Catholic Church. My mother was never quite able to forgive the Catholic Church for this. Because I am a gay man, my mother refused to accept the teachings of the Catholic Church that homosexuality is both a moral and an objective disorder. Her love for me trumped whatever the Catholic Church taught in this regard, and she chose to trust her love more than the official teachings of the Catholic Church. Nevertheless, although she no longer walked in the procession in honor or St. Gerard, my mother still went down to St. Lucy's Church every year during the annual *festa* and procession at which point she would go to the saint's shrine, light a candle, pin some money on the saint's statue, and make a prayer of thanksgiving before the procession would begin.

In October 1994, I began attending the annual *festa* and procession once again. My decision to do so was partly motivated by my graduate studies, and partly by my need to revisit the Italian Catholic tradition and culture of my heritage. This latter I did in the hope of understanding those aspects of that tradition and culture, which continue to have a deep hold on me spiritually, emotionally and physically. When my mother became ill in 1997, I began observing an earlier version of the family's vow on my mother's behalf. For the last three years of her life, I saved money and asked family members and close friends to give me money so that I could make a ribbon out of it, which I wrapped around the statue of the saint at a particular point along the procession route.

My training as an anthropologist of religion and a scholar does not render me immune to religion's capacity to stir feelings of deep devotion or its capacity to make meaning of the mysteries of life—birth, death, as well as what precedes and follows them—or to provide insight into the nature of "Ultimate Reality" or what most Christians call "God." Despite my scholarly education, I am nevertheless a spiritually engaged person who understands myself to be culturally Catholic even if I dissent from some of the official teachings of the Church on human sexuality and on the status of other religious traditions. Therefore, I sought to use the observance of my family's vow as a means whereby the rich symbolism and rituals of the Catholic tradition and the material culture associated with the devotion to St. Gerard Maiella could be used as a lens by which devotion to St. Gerard could become intelligible, emotionally accessible, and spiritually significant to my readers through my personal firsthand experience of the devotion.

In the process of doing fieldwork, I came to understand myself as "hard-wired" Roman Catholic[22] despite the fact that I have explored many other forms of Christianity, including Eastern Orthodox Christianity, Episcopalian Christianity, and the Quaker tradition. I have also explored non-Christian traditions, such as Buddhism (Zen and Tibetan) and Sufism (Islamic mysticism). "People learn . . . religion not through the exegesis of important concepts but primarily through observation and enactment," writes Michael Mason.[23] I, too, am convinced that in order to understand the profundities and lived nature of a religious tradition, one must have a firsthand experience of it, in as much as it is possible, or "observation and enactment," as Mason rightly notes. Thus, in revisiting my family's devotion to St. Gerard, I sought through the reenactment of the ritual and devotional practices associated with the Roman Catholic cult of the saints, to arouse emotionally and physically what had been dormant during the many years of my having been away from active involvement with the Catholic religion of my childhood and an even larger part of my early adult life. The end result of this process was a fuller understanding of what it means to be both Catholic and Italian, spiritually, emotionally, and physically.

As part of my ethnographic research project, which eventually became the foundation for my Ph.D. dissertation on devotion to St. Gerard, I volunteered at the National Shrine of St. Gerard. Every Wednesday for two years, I went down to the saint's shrine at St. Lucy's Church and under the guidance of two of St. Gerard's principal devotees, Carmine and Gilda Signorelli, I cleaned the shrine, removed burned-out votive lights and replaced them with fresh ones, learned to care for the statue of St. Gerard, and participated in the preparation of the shrine for the annual *festa* and procession and for Christmas and Easter. As a result of my volunteering, I was invited to attend the annual changing of St. Gerard's clothes in both 1999 and 2000. During the time that I did fieldwork at St. Lucy's Church, I conducted formal life history interviews with many of St. Gerard's devotees, who are central participants in the changing of the saint's clothes. I also had informal conversations with many more devotees both during the ritual of changing St. Gerard's clothes and in many other venues over the course of my approximately four years of ethnographic research. Thus, all that follows is derived from formal interviews and informal conversations through my participation in the devotions to St. Gerard and my own personal reflections on those experiences.

Devotees' Accounts of Changing St. Gerard's Clothes

Devotees' descriptions of the changing St. Gerard's clothes are somewhat similar although their interpretations of the meaning of the ritual are often different. Some offer a window into the rich subjective emotional/spiritual life of a particular devotee. Others

are detailed accounts of the history and rubrics of the ritual, the material culture associated with it, and/or social commentary or grassroots theologizing. The accounts that
follow are by devotees I interviewed during 1995–2000.

The first is by Emilio, a central player in the life of St. Lucy's Church, in the community of devotees to St. Gerard and in the changing of St. Gerard's clothes. Like many of
St. Gerard's devotees who are intimately involved in the devotion to the saint and in
the life of St. Lucy's itself, Emilio, who was in his 50s at the time of my interviews and
conversations with him, grew up in the Old First Ward of Newark. He comes from a
family with long history of devotion to the saint. At the time of my interview, Emilio
lived just a few short blocks from St. Lucy's. Emilio is also an openly gay man who has
managed to reconcile his sexual orientation with his Roman Catholic faith. As of this
writing (2009), he lives with his partner, Tom, who is also involved in the devotion to
St. Gerard. Tom was also present at the changing of St. Gerard's clothes in both 1999
and 2000.

> It's usually private and personal. But of course I can share it, since I've done it so many
> times. It's a group of people, headed by Carmine Signorelli, who has taken on this vow
> from his mother, and other older women from the parish. The saint is taken down from
> the pedestal, usually put in the middle of the chapel, and undressed. We take his habit
> off of him. Under his habit, there is a shirt and a pair of slacks. It's a form. His arms, his
> face, his hands are washed with cream, or half-and-half. We go into his ears with cotton
> swabs. Prepare him as we would one of our loved ones, a child, a grown up, as we go
> along. And his shirt is placed on him. Of course, it's with snaps and zippers, because of
> course we can't move his arms as we move our own. Put his slacks on and then his habit
> with a collar. And he's dressed. And he has his belt with the initials on it, and then his
> rosary. His rosary is always placed on his belt. And if you look closely, it's always in the
> form of an M, for Mary, our Mother.[24]

The second account is by Emilio's partner, Tom. Tom is not Catholic, but a Presbyte-
rian. He participates in the ritual changing of the saint's clothes, and in the devotion to
St. Gerard, because of his relationship with Emilio. Since I had this conversation with
both Emilio and Tom, Emilio moved from the Old First Ward of Newark. However,
they both remain active in the devotion to St. Gerard and in the parish of life of St.
Lucy's Church.

> They have to special-order the outfit that goes on the saint. And it comes from a place in
> Italy. There's only one man that makes it. And usually what they do is they have one
> family, one person they've asked to donate the outfit that he [St. Gerard] will wear for the
> entire year. When they take the clothes off, it is funny, there are no women present . . .
> only men. They [the women] are in the church, but where the saint is undressed, it is
> only men.
>
> It is good, and it is bad. You get to see literally how St. Gerard, I want to say "the
> statue," is made. I think if I remember it right, he's almost 85 to 90 years old when they
> sent him over from Italy. So he's got a little wear and tear. He's got a bandage. He's got
> some gauze. So you see how the statue is literally made. But they take the clothes . . .
> certain pieces of garment come off in different ways. . . . They always take his cloak off,

then they take his jacket, his shirt, his pants, he does not have underwear on, he does have everything else that you would wear. Then they . . . very neatly take the clothing, and then what they do with it afterwards is, there is a group of women, they sit and they cut the shirt, and they cut the pants, the jacket, everything up into little pieces so that people can literally have a piece of St. Gerard to pray with later on.

I think they change the outfit a week before [the Novena prior to the annual *festa* and procession]. And then the clothing is ready for when we have the procession. There is one lady, a husband and wife team that do the cutting up. There's been different people, but I know they've been doing it recently. Then they put the clothing back on, and during and in between the priest comes and he is blessed, the statue is re-blessed. He's re-dressed from top to bottom. He's washed down in-between with milk, because the milk won't take any of the paint away from the statue getting old. They don't want to repaint him. He has a beautiful face. You see different forms of him, pictures and things like that. But he does have a beautiful face when you look at him, and his hands.

His legs, the pants are special-made, they're cut in the back, so they snap around. So that's why . . . the man who does it in Italy knows exactly the form. And I think the last time the man was very sick, so they had like five outfits made in one shot, so they'll know this is this year, this is next year, this is the following year. And who donates it every year. It's kind of an extra blessing they do have.

And it sounds terrible . . . there's special people that have been able to put them [the clothes] on. It's not everybody that puts them on. Then he's taken down from his normal stance to do this. Then he's put back. The Monsignor comes back in and they bless the entire chapel all over again.[25]

The last is a description of the ritual given by Donato, another gay man. Unlike Emilio, Donato is deeply conflicted about his Catholic faith in light of the Church's stance on homosexuality and its position on the ordination of women to the priesthood. Donato was in his early 30s at the time of my interview with him. He is also a native of Newark although he did not grow up in the Old First Ward of Newark. Rather, his family settled in another part of the city, located in the East Ward and commonly called "The Ironbound" section of Newark because it is flanked on all sides by train tracks. Donato identifies himself as a Christian, but over the years, he has gone back and forth between the Roman Catholic Church and the Episcopal Church.

Anyway . . . the one major group of people that are . . . involved in this feast, is this group of very, very closeted gay men . . . who have this incredible devotion to St. Gerard, within the confines of Catholicism, but, their idolatry of St. Gerard moves way beyond anything that's even considered appropriate for Roman Catholicism. One central tenet to Catholicism is adoration of the Blessed Sacrament, which is the Eucharist. That tenet is practically irrelevant to this group. They're much more concerned with adoration of this statue and its clothing. And I can tell you some anecdotes about that. . . . This group of guys will do things like . . . when the statue's clothes, clothing needs to be replaced because of just wear, or dry rotting, they cut the clothing up and consider it a first class relic of the saint. They have been known to wash the statue in milk, because it's such a holy piece of something. . . . They have been known to drive the statue to get re-dressed or re-painted in the back of a station wagon, and they've had people lying down with it so that it doesn't stir. It looks to me like they really believe they are dealing with St. Gerard here rather than a lump of clay and some material to cover it.[26]

Although Donato does not participate in the changing of St. Gerard's clothes, he considers himself qualified to speak about devotion to St. Gerard because his paternal grandmother was a devotee of St. Gerard, and his father was remotely involved with the devotion to St. Gerard. Coincidentally, Donato's father's name was Gerard because he was born on October 16, St. Gerard's Feast Day. Donato shares what he has heard about the changing of St. Gerard's clothes from the gay male friends he knows who regularly participate in the changing of St. Gerard's clothes.

Finally, I offer here my account of the annual changing of St. Gerard's clothes: At the beginning of the ritual, St. Gerard's statue is lifted down from the pedestal situated on the altar in his shrine. Then the statue is slowly undressed. His hands, arms, and head are made of teakwood. The torso and legs are made of plaster. The statue has been repaired many times with the plaster gauze that is used in hospitals to make casts. In 1999, there was a medical doctor there. She was there because if and when St. Gerard (the statue) is in need of repair, she repairs it. Interestingly enough, both the diagnosis and the repair are all performed using medical metaphors such as "the saint has a wound on his right arm which is in need of treatment." If the saint is in need of "treatment," the statue is clothed in a hospital gown. In 1999, the doctor made the diagnosis that St. Gerard was in need of "treatment" on the wrist of his right arm. She carefully and tenderly applied some plaster gauze to his wrist.

There are also many gold chains with lockets and medallions that hang around the neck of the statue of the saint. One of the medallions that hangs around his neck reads "100% Italian." There was quite a bit of joking by those in attendance about St. Gerard having his own doctor. Devotees also referred to him as "GQ St. Gerard," a reference to the men's magazine *Gentlemen's Quarterly*, because of the jewelry and fine clothing the statue wears. However, the joking was accompanied by a deep sense of affection for the saint, which gave me goose bumps. Then the saint's rosary beads are washed in holy water. A mixture of half-and-half and holy water is used to clean St. Gerard's face, hands, and arms. This process is done very gently with cotton balls. This action is based both on devotion, since it is done with such tenderness and affection, and on the practical fact that half-and-half removes grime and soot from painted furniture. It is also not lost on me, though it may not have occurred to some of St. Gerard's devotees, that there is some symbolic significance to the use of half-and-half and St. Gerard's association with fertility and childbirth, for in many religious traditions milk or half-and-half are symbols of both mother's milk and semen.

When it came time to dress St. Gerard in his new clothes, cuff links with the initials SGM (for *St. Gerard Maiella*) were put on him. When the dressing was complete, one of the women collected one dollar from each of us and put the money in St. Gerard's shirt pocket. I was told that the money would be used as a donation to commission a special mass next year for those of us who contributed the dollar. The people who did most of the dressing of St. Gerard are longtime devotees who have participated in the changing of St. Gerard's clothes for a number of years. Some of them are Carmine and Gilda Signorelli; Dr. Concini, the medical doctor who examined St. Gerard and determined that his arm was in need of treatment; Lucia; Genevieve; Emilio; and Mario; all of whom are longtime members of the parish and who play active roles in the various sodalities of the church. Each of these people also grew up in the Old First Ward and come from Italian families who have been devoted to St. Gerard for generations. They range in age from late 60s to early 30s. Many of them still work in Newark although none of them any longer live in the city.

There were also other people present who come to scrub the chapel of St. Gerard: Rafaello Gambucci and Anna Costenza. Rafaello Gambucci, a longtime devotee to St. Gerard, who was first introduced to the devotion to St. Gerard by Anna Costenza, a neighbor to his family when they all still lived in the Old First Ward. Every year, Rafaello collects large amounts of money from others. He then weaves the money into elaborate and very long blankets, sometimes two or three of them, that together he and Anna Costenza wrap around the statue of the saint. The blankets of money they make to wrap around the saint's statue are so long that they have to roll them on large cardboard tubes used to wrap carpets. It often takes at least 45 minutes to an hour for Rafaello and Anna to complete wrapping the statue of the saint with the blankets they offer to him as a sign of their devotion. Anna Costenza was a childhood friend of my father and my father's first wife. Since he died when I was seven years old, she was able to tell me about my father as a young man growing up in the Old First Ward of Newark. Quite coincidentally, my mother was a friend of Anna Costenza's brother, a local political figure of some controversy who commanded quite a bit of loyalty from St. Gerard's devotees, especially from those who were still living in Newark at the time of the so-called "riots" of 1967, until he died in the early 2000s.

A young pregnant woman was allowed to put a silver pendant with black onyx in the center of it around St. Gerard's neck, thus also playing on the fertility motif associated with devotion to St. Gerard. In 2000, they did not remove St. Gerard's pants. Apparently, they are having trouble finding someone to make his clothes each year. Fortunately, Carmine Signorelli had the tailor he usually commissions make three or four new habits for the saint's statue so that they have a supply, which will last for at least that many years. Subsequently, they have been forced to buy some of the new clothing for the saint's statue from retail chain stores. Carmine's wife, Gilda, then alters the clothes to fit the statue as best she can. Also, the paint on the statue's face is starting to crack. A few people suggested that a mold of his face be made soon so that if necessary a new statue can be made to replace the old one that is at least 88 years old.

As already mentioned, some of the central participants in this ritual are gay men. Emilio was helpful in that he identified for me those men who he knew to be gay for certain and those whom he suspected. I also suspected that some of the women are lesbian; and I turned out, eventually, to be correct in my assumption, confirmed by both Emilio and by some of the women themselves.

In October 2000, while talking with Mario (another central player in the devotion to St. Gerard by virtue of family heritage) and Emilio during the ritual changing of St. Gerard's clothes, the gay theme—and the camp often associated with gay humor—came up spurred by an incident that occurred in relation to the statue of the saint. As Mario, Emilio, and I glanced over at the statue of St. Gerard, we noticed that at his feet were lying a purse and a woman's sweater, inadvertently placed there by one of the women in attendance at the ritual. After a series of gestures, eye movements, and other nonverbal cues (often a central element of gay humor, most especially in mixed company of straights and gays, or in settings not hospitable to open expressions of gay identity and culture), we three joked that perhaps St. Gerard really was gay after all. This was a reference to the fact that many of the gay men devoted to saint have speculated that the saint was gay, and this despite the fact that there simply is no evidence for such speculation about St. Gerard's sexual orientation. Then Mario said that someone had recently told him that he heard St. Gerard was the saint that all the gay boys followed. This upset Mario very much. He proceeded to tell us that he defended St. Gerard and that it wasn't true. While Mario laughed with us, this incident also gave him an opportunity to tell us that he set the person "straight" (pun intended) who had made the claim that St. Gerard is the saint that all the gay boys follow.

Most of the speculation about St. Gerard being gay is drawn from incidents in the various hagiographies that have been written about the saint and which I have addressed in both my dissertation[27] and in a separate chapter included in an anthology entitled *Gay Religion.*[28] Although it is not possible to delve into the specifics here, in these other writings, I have made the argument that some of these incidents in the saint's life have become fertile ground for the gay male imagination. Additionally, further speculation that St. Gerard is gay is based upon the style in which many of the images of the saint are painted known as the *l'art Saint-Sulpice* style.[29] This style is characterized by its feminization of all Catholic religious images, including images of Jesus, the Apostles, and male saints. It is the *l'art Saint-Sulpice* style that makes St. Gerard look effeminate and as though his lips are red with lipstick in both pictures and statuary. As I have written elsewhere, speculation by gay male devotees about St. Gerard's alleged gayness is primarily based upon the *l'art Saint-Sulpice* style of images depicting him. Rare it is that I have not met a gay man who, upon seeing one of these images of St. Gerard, has not said, "He looks so gay!" Unfortunately, doing so reinforces some of the stereotypes that all gay men are effeminate, sexually passive, and drag queens.[30]

Carmine Signorelli put the finishing touches on the newly dressed statue by gently washing St. Gerard's face with cotton balls dipped in heavy cream (yet another symbol of fertility) and holy water. The latter, too, is symbolically associated with motherhood and birth in that the onset of labor is often accompanied by the mother's "water breaking." As Carmine was putting the finishing touches on the statue, he began to tell stories about an elderly Italian woman devotee to the saint and about his mother, from whom Carmine inherited his devotion to St. Gerard and to the ritual of changing St. Gerard's clothes. Carmine used the stories to lecture those of us in attendance about how we don't do enough for St. Gerard the way that people used to years ago. As Carmine was telling us this, people's cell phones and beepers began to ring and sound off, thus bringing the technology of the first years of the twenty-first century into direct contact with this devotion to St. Gerard that was at the time approximately 100 years old. It also added a certain carnivalesque atmosphere to this sacred ritual.

Carmine asked special people in the community to wash St. Gerard's hands. There was also lots of joking and sexual humor, not inappropriate for a saint who is so closely associated with human sexuality and childbirth. It is also a common feature of rituals in many of the world's sacred traditions that humor, tricksterism, and transgression of gender and sexual boundaries function as a pressure valve to the serious intensity of the ritual setting. A concrete example of this pressure valve release through humor—in this case, gay humor—occurred when Carmine Signorelli asked Rafaello Gambucci to tip the statue of St. Gerard on its side in order to lift the statue back on the pedestal on the altar. As Rafaello held the statue in his arms, St. Gerard's habit fell back like the train of a dress; after looking around to make sure that no one else was within ear shot, Rafaello said to Emilio, Mario, and me, "Look! It falls back like that actress' dress that just died. What was her name?" I chimed in, "Loretta Young."

An Interpretation of the Changing of St. Gerard's Clothes

What strikes me as interesting, even though I have not thoroughly exhausted all their possible meanings, is the different narratives simultaneously circulating in each of the accounts of the ritual just presented. Some devotees' voices speak past others; some are in theological and moral debate with others, or are at least at cross-purposes. For example, Donato introduces elements of the gay and lesbian politics of "outing," by publicly exposing (which is what it means to "out") what he understands to be a group of hypocritical gay men who live openly gay lives when they are not "in church" caring for the statue of St. Gerard, but who do not challenge the Catholic Church's teachings on homosexuality, both to their detriment and to the detriment of gay men, lesbians, and all sexual minorities. Donato's critique definitely contains an extra-religious element drawn from the culture wars around human sexuality, as well as a critique of traditional Italian devotion to the saints from a post–Vatican II point of view. Similarly, the discussion about St. Gerard's sexuality that ensues between Mario, Emilio, and me—and the references by Rafaello to St. Gerard's habit and the train of Loretta Young's dress—draw upon both popular gay culture and the cult of celebrity. I like to think of these different voices as markers of "parallel universes" of religion and popular culture, with the ritual setting of the changing of St. Gerard's clothes as a place where these parallel universes encounter and intersect with each other in interesting and creative ways.

Discourses of humor, camp, traditional piety, local history, popular culture, theology, and critique are present in this ritual arena. All these diverse themes encounter each other; both mix and clash within the context of the ritual practice of changing St. Gerard's clothes. Religious, social, cultural, and political forces organize themselves around the devotion to the saint. Some are discourses that bring devotees together into one community that understands itself to be Roman Catholic, primarily Italian or Italian American, and displaced from the Old First Ward of Newark. Other discourses are local manifestations of a counterhegemonic discourse to the rigid theological, sexual, and gender-based categories of the Catholic Church and of wider society. Perhaps this is one of the ways in which the ritual setting accomplishes what years of discourse in other settings cannot: that is, the transformation of what is often presented as fixed and unchanging, traditional moral and religious values, within the context of a rapidly changing world.

In many ways, these sometimes harmonious and sometimes clashing parallel universes embodied in the discourse and ritual practices of St. Gerard's devotees function in their religious, social, cultural and political context along similar lines to that of the *Shikhat* (Moroccan female performers) of which Deborah Kapchan writes. They juxtapose ". . . in order to both define and, at least momentarily resolves crisis. . . ." "The plurality of messages in different symbolic venues," notes Kapchan, "acts to integrate and renew the community" in such a way that the contradictions and tensions are thus "celebrated and embodied and made into strength."[31]

In some cases, individual voices are both loyal and simultaneously use humor to critique some of the teachings of the church with regard to gender and sexuality, as indicated by the deployment of camp humor about whether St. Gerard is gay, or that the train of his habit falls to the floor like Loretta Young's dress. These devotees consider themselves to be good Catholics, yet their parodying suggests that there is tension among them in relation to the Church's teachings: They use humor as the pressure-release valve for the tension. Thus, the ritual changing St. Gerard's clothes becomes a site wherein this tension between devotees and the official teachings of the Church on homosexuality and gender binarisms is performed and worked out within the ritual space in which the changing of St. Gerard's clothes takes place.

As Mikhail Bakhtin reminds us, parody-travesty served a function. Historically, it was not understood as blasphemy, but rather as a necessary antidote to the over-formalized aspects of the culture of the "elites." Parody allowed a way for the frozen word and world that had become remote and out of touch with the everyday realities of the common folk to thaw and enter into the open-ended present, "to force men [*sic*] to experience . . . a different and contradictory reality."[32] Parodic-travestying made it possible for the dominant order to be turned upside-down, creating an opening for the masses, "to provide the corrective of laughter and criticism to all existing straightforward genres, languages, styles, voices,"[33] thus allowing possibilities for release and for renewal.[34]

The different topics discussed during the changing of St. Gerard's clothes cover a range of contemporary subjects and concerns. They bring together the sacred and the profane, the religious and secular. They intermingle traditional Catholic piety and values with popular culture through the use of humor and camp. And these allegedly separate spheres of existence mix with each other in ways that challenge the usual distinctly defined boundaries that are supposed to exit between them. All these disparate voices, uttering different concerns drawn from different aspects of human existence, organize themselves, even if uncomfortably, around the figure of St. Gerard, literally and figuratively. As a common, but not a unifying, presence, St. Gerard holds together differences between devotees in centrifugal tension with each other and with the institutional Church.

THE IMPORTANCE OF RECIPROCITY AND PATRONAL RELATIONSHIPS

The ritual changing of St. Gerard's clothes is one means by which the patronal relationship between St. Gerard and his devotees is annually renewed. Michael P. Carroll rightly

observes that the patronal relationship between a saint and his or her devotees is reciprocal. A patron saint is obliged, as are his devotees, to make good on his or her commit-
ments to the relationship. For all parties involved, a failure to live up to the terms of the
agreement brings with it stiff penalties.[35] A similar relationship dynamic is involved in
the expectations that both St. Gerard and his devotees have of each other. The expectations are played out every year in the ritual changing of St. Gerard's clothes and in the
honoring of vows devotees make to the saint.

The consequences for the failure to live up to such expectations are duly recorded
in the sacred biographies of St. Gerard. One of St. Gerard's hagiographers writes that
the failure on the part of a devotee to publicize the cure of a disease or other miracles
performed through the saint's healing powers would result in a relapse, the appearance
of another disease, or the visitation of other personal or familial tragedies.[36] In one
specific case, Antonio Addio of Arrienzo failed to live up to his vow to visit the saint's
shrine annually, and this resulted in renewed attacks of the disease.[37] The seriousness
of such obligations and the dire consequences of a failure to live up to them are never
absent from the minds of St. Gerard's devotees. As Carmine Signorelli told me, "Don't
fool around with the saints. Don't make promises to them unless you are certain that
you are going to keep them."[38]

The parodying humor, celebratory playfulness, and travestying camp that is also a
feature of this culture of devotion reflects the other aspect of reciprocal relationships:
the intimacy, deep trust, and affection that exists alongside the obligatory and hierarchical power relations of these family-like systems. Although saints possess miraculous
powers that most humans do not, the relationship between a saint and his devotees is
markedly different from that between a devotee and God the Father, or Jesus, or the
Virgin Mary. One means of conceptualizing this difference is spatial: proximity versus
distance. The relationship between a saint and his devotee is more analogous to that of
an older sibling or a cousin. Even though there is still a power differential between the
older and the younger, the relationship between them is more intimate than that with
a parent. Among St. Gerard's devotees, it does seem that like a sibling, a cousin, or a
friend, St. Gerard is more accessible and more approachable than a mother or a father,
and surely more so than God or the Madonna. One devotee expresses this idea differently: "Some people might say, 'Why pray to a saint and not directly to Jesus?' The best
way I can answer is that when you go to court, you always take your lawyer with you.
What better lawyer to intercede for us than one of Jesus' special friends, St. Gerard?"[39]

THE IMPORTANCE OF MATERIAL CULTURE IN POPULAR
ITALIAN-AMERICAN CATHOLICISM

The new clothes; the gentle bathing of St. Gerard's statue with half-and-half and heavy
cream and holy water; the modesty with which his statue is disrobed; and the medical
attention lavished upon him, as indicated earlier in this chapter, all illustrate the rela-
tional obligations between St. Gerard's and his devotees. These ritual acts and the objects and substances used to perform them underscore the importance of material
culture in the devotion to St. Gerard. The performance of such simple, everyday activities expresses in ritual form awareness of the saint's formidable power to send calamity

on a recalcitrant devotee, but it is the statue of St. Gerard itself that becomes the actual physical vehicle by which such formidable power is both regulated and controlled by his devotees. Money, the supreme symbol of value in a capitalist society, sewn together into elaborate ribbons, capes, and blankets, some hundreds of feet long, is lavished upon the saint during the procession in his honor. Perhaps this practice is not only a sign of the tender loving care of the devotees, but also a form of tying or binding his miraculous power in order to secure it. During my formal interviews and informal conversations with those devotees in attendance at the ritual changing of St. Gerard's clothes, I did not directly ask whether this was so for fear of influencing with theory what might not be true in practice. Thus, I admit it is purely conjecture on my part, but it is not an uninformed conjecture. While devotees expressed great love and trust in St. Gerard's kindness, they also expressed both in word and in ritual actions an awareness of his sacred power and a fear of its consequences.

David Freedberg noted that the binding, tying, or chaining of sacred images is a practice found in many diverse cultures and religious traditions. "The phenomenon," he writes,

> . . . is not a surprising one. If statues are invested with life, or work miracles, or are capable of being dangerous, why should attempts not be made to bind them? They are chained in order to stop them from getting away—either because they can do harm or because they bring good fortune to their owners or to the adherents of their cult (who consequently do not wish to lose them).[40]

One particular means by which the statue of St. Gerard is invested with life by his devotees is by dressing the saint's statue in actual clothing. In his discussion of the function of clothing in Byzantine iconography, Henry Maguire notes that "the clothes make the man," and thus conveys the very nature of the saint's body.[41] St. Gerard's devotees have taken this idea to another level. By dressing the statue of St. Gerard in actual clothing, they empower the statue and make the saint's sacred presence tangible. His corporeality is palpably revealed; his body is rendered accessible to his devotees. By the very folds of the clothes in which they dress him, the statue of the saint appears animated with sacred power. The currents of "grace" by which St. Gerard imparts the "force" of his supernatural power are deployed for those who care for his statue and who honor the reciprocal obligations required of the patronal relationship expressed through the annual ritual changing of St. Gerard's clothes. In exchange for their devotion and care of his Shrine and the statue that gives material form to his sacred but invisible presence, St. Gerard answers his devotees' petitions, protects them from hardship and calamity, and provides comfort and strength during trying times.

Embodiment: St. Gerard's Statue, His Body, and His Devotees' Bodies

In the devotion to St. Gerard, I suggest that the statue functions as a stand-in for his physical presence. In this regard, there is more to the relationships devotees have with the statue of St. Gerard than well-meaning or "superstitious" idolatry.[42] It points to the important role material culture plays in making the supernatural present in palpable ways. As Joseph Sciorra notes, "The degree to which a statue is enhanced and cared for is seen by the community as reflecting the intensity of an individual's or a family's relationship with the supernatural."[43] In terms of ritual practice, one of the ways that the conflation of St. Gerard with the statue that gives him embodied form operates is that when the ritual changing of St. Gerard's clothes is conceived as a "performance," the statue of St. Gerard operates as a prop by which the ritual ". . . makes its proponents especially sensitive to the processes whereby performance transforms the social, psychological, and emotional being while, at the same time, it experientially enfolds the individual into the group."[44]

When asked about the statue of St. Gerard, the general consensus among his devotees is, "We speak of his statue as 'The Saint' because for us the statue is not just a statue. It is he. The statue is St. Gerard. It makes him real for us."[45] As Emilio describes it: "We refer to him as St. Gerard. The Saint. The Saint. . . . He's not a statue to us. He's real. I can't say anything else except that."[46] The statue and all the material objects that go along with it are then the means by which devotees make tangible contact with St. Gerard. This is how they maintain an embodied connection with him and, therefore, how they express their deepest desires, fears, and hopes in a concrete way. Through their relationship with "The Saint," embodied through his statue, and animated by the clothes he wears, they bring into the devotion their emotions and their deepest spiritual aspirations through the clothing and the gifts that they lavish upon him. Furthermore, numerous prayers are written on pieces of paper of every shape and size, which they pin on the underside of the religious habit that the statue wears and on the legs of the trousers beneath the habit so that the saint "will not forget" them. Most of all, they do this through displays of physical affection lavished upon "The Saint." More than just simple displays of physical affection, these bodily acts construct and condition a culturally and religiously specific way of being embodied.

Devotees also pin photographs of themselves and those for whom they pray onto the statue of the saint along with notes asking for the saint's assistance. Often, they pin the photo on that part of his statue that corresponds to the sick part of their own or another's body. Flowers, pieces of clothing, or some object belonging to a devotee or the person for whom he or she prays are also placed on or near St. Gerard's statue. For example, every year, Emilio places a bouquet of flowers on the saint's statue near the right breast. On the ribbons of the bouquet, he pins fresh dollar bills as a gift of thanksgiving to the saint for having seen his mother through breast cancer. The bouquet is specifically placed on the right side of St. Gerard's statue because that's where his mother's malignancy was.[47] In this devotional practice, there is an inversion of a traditional healing practice found in the sacred biographies of St. Gerard. There, pictures of the saint are placed on ailing bodies.

This need for bodily connection is also made through the pieces of clothing contemporary devotees pin to the statue. During the time I spent caring for the saint's statue as part of my fieldwork, I encountered pinned to the saint's clothes or left at his feet: socks, handkerchiefs, t-shirts, earrings, and even a small cup of what looked like bodily fluids.[48] These contemporary devotional practices are a variation of the practices recounted in the hagiographies. They further the symbiotic relationship between St. Gerard and his devotees who leave a part of themselves with the saint. Gifts to the saint operate metonymically. They function as stand-ins for a person's petitioning presence.

Conclusion

My descriptive analysis of the annual ritual of changing St. Gerard's clothes suggests complex religious, social, and cultural processes are at work. The act of ritualization provides a means for such processes to be encountered and assimilated by St. Gerard's devotees who embody cultural and religious values that are combinative of traditional Italian Catholicism, religious conservatism, and the cosmopolitanism of the wider community (both local and global) in which they live—all of which are simultaneously encoded in the bodies of the ritualized agents doing what ritualized agents do best: namely, ritualize.[49] Current theories used to analyze and explain ritual activity fail to embrace the full scope of the ritualizing process.[50] The processes that I describe and the analysis that I offer herein are based not only upon what various devotees have told me, but also on what I have observed and personally experienced while participating in the ritual. As such, I am not impervious to the effects of ritual performance in constituting my own localized and ritualized body in all its dimensions and complexity.

Here is yet another aspect of ritual devotional practice that is perhaps difficult to comprehend because it is so obviously simple: When a person grows up in a highly ritualistic and symbolically rich religious or cultural tradition such as Roman Catholicism—most especially, in a Mediterranean cultural context—ritualizing satisfies an almost built-in need to perform powerful feelings and beliefs in an embodied way. The processes in play, the issues being worked out, and the means by which they are accomplished are hardly at the level of conscious awareness of those devotees participating in the ritual. Quoting anthropologist Michael Jackson, Robert Orsi suggests that "to investigate beliefs or 'belief systems' apart from actual human activity is absurd because beliefs—even the most crucial—are quiescent most of the time, activated in crisis, but having no stable or intrinsic truth values that can be defined outside of contexts of use."[51] It is during the course of the ritual changing of St. Gerard's clothes itself and the conversations devotees hold with each other during its performance that their quiescent beliefs are activated, investigated, and challenged.

Cursed Flesh

FAITH HEALERS, BLACK MAGIC, AND (RE-MEMBERING)
DEATH IN A CENTRAL ITALIAN TOWN

Luisa Del Giudice

For Marzia and Giuseppe Otello Poldi

In memory of Giuseppe Poldi, their father

This chapter is equal parts: commemoration of a deceased brother-in-law, Giuseppe (Pep) Poldi; personal journal; and ethnographic voyage into death and cultural darkness. Although I turned to the theme of death with dread—approaching the coffin with great caution, so to speak—I also knew I could not avoid the topic indefinitely. It required understanding and closure. This chapter is also a fulfillment of a death-bed promise: As godmother to Pep's son, Otello, I promised to help keep his memory alive in his children.

My intricately entwined roles as ethnographer and family member forced me to closely examine my role as participant and as observer. All this was overlaid by a complex "immigrant syndrome," in which distorted and recovered memory frequently played a part. Here, for instance, I unearthed a buried part of my family history: Specifically, I learned that a grandmother and a great aunt (both bearing my own name) were healers—that healing was, in fact, a part of my family history. Unexpectedly, therefore, this paper became both an exercise in spiritual archaeology and a reconstruction of a matrilineage.

The catalyst for recovering this history was Giuseppe Poldi, born and raised in Terracina (province of Latina, region of Lazio), on the west coast, roughly equidistant between Rome and Naples. He came to Toronto as an adult and married my sister, Franca, and they returned to Terracina shortly after. Pep became a direct bridge between memorial culture of immigrant parents and contemporary Terracina: a mediator and guide. But the relationship was a dyadic one because as an emerging ethnographer, *I* helped newly focus *his* attention on local cultural phenomena. We were each mediating Terracinese culture for the other. This chapter explores the "porous" border between ethnographic research and personal identity, the interplay between observer and observed, and the role of memory—both personal and communal—in shaping this narrative.

Giuseppe Poldi's niche at the Terracina cemetery, with inscription "Terracina: cogli il tuo figlio nobile e devoto" in an aesthetically unfortunate bubble lettering. (Photograph by the author.)

This chapter also explores another border crossing, the one implied in diasporic or immigrant narrative. In this dyadic, trans-Atlantic discourse, I discovered that it is not safe to assume that the "roots" experience is confined to digging in Italian soil. Indeed, it is frequently the case that greater, or equal, "treasure" is to be unearthed—to continue the archaeological metaphor[1]—on *this* side of the Atlantic and among immigrants. In any case, the dialogue might theoretically be a two-way communication although in practice, it is typically the immigrant who initiates such a dialogue. Indeed, few are the Italians enquiring among Italian immigrants to more fully understand their own cultural identity although there appear to be recent, modest signs that the situation may be changing.

Terracina, in the midst of the once-malarial Pontine Marshes, has a grim heritage of blood disorders. It was a myelodysplastic anemia type B that claimed Pep at the age of 38, in 1989. Pep began an odyssey into the world of faith healers and the occult as he grappled with his approaching death.[2] His disease was diagnosed by at least one healer as having been caused by the cursing of animal flesh: that it was, in fact, incurable, because the spell had not been broken in time. His blood—*sangue legato*—had been "bound" or "tied"[3] so that as the animal flesh rotted, so would his human flesh degenerate by degrees, until his death. By degrees, Pep came to concur with this diagnosis and wove together a complex web of anxieties and tensions: attributing his disease to the malice of scheming neighbors, even envious relatives (in a perennial battle over land rights and boundaries), or possibly to a spurned lover who had claimed his paternity of her son.[4]

Pep fought death and sought a cure on a variety of fronts, from modern medicine (including a visit to the UCLA Medical Center) to traditional practices, both local and exotic. Monsignor Milingo, Archbishop of Lusaka, Zambia (whom the Church had "exiled" to Italy) visited Terracina to exorcise Pep's and Franca's house—which, many were convinced, had been cursed.[5]

Franca's role in this research has been critical. I came to learn much about Terracina through her life there. Like Franca, I was born in Terracina but was raised in Toronto, Canada. We often considered Terracina lost in the Dark Ages, where belief systems and gender relations remained archaic. We were both insider/outsiders, coming to terms with what *was* and *wasn't* our cultural heritage. She, nonetheless, became increasingly resigned to that world and belief system, ultimately actively participating in the healing arts herself because it all became very real and tangible, she said, even for a skeptic like herself.

It took some coaxing for Franca to participate in this research. She believed that this was "my" story, and that "[I] should tell it as [I] saw it." Her readings, however, provided a reality check. For instance, an abstract I wrote prior to reading this chapter at an academic meeting stated that healing was an "*unacknowledged* part of our family history."[6] Franca however noted that "there always *had* been references made to healers in our past but we didn't understand these references." Further, she implied that I continued to ignore its reality because the gift of healing had indeed survived into our generation: namely, in Franca herself, and she added, "Who knows who else, this is yet to be discovered!"

My study became unavoidably and intensely personal. I both cringed at the potential solipsism of "I-centered" ethnographic discourse yet marveled at the complexity and value of exploring, not merely the anthropology *of* emotion, but the emotions *in* anthropological process and discourse. Listening to the narratives about female healers in my family, for instance, had a profound impact upon me, precipitating a form of crisis into which I began heading in 1997 and out of which I have recently found my way.[7]

Here is my grandmother Luisa ("Lisetta") Del Giudice's story, as told by her daughter, my aunt Rosaria:

> Grandma [mom] was about ten years old. She was walking alone to the vineyard to take her stepfather his lunch. An old and ugly woman came out of nowhere and asked her: "Pretty young girl, where are you going?" "I'm going to the vineyard to take *tata* his bread." (That's what one called a father in those days.) "Alone?" she asked. "Yes, the vineyard is close by." The woman then took her hand and said, making a terrible gesture, just as though she were a witch [here her voice shifts to a cackle]: "This hand here will do much good in all things"—as though it were a holy hand. She [Lisetta] was afraid. As she turned to look again, the woman had vanished. She started to run. When she got to the vineyard, her stepfather saw her trembling and asked her what was wrong. Mom explained about the old woman. He answered that she should not pay any attention to such things.

So it ended, and she didn't think about it anymore until after she was married and had children. One day, she started to discover these things. There was a man, Mario Trocchei, whose son, Carlo, was sickened by the evil eye. She called Mario to her and asked him where he was taking the boy. He was taking him to the pharmacy for medicine, he answered. "What's wrong with him?" she asked, but he didn't know. The boy had a swollen ear (*orecchioni*, mumps) and had a fever, evil eye (*malocchio*), and other things. She asked him to bring the boy to her. She remembered then what the old woman had told her. She performed a cure for the evil eye (not in the usual way but merely with her hands over the boy's eyebrows, saying prayers), and "marked" the swollen ears with her wedding band.[8] As she did all these things, the little boy of five or six years wanted to get down and run around. He felt well. The boy's father, then remarked: "Oh Lisetta, you have holy hands like these, and you didn't tell anyone before?" Mom answered: "But I've never done anything like this before; I just remembered this from when I was a child." And from that moment on, one person told the next, and as children got sick they went to her, for worms, evil eye, realignment of bones.

Such healing powers were normally bequeathed only on one's deathbed, or during Christmas Eve, through the female line. In my grandmother's case, however, the gift appeared, *ex novo* through *La Fortuna* (Lady Luck). Yet, because none of her daughters apparently wanted such powers, so it ended with her death in 1974. Such gifts proved a source of much conflict within traditional male-dominated marriages because healing raises the question of modesty and reputation management. Lisetta, however, defended her craft as an act of public charity (particularly toward children and women): She would not accept payment. Further, she treated illnesses *publicly*, never behind a closed door. The prayers and incantations, however, remained secret.

The second narrative regards my great aunt (on my paternal side), Luigina Del Giudice (n.b., *Luigia* is a variant of *Luisa*),[9] whom Pep and Franca visited regularly and whom I met only once in the mid-1980s. Here is her narrative.

At the age of nine, Luigina saw the Madonna everywhere, and she was afraid. In an interesting role reversal, her first healing experience was for her mother. As a married woman and mother, Luigina talked regularly to Mary and Jesus, as had her mother, Teresina, before her. She both heard voices and saw visions of Mary and of her son, who instructed her on how to counsel her large following.

She claimed for herself, and the entire Del Giudice family, a direct lineage from the Virgin Mary. I contend that she was here creating a symbolic matrilineage, fixing in this ideal ancestor a link between herself and an archetypal mother and healer. She had therefore, in her own view, inherited healing from biological *and* spiritual mothers.

She began to practice her variety of faith healing only after her husband died, at which point, time stood still and she became a sort of Miss Haversham from *Great Expectations*. She sold no more of the inventory in her housewares shop, but left everything exactly as it was. Instead, she began receiving the sick and the needy every night at 6 P.M. They waited in a line, which spilled into the main street of the old town, Corso Anita Garibaldi (presently occupied by the restaurant "Ai Trioni"). Luigina's *bottega* (shop) became something of a clearing-house from which she redistributed the wealth: Gifts brought to her (including a stock of pharmaceuticals) would in turn be given to

Luigina Del Giudice, faith-healer, in her bottega *in Terracina* alta *(the Medieval part of town).*

others. Luigina reputedly cured people of everything from minor skin disorders to infertility and even blindness. Some disparagingly called her *la santa* (the saint).

The management of reputation became critical here, too. Some accused her of practicing for gain although she apparently accepted only gifts "in kind."[10] Luigina was careful to align her healing within the Catholic matrix. Although she conceded that evil powers existed, she would not listen to stories about spells and the evil eye, insisting that all her powers came from Mary and Jesus. Indeed, with regard to Pep, she was the only healer who never ventured a guess as to *why* he had become sick. And she so eschewed fortune telling with cards, for instance, that not even at Christmastime would she allow *tombola* (a traditional card game, in its Terracinese variant) to be played in her house.[11]

There are common threads in the two narratives. In both instances, the healer was prepubescent when she received a sign of her calling, marking the passage into womanhood with attendant fear and confusion—a sort of re-enactment of the Marian Annunciation.[12] The full exercise of the gift however, came only with *motherhood*. Opposition from a spouse was overcome, either by standing firm or by waiting for widowhood. Both practiced openly (Luigina literally keeping an open-door policy), became mothers to the wider community, and perceived their work as acts of public charity.

The experience of maternity, the maternal (Marian) model, and the matrilineage seem here to have had much to do with healing. Nevertheless, neither my grandmother

nor my great aunt, apparently, found any manifest inheritors of their healing knowledge. There seem to be broken lines of inheritance in both cases. Although Luigina
prophetically believed that these powers descended through the seventh generation, no
one was quite certain how this occurred. Some conceded that this gift of God might be
transmitted genetically (as potential) and therefore might, or might not, be "revealed"
in time.

Reflections on the I-Narration

No other folkloristic work that I had previously done has merged so many areas of my
private experience, family history, and professional identity as this writing on death,
belief, and healing. In remembering a *single* death, I began reassembling *many* life
narratives. I literally began rummaging through an attic of long-forgotten memory
drawers: boxes containing bits of paper on which, as far back as my early teens, I had
scribbled proverbs, recipes, nicknames, songs, dreams—a chaotic archive made audible
only more recently through recorded interviews. As a double immigrant (two decades
in Toronto and another two in Los Angeles), it was only in Los Angeles—and hence at
the greatest distance in my existential triangle (Canada-Italy-USA)—that I began exploring and reordering these fragments. It became evident that this accumulated past was
present still and that, in gathering up these bones of memory, new life was being
breathed into them.

Among the narrated family biographies, my own began emerging in an unavoidable
way. I began to have the eerie and powerful feeling that a secret voice was "calling"
me.[13] Why was this knowledge finding me now? Was my feminist consciousness and
my exploration of female spirituality coming together in a revelatory way?[14] Was I
being prompted to examine my matrilineage for a reason? Or could the focus on the
emergence of my identity as a folklorist in the early 1980s have been a response to a
recurring professional (and approaching mid-life) crisis? I began to question what I did
as a folklorist—and why. How had it all begun? And where was it leading? This re-
visitation marked a life passage for me. In mourning Pep, I also grieved fresh begin-
nings, lost youth, scattered family, the severed link to Terracina, and professional
disappointments.

I began discovering how ancestors do speak. Part of that communication came in
the form of objects and images. For instance, the only *tangible* inheritance from my
grandmother, Lisetta, was a crystal-beaded rosary that had somehow ended up in my
hands; and from Luigina, a typewritten prayer brought back from a pilgrimage and
given to me directly. To me these gifts seemed symbolically "loaded." I had not said the
rosary in decades.[15] I was not even a member of the Catholic Church any longer. Further, Luigina, whom I met but once, gave me greater "knowledge" about Del Giudice
genealogy (both real and apocryphal), which somehow fixed the significance of names
in my mind.

What was in a name, anyway? I have had a long and troubled relationship with
mine (as one can imagine). My name struggled to assert itself all through my early
school days in English Canada. I have since defended it against erosion and distortion,
feeling that its fate was directly linked to mine. At a young age, I knew that I would

The author's grandparents Luisa (Palmacci) Del Giudice (family nickname: "Paguèlæ," a lisped distortion of fagioli *[beans]) and Giovanni Francesco Del Giudice (family nickname: "Carbonæe" [charcoal]), with the rosary inherited by her grandmother draped over their photographs.*

never change it, not even upon marrying, for this would plunge me into an identity crisis. I have passed on my surname to both daughters as middle names—hardly an Italian custom.

I was convinced that it locked within itself a secret that I would eventually learn. I discovered one day that re-segmented, my name had *another* meaning: that it formed a complete, if cryptic, sentence: *Lui sa del giudice* (He knows about the judge). This was an epiphany . . . until I began to interrogate it: But *who* was this judge? and *who* was it that had this knowledge? and *what* precisely was the knowledge? I was the first and remain the only female in our entire clan (now more than 150) to have inherited my grandmother's name. Was I "marked" by that name and by my grandmother (see photo above)?[16] It is in this sense that this research project became one of spiritual archaeology. Or call it *bricolage*. I found myself reassembling, possibly inventing, a fragmented religious-magical inheritance about which I had known little.[17]

Was a religious path calling me?[18] I could choose to merely transfer and thereby deflect some of its impact: that is, suppose I did miss my calling as a healer. On the other hand, I began to rationalize, if healing were taken less literally, my work as a folklorist might be construed as a form of healing. I have no magical techniques, of course, but perhaps a portion of my folklore advocacy did attempt to "heal" broken identities through historical and geographic mending. And like my grandmother, much of my work has been an act of public charity because so little of it has ever been remunerated. Further, many of my community cultural and educational activities, directly served (and continue to serve) girls' and women's issues.[19]

Folklorists may heal, but in the final analysis (and with less grandiosity), I can claim that folklore work has proved profoundly *self*-healing. It has literally *grounded* me in a sense of my personal and cultural identity, and in historic and geographic *place*. Pep, in death, as in life, assisted in that passage. Pep knew where *he* belonged. For me, it has taken years of research and writing. For Pep, a few years in Canada were sufficient to clarify his values, his identity, his place. In fact, he returned home and never looked back. I envied this certainty and ease. I was asked to write Pep's epitaph. In attempting to capture the core of Giuseppe Poldi's life—both an honor and an onus—it occurred to me that it resided in the fact that the man embodied the place. They were inseparable. I settled on *Terracina, cogli il tuo figlio nobile e devoto* (Terracina, gather up your noble and devoted son).

Several years after Pep's death in 1989, I returned to the house on Via Panoramica, with its commanding vista of the sea, and the Roman temple to Jupiter on Montegiove, separated from the house by a vast olive grove. I realized that I was the first family member to reanimate the dead man's home and help fill it with light and sound again. I returned with my two-year-old daughter, Elena, because I knew that a child's laughter and noise would dispel any darkness lingering there. This chapter continues the effort of bringing life to memories that should not die, and light to the darkness that I feared. It has also helped me recover my various mothers.

In an anxiety-provoking dream recorded many years ago, I remember saying to my mother, Liliana (whom I imagined was dying), and to my grandmother Luisa that I barely knew them and had so much to ask and learn. Couldn't they please stay longer? My grandmother, who actually was dead, smiled and said that no, she couldn't stay. I know now that she didn't really mean it.

Imagining the *Strega*

FOLKLORE RECLAMATION AND THE CONSTRUCTION OF ITALIAN-AMERICAN WITCHCRAFT

Sabina Magliocco

The expansion of Neo-Paganism and revival Witchcraft[1] in North America is among the most interesting outgrowths of the contemporary "New Age" movement.[2] Italian folk magic is among those which have received considerable attention, spawning a proliferation of books, Web sites, and small groups of practitioners. Still, these re-claimed magical practices bear only a slight resemblance to the folk magic that existed (and, in some cases, continues to exist) in Italian-American ethnic communities. In this chapter, I trace the development of *Stregheria*, or Italian-American revival Witchcraft, showing how it has been constructed by combining traditional Italian folk beliefs and practices with historical and ethnographic materials, New Age concepts, and frame-works for religious ecstasy to create a completely new religion that serves the needs of contemporary Italian-American spiritual seekers. I will argue that it codifies and reval-ues traditional Italian folk beliefs and magical practices, placing them in a form that is friendly to the values of second-, third- and fourth-generation Italian Americans, but is significantly different from folk magic as practiced in rural Italy and brought to North America by Italian immigrants. I am particularly interested in the ways how the cre-ators of Italian-American Witchcraft have made use of scholarly literature on Italian history and ethnography in ways that are quite different from what the producers of knowledge may have intended. I will also examine the implications of the emergence of Italian-American revival Witchcraft at this particular historical juncture in terms of what it can tell us about the nature of ethnic identity in the United States at the begin-ning of the twenty-first century.

I base my analysis on the literature that emerged from the postmodern historical critiques of cultural categories previously understood as natural or essential.[3] According to this theoretical strain, categories such as gender, race, nationality, and ethnicity—which, at first glance, appear inherent—can be regarded as inventions, in the sense of "widely shared, though intensely debated, collective fictions that are continually rein-vented."[4] By adopting this stance, I am neither denying the existence of real cultural differences between groups nor asserting that expressions of ethnic identity are not genuine for tradition-bearers. Instead, I posit that ethnic groups as we conceive of them today—rather than being natural, static, stable entities that possess an essential set of traits that exist relatively unchanged through time—are actually of fairly recent origin, tied to the emergence of the modern nation-state.[5] Our assumptions about ethnic groups carry the legacy of European romanticism and its emphasis on the concept of authenticity.[6] However, as Michael Fischer suggests, "ethnicity is something reinvented and reinterpreted in each generation [and] by each individual," often in ways that remain fairly obscure and impenetrable even to the artists and re-creators themselves.[7]

Italian-American Witchcraft is one among many reinterpretations of Italian-American ethnicity emerging in the late twentieth century. Although based in traditional folk-magical practices brought to North America by Italian immigrants, it is essentially a case of "folklore reclamation," a term that describes a particular kind of folklore revival that attempts to reclaim, albeit in a new cultural context, aspects of folk tradition stigmatized by a dominant discourse. Like other forms of revival and "invented tradition," folklore reclamation generally signals a break with tradition and the deep-seated need to erase that break from collective memory, or at least make it more palatable. What distinguishes folklore reclamation from similar forms of cultural revival is its focus on forms, elements, and even words formerly marginalized, silenced, and discredited by the dominant culture. Through the process of reclamation, these previously repudiated elements are reappropriated, reinterpreted, and given a new and illustrious context in which they function as important symbols of identity and pride. This identity is consciously oppositional to the one portrayed in the dominant culture's representations.

Folklore reclamation is not unique to Italian Americans; in fact, the process seems to emerge as part of identity politics in the larger context of globalization. In the case of *Stregheria*, folklore reclamation is taking place as the status of Italian Americans in North America is changing. Once reviled as the newest wave of unacculturated immigrants, many have now become part of the middle classes and find themselves targets of hostility from immigrant groups who see them as white oppressors, blaming them (through Christopher Columbus) for the genocide of Native American peoples and the destruction of their cultures. At the same time, the projection of contemporary nationalisms into the past has allowed other European ethnics to vilify Italian Americans as the descendants of imperial Romans, responsible for the first wave of European colonialism and cultural destruction. I argue that the discourse of Neo-Paganism allows Italian Americans and other European Americans to create identity in part by aligning themselves against the dominant cultural and religious paradigms, and with oppressed minorities, by reclaiming traditions previously abandoned in shame. My interest lies precisely in how contemporary artisans of the tradition create the impression of ethnic authenticity through text and practice, and on the role of scholars in helping to construct tradition, albeit sometimes unwittingly.

I want to make very clear that my goal is *not* to de-authenticate Italian-American Witchcraft. Contemporary folklorists and anthropologists have recognized that authenticity is always a cultural construct: what is considered "authentic" is a result of how we construe our relationship to the past, and how we interpret that past in light of present concerns.[8] Moreover, all traditions are perpetually in flux as their bearers constantly reinterpret and reinvent them with each individual performance. Revival and reclamation are part of the process of tradition, even when the result is different from the original practice itself. Thus *all* traditions are authentic, and the historicity of a tradition has nothing to do with its efficacy for any given group of people.

The Stigmatization of Italian Folk Magic in America

By far, the largest number of Italians who immigrated to North America were *contadini* (peasants) from the south who brought with them a folk religion that while nominally Catholic, had little to do with the dogma and doctrine of the Church, but was "a syncretic melding of ancient pagan beliefs, magical practices, and Christian liturgy."[9] Their universe was animated by angels, demons, and saints as well as a variety of local spirits who could be invoked to help survival, but who could also be dangerous at times. Much of their religious devotion was focused upon the local saint, especially the patronal feast, whose secular, celebratory aspects also included expressions of religious passion and ecstasy through which worshippers experienced direct contact with the sacred.[10]

The immigrants also brought with them a rich tradition of folk magic, especially a pervasive belief in *malocchio* (the evil eye). All manner of illnesses and social conditions could be attributed to it, and Italians had an arsenal of amulets and folk cures to protect against it. Most rural communities had folk healers whose craft was learned in the family; these specialists, called by various dialectical terms, knew both herbal and magical charms to help their fellow villagers, but were often reputed to be able to cause harm as well. Italian peasants also had a plethora of folk legends and beliefs regarding *streghe* (witches), individuals with a supernatural ability to do evil. The witches of legend performed feats that were obviously preternatural: They could change shape, transforming into animals; fly through the night sky to the walnut tree of Benevento, their secret meeting place; enter homes through the keyhole, steal milk from nursing mothers and livestock; suck the blood of living beings; and paralyze people in their sleep.[11] At times, the popular imagination conflated folkloric witches with folk healers, leading to accusations of witchcraft.

Italian immigrants' folk Catholicism and magical practices encountered tremendous hostility from the dominant American culture. "American Protestants and Catholics agreed that the Italian immigrants were characterized by ignorance of Christian doctrine, image worship, and superstitious emotionalism," and branded the immigrants pagans, heathens, and idolaters.[12] Educated Italian Americans, embarrassed by the apparent vulgarity of religious displays, echoed this sentiment, and suggested that working class Italian Americans replace their devotion to saints with the celebration of prominent Italian historical figures such as Christopher Columbus and Giuseppe Garibaldi—something that many Italian American communities evidently took to heart.[13]

While many clergymen and educators simply disparaged Italian-American folk religiosity and despaired of ever educating the immigrants, others turned to anthropological and folkloristic theory of the time to explain the strange beliefs and practices. Foremost among these was the theory of survivals, which postulated that seemingly incomprehensible and irrational beliefs and practices were actually the vestiges of a previous savage or primitive stage in the unilinear evolution of culture. Survivals, it was thought, would eventually disappear as populations became educated and more rational, scientific practices took hold. The theory of survivals, first developed by anthropologist Edward B. Tylor and applied to Italian folk customs by early ethnographers, was adopted enthusiastically by American clergy, educators, and social workers struggling to understand unfamiliar ideas and practices. For example, Phyllis H. Williams wrote in *South Italian Folkways in Europe and America: a Handbook for Social*

Workers, Visiting Nurses, School Teachers and Physicians (1938, 1969): "The religious practices of the South Italians preserved in modified form many elements . . . associated with ancient Greek, Roman and Mohammedan beliefs" (135). She argued that saints were in fact "folk substitutes for the old Greek and Roman gods and spirits of the woods and rivers. . . . The polytheism of the old departmental deities survived in the veneration of local saints" (136). While survivalism began as an attempt to account for these practices, it ultimately worked to disenfranchise the folk religion of Italian Americans, even as it appeared to romanticize it. The practices remained stigmatized: "These ethnic survivals cause us to be laughed at, even disdained, exposed to sarcasm of the Americans. . . ." wrote an Italian American commentator of the time.[14]

Despite this social stigma, many Italian folk magical and religious traditions did not die out. Patronal feasts remained the most lively, vivid expressions of folk religiosity, but folk magical practices continued to be documented well into the 1970s although Malpezzi and Clements argue that by the late 1980s, some had fallen into disuse.[15] Yet, many Italian Americans still remember a *nonna* (grandmother) or other relative who knew how to remove the evil eye, cure common ailments with charms and prayers, or purify the house with salt. Often the younger generations adopted the view of the dominant culture, that these were "only a lot of fish stories."[16] The term *strega* (witch) was sometimes used disparagingly by family members to refer to the bearers of these "superstitious" practices. "My twenty-seven-year-old son calls us a bunch of witches," said a second-generation Italian-American woman who used amulets to ward off the evil eye.[17]

Even when Italian Americans continued their traditional folk religious practices, it is clear that by the late twentieth century, these existed in a context quite different from that of the peasant villages from which most immigrants had come. The changed sociocultural context combined with the stigmatization of folk practices to form a veil of secrecy and mystery around them. For many second-, third-, and fourth-generation Italian Americans, the word *strega* and the elements of folk magic became whispers in family legends—decontextualized, marginalized, silenced, but still powerful in the imagination, and ripe for reclamation.

Neo-Paganism and Revival Witchcraft

In 1977, Rudolph Vecoli wrote: "With the current revival of interest in witchcraft and demonology, American culture appears to be catching up to the *contadini* of a century ago."[18] And indeed he was correct. Although the Italian-American witchcraft revival was still in its infancy, revival Witchcraft had already exploded onto the American counter-cultural scene. Revival Witchcraft and Neo-Paganism, the larger movement of which it is part, include a number of ecstatic mystery religions whose aim is to revive, re-create, and experiment with pre-Christian forms of polytheistic worship. While encompassing a wide variety of beliefs and practices, these religions generally seek a direct, embodied experience of the sacred, often through altered states of consciousness achieved in ritual. They also seek harmony with the environment and an emphasis on the feminine divine (which they locate in pre-Christian practice and in the religions of indigenous peoples), qualities that they do not find in mainstream Christianity. Contemporary Witches see themselves as the spiritual or actual descendants of witches burned during the European witch hunts, whom they believe were practicing the remnants of a pre-Christian nature religion. While rooted in a Western mystery tradition going back to Neoplatonism and containing a number of traditional folk magical practices, these religions are essentially of recent invention, and constitute an important form of cultural critique.

While lacking any single scriptural text, revival Witchcraft nevertheless grew from a literate and literary tradition, and folklorists played no small part in formulating its essential premises.[19] British civil servant and folklorist Gerald B. Gardner is credited with establishing the basic parameters of this religion in *Witchcraft Today* (1954), in which he interpreted the practices of a British occult group as survivals of an ancient pre-Christian fertility religion. Along with one of his initiates, Doreen Valiente, Gardner developed a ritual framework that involved casting a sacred circle, invoking the four cardinal points, calling the names of a goddess and god, and a shared meal of cakes and wine. Direct experience of the deities through ecstatic states was the climax of ritual. Gardner also contributed the eight sabbats, or holy days, to the Wiccan year cycle. "Gardnerian" Witchcraft, or Wicca, entered North America in the late 1950s. Buoyed by the 1960s counterculture, it soon diffused, giving rise to numerous variants.[20] Conservative estimates count approximately 600,000 Neo-Pagans and Witches in North America today, most of whom are part of the urban middle classes. The number of Italian-American Witches is much smaller, but books on the topic have sold about 60,000 copies since publication, suggesting that a small but substantial minority of Neo-Pagans are either of Italian extraction, or are interested in ethnic variants of revival Witchcraft. The number of initiated, practicing Italian-American Witches is probably very limited, around the order of several hundred.

Charles G. Leland and the Witchcraft Revival

One of the earliest texts of the modern Witchcraft revival has also been extremely influential in the development of Italian-American Witchcraft. In 1899, amateur folklorist Charles G. Leland published *Aradia, or The Gospel of the Witches*, a series of Italian spells, conjurations, and legends collected from a Florentine fortuneteller whom Leland called "Maddalena." This text, which Maddalena reportedly gave Leland as a manuscript, presents Italian witches as worshipping Diana—goddess of the moon, Queen of the Witches, and "protectress of the oppressed, the outcast, the ungodly and the godforsaken"[21]—along with her brother and lover, Lucifer. The two have a daughter named Aradia (derived from Herodias, a legendary figure associated with Diana in early medieval witch trial transcripts) who is sent to Earth to enlighten humans and teach them to resist the oppression of wealthy and powerful landowners through sorcery. In accordance with Aradia's teachings, witches gather in the woods during the full moon, where they worship naked as a sign that they are free from the bonds of social class. There they hold a witches' supper with cakes of meal, salt, and honey, shaped like half-moons. Leland called their religion *la vecchia religione* (the old religion).

Charles Godfrey Leland (1824–1903), amateur American folklorist and author of Aradia, or the Gospel of the Witches *(1899).*

The *Vangelo* (Gospel) also contains a number of spells or conjurations, many intended to avert the evil eye or bring good luck. The tone of these spells emphasizes a clientilistic relationship between Diana and her worshippers not unlike that familiar to scholars of folk Catholicism: The deity can be threatened if she does not help fulfill the supplicant's prayers. Leland translated the texts and strung them together with interpretations based on prevailing folklore theories of his time, suggesting that they were survivals of a pagan religion dating back to the days of ancient Rome and Etruria.

From the very beginning, *Aradia* has been surrounded by controversy. Among Neo-Pagans and revival Witches, the text has been vilified because of its linking of Diana with the character of Lucifer—a name for the Christian devil—and the presence of manipulative magic, which suggests the imposition of one's will on gods and humans.

"Maddalena," Charles G. Leland's informant and alleged source of the material in Aradia.

These concepts sharply contrast with the "harm none" ethic of revival Witchcraft, and the egalitarian, collaborative relationships between humans and gods that characterize this group of religions.[22] Likewise, scholars have rejected its historicity. Because there are no analogues to the text as a whole in Italian collections or archives, Leland was suspected of having fabricated it himself out of bits and pieces of folklore, as well as having invented his key informant. Even those who accepted her existence believed that Maddalena, a Florentine fortune-teller of dubious reputation, may have concocted material to satisfy the American folklorist who was paying her for information. A more likely interpretation, proposed by Robert Mathiesen, suggests that we regard *Aradia* as dialogic and intersubjective: "Maddalena to a certain extent invented herself in response to the interests and enthusiasms of . . . Leland, . . . adapt[ing] from the vast amounts of lore at her disposal precisely those texts and practices, those legends and spells, which would most fascinate her patron."[23]

Despite these controversies, *Aradia* became a fundamental text in the twentieth-century Witchcraft revival. Its influence extends from very particular practices of modern Witchcraft (the full moon meetings; the "Charge of the Goddess," later rewritten by Doreen Valiente; the goddess name, which in Garnderian Craft remained "Aradia" until the early 1960s; and ritual nudity)[24] to the more general notions of witchcraft as a continuation of pre-Christian religion, cultural critique, and peasant resistance.

Perhaps the most important idea for Italian-American Witchcraft revivalists has been the linkage of folk magic with an ancient Italian religion involving goddess worship. The presence in the text of a number of items with clear analogues in Italian folklore (for example, the "conjuration of lemon and pins," in which a lemon is stuck with pins to cause harm to an enemy; the children's rhyme to catch fireflies; the blessing of the flour) allowed Italian Americans reading Leland to interpret their family magical practices as vestiges of an ancient pagan religion and forms of peasant resistance.

Stregheria, or Italian-American Witchcraft

Among the first to openly identify himself as a practitioner of Italian witchcraft was the late Dr. Leo Louis Martello. Born in the 1930s in Massachusetts to Sicilian immigrant parents, he claimed to have been initiated by a cousin of his father's in 1951.[25] In his writings, he describes Sicilian tradition as being practiced solely among family members; initiation takes place at puberty; and the goddess and god are not part of the Roman pantheon. He stops short of revealing exact rites and practices transmitted by his family because initiates must take a blood oath never to reveal its secrets to outsiders.[26] Martello describes his family tradition as essentially domestic, family-based, and oath-bound, yet he also founded the Trinacrian Rose Coven, a more public group that emphasizes the Sicilian deities and practices yet in other ways resembles Gardnerian-based groups.

Although Martello probably never intended to become a popularizer of Italian-American Witchcraft, in many ways, he laid the groundwork for the development of later variants. In *Weird Ways of Witchcraft* (1972), he is the first to reproduce an engraving of the *mano fica* (a fist with the thumb between the first and second fingers), calling it the "fig gesture" and attributing it to Italian magic-workers who used it to turn back evil spells.[27] In *Witchcraft, the Old Religion* (1975), he describes Sicily as the home of the goddess Demeter, her daughter Persephone, and their mystery cult, deities brought to the island by the ancient Sikels, the original settlers, whom he conflates with the Etruscans and the founders of Rome.[28] He sees Sicilian Catholics' devotion to the Virgin Mary as a continuation of their devotion to earlier goddesses: In describing the statue of the Madonna and child in the church near the Temple of Demeter at Enna, he characterizes the child as female, and says "The sculptor who made the statue belonged to '*la vecchia religione.*'"[29] He further insists that Catholicism, especially Marian worship, was used by witch families to conceal their continuing veneration of Demeter and Persephone. Long before its translation into English, he cites Carlo Ginzburg's work *The Night Battles: Witchcraft and Agrarian Cults in the 16th and 17th Centuries* (1983), on the *benandanti,* a group of sixteenth-century Friulian men who belonged to a secret brotherhood that fought against *malandanti* (evil sorcerers) for the fertility of crops. Inquisitors, at first puzzled by this legend, finally interpreted it as a form of witchcraft, and executed the *benandanti*. Martello was also the first Neo-Pagan author to mention the Neapolitan word for witch—*janara*—and to point out its linguistic connection to those who worshipped Diana.[30]

Perhaps Martello's most startling claim is that the old religion was linked with the *Mafia*. He explains the origin of the word *Mafia* as a combination of *mater* and *fidelitas*—faith to the mother (goddess)—or *mater* and *filia*, mother (Demeter) and daughter (Persephone).[31] In fact, many aspects of Martello's presentation of Sicilian craft are reminiscent of this particular pernicious Italian stereotype: the emphasis on family, blood oaths, honor, and vendetta. "Sicilian *streghe* live by the concepts of *omertà* and vendetta, and do not believe in 'turning the other cheek,'" he writes.[32] It is likely that contemporary constructions of Italian-American identity—most notably, the publication of Mario Puzo's *The Godfather* and its subsequent film version—may have influenced Martello's interpretation and framing of his traditions. In this classic example of folklore reclamation, Martello successfully reclaims a negative stereotype and infuses it with a new, positive meaning.

Another important contributor to the emergence of Italian-American Witchcraft is Lori Bruno. Born in 1940 in New York City, she traces her ancestry to the Dominican monk Giordano Bruno, burned at the stake in 1600 for heresy, and to a woman executed in Catania for lancing the swellings associated with the bubonic plague.[33] Bruno grew up in a family where many forms of folk magic were practiced: Both her mother and grandmother were healers, and her grandmother was also a midwife in the area of Nola (Campania), near Naples. Divination, the removal of the evil eye, the magical cutting away of illness with a special knife, and the use of prayer to heal were all part of Bruno's everyday childhood experience. This form of folk magic was, like Martello's, a secret tradition, handed on from one relative to another: "a sacred priesthood," she calls it, rooted in ethical principles of honor and respect. Bruno's family also seems to have practiced some form of altered consciousness which was used in healing: "My parents told me, 'When you need to leave [your body], it will happen. And when they touch us, we feel them with a warmth that touches, that fills your whole body. And we walk with them—we walk with the gods.'"[34] Bruno movingly described her use of this technique to save her granddaughter, who was born with a heart defect and hovered near death for days afterward. "I called on Aesclepius, Apollo—I walked with them," she explains. Today, the child is healthy.[35]

In addition to her private, family-based practices, Bruno co-founded the Trinacrian Rose Coven with Martello. Here, Sicilian traditions are modified and combined with a more standardized magical practice, which includes group worship in a circle, the observance of the eight sabbats, and a commitment to political and social action. Although the coven does initiate members, Bruno declared: "I cannot make a Strega. Do you know who makes the Strega? It is the gods and goddesses—the hand that touches you that causes the quickening, that wakes your memories of a different life."[36] In other words, although techniques and rituals can be learned, Bruno maintains the Old World belief that a certain part of Witchcraft is inborn—one must "have the light in

them," as she says, to be a *Strega*. This attitude closely mirrors that of Italian practitioners of vernacular healing and magic, and reflects a cosmology transmitted through
Bruno's family traditions.

Leo Martello and Lori Bruno were among the first Italian Americans to combine
Italian folk magic traditions with more public forms of Neo-Pagan worship, and to
interpret their practice as an ancient pre-Christian religion, but the real architect of
Italian American revival Witchcraft is Raven Grimassi. Raven, who was born in Pittsburgh in 1951, is the son of an American GI and an Italian woman who met during the
Allied occupation of Naples. Grimassi's mother was born into a middle class family in
the town of Pagani (Campania); soon after her birth, the family relocated to Naples, a
center of occultism in Italian popular culture. Her family preserved a number of magical traditions, including removal of the evil eye, divination, and the making of curative
liqueurs and tonics by steeping herbs in olive oil. Grimassi's mother is also an active
bearer of folktales, one of which features the moon becoming pregnant by the morning
star, called *Lucino* or *Lucifero*. It is easy to see how Grimassi connected this folktale to
Leland's legend of Diana and Lucifer, and began to interpret many aspects of his mother's folk culture as evidence of *la vecchia religione*.

Grimassi says he was initiated as an adolescent into the family tradition of magical
practice by an aunt—in reality, not a blood relative, but a close family friend. Echoing
Martello and Bruno, he describes this tradition as hereditary, limited to family members, based upon some inherent magical talent or ability, domestic, and secret. This fits
well with what we know about folk magical practice from the ethnographic record in
Italy. He also maintains that a maternal uncle taught him aspects of ceremonial magic
and what perhaps were Masonic practices; this is not unlikely because Naples has a
strong tradition of interest in ritual magic and the occult, and the Masons continue to
be an important networking organization for middle-class men, especially in southern
Italy. However, in his popular books *The Ways of the Strega* (1995), *Hereditary Witchcraft* (1999), and *Italian Witchcraft* (2000), he presents very different traditions. These
lay out in detail a system of beliefs, rituals, and practices that he claims hearken back
to *la vecchia religione*, which "survived relatively intact throughout Italy,"[37] but in
most ways resemble Wicca. Building upon Leland, his intent is to "restore the original
Tradition which Aradia had returned to the people"[38]—that is, nothing short of re-
creating the ancient religion of the Etruscan[39] and pre-Etruscan Italic peoples. However,
the context in which that religion existed is gone, as is the context in which Italian folk
magic existed before its journey to North America. Contemporary Italian Americans
who want to understand the magico-religious practices of their elders have little to go
on to reconstruct this original context. To make these folk practices understandable as
part of an ancient religion, Grimassi must build a coherent system that his contempo-
raries can understand and adapt for their own magical practice. That system is fundamentally Wiccan in structure.

In our conversations, Grimassi was surprisingly candid about his role as an inventor
of much of what appears in his books. Motivated partly by a desire to share some of
his family's folk traditions, he is nevertheless aware that much of that knowledge does
not translate well into a popular New Age format. Many of his family practices pertain
to rural life; others include manipulative magic and counter-magic that violate modern

Author Raven Grimassi (1951–), creator of modern Stregheria, *or Italian-American revival* Witchcraft. *(Photograph courtesy of Raven Grimassi.)*

Wiccan ethics about harming none. Others still are so rooted in a peasant context that contemporary American Neo-Pagans find them disturbing. For example, he described a classic folk cure that involves rubbing the body all over with a piece of meat or pork fat. The meat, having absorbed the illness through the magical principle of contagion, is buried or is thrown into the ocean, symbolically taking away the disease. Contemporary Witches are grossed out by this, he observed, and he jokingly imagined their reaction if he were to publish such a spell in his books: "I'm vegan; can I use broccoli instead? Can I use tofu?" Not the least of his hesitations is that his mother, a formidable woman, is distressed by the idea that her son could reveal secret magical practices to nonfamily members. So, instead of collecting and preserving his family's folklore,[40] he elaborates on it, using scholarly sources to reconstruct the missing historical and ethnographic context. When he cannot reconstruct, he invents.

Grimassi presents Italian Witchcraft as consisting of three traditions, or clans, as he calls them: the northern-Italian *Fanarra* and the central-Italian *Janarra* and *Tanarra*. In Campania, *janara* is a dialectical word for "witch," but I could find no evidence of the other terms in Italian dialectical dictionaries. Interestingly, he makes no reference to southern-Italian traditions even though the largest percentage of Italian immigrants to North America, including his own mother, came from that area. Each tradition is led by a *Grimas* (leader)[41] and organized into *boschetti* (groves). The *streghe* of Grimassi's *Stregheria*, like Gardnerian Witches, worship in sacred circles, cast with elaborate formulas and gestures, and are watched over by *Grigori* (guardians). They worship a goddess-and-god pair variously called Diana and Dianus, Fana and Faunus, or their Etrurian counterparts Tana and Tanus. They celebrate eight sabbats: *la festa dell'ombra* (the feast of the shadow, October 31), *la festa dell' inverno* (the feast of winter, December 21), *la festa di Lupercus* (the feast of Lupercus, February 2), *l'equinozio della primavera* (Spring Equinox, March 21), *la giornata di Diana* (Diana's day, May 1), *la festa dell'estate* (the feast of summer, June 21), *Cornucopia* (August 1), *l'equinozio d'autunno* (Fall Equinox, September 21), and the full moons; and have life-cycle rites for initiations, weddings, child blessings, and funerals. In other words, except for their Italian names, their rituals are in many ways much like those of other revival Witches. This renaming of tradition to make it seem Italian is part of an authenticity-creating process that I noted previously in regard to foodways.[42] *Stregheria* differs from non–Italian-American Witchcraft mostly in its focus on Italic deities, its emphasis on *lasa* or *lares* (ancestor spirits), and its Italian-centered mythology.

Some of what Grimassi presents is clearly drawn from his own family's knowledge and practice, and has many analogues in Italian folklore collections. He gives several spells, which have analogues in Italian folklore collections, to turn away the evil eye,[43] as well as one to St. Anthony to retrieve lost objects, and another to Sts. Peter and Blaise to bless a holy stone.[44] His "Nanta Bag"[45] seems to be a rendition of Italian *brevi*, small pouches holding sacred objects hung around the neck for protection. He also describes divination using oil and water or cards that is in keeping with documented Italian and Italian-American folk practices. However, the majority of his materials are culled from historical or ethnographic sources, which he reinterprets to suit his particular bent. From Leland's *Etruscan Roman Remains* (1980; originally published in 1892), he borrows the names of the ancient Etruscan deities and the importance of ancestor spirits in early Italic religion. He adapts the Etruscan alphabet, which he restyles as a secret *Strega* alphabet, from works of popular archeology. The Inquisitorial reports of the society of Diana and the *benandanti* are drawn from the works of historian Carlo Ginzburg. Grimassi borrows the concept of the *veglia*, an evening of traditional story-telling, from Alessandro Falassi's *Folklore by the Fireside* (1980) and reinterprets it as a witch family practice during which a kind of credo is recited. I even found in *Hereditary Witchcraft* a spell against the evil eye drawn verbatim from Frances Malpezzi's and William Clements' *Italian American Folklore* (1992), which is probably a result of my signaling that book to him as part of an extended e-mail exchange in 1996.[46] Although Malpezzi and Clements present it as Piemontese, Grimassi calls it a Sicilian spell passed on orally on the winter solstice.[47]

To be fair, Grimassi never claims to be reproducing exactly what was practiced by Italian immigrants to North America. He admits that Italian-American Witches "have adapted a few Wiccan elements into their ways"[48] and acknowledges that he has expanded upon the traditions that he learned from his mother to restore the tradition to its original state.[49] In attempting to restore an ancient tradition, though, Grimassi has in fact created a new one: a potpourri of folklore, revised history, and contemporary magical practice that bears little resemblance to anything that was ever practiced in Italy, before or after the Inquisition. The now-diffuse Wiccan rituals and practices are reworked, renamed, and recast as Etruscan worship; scholarly work is used to create a link between ancient religion, medieval belief, and contemporary revival; and folk magic is reinterpreted as the practice of an archaic cult. Almost any folk custom can be reinterpreted as evidence of the preservation of the old religion. For instance, Grimassi told me his family kept a *lararium* (ancestor shrine). When I asked him to describe it in detail, he described a niche or shelf on the wall where photographs of dead relatives were kept, on which his mother would put a candle or some flowers in water—the classic configuration found in many Italian and Italian-American homes. Grimassi has reinterpreted a standard folk practice in light of his survivalist views.

Grimassi's books (published by Llewellyn, a New Age press) have been quite successful, selling about 60,000 copies apiece and spawning numerous Web sites and imitators. Raven himself has initiated many individuals through classes and magic circles, which meet in a room behind his well-appointed, pristine occult shop in Escondido, California.[50] These individuals in turn have initiated others, bringing the total number of initiates in his line to about 70. Only one-third of his initiates are of Italian extraction; the rest become Italian through a special adoption ritual.

Although it is difficult to assess the influence of Martello, Bruno, and Grimassi on Italian Americans as a whole, I will present a few examples of how certain individuals have interpreted their own experiences in light of their reading of these authors.

FABRISIA

Fabrisia, an early—albeit currently alienated—disciple of Raven Grimassi, is a third-generation, Italian American born and raised in Massachusetts. She now lives in Florida, where she and her husband operate a chicken farm. Fabrisia considers herself a hereditary witch; although her family did not formally initiate her into the practice, she believes that her grandmother was a *strega*, albeit under a veneer of Catholicism.

My grandmother Adelina [was] from Livorno, Italy and [my other] grandmother Mariona and grandfather Primo were from Parma. [They] were very closed and withdrawn to ANYONE who wasn't Italian, and I mean "off the boat." My grandmother had the "obligatory" Catholic statues. I remember my grandmother always had a wonderful herb garden, and on one side of it was a statue of Mary. When she cut herbs or worked in the garden, she always turned the statue away from her work. . . . I remember them working potions and charms, always in Italiano, so as a child, I only got bits and pieces of what they were doing. When my grandmother passed over in 1963, there was no Catholic "thing," only a simple ritual at her home. Her athame[51] was buried with her along with a variety of stones to "help her on her way." She was buried in a cemetery and flowers strewn over her grave. I was only eight years old and "knew" this was different.[52]

What is striking about Fabrisia's description is how closely it adheres to the parameters of the classic Italian-American experience. She describes *not* the elaborate sabbats of Grimassi but rather an herb garden, the making of herbal remedies and charms, the presence of a special knife, and a simple funeral, perhaps because of poverty or personal preference. She now sees these as conscious acts of resistance against Catholicism, evidence of the preservation of an ancient religion under the guise of conformity. She elaborates further on this when she narrates the story of her grandfather:

My grandfather Primo was a caretaker at a Catholic church. What a way to stay hidden. Primo's father Luigi was also a caretaker at this same church. Luigi's brother Salvatore was a priest and worked closely with many popes. . . . According to family "tales," many who attended this church were of The Ways.[53] Since my dad won't discuss this, I am at a loss to know for sure. . . .[54]

Here, Fabrisia interprets her relatives' religious activities as paganism hiding under the noses of the priests, even the Pope himself. Although she first says that according to family legends, her relatives practiced a pagan religion, she also adds that her father refuses to discuss these matters with her. Although the reasons for his silence remain a mystery, to Fabrisia, they suggest complicity in a secret magical tradition. The evidence that Fabrisia presents might be interpreted in a number of ways, yet she chooses to interpret it as a sign of her family's involvement with *la vecchia religione* and as an affirmation of her current spiritual path—one that does not include Catholicism, but strives to re-create an older, pre-Christian practice.

PHILIP

Forty-eight-year-old Philip, who does not state his ethnic background, grew up in a Fundamentalist Christian household; his father was the minister of a small church.[55] "I am a *benandanti* [sic]," he says. From the time that he was a small boy, Philip remembers a series of strange experiences in which he felt that he was leaving his body:

Before I could walk, I left my crib and traveled down the hall on legs not made of flesh. . . . When I was eight, I got up from my bed and crossed the room to turn on the light only to have my hand pass through the wall. Night after night, I was tormented by the electric, paralyzed feeling of being disincarnate and trying to cram myself back into my body knowing if I did not make it back by dawn I would die. . . . I've kept this to myself most of my life, a life that has been warped and twisted as I searched for an answer from religion and science. The former exorcised me, the latter operated on me for sleep apnea. Yet to this day, when I lay down to sleep, I don't know if I am going to dream or fly. . . . Nine years ago, I stopped fighting and let the night take me where it wanted me to go. I didn't have a name for it then, but that is when I became *benandanti*.

In search of an explanation for his unusual experiences, Philip came across Carlo Ginzburg's *The Night Battles* (1983), an account of the Inquisitorial persecution of the *benandanti*, literally "good walkers," who believed that they journeyed in spirit at certain appointed times of the year to fight evil sorcerers for the fertility of the crops. One became a *benandante* by being born with the amniotic sac intact, or "with the caul." Although the *benandanti* steadfastly denied accusations of witchcraft, Philip, inspired by Grimassi, interprets them as Witches, in the sense of "practitioners of a pre-Christian pagan religion." But here Philip departs from Grimassi's concept of initiatory traditions. Building upon the idea that *benandanti* were born, not made, he postulates a biogenetic component, perhaps related to birth trauma, which causes them to have out-of-body experiences. "*Benandanti* would appear in any culture, at any time, and into any social class without regard for or in reaction to the predominant religion," he postulates. "The shaman, mystic, prophet, seer, etc. reacts to an inner call. . . . These people stand outside of and in most cases, are antagonistic towards, the established religion." Here Philip's comments echo those of Lori Bruno, whose tradition incorporates altered states of consciousness and who believes that *Stregheria* is at least partly inborn. Although Philip's interpretations are problematic from an anthropological perspective, they allow him to see himself as part of an ongoing mystical tradition that exists in opposition to Christianity, much as he now sees himself in contrast to the Fundamentalist Christian tradition of his youth. The story of the *benandanti* has furnished Philip with a positive explanation for his frightening experiences, and a magical context in which to understand them.

Understanding the Appeal of *Stregheria*

What accounts for the growing popularity of this new religion and its construction of Italian ethnicity and identity? No single factor can explain the appeal of a new religion to a diverse group of people. However, I will focus on two principal mechanisms: the revaluing of traditional folk magical practices, and the politics of identity in North America in the 1990s, including the changing position of Italian Americans vis-à-vis other ethnic groups.

First and foremost, Neo-Pagan religions are frameworks for the practice of magic and ecstatic experience. As Philip's example demonstrates, it is that which pulls many participants away from mainstream religions and draws them toward contexts that provide opportunities to directly experience the sacred not available through official channels. For Italian Americans who, when they arrived in North America, experienced the stigmatization of their folk religious practices by the Irish-dominated Catholic clergy, *Stregheria* and its variants provide a way to reconnect with some of the ecstatic religious practices of their parents and grandparents. When these have been forgotten or buried, systems such as *Stregheria* furnish new traditions to replace them.

The first Italians to come to North America in large numbers at the end of the nineteenth century came primarily from the rural peasant class. They brought with them a body of traditional folk magical beliefs and practices that included a range of healing techniques, from the manufacture of tonics and philters to the use of prayers and spells, to family-based practices of vernacular magic that included divination and the use of altered states of consciousness. These traditions, which had helped *contadini* survive the harsh conditions of the Old World, were stigmatized and misunderstood in the New World as superstitious nonsense and markers of ignorance and backwardness. Representatives of the dominant culture, from social workers to Catholic clergy to educators, all decried the "superstitiousness" of Italian Americans and the tenacity with which they clung to their folk traditions. Instead of being a source of status within the community, folk-magic practices became a source of shame, and their practitioners increasingly hid their actions from prying outsiders and at times from family members, as well.

The scholarly investigation of folk-magic practices contributed to their stigmatization by ignoring their profoundly spiritual nature in an effort to appear more "scientific" and objective. Both Italian and American ethnographers have consistently failed to address the spiritual dimensions of folk practices, focusing instead on their relationship to social and economic structures. Folk magic has been portrayed either as a cultural survival (for example, by Giuseppe Pitrè) or as an emblem of underdevelopment or false consciousness (for example, by Antonio Gramsci and Ernesto De Martino). Italian-American revival Witchcraft represents a reclaiming of the interpretive structures as well as the practices themselves, adapting them to new social realities.

Stregheria and other forms of Italian revival Witchcraft revalue what has been devalued by these progressivist discourses. Instead of being viewed as signs of benightedness, folk-magic practices are recast as a complex system of occult and philosophical knowledge going back to the ancient Etruscans; rather than being regarded as superstitious nonsense, they become evidence of peasant resistance. Italian-American Witches can now interpret almost any folk practice in their family as a sign that they are the heirs to an ancient mystical religion—one that the Catholic Church helped to destroy.

This is particularly significant against the backdrop of the changing politics of identity in the 1990s. During the first half of the twentieth century, assimilationist paradigms dominated political approaches to ethnic identity: Immigrants were supposed to gradually give up their old ways and adopt the language, beliefs, and customs of the dominant Anglo-American culture. As a result of the Civil Rights movement of the 1960s, this model began to change. The new paradigm of multiculturalism emphasizes American society as a salad bowl, with each minority maintaining some ethnic distinctiveness while contributing to the flavor of the larger society. The Civil Rights movement also influenced the discourse of identity creation. Because African Americans, Native Americans, and others who struggled for civil rights had suffered egregiously at the hands of the dominant culture, discrimination and victimization became part of the mechanism for claiming a legitimate identity.

Many Italian Americans were caught in the middle of these shifting political sands. Most arrived at a time when the dominant paradigm emphasized acculturation and fitting in rather than ethnic resistance. Many shed or hid the practices that made them objects of discrimination. In creating an Italian-American ethnic identity, they often aligned themselves with Italian high culture, organizing Columbus Day celebrations and emphasizing Italian contributions to the arts. In the 1990s, though, this strategy increasingly backfired. Columbus Day parades as celebrations of Italian-American pride have been criticized as expressions of white imperialism and colonialism. In contrast with nonwhite immigrant groups that are perceived as having "authentic" cultural difference from the mainstream, Italian Americans have become subsumed under the category of dominant whites, often collectively labeled as "Anglo." In some cases, the new paradigm becomes an excuse for Italian-bashing by other European Americans: Grimassi began to explore Italian traditions after being attacked by Celtic Wiccans who blamed the Romans—and, by association, Italians—for the destruction of Celtic culture in Britain and Gaul. Yet, many Italian Americans remember times not long ago when they were targets of prejudice, discrimination, and hate crimes.

Although adherents are generally not consciously adopting this strategy, revival Witchcraft and Neo-Paganism create identity in part by aligning participants with oppressed indigenes and against the dominant cultural and religious paradigms. As Chas Clifton suggests, these religions "turn the literate, often college-educated modern witch into a noble savage."[56] *Stregheria* and allied forms use the folk traditions of Italian peasants as markers of authenticity against a cultural backdrop in which identity claims are more legitimate if they are framed by reclaiming the histories of the forgotten and the oppressed rather than by making reference to the products of elite culture. They at once ennoble folk traditions by giving them an illustrious pedigree; and they also disassociate Italians from the imperial heritage of Rome and, later, the Catholic Church, which have become politically incorrect and embarrassing to many Italian Americans.

On the surface, this approach to constructing identity appears to be the very opposite of the strategy employed by Italian Americans of earlier generations, who preferred to distance themselves from their peasant roots by aligning themselves with great men in Italian culture: Leonardo da Vinci, Michelangelo, Christopher Columbus, and the like. Yet ultimately, *Stregheria* substitutes one set of famous Italians for another: Aradia di Toscano and Giordano Bruno have simply replaced the earlier heroes. It also continues the Italian tradition of prejudice against, and erasure of, southern Italy by emphasizing the Tuscan (and thus central Italian) origin of magical traditions. As Tuscany is typically considered the birthplace of Italian literary and gastronomic culture, the imagined *Strega* is located in an Italian region with a prestigious and celebrated history.

At the same time, it is important to note that although *Stregheria* longs to create solidarity with the experiences of Italian peasants, it is a far cry from their cultures. Many *Streghe*, Grimassi included, do not speak, read, or write Italian, and are relatively uninformed about Italian history. Few *Streghe* have traveled to Italy, and of those, even fewer have actually visited rural villages where traditions of vernacular magic can still be found. Not all *Streghe* are of Italian descent, and those who are of Italian descent are often several generations removed from the immigrant experience. Perhaps as a result of this lack of direct contact with Italian culture, *Stregheria* tends to romanticize the Italian peasant past. Its image of rural Italian life has more in common with an Olive Garden (a national chain of Italian restaurants) commercial than with lived experience. It portrays Italian peasants as living in a land of plenty in harmony with nature, whereas the Italian peasant experience was generally one of hunger, poverty, and privation. It also removes the Christian element from Italian and Italian-American folkways, distorting their context and meaning in a way that renders them unrecognizable to their actual practitioners.

At root, this paradox may signal the ambivalence that Americans feel about issues of ethnicity. Many Americans would like to enjoy what they imagine as the benefits of belonging to an ethnic community: the warmth of a ready-made extended family; a feeling of being part of something greater than oneself; a connection to a noble heritage; and of course, colorful folk customs. However, few want to experience the limitations that accompany life within the confines of a small group, and even fewer the prejudice, discrimination, and poverty that are often part of the American ethnic experience. More to the point, because American discourses of ethnicity and class are inextricably intertwined, many Americans feel tremendous ambivalence about ethnicity: They want the feeling of belonging to an ethnic group without the inconvenience of belonging to the lower classes. Many positive representations of ethnicity are thus stripped of their class markers: sanitized, commodified, and rendered nonthreatening to a white, middle-class audience. In this, *Stregheria* is not different from other ethnic varieties of Neo-Pagan Witchcraft, or, for that matter, from other positive representations of ethnicity in the public view.

The reclamation of *Stregheria* also allows Italian Americans to reinterpret existing negative stereotypes, recasting them as positive: Martello turns the infamous Mafia into a secret society of goddess-worshippers, while Grimassi transforms the epithets of "witch," "heathen," and "pagan" into evidence of spirituality and devotion that have survived millennia. In the course of this, Italian folk-magic traditions are finding a new and unexpected life. Through this process, folk-magic practice has been transformed into a source of ethnic pride and distinctiveness in the face of an increasingly homogenizing mass culture.

Notes

Introduction: Listening with an Accent JOSEPH SCIORRA

I am grateful to Rosangela Briscese, George De Stefano, Jennifer Guglielmo, Leonard Primiano, Laura Ruberto, and Anthony Tamburri for offering their comments on an earlier version of the introduction.

1. Antonio Gramsci, *Selections from Cultural Writings* (Cambridge, Mass.: Harvard University Press, 1991). Folklore was an important component to Italian Marxist Antonio Gramsci's thoughts on the subaltern and hegemony. He viewed folklore as "a 'conception of the world and life' implicit to a large extent in determinate (in time and space) strata of society and in opposition also for the most part implicit, mechanical and objective to 'official' conceptions of the world" (ibid., 189). Because of the subjection of working people, the subaltern's conceptions of life were by definition "contradictory and fragmentary" (ibid., 194). "Not only does the people have no precise consciousness of its own historical identity, it is not even conscious of the historical identity or the exact limits of its adversary" (Antonio Gramsci, *Selections from the Prison Notebooks* [London: Lawrence and Wishart, 1976]). For Gramsci, folklore needs to be understood so that it can be "overcome" and "uproot[ed]" so as to "replace" it with "conceptions which are deemed to be superior" for the edification of the broad masses of people and radical social change. See Kate Crehan's elaboration on Gramsci in context of anthropology, *Gramsci, Culture and Anthropology* (Berkeley: University of California Press, 2002), and Laura E. Ruberto's *Gramsci, Migration, and the Representation of Women's Work in Italy and the U.S.* (Lanham, Md.: Lexington Books, 2007) for a Gramscian analysis of the cultural work of women in Italy and within the Italian diaspora.

2. Donna R. Gabaccia, *Italy's Many Diaspora* (Seattle: University of Washington Press, 2000), 177.

3. Joseph Sciorra, "Yard Shrines and Sidewalk Altars of New York's Italian-Americans," in *Perspectives in Vernacular Architecture* III, ed. Thomas Carter and Bernard L. Herman (Columbia: University of Missouri Press, 1989), 185–98.

4. In her article on the term "group" within folklore studies, Dorothy Noyes discusses the enactment of myriad affiliations and exclusions around the ceremonial climbing of a "greased pole" during the 1988 "Italian Market Days" festival in Philadelphia. Dorothy Noyes, "Group." *Journal of American Folklore* 108.429 (1995): 449–78.

5. Joseph Sciorra, "'We Go Where the Italians Live': Religious Processions as Ethnic and Territorial Markers in a Multi-ethnic Brooklyn Neighborhood," in *Gods of the City*, ed. Robert A. Orsi (Bloomington: Indiana University Press, 1999), 310–40.

6. Harris M. Berger and Giovanna P. Del Negro, *Identity and Everyday Life: Essays in the Study of Folklore, Music, and Popular Culture* (Middletown, Conn.: Wesleyan University Press, 2004), 3–22. For the purposes of this introduction, I have relied upon the more common term "folklore," although "folklife" is a more inclusive approach to expressive culture and one that I embrace. For further discussion of the disciplinary history of folklife, see Don Yoder, *Discovering American Folklife: Studies in Ethnic, Religious, and Regional Culture* (Ann Arbor: UMI Research Press, 1990) and Leonard Norman Primiano, "Folklife," in *Folklore: An Encyclopedia of Beliefs, Customs, Tales, Music and Art*, Vol. 1, ed. Thomas A. Green (Santa Barbara, Calif.: ABC-CLIO, 1997), 322–31. A useful introduction to folklore scholarship is Burt Feintuch, ed., *Eight Words for the Study of Expressive Culture* (Urbana: University of Illinois Press, 2003).

7. Richard Bauman, *Verbal Art as Performance* (Prospect Heights, Ill.: Waveland Press, 1977); Richard Bauman, "Performance," in *The International Encyclopedia of Communications*, Vol. III, ed. Erick Barnouw (Oxford: Oxford University Press, 1989), 262–66; Deborah A. Kapchan, "Performance." *Journal of American Folklore* 108(430) (1995): 479–508.

8. Alan Lomax, "Saga of a Folksong Hunter: A Twenty-year Odyssey with Cylinder, Disc and Tape." *HiFi Stereo Review*, May 1960. Reprinted online at http://www.culturalequity.org/alanlomax/ce_alanlomax_saga.jsp.

9. Pellegrino D'Acierno, "Cultural Lexicon: Italian American Key Terms," in *The Italian American Heritage*, ed. Pellegrino D'Acierno (New York: Garland Publishing, Inc., 1999), 708.

10. Mario Puzo, *The Fortunate Pilgrim* (New York: Bantam, 1985), 48.

11. D'Acierno, "Cultural Lexicon," 754.

12. Gloria Nardini, *Che Bella Figura! The Power of Performance in an Italian Ladies' Club in Chicago* (Albany: SUNY Press, 1999), 7.

13. Nardini, *Che Bella Figura!*, 18.

14. The cultural concept *gavon/cafone* is discussed in D'Acierno's "Cultural Lexicon," 711–12.

15. Luisa Del Giudice, ed., *Studies in Italian American Folklore* (Logan: Utah State University Press, 1993), 237–45.

16. The term has also been translated as a "suppressed" or "denied" culture. Birnbaum introduced Carbonaro and Nesti's Gramscian term to English readers. D'Acierno expanded upon the concept in his writing about Italian-American culture. Lucia Chiavola Birnbaum, "red, a little white, a lot of green, on a field of pink: a controversial design for an Italian component of a multicultural canon for the United States," in *From the Margin: Writings in Italian Americana*, ed. Anthony Julian Tamburri, Paolo A. Giordano, and Fred L. Gardaphé (West Lafayette, Ind.: Purdue University Press, 1991), 282–93; Antonio Carbonaro and Arnaldo Nesti, *La cultura negata: Caratteri e potenzialità della cultura popolare* (Rimini: Guaraldi Editore, 1975); Pellegrino D'Acierno, "The Making of the Italian American Cultural Identity: From *Cultura Negata* to Strong Identity," in *The Italian American Heritage*, xxxiii–liv.

17. Barbara Grizzuti Harrison, *Italian Days* (New York: Ticknor & Fields, 1989), 390–91; 143; 103.

18. Ibid., 77.

19. Ibid.

20. Anna L. Chairetakis, Liner notes for *"Chesta e La Voci Ca Canuscite*—This Is the Voice You Know: Southern Italian Mountain Music from Calabria, Campania, Basilicata and Abruzzo." Global Village C675." *New York Folklore* 25 (1–4) (1999), 110; Robert F. Harney, "Caboto and Other *Parentela*: The Uses of the Italian Canadian Past," in *From the Shores of Hardship: Italians in Canada. Essays by Robert F. Harney*, ed. Nicholas De Maria Harney (Welland, Ont.: Éditions Soleil, 1993), 10–13.

21. Robert Glenn Howard, "Electronic Hybridity: The Persistent Processes of the Vernacular Web." *Journal of American Folklore* 121(480) (2008): 203.

22. Elizabeth Mathias, "The Italian-American Funeral: Persistence through Change." *Western Folklore* 33(1) (1974): 35–50.

23. Philip V. Cannistraro, "The Duce and the *Prominenti*: Fascism and the Crisis of Italian and Italian American Leadership." *Altreitalie* 31 (July–December 2005): 76–86; see also Dorothy Noyes, "From Paese to Patria: An Italian American Pilgrimage to Rome in 1929," in *Studies in Italian American Folklore*, 127–52; see also Joan L. Saverino's essay in this book.

24. Mark I. Choate, *Emigrant Nation: The Making of Italy Abroad* (Cambridge, Mass.: Harvard University Press, 2008); Simone Cinotto, *"Glocal Italies: Un possible nuovo percorso per lo studio storico delle comunità italoamericane." Altreitalie* 32 (January–June 2006), 38–51; Pasquale Verdicchio, *Bound by Distance: Rethinking Nationalism through the Italian Diaspora* (Rutherford, N.J.: Fairleigh Dickinson University Press, 1997); Robert Viscusi, *Buried Caesars and Other Secrets of Italian American Writing* (Albany: SUNY Press, 2006).

25. Alessandra Belloni, *Tarantata: Dance of the Ancient Spider*. CD STA MM00117D. Boulder: Sounds True, 2000; Laura Biagi, "Spider Dreams: Ritual and Performance in Apulian Tarantismo." PhD diss., New York University, 2004; Birnbaum, "red, a little white, a lot of green, on a field of pink," 282–93; Lucia Chiavola Birnbaum, *Black Madonnas: Feminism, Religion & Politics in Italy* (Boston: Northeastern University Press, 1993); Luisa Del Giudice, "The Folk Music Revival and the Culture of Tarantismo in the Salento," in *Performing Ecstasies: Music, Dance, and Ritual in the Mediterranean*, ed. Luisa Del Giudice and Nancy van Deusen (Ottawa: The Institute of Mediaeval Music, 2005), 260–61; Luisa Del Giudice, "Alessandra Belloni: In Her Own Words," in *Oral History, Oral Cultures, and Italian Americans*, ed. Luisa Del Giudice (New York: Palgrave McMillan, 2009), 193–251; I Giullari di Piazza. *Earth, Sun & Moon*. CD LYRCD 7427. New York: Lyrichord, 1995; see Sabina Magliocco's essay on witchcraft in this book.

26. Richard Handler and Jocelyn Linnekin, "Tradition, Genuine or Spurious." *Journal of American Folklore* 97(385) (1984): 273–90.

27. D'Acierno, "The Making of the Italian American Cultural Identity," 604.

28. See Michael McCabe, *New York City Tattoo: The Oral History of an Urban Art* (Honolulu: Hardy Marks Publications, 1997) and Joseph Sciorra's "'Hip Hop from Italy and the Italian Diaspora': A Report from the 41st Parallel," *Altreitalie* 24 (January–June 2002): 86–104 and "The Ethnoscape of Hip Wop: Alterity and Authenticity in Italian-American Rap Music," in *Global Media, Culture, and Identity*, ed. Rohit Chopra and Radhika Gajjala (New York: Routledge, in press). The Italian-American contribution to subway art and rap music was the theme of the symposium "Eye-talian Flava: The Italian American Presence in Hip Hop," sponsored by the Calandra Institute and New York University's Casa Italiana Zerilli-Marimò, October 5, 2002.

29. Donald Tricarico, "Guido: Fashioning an Italian American Youth Subculture." *The Journal of Ethnic Studies* 19(1) (Spring 1991), 41–66; Donald Tricarico, "Youth Culture, Ethnic Choice, and the Identity Politics of Guido." *VIA* 18(1) (2007), 34–88; Donald Tricarico, "Dressing Italian Americans for the Spectacle: What

Difference Does Guido Perform?" in *The Men's Fashion Reader*, ed. Andre Reilly and Sarah Cosbey (New York: Fairchild Books, 2008), 265–78.

30. Berger and Del Negro, *Identity and Everyday Life*, 19–20; Luisa Del Giudice, "Folklore, Folklife," in *The Italian American Experience: An Encyclopedia*, ed. Salvatore J. LaGumina, Frank J. Cavaioli, Salvatore Primeggia, and Joseph A. Varacalli, (New York: Garland Publishing, Inc., 2000), 237–45; Leonard Norman Primiano, "'The Consciousness of God's Presence Will Keep You Well, Happy, and Singing': The Tradition of Innovation in the Music of Father Divine's Peace Mission Movement," in *The New Black Gods: Arthur Huff Fauset and the Study of African American Religions*, ed. Edward E. Curtis IV and Danielle Brune Sigler (Bloomington: Indiana University Press, 2009), 91–115.

31. Sciorra, "The Ethnoscape of Hip Wop."

32. Edvige Giunta, *Writing with an Accent: Contemporary Italian American Women Authors* (New York: Palgrave, 2002), 2.

33. Del Giudice, ed., *Studies in Italian American Folklore*; Del Giudice, ed., *Oral History, Oral Cultures*; Frances M. Malpezzi and William M. Clements, *Italian-American Folklore* (Little Rock: August House, 1992); Elizabeth L. Mathias and Richard Raspa, *Italian Folktales in America: The Verbal Art of an Immigrant Woman* (Detroit: Wayne State University Press, 1985); Dorothy Noyes, *Uses of Tradition: Arts of Italian Americans in Philadelphia* (Philadelphia: Philadelphia Folklore Project, 1989); David A. Taylor and John A. Williams, eds., *Old Ties, New Attachments: Italian-American Folklife in the West* (Washington: Library of Congress, 1992). Increasingly non-folklore scholars within Italian-American studies are turning their thoughts to vernacular culture, such as Mary Jo Bona, *By the Breath of Their Mouths: Narratives of Resistance in Italian America* (Albany: SUNY Press, 2010); D'Acierno, ed., *The Italian American Heritage* (1999); Fred L. Gardaphé, *Italian Signs, American Streets: The Evolution of Italian-American Narrative* (Durham, N.C.: Duke University Press, 1996); and Ruberto, *Gramsci, Migration, and the Representation of Women's Work in Italy and the U.S* (2007).

"Sunday Dinner? You Had to Be There!": The Social Significance of Food in Italian Harlem,

1920–40 SIMONE CINOTTO

This chapter was originally part of the interuniversity research project "Public and Private in Twentieth Century American History: State, Family and Subjectivity in Comparative Perspective" funded by the Italian Ministry of the University and Scientific Research (2001). My research was also made possible by a one-month fellowship from The Balch Institute for Ethnic Studies, Historical Society of Pennsylvania, Philadelphia (2000). I especially benefited from the insightful comments of Gerald J. Meyer, Joseph Sciorra, and Maurizio Vaudagna.

1. Herbert J. Gans, *The Urban Villagers: Group and Class in the Life of Italian Americans* (New York: The Free Press of Glencoe, 1962), 33.

2. Richard Gambino, *Blood of My Blood: The Dilemma of the Italian-Americans* (Garden City, N.Y.: Anchor Press, 1974), 17–23. For a narrative, autobiographical account of the food–family relationship see, among others, Jerre Mangione, *Mount'Allegro* (New York: Knopf, 1952); and, for a conscious "ethnic revivalist" point of view, Helen Barolini, *Festa: Recipes and Recollections of Italian Holidays* (San Diego: Harcourt Brace Jovanovich, 1988). Harvey Levenstein, one of the early historians of Italian-American food habits, insists upon the resistance to change by Italian immigrants in matters of food, in particular against the efforts of different agencies to "Americanize" their diet. Harvey A. Levenstein and Joseph Conlin, "The Food Habits of Italian Immigrants in America: An Examination of the Persistence of a Food Culture and the Rise of 'Fast Food' in America," in *Dominant Symbols in Popular Culture*, ed. Ray Browne et al. (Bowling Green, Ky.: Bowling Green Popular Culture Press, 1990); Harvey A. Levenstein, "The American Response to Italian Food." *Food and Foodways* 1(1) (1985).

3. On this last point, see Donna R. Gabaccia, *From Sicily to Elizabeth Street: Housing and Social Change Among Italian Immigrants, 1880–1930* (Albany: SUNY Press, 1984); and Maddalena Tirabassi, "Trends of Continuity and Signs of Change Among Italian Migrant Women," in *Le stelle e le strisce: studi americani e militari in onore di Raimondo Luraghi*, ed. Valeria Gennaro Lerda, (Milan: Bompiani, 1998), 283–98.

4. On Italian Harlem history, see Robert A. Orsi, *The Madonna of 115th Street: Faith and Community in Italian Harlem, 1880–1950* (New Haven: Yale University Press, 1985); Gerald J. Meyer, "Italian Harlem: Portrait of a Community," in *The Italians of New York: Five Centuries of Struggle and Achievement*, ed. Gerald J. Meyer and Philip V. Cannistraro (New York: New-York Historical Society and John D. Calandra Italian American Institute, 1999); and Nadia Venturini, *Neri e italiani ad Harlem: gli anni Trenta e la Guerra d'Etiopia* (Rome: Edizioni Lavoro, 1990).

5. Covello's dissertation was published years after his defense: Leonard Covello, *The Social Background of the Italo-American School Child: A Study of the Southern Italian Family Mores and Their Effect on the School Situation in Italy and America* (Leiden, The Netherlands: Brill, 1967). The Covello Papers consists of more than 100 boxes of the written and photographic material he collected throughout his life. The collection is maintained by The Balch Institute for Ethnic Studies, Historical Society of Pennsylvania, Philadelphia. Covello died in Messina, Sicily, in 1982.

6. On the emergence of a distinct youth subculture in the 1920s, see Paula S. Fass, *The Damned and the Beautiful: American Youth in the 1920s* (New York: Oxford University Press, 1977).

7. Werner Sollors, "'Of Plymouth Rock and Jamestown and Ellis Island'; or, Ethnic Literature and Some Redefinitions of 'America,'" in *Immigrants in Two Democracies: French and American Experience*, ed. Donald L. Horowitz and Gérard Noiriel (New York: New York University Press, 1992), 221–22.

8. Leonard Covello, "Language Usage in Italian Families." *Atlantica* (October 1934): 329.

9. Helen Barolini, "Heritage Lost, Heritage Found." *Italian Americana* 16(2) (1998): 127.

10. B. V., quoted in Covello, *The Social Background*, 339.

11. Harvey A. Levenstein, *Revolution at the Table: The Transformation of the American Diet* (New York: Oxford University Press, 1988), 109–20.

12. Diane Ravitch, *The Great School Wars, New York City, 1805–1973: A History of the Public Schools as Battlefield of Social Change* (New York: Basic Books, 1974), 178.

13. Archie Bromson, "The Italian Peg and the American Hole," "Adjustment," folder 2, box 92, Covello Papers.

14. D. diB., quoted in Covello, *The Social Background*, 341.

15. Vito Teti, "Le culture alimentari nel Mezzogiorno continentale in età contemporanea," in .*Storia d'Italia: Annali*, ed. Alberto Capatti, Alberto De Bernardi, and Angelo Varni, 13: *L'alimentazione* (Turin: Einaudi, 1998), 137.

16. Claude Fischler, "Learned Versus 'Spontaneous' Dietetics: French Mothers' Views of What Children Should Eat." *Social Science Information* 25(4) (1986).

17. C. G., quoted in Covello, *The Social Background*, 315.

18. "Italian Family in America," folder 12, box 67, Covello Papers.

19. Edward Corsi, "My Neighborhood." *Outlook* (September 16, 1925): 92.

20. "Miss S.—20 years. Born in Italy. Came to U.S. at age of 7," "Girls," folder 2, box 68, Covello Papers.

21. Lucy H. Gillett, "Factors Influencing Nutrition Work Among Italians." *Journal of Home Economics* (January 1922): 16.

22. "Study of a Family," "Family in America," folder 17, box 93, Covello Papers.

23. Michael J. Eula, *Between Peasant and Urban Villager: Italian-Americans of New Jersey and New York, 1880–1980: The Structures of Counter-Discourse* (New York: Lang, 1993), 159–94.

24. Marie Concistre, "A Study of a Decade in the Life and Education of the Adult Immigrant Community in East Harlem" (PhD diss., New York University, 1943), 345.

25. Victor J. Vicesvinci, "The Italian Pattern in a Family That I Know Well," folder 23, box 67, Covello Papers.

26. Vicesvinci, "The Italian Pattern in a Family That I Know Well," folder 23, box 67, Covello Papers.

27. Velma Phillips and Laura Howell, "Racial and Other Differences in Dietary Customs." *Journal of Home Economics*, 41 (Sep. 1920): 405; Gertrude Gates Mudge, "Italian Dietary Adjustments." *Journal of Home Economics*, 15 (April 1923): 183–84; and Dorothy Wiehl, "The Diets of Low Income Families in New York City." *Milbank Memorial Fund Quarterly Bulletin* 11 (October 1933): 317–22.

28. Covello, *The Social Background*, 340.

29. "Life History, T. B., 1938," "Retention of Family Tradition in the 3rd Generation," folder 9, box 68, Covello Papers.

30. Peter Rofrano interview by Simone Cinotto, November 21, 1998, audiotape (in Simone Cinotto's possession), side 1.

31. Orsi, *The Madonna of 115th Street*, 77.

32. Mangione, *Mount'Allegro*, 136.

33. Leonard Covello, *The Heart Is the Teacher* (New York: McGraw-Hill, 1958), 36.

34. C. L. Tepedino, "Italo-American Family Problems, Jan. 1941," folder 18, box 93, Covello Papers.

35. "Louis Pesce," "Friends etc. in America," folder 2, box 68, Covello Papers; "C.V., 2nd gen. female, college grad.," "Family concept of friends America," folder 4, box 68, Covello Papers.

36. Mangione, *Mount'Allegro*, 24–25.

37. Tirabassi, "Trends of Continuity," 287–88.

38. Gambino, *Blood of My Blood*, 24. For an ethnographic account of the work of accumulation of social capital performed by Italian-American women in the family sphere, see Micaela Di Leonardo, *The Varieties of Ethnic Experience: Kinship, Class, and Gender among California Italian Americans* (Ithaca, N.Y.: Cornell University Press, 1994), 191–229.

39. Marzio Barbagli, *Sotto lo stesso tetto: mutamenti della famiglia in Italia dal XV al XX secolo* (Bologna: Il Mulino, 1984), 115–21; Giovanna Da Molin, *La famiglia nel passato: strutture familiari nel Regno di Napoli in età moderna* (Bari: Laterza, 1990); and Francesco Benigno, "Famiglia mediterranea e modelli anglosassoni," *Meridiana* 6 (May 1989).

40. Gabaccia, *From Sicily to Elizabeth Street*, 115.

41. Robert A. Orsi, "The Fault of Memory: 'Southern Italy' in the Imagination of Immigrants and the Lives of Their Children in Italian Harlem, 1920–1945." *Journal of Family History* 15(2) (1990): 133–47.

42. "C. G., 1st Generation, Came to America at Age of 30," "La famiglia in America," folder 4, box 68, Covello Papers.

43. Mangione, *Mount'Allegro*, 18–19.

44. Steven Mintz and Susan Kellogg, *Domestic Revolutions: A Social History of American Family Life* (New York: Basic Books, 1988), 113–19.

45. "Family," "Person Interviewed: Man, 58 years of Age. Came to America about 1908, Married Here. Locality—Girgenti, Sicily. Class—Landless Workers," folder 10, box 68, Covello Papers.

46. "Marriage Concepts of Italian Girls," "Italo-American 42 Years Old, Came to US as a Boy of 3, Father of 5 Girls, 1 Boy," folder 1, box 68, Covello Papers.

47. "C. G.," Untitled, folder 6, box 68, Covello Papers; "Endogamy among Italo-Americans. Old Man, Born Near Bari, Apulia," folder 1, box 68, Covello Papers.

48. "Case Study, R. M., 1943," "Persistence of Italian Family Tradition," folder 7, box 68, Covello Papers.

49. "Cultural Changes, from Life History, Vito Maglio, H. S. grad male," folder 1, box 68, Covello Papers.

50. Eula, *Between Peasant and Urban Villager*, 174–75; "Classification of Nationalities by Proportion of Intermarriage: Men and Women of 1st, 2nd, and 3rd Generations, 1908–1912," folder 18, box 65, Covello Papers.

51. "Tony the Cleaner," "Marriage among Italo-Americans," folder 5, box 68, Covello Papers.

52. "Life History," quoted in Covello, *The Social Background*, 347.

53. "Retention of Old Customs," "From Case Study, 1938," folder 9, box 68, Covello Papers.

54. Robert A. Orsi, "The Religious Boundaries of an In-between People: Street *Feste* and the Problem of the Dark-Skinned Other in Italian Harlem, 1920–1990." *American Quarterly* 44(3) (September 1992): 313–47. On the acceptance of the racist discourse as a fundamental passage of the process of construction of an Italian-American identity, see also Jennifer Guglielmo and Salvatore Salerno, eds., *Are Italians White? How Race Is Made in America* (New York: Routledge, 2003) and David A.J. Richards, *Italian American: The Racializing of an Ethnic Identity* (New York: New York University Press, 1999).

55. L. V., quoted in Covello, *The Social Background*, 350.

56. Vito Teti, *La razza maledetta: origini del pregiudizio antimeridionale* (Rome: ManifestoLibri, 1993); and Peter D'Agostino, "Craniums, Criminals, and the 'Cursed Race': Italian Anthropology in American Racial Thought, 1861–1924." *Comparative Studies in Society and History* 44 (2002): 319–43.

57. Matthew Fryre Jacobson, *Whiteness of a Different Color: European Immigrants and the Alchemy of Race* (Cambridge, Mass.: Harvard University Press, 1998), 56–62.

58. Donna R. Gabaccia, *We Are What We Eat: Ethnic Food and the Making of Americans* (Cambridge, Mass.: Harvard University Press, 1998); Levenstein and Conlin, "The Food Habits"; Levenstein, "The American Response."

59. Laurence R. Chenault, *The Puerto Rican Migrant in New York City* (New York: Columbia University Press, 1938); Federal Writers' Project, *New York City Guide* (New York: Random House, 1939), 265–68; Charles E. Hewitt Jr., "Welcome: Paupers and Crime: Porto Rico's Shocking Gift to the United States." *Scribner's Commentator* (March 1940); and Howard A. Rusk, "The Facts Don't Rhyme—An Analysis of Irony in Lyrics Linking Puerto Rico's Breezes to Tropic Diseases." *The New York Times*, September 29, 1957.

60. Thomas Sugrue, "The Toughest Street in New York." *New York Herald Tribune*, January 17, 1932; and Federal Writers' Project (eds., Roy Ottley and William J. Weatherby), "The Depression in Harlem," in *Hitting Home: The Great Depression in Town and Country*, ed. Bernard Sternsher (Chicago: Quadrangle Books, 1970).

61. Clarence Woodbury, "Our Worst Slum: Can We Save It from Going Red?" *The American Magazine* (September 1949): 31.

62. Peter Pascale, "East Harlem," in Jeff Kisseloff, *You Must Remember This: An Oral History of Manhattan from the 1890s to World War II* (New York: Schocken Books, 1990), 354.

63. Covello, *The Heart Is the Teacher*, 223.

Cuscuszu in Detroit, July 18, 1993: Memory, Conflict, and *Bella Figura* During a Sicilian-American Meal   JOHN ALLAN CICALA

I wish to thank my aunts and uncle (Katie, Rose, and Joseph), my grandmother (Leonarda), and my father (John Cicala), for allowing me to interview them and document *cuscuszu* preparation and meal that took place on July 18, 1993. I have benefited from discussions on the *cuscuszu* complex with these intimates; other relations (who wished not to be named); and with folklorists, including my dissertation advisor at the Folklore Institute, Indiana University, the late Warren Roberts, Simon Bronner, Michael Owen Jones, Henry Glassie, Robert Orsi, Janet Theophano, Susan Kalcik, Yvonne Lockwood, and Janet Langlois. I am especially indebted to editor Joseph Sciorra, whose critical uncompromising eye forced me to overcome my fear of breaking the Sicilian rule of silence concerning family affairs—*omertà*—by forcing me to stay focused on a very sensitive topic and carry it through to its logical conclusion.

1. Dennis Mack Smith, *Medieval Sicily: 800–1713* (New York: Dorset Press, 1968), 3–12.

2. Interview with Rosina Selvaggio, Roseville, Michigan, April 10, 1990.

3. Susan L. Scheiberg discusses the issues of doing fieldwork with one's family or friends in her "A Folklorist in the Family: On the Process of Fieldwork Among Intimates." *Western Folklore* 49(2) (April, 1990): 208–14.

4. For a discussion of the importance of the family in Sicily and America, see Richard Gambino, *Blood of My Blood: The Dilemma of Italian Americans* (Toronto: Guernica, 1997), 1–41.

5. The definition of behavioristics can be found in Simon J. Bronner, "Chain Carvers in Southern Indiana: A Behavioristic Study in Material Culture" (PhD diss., Indiana University, 1981), 56–62. For an overview of behaviorism's importance to theoretical folklore issues, see Michael Owen Jones, "L.A. Add-ons and Re-dos: Renovation in Folk Art and Architectural Design," in *Perspectives on American Folk Art*, eds. Ian M.G. Quimby and Scott T. Swank (New York: W. W. Norton & Co., 1980), 325–63. Case studies using the behavioral methodology include Michael Owen Jones, *Craftsmen of the Cumberlands: Tradition & Creativity* (Lexington: The University Press of Kentucky, 1989); Simon J. Bronner, *Chain Carvers: Old Men Crafting Meaning* (Lexington: The University Press of Kentucky, 1985); and John Michael Vlach, *Charleston Blacksmith: The Work of Philip Simmons* (Athens: The University of Georgia Press, 1981.)

6. Bronner, "Chain Carvers in Southern Indiana," 57.

7. See Simon Bronner, *Chain Carvers: Old Men Crafting Meaning*, 126–44.

8. Jones, *Craftsmen of the Cumberlands: Tradition & Creativity*, 154–95.

9. John Michael Vlach, "Folk Craftsmen," in *Handbook of American Folklore*, ed. Richard M. Dorson (Bloomington: Indiana University Press, 1983), 303–4.

10. Ibid., 301–5.

11. The application of artifactual behaviorist method to include ceremonial cooking is discussed in John Allan Cicala's dissertation, "The Folk Artist as Producer: A Behavioral Study of a Sicilian Immigrant Woman's Ceremonial Cooking Style" (PhD diss., Indiana University, 1995), 63–109.

12. Norman Count Roger christened Erice, Monte San Giuliano, when he dreamed of Saint Julian ridding the Saracens with a pack of dogs while his army was laying siege to the town in the twelfth century. See Vincent Cronin, *The Golden Honeycomb* (New York: E. P. Dutton & Company, 1965), 18. Mussolini changed it back to its original classical designation of Eryx. Information on Eryx is covered in M. I. Finley, *Ancient Sicily to the Arab Conquest* (New York: Viking Press, 1968), 135–36.

13. Detroit *Montese* often said that one characteristic of the older generation was a reticence even when strangers were not around. My grandmother's quiet behavior was traditional, not idiosyncratic. When I was finally able to meet members of my extended family, my younger Americanized cousins humorously referred to their parents' and grandparents' inability to talk. One said that the *Montese* wear black, sit in a rocking chair, gossip a little, and wait to die. Every once in a while, she continued, they would decide to cook and when they did, they would make the most fabulous dishes found in Italy.

14. Interview with Katie Deyoub, Warren, Michigan, July 10, 1993.

15. Bronner, "Chain Carvers in Southern Indiana," 61–62.

16. Interview with Katie Deyoub, Warren, Michigan, July 15, 1993.

17. Maria Grammatico and Mary Taylor Simeti, *Bitter Almonds: Recollections and Recipes from a Sicilian Girlhood* (New York: William Morrow and Company), 26–27.

18. Grammatico and Simeti.

19. Interview with Katie Deyoub, Warren, Michigan, July 16, 1993.

20. Ibid. Maria Grammatico describes similar patterns of behavior when she reviews a day in her life at the San Carlo Institute during the 1960s; see Grammatico and Simeti, *Bitter Almonds*, 29–49.

21. Interview with Katie Deyoub, Warren, Michigan, August 1, 1993.

22. This information was collected from my father, John Cicala, my uncle Joseph, and my aunt Rose between 1989 and 1993. I showed my aunt, Katie, the transcriptions concerning the Cicala family history on August 1, 1993. Five days later, August 6, 1993, we discussed the consistencies and inconsistencies in the narratives and decided on a version that contained the same elements in all the interviews.

23. Interview with Katie Deyoub, Warren, Michigan, August 1, 1993.

24. Ibid.

25. Ibid. Katie attributed this belief to her mother and to herself.

26. Gloria Nardini, *Che Bella Figura! The Power of Performance in an Italian Ladies' Club in Chicago* (Albany: SUNY Press, 1999), 7.

27. Interview with Katie Deyoub, Warren, Michigan, August 1, 1993.

28. Interview with Antonina DiCesare, at Katie's home in Warren, Michigan, December 20, 1992.

29. I describe in more detail the process that allowed me to get my grandmother's and my aunt's permission to show the photographs to Detroit *cuscuszu* makers for my research in my dissertation. See John Allan Cicala, "The Folk Artist as Producer," Chapter 3 "Field Strategies, Conflicts, and Ethics," 110–54.

30. Interview with Aurelia Tranchida, Birmingham, Michigan, February 10, 1993.

31. In Detroit, the fish-broth cure is made with a fish that Sicilians call *sadachi* and Americans refer to as "porgies." Detroit Sicilians may use other kinds of seafood, such as red snapper, whiting, and shrimp. The traditional Sicilian *cuscuszu* cooks in Detroit told me that it took three types of fish to make the *cuscuszu* cure: fatty, bony, and meaty. These would include *anguilla* and *bimorena* or eels for the fatty; *sarpa*, *scorfano*, and *cipolla* for the bony; and *sadachi*, *luali*, *occhiate*, *dendici*, and *merluzzo* for the meaty. These fish caught in Sicily made the most flavorful broth for the cure. See Cicala, "The Folk Artist as Producer," 226.

32. Interview with Katie Deyoub, Warren, Michigan, August 1, 1993.

33. Interview with Aurelia Tranchida, Birmingham, Michigan, February 10, 1993.

34. See Erving Goffman, *The Presentation of Self in Everyday Life* (Garden City, N.Y.: Doubleday, 1959), xi; and Mary Douglas, *Purity and Danger: An Analysis of the Concepts of Pollution and Taboo* (London: Routledge & Kegan Paul, 1966), 1–40.

35. Interview with Katie Deyoub, Warren, Michigan, August 10, 1993.

36. This is the implication I draw from her statement. See Nardini, *Che Bella Figura!*, 7.

37. Interview with Maria Rondello, Bloomfield Hills, Michigan, February 10, 1991.

38. Interview with Nina Selvaggio, Roseville, Michigan, March 15, 1992.

39. Interview with Katie Deyoub, Warren, Michigan, August 7, 1993.

40. The information from this section was derived from participant observation. The interpretation and analysis were the result of the conversations I had with Katie Deyoub, Warren, Michigan, August 1, 1993.

41. Ibid.

42. Ibid.

43. Ibid.

44. I was raised with the fear of revealing family secrets to the outside world. These secrets could consist of mentioning our vacation plans or that my father had gotten a new job. The secrecy was confined to my nuclear family, but it could also include the extended family as well. Talking about a family-oriented meal like *cuscuszu* to other relatives or friends—or even worse, making it known to the public through a publication— was forbidden even though no one ever said so explicitly. It was just something I knew, and the thought of talking about it made me tremble. However, this trend is changing. Recently, two Detroit Sicilian-Americans have written creative memoires that deal with affairs that formerly were so secret that they were not even discussed within the family circle. See Frank Viviano's *Blood Washes Blood*, in which he describes his personal journey involving his attempt to solve the murder of his great-grandfather (and namesake) near the Sicilian family village of Terrasini. More controversial is Karen Tintori's *Unto the Daughters*, which chronicles her effort to reclaim the identity of her great-aunt, who was raped, murdered, and thrown into the Detroit River by her brothers for refusing to marry her father's choice for a spouse, thereby dishonoring the family name.

45. Interview with Katie Deyoub, Warren, Michigan, August 1, 1993.

The Italian Immigrant Basement Kitchen in North America   LARA PASCALI

This article was originally published as "Two Stoves, Two Refrigerators, *Due Cucine*: The Italian Immigrant Home with Two Kitchens," *Gender Place and Culture: A Journal of Feminist Geography* 13, no. 6 (2006): 685–96. The paper was drawn from *Two Stoves, Two Refrigerators, Due Cucine: The Italian Immigrant Home with Two Kitchens* (Montreal: McGill University, 2004) written while I was a student in the Master of Architecture, Domestic Environments program at McGill University. This project was based on interviews and field-work conducted in Toronto, Montreal and New York, between January and September 2004 and was assisted by the McGill Centre for Research and Teaching on Women.

An immense number of people provided help with this research. I am especially indebted to all participants in this study who welcomed me into their homes. I would like to thank my friends and classmates who provided helpful commentary on preliminary drafts. In particular, I would like to thank Umberto and Erlinda Pascali and Joseph Sciorra for their invaluable assistance. Finally, I owe a very special thanks to Annmarie Adams for her never-ending guidance throughout this project.

1. I use the term "Italian" in the way that it is used colloquially among immigrants to signify a person of Italian origin/ancestry. Where the generation is unspecified, "Italian" refers to first-generation Italians: that is, Italians who immigrated to North America.

2. In Italy, homes with two kitchens are said to be a small trend, particularly in new housing units. In contrast, homes with two kitchens in North America are increasingly becoming obsolete.

3. The concept of invisible objects and their capacity to project ideologies is discussed in Daniel Miller, "Materiality: An Introduction," in *Materiality*, ed. Daniel Miller (Durham: Duke University Press, 2005), 1–50.

4. Michael Ann Williams, *Homeplace: The Social Use and Meaning of the Folk Dwelling in Southwestern North Carolina* (Athens: University of Georgia Press, 1991), 20.

5. February 23, 2004.

6. Gerald L. Pocius, "'Interior Motives': Rooms, Objects and Meaning in Atlantic Canada Homes." *Material History Bulletin* 15 (1982): 7.

7. September 2004.

8. This is the argument presented in Jennifer Lucchino, "Deciphering Italian American Kitchen Design," in *A Tavola: Food Tradition and Community Among Italian Americans*, ed. Edvige Giunta and Samuel J. Patti (Staten Island, N.Y.: American Historical Society, 1996), 55.

9. Luisa Del Giudice, "The 'Archvilla': An Italian Canadian Architectural Archetype," in *Studies in Italian American Folklore*, ed. Luisa Del Giudice (Logan: Utah State University Press, 1993), 79.

10. February 23, 2004.

11. September 27, 2004.

12. See Annmarie Adams, "The Eichler Home," in *Gender, Class and Shelter, Perspectives in Vernacular Architecture V*, ed. Elizabeth C. Cromley and Carter L. Hudgins (Knoxville: University of Tennessee Press, 1995), 164–78.

13. See Gwendolyn Wright, *Building the Dream: A Social History of Housing* (New York: Pantheon Books, 1981), 158–76; Dolores Hayden, *The Grand Domestic Revolution: A History of Feminist Designs for American Homes, Neighborhoods and Cities* (Cambridge, Mass.: The MIT Press, 1981), 57–58; Anthony King, *The Bungalow: The Production of a Global Culture* (London, Boston, Melbourne, and Henley: Routledge & Kegan Paul, 1984), 127–55; Peter Ward, *A History of Domestic Space: Privacy and the Canadian Home* (Vancouver and Toronto: UBC Press, 1999, 38–41); and Clifford E. Clark, *The American Family Home* (Chapel Hill and London: University of North Carolina Press, 1986), 171–92.

14. March 5, 2004. A number of Italian women prefer to cook downstairs because of the desire to hide the smells of cooking. Attitudes toward smell have changed according to cultural background and time period. See Elizabeth C. Cromley, "Transforming the Food Axis: Housing, Tools and Modes of Analysis." *Material History Review* 44 (1996): 8–22; and Constance Classen, David Howes, and Anthony Synnott, *Aroma: The Cultural History of Smell* (London and New York: Routledge, 1994). On cleanliness and germs, see Nancy Tomes, *The Gospel of Germs: Men, Women and the Microbe in American Life* (Cambridge, Mass.: Harvard University Press, 1998); and Ellen Lupton and J. Abbott Miller, *The Bathroom, the Kitchen and the Aesthetics of Waste: A Process of Elimination* (Cambridge, Mass.: The MIT List Press, 1992).

15. September 27, 2004.

16. Mary Douglas, *Purity and Danger: An Analysis of Concepts of Pollution and Taboo* (New York and Washington: Praeger, 1966), 7, 68.

17. See Elizabeth Shove, *Comfort, Cleanliness and Convenience: The Social Organization of Normality* (Oxford and New York: Berg, 2003).

18. See Cromley.

19. For a discussion of the Newfoundland kitchen, see Marylin Porter, "'She Was Skipper of the Shore Crew': Notes on the History of the Sexual Division of Labour in Newfoundland," in *Their Lives and Times: Women in Newfoundland and Labrador, a Collage*, ed. Carmelita McGraith, Barbara Neis, and Marilyn Porter (St. John's, Newfoundland: Killick Press, 1995); Gerald L. Pocius, *A Place to Belong: Community Order and Everyday Space in Calvert, Newfoundland* (Athens, Georgia, and London: University of Georgia Press; Montreal and Kingston: McGill University Press, 1991); and Robert Mellin, *Tilting: House Launching, Slide Hauling, Potato Trenching, and Other Tales From a Newfoundland Fishing Village* (New York: Princeton Architectural Press, 2003).

20. February 23, 2004.

21. Clifford E. Clark, "The Vision of the Dining Room: Plan Book Dreams and Middle-Class Realities," in *Dining in America: 1850–1900*, ed. Kathryn Grover (Amherst: University of Massachusetts Press, 1987), 142–72.

22. Katherine C. Grier, "The Decline of the Memory Palace: the Parlor After 1890," in *American Home Life, 1880–1930: A Social History of Spaces and Services*, ed. Jessica H. Foy and Thomas J. Scherlereth (Knoxville: University of Tennessee Press, 1992), 56. See also Grier, *Culture and Comfort: People, Parlors and Upholstery, 1850–1930* (Amherst: University of Massachusetts Press, 1988).

23. Pocius has noted in his study of Calvert, Newfoundland, that the homes in this community often have front rooms that display a family's best furniture but are almost never used. Instead, friends and family congregate in the back kitchen. See Pocius, *A Place to Belong*, 238–50.

24. Del Giudice, "The 'Archvilla,'" 56.

25. Interior embellishment has often been an important socioeconomic marker. The material culture of working-class immigrants in the United States at the turn of the twentieth century was characterized by a preference for what was considered more extravagant decorative treatments and furniture that embodied the ideal of upper-class European rural societies. See Lizabeth Cohen, "Embellishing a Life of Labor: An Interpretation of the Material Culture of American Working-class Homes, 1885–1915," in *Common Places: Readings in Vernacular Architecture*, ed. Dell Upton and John Michael Vlach (Athens, Georgia, and London: University of Georgia Press, 1986), 261–80.

26. As a community, Italians were particularly successful in achieving home ownership. The high percentage rates indicate the fundamental importance of home ownership to achieving success. For statistics, see Richard Harris, *Creeping Conformity: How Canada Became Suburban, 1900–1960* (Toronto, Buffalo, and London: University of Toronto Press, 2004), 28; and Nicholas De Maria Harney, *Eh Paesan! Being Italian in Toronto* (Toronto: University of Toronto Press, 1991), 28.

27. Women played key roles in the contribution and management of household incomes. In Toronto, many women took menial jobs to help support the family and contribute to purchasing a home. Women also drew upon inexpensive ways of generating food, such as growing vegetables and preserving foods. See Franca Iacovetta, *Such Hardworking People: Italian Immigrants in Postwar Toronto* (Montreal and Kingston: McGill–Queen's University Press, 1992), 90–93.

28. Orlando Barone also suggests that the division between upstairs and downstairs may be linked to what were considered elite notions of home.

29. Gloria Nardini, *Che Bella Figura! The Power of Performance in an Italian Ladies' Club in Chicago* (Albany: SUNY Press, 1999), 7.

30. For another example of an architectural marker among Italian immigrants, see Joseph Sciorra, "Yard Shrines and Sidewalk Altars of New York's Italian-Americans," in *Perspectives in Vernacular Architecture* III, ed. Thomas Carter and Bernard L. Herman (Columbia: University of Missouri Press, 1989), 185–98.

31. September 21, 2004.

32. September 21, 2004.

33. March 14, 2004. Translated from Italian by the author.

34. It is because of this lack of demand that in the early 1990s, Ennio Di Fiore stopped building homes with two kitchens.

35. March 1, 2004.

36. March 5, 2004.

37. March 14, 2004.

Creative Responses to the Italian Immigrant Experience in California: Baldassare Forestiere's Underground Gardens and Simon Rodia's Watts Towers   KENNETH SCAMBRAY

1. Although Metz used the term "grassroots art" to describe Rodia's Watts Towers, she explains that the term "grassroots art" has now been replaced by the more recent "outsider art." She points out that her husband and colleague, Bob Foster, continues to use the term "folk art environments." See *Outsider Architectures: Laboratories of the Imaginary*, special issue of *The Southern Quarterly: A Journal of the Arts in the South*, ed. Frédéric Allamel, No. 1–2 (Fall-Winter 2000/2001). I would like to thank Joseph Sciorra for bringing Metz' presentation at the Calandra Institute and her article to my attention.

2. *Outsider Architectures*, 215.

3. *Watts Towers*. Los Angeles: Getty Conservation Institute and J. Paul Getty Museum, 1997, 13, 15, and 63. See also Roger Cardinal's *Outsider Art* (London: Studio Vista, 1972) and William Seitz's *The Art of Assemblage* (New York: Museum of Modern Art, 1961.) The term "nonacademic art" is from John Maizels' *Raw Creation, Outsider Art and Beyond* (London: Phaidon, 1996) and is also cited in Goldstone and Goldstone, *Watts Towers* (Los Angeles: Getty Conservation Institute and J. Paul Getty Museum, 1997), 108.

4. Rose Basile Green, *The Italian-American Novel: A Document of the Interaction of Two Cultures* (Rutherford, N.J.: Fairleigh Dickinson University Press, 1974).

5. John Higham, *Strangers in the Land: Patterns of American Nativism, 1860–1925* (New Brunswick, N.J.: Rutgers University Press, 1988), 234–64.

6. Rudolph J. Vecoli, "The Search for an Italian American Identity: Continuity and Change," in *Italian Americans: New Perspectives in Italian Immigration and Ethnicity*, ed. Lydio Tomasi (New York: Center for Migration Studies, 1985), 94–95.

7. Jerre Mangione, *Mount Allegro: A Memoir of Italian Life* (New York: Harper & Row, 1981), 204.

8. Elena Faulks. Telephone interviews by Kenneth Scambray, July 1998 and 2001. Elena is Baldassare Forestiere's niece and Ric Forestiere's sister. Baldassare had five siblings: in their order of birth, Antonio, Baldassare, Giuseppe, Rose, Vincenzo, and Nicolina. Vincenzo settled in Boston, and Giuseppe settled in Fresno. After leaving Fresno, Rose lived in northern California, where Elena currently resides. Only Nicolina remained in Italy.

9. Silvio Manno, *The Forestiere Underground Gardens: A Pictorial Journey* (Fresno: Ionian, 2006), 3. Manno's photographs represent well both the dimensions of the grottoes and Forestiere's craftsmanship in his construction of walls, arches, and domed ceilings with the "bricks" that he fashioned from the hardpan he dug from the site. *The Forestiere Underground Gardens* is based on Manno's earlier manuscript, which includes a forward, "California: Earthly Paradise" (unpublished ms.), on which I have drawn for valuable details not included in the published version. The unpublished ms. is cited as "Forward" throughout. Unless otherwise indicated, all other Manno citations are from *The Forestiere Underground Gardens*. Rosario "Ric" Forestiere contribution and Italian translation by Silvio Manno, "In Search of Baldassare: Twelve Days in Sicily," travel diary, September, 10–21, 1999 (unpublished ms.), 6. Hereafter, "In Search of Baldassare" is cited as Forestiere. Ric Forestiere is the son of Giuseppe Forestiere, Baldassare's brother. Ric and Silvio Manno, the Underground Gardens' docent, traveled to Filari in 1999. Filari has been abandoned and is now in ruins. For the economic context of Baldassare's life in Sicily, see Denis Mack Smith, *A History of Sicily: Medieval Sicily 800–1713*, vol. 1; *A History of Sicily: Modern Sicily After 1713*, vol. 2 (New York: Dorset, 1968), 499–501.

10. Faulks.

11. Manno, 3; Rolle, *The Italian Americans: Troubled Roots* (Norman, Oklahoma: University of Oklahoma Press, 1980), 34.

12. Manno, "Forward," 3.

13. Manno, "Forward," 3.

14. Manno, "Forward," 24.

15. Rolle, *The Italian Americans*, 35; Charles Hillinger, "The Human Mole," in *Dream Streets: The Big Book of Italian American Culture*, ed. Lawrence DiStasi (New York: Harper & Row, 1989), 21.

16. Rolle, *The Italian Americans*, 35.

17. Faulks.

18. Faulks. Also, Silvio Manno, docent, Underground Gardens, visit by Kenneth Scambray, July 15, 2001. All further references to the July 15, 2001 visit are listed as Manno, docent.

19. Garibaldi Lapolla, *The Grand Gennaro* (New York: Vanguard Press, 1935), 63.

20. Michael La Sorte, *La Merica: Images of Italian Greenhorn Experience* (Philadelphia: Temple University Press, 1985), 37–60.

21. Micaela Di Leonardo, *The Varieties of Ethnic Experience: Kinship, Class, and Gender among California Italian-Americans* (Ithaca: Cornell University Press, 1984), 93–94; in *Fulfilling the Promise of California: An Anthology of Essays on the Italian American Experience in California*, ed. Gloria Ricci Lothrop (Seattle: California Italian American Task Force: Arthur H. Clark, 2000), 235.

22. Faulks.

23. Manno, docent; Faulks.

24. Manno, 5.

25. Faulks.

26. Faulks.

27. Lapolla, 277.

28. Manno, "Forward," 17. See also, Gloria Ricci Lothrop, "Unwelcome in Freedom's Land: The Impact of World War II on Italian Aliens in Southern California" and Lawrence DiStasi, "How World War II Iced Italian American Culture," in *Una Storia Segreta: The Secret History of Italian American Evacuation and Internment during World War II*, ed. Lawrence DiStasi (Berkeley: Heyday, 2001), 161–94, 303–12.

29. Faulks.

30. Thomas Bulfinch, *Bulfinch's Mythology* (New York: Harper & Row, 1970), 237–40, 920.

31. Forestiere, 12.

32. Manno, "Forward," 28–29.

33. Forestiere, 3. See also Manno, 5.

34. David D. Hume, *About Sicily: Travelers in an Ancient Land* (Exeter, N.H.: J. N. Townsend, 1999), 141.

35. Smith, vol. 2, 475–77.

36. Manno, "Forward," 30.

37. Manno, docent.

38. Manno, "Forward," 24.

39. Joseph Sciorra, "Multivocality and Vernacular Architecture: "The Our Lady of Mount Carmel Grotto in Rosebank, Staten Island," in *Studies in Italian American Folklore*, ed. Luisa Del Giudice (Logan: Utah State University Press, 1993), 204.

40. Manno, docent.

41. Manno, docent.

42. Manno, docent.

43. Teresa Fiore, "*Il giardino sotterraneo.*" *America Oggi* (September 19, 1999): 16B; Manno, docent.

44. Manno, 5. Because it cannot always be determined where one room or tunnel leaves off and another begins, it is difficult to establish the exact number of rooms. Manno counts "more than ninety underground rooms," 5. As docent, Manno reported that recent discoveries adjacent to the Gardens have uncovered more Forestiere grottoes. He also dug a grotto on his Coalinga property. See also Rolle, *The Italian Americans*, 34.

45. Manno, 7.

46. Manno, "Forward," 24.

47. Manno, 6.

48. Luisa Del Giudice, "The 'Archvilla': An Italian Canadian Architectural Archetype," in *Studies in Italian American Folklore*, ed. Luisa Del Giudice (Logan: Utah State University Press, 1993), 55.

49. Del Giudice, 55.

50. Manno, 5.

51. Manno, docent. The names of all rooms are from Manno.

52. Faulks.

53. Del Giudice, 61.

54. Smith, 8.

55. Smith, 473, 497.

56. Forestiere.

57. Manno, 5–6.

58. Manno, docent.

59. Catherine Morison Rehart, *The Valley's Legends & Legacies* (Fresno: Word Dancer, 1996), 189.

60. Manno, 100–02.

61. Manno, 100.

62. Lapolla, 323.

63. Jo Pagano, *Golden Wedding* (1943; repr., New York: Arno, 1975), 4.

64. Del Giudice, 55. "In a home of one's own, each one is king," Del Giudice, 92.

65. Pagano, 263.

66. Angelo Pellegrini, *American Dream* (San Francisco: North Point, 1986), 5–6.

67. Lothrop, ed., *Fulfilling the Promise of California*, 259.

68. David Fine, *Imagining Los Angeles: A City in Fiction* (Albuquerque: University of New Mexico Press, 2000), 7.

69. Pagano, 284.

70. Goldstone, 27–35.

71. Goldstone, 84.

72. Rob Haeseler, "The End of the Line," in *Dream Streets: The Big Book of Italian American Culture*, ed. Lawrence DiStasi (New York: McGraw-Hill, 1971), 18.

73. Goldstone, 39.

74. Rosalind Giardina Crosby, "The Italians of Los Angeles, 1900," in *Struggle and Success: An Anthology of the Italian Immigrant Experience in California*, ed. Paola A. Sensi-Isolani and Phylis Cancilla Martinelli (New York: Center for Migration Studies, 1993), 39.

75. Goldstone, 28.

76. Goldstone, 29; Di Leonardo, 18.

77. Lothrop, ed., *Fulfilling the Promise of California*, 235.

78. Haeseler, 18; Goldstone, 31.

79. Andrew Rolle, "Introduction," in *Fulfilling the Promise of California*, ed. Gloria Ricci Lothrop, 16.

80. *American Dream*, 8.

81. Andrew Rolle, *The Immigrant Upraised* (Norman: University of Oklahoma Press, 1968), 3. Reprinted as *Westward the Immigrants* (Ninot: University Press of Colorado, 1999).

82. Goldstone, 28.

83. Di Leonardo, 104–6.

84. *American Dream*, 6.

85. Crosby, 38–40.

86. Rolle, *The Immigrant Upraised*, 292.

87. Franklin Walker, *A Literary History of Southern California* (Berkeley: University of California Press, 1955), 5.

88. Walker, 5.

89. The Los Angeles Historic Hall Foundation. www.italianhall.org/history.php. See also Crosby, 40–44, for the demographic distribution of Italians in Los Angeles.

90. *Golden Wedding*, 208–9.

91. Crosby, 41–44.

92. Dick Rosano, *Wine Heritage: The Story of Italian American Vintners* (San Francisco: Wine Appreciation Guild, 2000), 56–68; in *Fulfilling the Promise of California*, ed. Gloria Ricci Lothrop, 243–46.

93. Goldstone, 80.

94. Goldstone, 68.

95. Crosby, 42–43.

96. Gerald Mast, *A Short History of the Movies* (Indianapolis: Bobbs-Merrill, 1996), 118.

97. Pagano, 284.

98. Mast, 118.

99. Fine, 12–13.

100. Richard Huber, *The American Idea of Success* (New York: McGraw-Hill, 1971), 184.

101. Goldstone, 66.

102. Goldstone, 56.

103. Goldstone, 70–74.

104. Steve Varni, *The Inland Sea* (New York: William Morrow, 2000), 223, 264.

105. Goldstone, 18.

106. Goldstone, 64.

107. Goldstone, 50.

108. I. Sheldon Posen and Daniel F. Ward, "Watts Towers and the *Giglio* Tradition," in *Folklife Annual 1985*, ed. Alan Jabbour and James Hardin (Library of Congress: Washington), 144–45.

109. Pascal D'Angelo, *Son of Italy* (1924; repr., Toronto: Guernica, 2003), 72.

110. Lapolla, 5.

111. Goldstone, 36.

112. Goldstone, 60.

113. Goldstone, 19.

114. John Auchard, ed., *Italian Hours* (University Park: Pennsylvania State University Press, 1992), 9.

115. A version of this section on Rodia's Watts Towers appears as "The Literary and Immigrant Contexts of Simon Rodia's Watts Towers," in *Sabato Rodia's Watts Towers: Art, Migrations, Community Development*, ed. Luisa Del Giudice (forthcoming).

Landscapes of Order, Landscapes of Memory: Italian-American Residential Landscapes of the New York Metropolitan Region   JOSEPH J. INGUANTI

1. "A Tree Dies in Brooklyn (Alas It's a Fig)." *The New York Times,* June 20, 2004.

2. Joseph Manzo, "Italian American Yard Shrines." *Journal of Cultural Geography,* 4 (1983): 119–25.

3. Robert A. Orsi, *The Madonna of 115th Street: Faith and Community in Italian Harlem 1880–1950* (New Haven: Yale University Press, 1985); Joseph Sciorra, "Yard Shrines and Sidewalk Altars of New York's Italian-Americans," in *Perspectives in Vernacular Architecture* III, ed. Thomas Carter and Bernard L. Herman (Columbia: University of Missouri Press, 1989), 185–98.

4. Jerome Krase, "Polish and Italian Vernacular Landscapes in Brooklyn." *Polish American Studies,* 54(1) (1997), 9–31; Jerome Krase, "Italian American Urban Landscapes: Images of Social and Cultural Capital." *Italian Americana* 22(1) (2004): 17–44.

5. Joseph J. Inguanti, "Domesticating the Grave: Italian American Memorial Practices at New York's Calvary Cemetery." *Markers: Annual Journal of the Association for Gravestone Studies,* XVII (2000): 8–31.

6. I generally eschew the word "garden" for the more inclusive term "landscape" here. To most Americans, "garden" has come to connote only a small section of the domestic landscape used for vegetables or flowers.

7. Folklorists might take issue with the limited number of quotes from the landscapers whose work is discussed here; this is a function of methodological choices on my part. I did not record interviews electronically, and I tended to favor the visual evidence itself over the landscapers' "on the spot" explanations of their work.

8. Most of the Italian-American home shrines I have seen feature at least some degree of symmetry. Scholarship on home altars reveals an enormous diversity of forms across cultures. See Kay Turner, *Beautiful Necessity: The Art and Meaning of Women's Altars* (New York: Thames and Hudson, 1999.)

9. Dorothy Noyes, *Arts of Italian Americans in Philadelphia* (Philadelphia: Philadelphia Folklore Project and Samuel S. Fleisher Art Memorial, 1989), 67.

10. Ibid., 70.

11. Sciorra, 188.

12. Inguanti, 23–24.

13. Orsi, 75–106.

14. Roger D. Abrahams, "The Language of Festivals: Celebrating the Economy," in *Celebration: Studies in Festivity and Ritual,* ed. Victor Turner (Washington: Smithsonian Institution Press, 1982), 176.

15. Jack Santino, "Tradition and Creativity in Halloween Folk Art," in *Folk Art and Art Worlds* (Ann Arbor: UMI Research Press, 1986), 161.

16. Oteri's character, the hard-boiled Italian-American woman Rita DelVecchio, appears in "Rita's Nativity," which aired on December 14, 1996.

17. Albert Forbes Sieveking, *Gardens Ancient and Modern: An Epitome of the Literature of the Garden Art* (London: J. M. Dent and Company, 1899), 9, 17, 21.

18. Luisa Del Giudice, "The 'Archvilla': An Italian Canadian Architectural Archetype," in *Studies in Italian American Folklore,* ed. Luisa Del Giudice (Logan: Utah State University Press, 1993), 53–105.

19. Elizabeth Barlow Rogers, *Landscape Design: A Cultural and Architectural History* (New York: Harry N. Abrams, 2001), 24.

20. Simon Schama, *Landscape and Memory* (New York: Alfred A. Knopf, 1995), 82.

21. Vincent Scully, conversation with author, June 27, 2005.

22. I am indebted to Dr. Richard Iversen of the Ornamental Horticulture Department at Farmingdale State College of New York for guiding me through the Italian-American enclave of Astoria and for his insights on its horticultural history.

23. Colleen J. Sheehy, *The Flamingo in the Garden: American Yard Art and the Vernacular Landscape* (New York: Garland Publishing, 1998), 149.

24. "A Tree Dies in Brooklyn" op. cit., 33.

25. Technically speaking, the two Connecticut landscapes discussed here fall outside the U.S. Federal Government's definition of the New York metropolitan area, officially called the "New York, Newark, Bridgeport, NY-NJ-CT-PA Combined Statistical Area." However, because they lie in an adjacent county and share a common design idiom with Italian-American landscapes of the larger region, I have considered them appropriate for inclusion here.

26. This aesthetic is not limited to southern Italy and southern Italian enclaves in America. Falassi states, "The external borders [of the traditional Tuscan farm] were always exactly defined, so that the indeterminate and the unknown were denied." Alessandro Falassi, *Folklore by the Fireside: Text and Context of the Tuscan Veglia* (Austin: University of Texas Press, 1980), 17.

27. Cesare Ripa, *Baroque and Rococo Pictorial Imagery: The 1758–60 Hertel Edition of Ripa's Iconologia with 200 Engraved Illustrations*, ed. Edward A. Maser (New York: Dover, 1971), ix. I wish to thank John Monahan of Yale University for facilitating my viewing of early editions of Ripa and for his generous assistance in obtaining other bibliographic sources for this chapter.

28. Cesare Ripa, *Iconologia* (Padua: Pietro Paolo Tozzi, 1618; facsimile Turin: Fògola Editore, 1988), 55.

29. Ripa, *Baroque and Rococo*, 154.

30. Anthony Esposito, conversations with author, October 2001.

Locating Memory: Longing, Place, and Autobiography in Vincenzo Ancona's Sicilian Poetry   JOSEPH SCIORRA

I am grateful to Rosangela Briscese, Edvige Giunta, Chiara Mazzucchelli, Rosina Miller, Laura Ruberto, Joan Saverino, and Anna Lomax Wood for their critical readings of an earlier draft of this essay. I am indebted to Chiara Mazzucchelli and Antonio Provenzano for their generous and invaluable assistance with translations.

1. Salman Rushdie, *Imaginary Homelands: Essay and Criticism, 1981–1991* (New York: Granta Books, 1991), 10.

2. Jack Kerouac, *Dr. Sax* (New York: Grove Press, 1975), 5.

3. For more information on Ancona's wire dioramas, see Joseph Sciorra, "Reweaving the Past: Vincenzo Ancona's Telephone Wire Figures." *Clarion* (Spring/Summer 1985): 48–53; Vincenzo Ancona, *Malidittu La Lingua/Damned Language: Poetry and Miniatures*, ed. Anna L. Chairetakis and Joseph Sciorra, trans. Gaetano Cipolla (New York: Legas, 1990; republished 2010); and Mary Hufford, Marjorie Hunt, and Steve Zeitlin, *The Grand Generation: Memory, Mastery, Legacy* (Washington, DC: Smithsonian Institution, 1987), 56–57, 61, 66–67.

4. The quoted excerpts of Ancona's Sicilian poetry (with the exception of *"La storia d'un briganti"*) are taken from his bilingual collection *Malidittu La Lingua/Damned Language* (1990). I have retranslated Ancona's excerpted poetry for this publication. My goal was to provide a more literal—not better—translation.

5. Ancona's poetry tackled a wide range of subjects. He maintained and demonstrated an intimate connection to the repertoire of oral artistry by reworking and composing verse based on traditional proverbs, jokes, and stories, such as *"Santu Roccu e lu picuraru"* ("Saint Roch and the Shepherd"), *"Frati Marcu nni lu Papa"* ("Brother Mark and the Pope"), and *"Tri grazzi di 'nna fata"* ("A Fairy's Three Wishes"). He also addressed a host of topical issues. He was fascinated by space exploration and composed *"L'omu nta la luna"* ("Man on the Moon") and *"Sciagura astronautica"* ("Astronautic Disaster") after the first moon walk and the explosion of the NASA space shuttle *Challenger*, respectively. He took on the theme of interracial love in the work *"La ceca di Messina"* ("The Blind Girl of Messina"). These aspects of Ancona's poetry warrant further study.

6. Howard S. Becker, *Art Worlds* (Berkeley: University of California Press, 1982), 34–35.

7. Maurice Halbwachs, *On Collective Memory*, ed. and trans. Lewis A. Coser (Chicago: University of Chicago Press, 1992), 49.

8. Barbara Kirshenblatt-Gimblett, "Authoring Lives." *Journal of Folklore Research* 26(2) (1989): 123–49.

9. Kirshenblatt-Gimblett, "Authoring Lives": 123–49.

10. Maurice Halbwachs, *The Collective Memory* (New York: Harper Colophon Books, 1980), 50–51.

11. Pierre Nora, "Between Memory and History: Les Liex de Mémoire." *Representations* 26 (Spring 1989): 7.

12. Halbwachs, *On Collective Memory*.

13. Arjun Appadurai, *Modernity at Large: Cultural Dimensions of Globalization* (Minneapolis: University of Minnesota Press, 2003), 31–33.

14. Interview, March 4, 1982. Portions of Ancona's biography and descriptions of his artistic production were originally featured in Anna L. Chairetakis and Joseph Sciorra, "Vincenzo Ancona: Poet of Two Worlds/ Vincenzo Ancona: poeta di due mondi," Ancona, *Malidittu La Lingua/Damned Language*, 26–41.

15. Maxwell noted that known Communists or opponents of the then-ruling Christian Democrat Party were not included in these figures despite the fact that leftists were to be found among the destitute. Gavin Maxwell, *The Ten Pains of Death* (New York: E. P. Dutton & Co., 1960), 63.

16. Maxwell, 16.

17. Maxwell, *The Ten Pains of Death*, 62.

18. Maxwell dedicated three individual chapters to the grain, grape, and olive harvests.

19. Social activists Danilo Dolci calculated the daily wage for 12 to 13 hours was $1.25 US in Trappeto in 1952. The following year wages rose to $1.50 US Danilo Dolci, *Sicilian Lives* (New York: Pantheon, 1981), xvii. American folklorist Alan Lomax observed that in 1951, the daily wage for Sicilian agricultural workers was 600 or 700 lire, which was calculated at "less than $1.00 US." Goffredo Plastino, *Italian Treasury: Sicily*, liner notes. Rounder 11661-1808-2, 2000. It is interesting to note that 700 lire was the cost for a panegyric mass at the time, according to a priest Maxwell interviewed in an unspecified town. Maxwell, *The Ten Pains of Death*, 188.

20. The plight of Sicilian fishermen was dramatized in Luchino Visconti's 1949 neo-realist film *La terra trema*.

21. Maxwell, *The Ten Pains of Death*, 65–67.

22. See Jane C. Schneider and Peter T. Schneider's *Reversible Destiny: Mafia, Antimafia, and the Struggle for Palermo* (Berkeley: University of California Press, 2003), 30–32, for a discussion of the relationship between brigandage and the *mafia*. In 2006, *Daily News* reporter Helen Kennedy chronicled the town's legacy as an exporter of mafiosi to the United States. "Don-town New York." *New York Daily News*, November 19, 2006, 34–35.

23. Personal conversation, February 23, 2004.

24. Salvatore Salomone-Marino, *Customs and Habits of the Sicilian Peasants*, ed. and trans. Rosalie N. Norris (Rutherford, N.J.: Fairleigh Dickinson University Press, 1968), 65.

25. For more information on oral poetry in Sicily and in Italy, see Benedetto Croce, *Poesia popolare e poesia d'arte* (Bari: Laterza, 1933); Alessandro D'Ancona, *La poesia popolare italiana* (Livorno: Giusti, 1906); Luisa Del Giudice, "The Sicilian Oral and Literary Traditions," in *Malidittu La Lingua/Damned Language*, 16–25; Ferdinando D. Maurino, "Italian Popular Poetry: Origin and Definition." *Journal of the Folklore Institute* 7 (1970): 36–46; and Giuseppe Pitrè, *Studi di poesia popolare* (Palermo: Il Vespro, 1875, 1978). See Hermann W. Haller's *The Hidden Italy: A Bilingual Edition of Italian Dialect Poetry* (Detroit: Wayne State University Press, 1986); *The Other Italy: The Literary Canon in Dialect* (Toronto: University of Toronto Press, 1999); and *La festa delle lingue: La letteratura dialettale in Italia* (Rome: Carocci editore, 2002) for a discussion of written dialect literature.

26. Ancona's parody was not the only example of anti-hegemonic verse created in Castellammare. The illiterate farmer Vito Monticciolo also improvised trenchant verse, such as "Ode a Don Caloriu Finuri," to challenge local *signori*. Joey Skee (aka Joseph Sciorra), "Ottava Rima in Bensonhurst" (blog post). http://www.i-italy.org/bloggers/988/ottava-rima-bensonhurst, December 27, 2007).

27. Barbara Kirshenblatt-Gimblett, "Studying Immigrant and Ethnic Folklore," in *Handbook of American Folklore*, ed. Richard Dorson (Bloomington: Indiana University Press, 1986), 39–41.

28. Elizabeth Mathias and Richard Raspa, *Italian Folktales in America: The Verbal Art of an Immigrant Woman* (Detroit: Wayne State University Press, 1985), 60; Fred L. Gardaphé, *Italian Signs, American Streets: The Evolution of Italian American Narrative* (Durham, N.C.: Duke University Press, 1996), 29; Graziella Parati, *Mediterranean Crossroads: Migration Literature in Italy* (Madison, N.J.: Fairleigh Dickinson University Press, 1999), 21; William Boelhower, *Immigrant Autobiography in the United States* (Verona: Essedue Edizioni, 1982).

29. Celia Jaes Falicov, "Immigrant Family Processes," in *Normal Family Processes: Growing Diversity and Complexity*, ed. Froma Walsh (New York: The Guilford Press, 2003), 293.

30. Kirshenblatt-Gimblett, "Authoring Lives," 123–49.

31. Halbwachs, *On Collective Memory*, 40.

32. Joseph Sciorra, "Imagined Places, Fragile Landscapes: Italian American *Presepi* (Nativity Crèches) in New York City." *The Italian American Review* 8(2) (Autumn/Winter 2001): 141–73.

33. Barbara Kirshenblatt-Gimblett, "Objects of Memory: Material Culture as Life Review," in *Folk Groups and Folklore Genres: A Reader*, ed. Elliot Oring (Logan: Utah State University Press, 1989), 331–32; see also Bruce M. Ross, *Remembering the Personal Past: Descriptions of Autobiographical Memory* (New York: Oxford University Press, 1991), 171.

34. Halbwachs, *On Collective Memory*, 60.

35. James Clifford, "On Ethnographic Allegory," in *Writing Culture: The Poetics and Politics of Ethnography*, ed. James Clifford and George E. Marcus (Berkeley: University of California Press, 1986), 115; see also Kirshenblatt-Gimblett, "Authoring Lives," 123–49.

36. Steven Feld and Keith H. Basso, "Introduction," in *Senses of Place*, ed. Steven Feld and Keith H. Basso (Santa Fe, N.M.: School of American Research Press, 2000), 11.

37. Robert A. Orsi, "The Fault of Memory: 'Southern Italy' in the Imagination of Immigrants and the Lives of Their Children in Italian Harlem, 1920–1945." *Journal of Family History* 15(2) (1990): 140.

38. Feld and Basso, "Introduction," 11.

39. Halbwachs, *The Collective Memory*, 131.

40. Ancona's verse, song, narrative, and sculpture were reminiscent of the ancient mnemonic device *loci memoriae*, which bound ideas and sentiments to a fictitious place for later recall. Frances A. Yates, *The Art of Memory* (Chicago: University of Chicago Press, 1974), 1–26.

41. David Gross, *Lost Time: On Remembering and Forgetting in Late Modern Culture* (Amherst: University of Massachusetts Press, 2000), 21.

42. Gross, *Lost Time*, 20–22; Ross, *Remembering the Personal Past*, 182–96.

43. Gross, *Lost Time*, 30–38.

44. Gross, *Lost Time*, 30–38.

45. Susan Stewart, *On Longing: Narratives of the Miniature, the Gigantic, the Souvenir, the Collection* (Baltimore: The Johns Hopkins University Press, 1984), ix.

46. Roy Cashman, "Critical Nostalgia and Material Culture in Northern Ireland." *Journal of American Folklore* (119) 472 (Spring 2006): 137–60.

47. Kathleen Stewart, "Nostalgia—A Polemic." *Cultural Anthropology* 3(3) (1988): 227.

48. Stewart, "Nostalgia," 227.

49. Stewart, "Nostalgia," 228.

50. Stanislao Pugliese, "The Culture of Nostalgia: Fascism in the Memory of Italian-Americans." *The Italian American Review* 5(2) (1996/1997): 17; see also Cashman, "Critical Nostalgia and Material Culture in Northern Ireland," 155.

51. Stewart, "Nostalgia," 239; see also Graziella Parati, *Migration Italy: The Art of Talking Back in a Destination Culture* (Toronto: University of Toronto Press, 2005), 23–53.

52. Pugliese, "The Culture of Nostalgia," 17.

53. See D'Acierno (1999, 743) and Viscusi (1990, 1–13) for discussion of *omertà* in Italian-American social life.

54. Pasquale Verdicchio, *Bound by Distance: Rethinking Nationalism through the Italian Diaspora* (Rutherford, N.J.: Fairleigh Dickinson University Press, 1997), 90–99.

55. Verdicchio, *Bound by Distance*, 90–99; Nancy C. Carnevale, *A New Language, A New World: Italian Immigrants in the United States, 1890–1945* (Urbana: University of Illinois Press, 2009), 31–32.

56. Ancona can be heard singing this song on "In Mezz'una Strada Trovai una Pianta di Rosa: Italian Folk Music Collected in New York and New Jersey, vol. 1." Folkways Records FW34041, 1979.

57. Kirshenblatt-Gimblett, "Authoring Lives," 128; see also Hufford, Hunt, and Zeitlin, *The Grand Generation*, 43–60.

58. He was also known as "Turrigiano," "Turriciano," and "Turricianu," the names that Ancona uses. Gaetano Falzone, *Storia della Mafia* (Milan: Pan Editrice, 1978), 109–11. My thanks to Jane Schneider for this reference.

59. These documents included an 11-page typed document entitled "*Storia del Brigante (Turriciano)/Leggenda e Realta.*"

60. Dickie cites an example from the 1860s of brigands recounting stories about brigands. He writes, "Before they become brigands, peasants are tellers of brigand stories." John Dickie, *Darkest Italy: The Nation and Stereotypes of the Mezzogiono, 1860–1900* (New York: St. Martin's Press, 1999), cf. 81, 165–66.

61. Dickie, *Darkest Italy*, 49.

62. Stewart, *On Longing*, 236.

63. Mikhail Bakhtin, *Rabelais and His World* (Bloomington: Indiana University Press, 1984), 472.

64. Mikhail Bakhtin, *The Dialogic Imagination* (Austin: University of Texas Press, 1988), 360.

65. For more on Italo-English, see Carnevale (2000, 51–56); Anthony M. Gisolfi, "Italo-American." *Commonwealth* (July 21, 1939), 311–313; Gisolfi (1939, 311–13); Michael La Sorte, *La Merica: Images of Italian Greenhorn Experience* (Philadelphia: Temple University Press, 1985), 159–88; and Anthony M. Turano, "The Speech of Little Italy." *American Mercury* 26 (July 1932), 356–59. See also Haller's *Una lingua perduta e ritrovata: L'italiano degli italo-americani* (Scandicci: La Nuova Italia, 1993) and "The Dialects Abroad," in *The Dialects of Italy*, ed. Martin Maiden and Mair Parry (New York: Routledge, 1997), 401–11, for discussion of Italian and dialect among immigrants in the United States in the latter half of the twentieth century.

66. During an outdoor panegyric mass held in front of the Castel del Golfo Social Club as part of the celebration of the 1988 *festa* in honor of the Madonna del Soccorso, Father Raffaele Zaccagnino of Regina Pacis–St. Rosalia Church proclaimed to the approximately 150 people in attendance, "*Questa è la vostra piazza. Questo è il vostro Castellammare*" ("This is your piazza. This is your Castellammare").

67. Appadurai, *Modernity at Large*, 33–34.

68. Vincenzo Ancona, *Casteddammari Meu* (Alcamo: Edizioni Campo, 1984).

69. Bakhtin, *The Dialogic Imagination*, 304.

70. This long-standing debating tradition in Sicily has been considered the basis for the prodigious number of lawyers and judges who emerged from the Santa Margherita di Belice immigrant community of Bushwick, Brooklyn. Kirk Johnson, "Sicily's Judicial Legacy to New York." *The New York Times*, March 14, 1986, section B, 1, 6.

71. This publication could be found for sale in Manhattan's Little Italy store Rossi & Co. as late as the 1990s.

72. Bakhtin, *Rabelais and His World*, 434.

73. Bakhtin, *Rabelais and His World*, 434.

74. Cashman, "Critical Nostalgia and Material Culture in Northern Ireland," 155.

75. Bakhtin, *The Dialogic Imagination*, 1988.

76. As early as the mid-1950s, the town was beginning to feel the impact of tourism. Maxwell (61) described the town as one of "extreme contrasts, in which the middle ages and the mid–twentieth century meet face to face," with tourists from Trapani and Palermo swimming at the local beach in skimpy bikinis next to local women bathing fully dressed in everyday clothes.

77. Anthropologist Charlotte Gower Chapman briefly describes this tension in the oral tradition from the late 1920s. *Milocca: A Sicilian Village* (Cambridge, Mass.: Schenkman Publishing Co., 1971), 111–12. She also discusses and reproduces, in part, a translation of a broadside poem about a quarrel between a mother and a daughter (239–43).

78. Orsi, "The Fault of Memory," 133–47.

79. Interview, April 8, 1987.

80. Appadurai, *Modernity at Large*, 35–36.

81. Halbwachs, *The Collective Memory*.

82. Halbwachs, *On Collective Memory*, 39.

83. Halbwachs, *On Collective Memory*, 53.

84. Bakhtin, *The Dialogic Imagination*, 356.

85. Kirshenblatt-Gimblett, "Authoring Lives," 125.

86. Hufford, Hunt, and Zeitlin, *The Grand Generation*, 66.

87. Kirshenblatt-Gimblett, "Objects of Memory," 332.

88. Michael Cooper, "Honors for a Poet Who Turns Life Into Verse in Bensinosti." *The New York Times*, May 14, 1995, Sec. City, 9.

89. Ray Oldenburg, *The Great Good Place: Cafes, Coffee Shops, Bookstores, Bars, Hair Salons, and Other Hangouts at the Heart of a Community* (New York: Paragon House, 1991); Ray Allen, Joseph Sciorra, and Steve Zeitlin, "'Welcome to Your Second Home': Ethnic Social Clubs in New York City." *New York Folklore* 25(1–4) (1999): 17–24.

90. Nora's work is problematic for its romantic notion of "true memory" or "integrated memory" in "primitive and archaic societies" (1996, 2) and its "focus on the national at the expense of the local" and its general "top-down approach." Hue-Tam Ho Tai, "Remembered Realms: Pierre Nora and French National Memory." *The American Historical Review* 106(3) (2001): 920–21.

91. Pierre Nora, "The Reasons for the Current Upsurge in Memory." *Transit-Europaeische Revue*, Vol. 22. (2002). http://www.iwm.at/t-22txt3.htm (accessed November 26, 2003).

92. Pierre Nora, "Between Memory and History: Les Liex de Mémoire." *Representations* 26 (Spring 1989): 7–8.

93. Pierre Nora, "General Introduction: Between Memory and History." *Realms of Memory*, vol. I: Conflicts and Divisions, ed. Lawrence D. Kritzman, trans. Arthur Goldhammer (New York: Columbia University Press, 1996), 6.

94. Nora, "General Introduction," 7.

95. Nora, "General Introduction," 7.

96. Nora, "General Introduction," 7.

97. "*Sicilia Bedda*" ("Beautiful Sicily") sentimentally extolled the island's natural beauty in "*stu chiantu chi t'arriva di luntanu/d'un figghiu di sangu sicilianu*" ("a cry that arrives from far away/from a son with

Sicilian blood"), while his aforementioned parody *"Italia! Italia Mia!"* professes a longing that is no longer conceived as local: that is, Sicilian. Written in Italian, *"In Occasione del Bicentenario: Italiani onoriamo L'America"* celebrates the American Bicentennial by naming the Italian explorers Columbus, Vespucci, Cabot(o), and Verrazzano, as well as the anonymous "multitude" who are "proud to be Italian Americans."

98. Halbwachs, *The Collective Memory*, 86.

99. Halbwachs, *The Collective Memory*, 78–79; Nora, "General Introduction," 3. "General Introduction," 3.

100. Natalie Zemon Davis and Randolph Starn, "Introduction." *Representations* 26 (Spring 1989): 5.

101. Nora, "Between Memory and History," 23; see Tai, "Remembered Realms," 920–21.

Valtaro Musette: Cross-Cultural Musical Performance and Repertoire Among Northern Italians in New York MARION S. JACOBSON

1. Brugnoli's region of origin, Emilia, is now known as Emilia-Romagna, as it merged with Romagna to become a single administrative region of Italy in 1947. Until Italy unified in 1861, Emilia had been part of the Duchy of Parma. For more specifics, see "Emilia Romagna," http://www.italyworldclub.com/emilia. Last accessed December 31, 2008.

2. Carol Spagnoli Schiavi, "Peter Spagnoli: New York Valtaro Accordionist." *Washington Area Metropolitan Accordion News*. www.washingtonaccordions.org/ValTaro.htm. Last accessed March 1, 2010.

3. See Gloria Nardini, *Che Bella Figura! The Power of Performance in an Italian Ladies' Club in Chicago* (Albany: SUNY Press, 1999); Donald Tricarico, *The Italians of Greenwich Village: Social Structure and Transformation of Community* (New York: Center for Migration Studies, 1984); and Caroline Farrar Ware, *Greenwich Village, 1920–1930* (New York: Harper & Row, 1965).

4. A pair of ethnic dance music folios for accordion published by Ernest Deffner in 1953 (Val-Taro Musette Orchestra 1953a and 1953b).

5. Helmi Strahl Harrington and Gerhard Kubik, "The Accordion," in *New Grove Encyclopedia of Music and Musicians*, ed. Stanley Sadie (New York: Grove's Dictionary of Music, 2003), 1096.

6. Beniamino Bugiolacchi, *A Man and His Dream: An Illustrated History of the Accordion* (Castelfidardo, Italy: Loreto Cassa di Risparmio Foundation, 2005), 2.

7. Cyril Demian accordion patent, Graz, Austria, 1829, available online at http://www.accordion-online.de/instrum/demian.htm. Last accessed March 1, 2010.

8. Beniamino Bugiolacchi, "Castelfidardo: International Centre of Accordion Production in Italy." http://www.accordions.com/index/his/his_it.shtml. Last accessed Dec. 31, 2008.

9. Ibid.

10. The Hohner company began making accordions at the turn of the century. Their instruments are also well regarded for tone quality and durability.

11. Marion Jacobson, "Searching for Rockordion: The Changing Image of the Accordion in the United States, 1921–1963." *American Music* 25 (2007): 216–43. For more detailed history of the accordion in Europe and the United States, see my book *Squeeze This! A Social History of the Piano Accordion* (Champaign–Urbana: University of Illinois Press, forthcoming 2011).

12. Tricarico, *The Italians of Greenwich Village*, 78.

13. Bugiolacchi, *A Man and His Dream*.

14. On this point, see Patrizia Audenino, "Paths of the Trade: Italian Stonemasons in the United States." *International Migration Review* 20 (1986): 779–95; and John E. Zucchi, *Little Slaves of the Harp: Italian Child Street Musicians in 19th-Century Paris, London, and New York* (Montreal & Kingston: McGill–Queen's University Press, 1992).

15. Ronald Flynn, *The Golden Age of the Accordion* (Schertz, Tex.: Flynn Publications, 1984).

16. The musette as a repertoire and style (as opposed to a switch on the accordion) references French culture. Many pieces in the Valtaro repertoire are shared by Northern Italian accordionists who migrated to Paris, as John Brugnoli did, and learned popular French accordion music. This repertoire was, in turn, adopted from the *musette* (bagpipe) traditions of immigrants from the Auvergne region.

17. Jerre Mangione and Ben Morreale, *La Storia: Five Centuries of Italian American Experience* (New York: HarperCollins, 1992), 112.

18. Donald Tricarico, *The Italians of Greenwich Village: Social Structure and Transformation of Community* (New York: Center for Migration Studies, 1984), 87.

19. For an account of the Deiro brothers' careers and their significance in popularizing the piano accordion in America, see Muir 2001 and 2002, and Guido Deiro's unpublished autobiography, "My Life" (www.guidodeiro.com). Last accessed March 1, 2010.

20. See Louis Erenberg, *Swingin' the Dream* (Chicago: University of Chicago Press, 1999) for an exploration of the jazz scene in the 1920s and 1930s.

21. *World of Music* 3, 2008.

22. Cathy Ragland, "La Voz del Pueblo Tejano: Conjunto Music and the Construction of Tejano Identity in Texas," in *Puro Conjunto! An Album in Words and Pictures*, ed. Juan Tejeda (Austin: Center for Mexican American Studies, The University of Texas at Austin, 2001), 200–12.

23. This event was held at the City University of New York's Graduate Center on March 23, 2001, sponsored by the Joseph Calandra Italian American Institute at Queens College and the Center for the Study of Free-Reed Instruments (CSFRI).

24. William Schimmel, personal communication, New York City, August 13, 2008.

25. James Periconi, "*Vergogna e Risorgimento*: The Secret Life of an Italian-American Accordionist." *The Free-Reed Journal* 4 (2002): 49–58.

26. Maria Sonevytski, "Learning from Lawrence Welk: The Accordion and Ethnic Whiteness." *World of Music* 3 (2008): 105.

27. As we know from Frank Zucchi's (1992) account of the Italian child street musicians in Paris, London, and New York, the instrument of choice for these early Italian buskers was the harp.

28. See Jacobson, "Searching for Rockordion," for insights into the American accordion phenomenon and its impact on popular culture at midcentury.

29. Christopher Small, *Musicking: The Meanings of Performing and Listening* (Middletown, Conn.: Wesleyan University Press, 1998): 184.

30. For insights into the reception of opera and Italian song by Italian immigrants in North America, see Simona Frasca, *La Follia di New York: La canzone napolitana negli anna dell'emigrazione di masa* (Rome: University of Rome, 2006); and Luisa Del Giudice, "Italian Traditional Song in Toronto: From Autobiography to Advocacy." *Journal of Canadian Studies* 29 (1994): 74–89.

31. Unsigned review, dated May 11, 1911. Guido Deiro Archives, New York City.

32. Guido Deiro, "My Life." Unpublished manuscript from the Center for the Study of Free Reeds Archives, City University of New York Graduate Center, New York.

33. Del Giudice, "Italian Traditional Song in Toronto," 75.

34. In my forthcoming book manuscript, I explore Pietro Deiro Jr.'s efforts to "elevate" the instrument through his arrangements of classical and popular music, and his development of improved teaching methods.

35. Ove Hahn, *Anthony Galla-Rini: On His Life and the Accordion* (Stockholm: Nils Fläcke Musik, 1986).

36. Erenberg, *Swingin' the Dream*.

37. Ware, *Greenwich Village, 1920–1930*.

38. Mary Boatti, personal communication, New York City, December 3, 2008.

39. Tricarico, *The Italians of Greenwich Village*, 46.

40. Mangione and Morreale, *La Storia*, 112.

41. With the exception of 90-year-old Mary Boatti, a resident of Flushing, and her son Stephen, who lives in Manhattan.

42. Mary and Stephen Boatti, personal communication, August 11, 2007.

43. Tricarico, *The Italians of Greenwich Village*, 312.

44. His photo, although at first glance a generic image of success and elegance, is revealing about common perceptions and myths about Italians and musicians. He is looking down, introspectively, as if caught up in a lofty reverie about art and beauty. Many Italian musicians who immigrated to the New World were dogged by stereotypes of the itinerant singer or low-class organ grinder. No doubt Brugnoli (like Deiro and other accordionists) aimed to project instead the image of a fine artist with "European cachet," in their music as well as their self-presentations.

45. Dominic Karcic, "John (Gianod Scud'lein) Brugnoli's Val-Taro Musette Orchestra." *Washington Metropolitan Accordion Club News*, http://www.washingtonaccordions.org/ValTaro.htm#brugnoli. Last accessed February 11, 2009. This article also appeared, in Italian in the *Gazzetta de Parma* on September 10, 2002.

46. For further exploration of the *ballo liscio* tradition and its repertoire, see Goffredo Plastino, jacket notes to *Italian Journey: Emilia-Romagna*. Alan Lomax's historic 1950s recordings from the region of Central Italy. Rounder CD, 2002.

47. Schiavi, "Peter Spagnoli: New York Valtaro Accordionist."

48. Ibid.

49. Ibid.

50. Interview, Pete Spagnoli, February 11, 2006, Whitestone, New York.

51. Ibid. This number is not likely to be exaggerated. A look at Pete Spagnoli's manuscript files, containing at least 1,000 songs that he transcribed himself, supports this claim. He had to have "known" or memorized most of these songs, as the Valtaro musicians did not generally play from sheet music.

52. As part of an ongoing research project on Valtaro music, I am presently interviewing people who identify with Northern Italian culture about their musical choices and preferences.

53. Schiavi, "Peter Spagnoli: New York Valtaro Accordionist."

54. In her 2002 address to the Society for Ethnomusicology meeting in Toronto (published in *Ethnomusicology* journal in 2005), Barbara Kirshenblatt-Gimblett highlighted folklorization as a process by which artists strategize ways to add value to their work by highlighting its authenticity. See Barbara Kirsehnblatt-Gimblett, "Theorizing Heritage." *Ethnomusicology* 39(3) (1995): 367–80.

55. Del Giudice, "Italian Traditional Song in Toronto," 82.

56. See Gay Talese, *Unto the Sons* (New York: Random House 1992) for further exploration of these stereotypes. However, in her notes on the popular Italian songs she recorded among Italian American immigrants, Anna Chairetakis parses "blond" as flighty and loose, in opposition to the sincere and faithful brunette. See Anna Lomax Chairetakis, jacket notes to *Cantate Con Noi: Choral Songs from Istria and the Alps and Vintage Popular Songs from South Central Italy* (New York: Global Village Music, CVM 678 and C 678, 1986).

57. Ernest Hemingway, who served in Italy in World War II, was said to have counted "Tutti Mi Chiamano Bionda" as one of his favorite songs. According to various biographical accounts, the author had cheerfully joined his wife in singing the tune, on morning of the day he committed suicide at his home in Ketchum, Idaho, on July 2, 1961.

58. Schiavi, "Peter Spagnoli: New York Valtaro Accordionist."

59. Translation by the author. The complete lyrics to *"Tutti Mi Chiamano Bionda"* are available on www.istria.net. Various recordings of the song have been circulated: the "original" having been released on the Colonial label (Valtaro Musette Orchestra). *"Tutti Mi Chiamano Bionda"* is most recently featured on Mario Tacca/Maria Mancini, *Nostalgia.*

60. Rounder's *Italian Treasury* series of recordings by Alan Lomax and Diego Carpitella contains some representative performances of Italian polkas.

61. See www.istrianet.org/istria/music/lyrics/index.htm for more information about this song, as well as audio files.

62. The same might be said of Valtaro singers Mario Nicolich and Eugene Gercovich, who performed on the Colonial Italian sing-along albums. Nicolich, a native Italian speaker, was born in a part of Croatia that was formerly under Italian rule. Although Croatian, he considers himself to be an admirer of and advocate for Italian culture and Valtaro music specifically, and continues to perform the Valtaro repertoire today.

63. Dominic Karcic, "Il Sirio." *Newsletter of the American Accordionists Association* (July 2006), 4.

64. Each year, the *Sirio* tragedy is recognized on Joe Farda's American Italian Music Hall radio program on 93.5 FM in the Hudson Valley.

65. Schiavi, "Peter Spagnoli: New York Valtaro Accordionist."

66. Mario Tacca and Maria Mangini, *Nostalgia: Dance to the Music of Northern Italy* (Gioia Productions CD, 2006).

67. See Richard March and James Leary, "Dutchman Bands: Genre, Ethnicity, and Pluralism in the Upper Midwest," in *Creative Ethnicity: Symbols and Strategies of Contemporary Life*, ed. Stephen Cicala (Logan, Utah: Logan State University Press, 1991), 21–47.

68. Without explaining why, my accordion teacher—who had played with a Polish polka band in Dearborn, Michigan—always instructed me to select a single reed switch (Clarinet) or the two-reed switch (Bandoneon).

69. Alan Polivka's article on wet versus dry tuning provides some useful insights into the cultural construction of texture in accordion playing (www.accordionpage.com/wetdry.html).

70. See Polivka, www.accordionpage.com/wetdry.html.

71. The unique role that opera—both recordings and live performances—has played as a form of popular culture in the Italian-American community is a topic worthy of further exploration. See Del Giudice, "Italian Traditional Song in Toronto," for an analysis of the "cult of opera" among the Italian *prominenti*.

72. Accordionist Ray Oreggia has claimed that he was "listening to Valtaro before he was born" (Schiavi 2007, 8).

73. Karcic refers to one of the most commonly found chord progressions in Western folk and popular musics. The numbers I-V-IV refer to chords built on the tonic, dominant, and subdominant pitches of the major scale.

74. Personal communication, Dominic Karcic, Commack, New York, February 11, 2006.

75. On this point, see Joan Saverino, "Italians in Public Memory: Pageantry, Power, and Imagining the Italian American." *The Italian American Review* 8 (2001–2002): 85–111; and Anthony R. Rauche, "Festa Italiana in Hartford, Connecticut: The Pastries, the Pizza, and the People Who 'Parla Italiano,'" in *We Gather Together: Food and Festival in American Life*, ed. Theodore C. Humphrey and Lin Humphrey (Ann Arbor: UMI Research Press, 1990), 205–17.

76. These thoughts came through in discussions with Pete Spagnoli, his wife, and his daughter (Carol Schiavi) (February 11, 2007). I thank the family for their insights.

77. For a discussion of the "twilight" phenomenon, which has been disputed by other scholars, see Richard Alba, *Italian Americans: Into the Twilight of Ethnicity* (New York: Prentice-Hall, 1985); for another perspective, see Rudolph Vecoli, *Italian Ethnicity: Twilight or Dawn? The Italian American Immigrant Experience* (Thunder Bay, Ont.: Canadian Historical Association, 1988).

78. Del Giudice, "Italian Traditional Song in Toronto," 81.

79. Although the resorts area of the Catskills is known most famously as the "Borscht Belt," this area was home to a number of resorts catering to Italian Americans, such as Villa Roma, Villa Bocilli, and Beverly Farms. Accordion music (solo and ensemble performance) was, according to Frank Toscano and Dominic Karcic, the featured musical entertainment at the Italian establishments, drawing clientele from other resort communities on weekends.

80. "Sing-Along in Italian" albums, such as Colonial LP 231and Colonial LP 212, are out of print and only available in private collections. I thank Peter Spagnoli for making his available.

81. Peter Spagnoli recorded two long-playing records on that label with John Brugnoli, featuring folk songs of Valtaro: *Balliamo e Cantiamo Con Valtaro*; *Cantano I Due Menestrelli* (Fiesta Records FLPS 1542); and an instrumental album, *Valtaro Musette: Popular Italian Favorites* (Fiesta Records FLPS 1515).

82. Joseph Sciorra, the editor of this volume, recalls that he came to know some of this repertoire through the performances of the song-and-comedy team The Gaylords.

83. Dominic Karcic was active during the summers as an accordionist at the Beverly, a family-owned Italian resort in East Durham, New York.

84. Filmmaker Dante Imperator's documentary film in progress will serve as a valuable record of Italian resort culture. It is entitled *The Last Resort*.

85. The Gaylords' *Italia* album features "Tutti Mi Chiamano Bionda," as do various recordings by Geraldine Farrar.

86. For insights into the Italian *festa* phenomenon, see Rauche, "Festa Italiana in Hartford, Connecticut: The Pastries, the Pizza, and the People Who 'Parla Italiano,'"; and Sabina Magliocco, "Playing with Food: The Negotiation of Identity in the Ethnic Display Event by Italian Americans in Clinton, Indiana," in *Studies in Italian American Folklore*, ed. Luisa Del Guidice, (Logan: Utah State University Press, 1993).

87. From the Web site for Milwaukee Festa Italiana, www.festaitaliana.com, last accessed January 10, 2010.

88. "Italian Family Festa in San Jose." www.letspolka.com/2006/09/italian-family-festa-in-san-jose. Last accessed January 10, 2010.

89. Sciorra, personal communication, August 1, 2008.

Italians in Public Memory: Pageantry, Power, and Imagining the "Italian American" in Reading, Pennsylvania JOAN L. SAVERINO

If this chapter approaches an accurate portrayal of the Italian-American community that existed, it is because of the people who so generously allowed me to interview them. I wish to thank Bob St. George for reading earlier versions of this essay and Philip Cannistraro for reading an earlier version of the section on Fascism. I also thank Joseph Sciorra for thinking of me in the first place, and thank him and Leonard Primiano for their comments and suggestions.

Versions of this chapter were presented at the Balch Institute for Ethnic Studies Faculty Forum, Philadelphia, March 1999; at the American Anthropological Association Annual Meeting, Washington, DC, November 1993; at the American Italian Historical Association Annual Meeting, Washington, DC, November 1992; and in the author's doctoral dissertation, Joan Lynn Savereno, "Private Lives, Public Identities: The Italians of Reading and Berks County, Pennsylvania, 1890–1940," University of Pennsylvania, 1996.

1. "Two-Ton Tony Likes Berks Spaghetti." *Reading Times*, 14 August, 1939.

2. David Kertzer defines ritual as "action wrapped in a web of symbolism. Standardized, repetitive action lacking such symbolization is an example of habit or custom and not ritual. . . . Through ritual, beliefs about the universe come to be acquired, reinforced, and eventually changed." David Kertzer, *Ritual, Politics and Power* (New Haven: Yale University Press, 1988), 9.

3. To read more about the 175th Anniversary of the Founding of Reading and other events, see Chapter Five: "Italians in Public Memory: Pageantry, Ceremony, and Celebration," 252–83, in the author's doctoral dissertation.

4. Allan R. Pred, "Space as Historically Contingent Process," in *Place, Practice, and Situation: Social and Spatial Transformation in Southern Sweden, 1750–1850* (Totowa, N.J.: Barnes & Noble, 1986), 6, quoted in Robert Blair St. George, *Conversing by Signs: Poetics of Implication in Colonial New England Culture* (Chapel Hill: University of North Carolina, 1998), 9.

5. John Bodnar discusses the construction of ethnic memory through commemorative events in Chapter 3, "The Construction of Ethnic Memory," in *Remaking America: Public Memory, Commemoration, and Patriotism in the Twentieth Century* (Princeton, N.J.: Princeton University Press, 1992). For performative studies of specific ethnic groups, see April R. Schultz, *Ethnicity on Parade: Inventing the Norwegian American through Celebration* (Amherst: University of Massachusetts Press, 1994) and Harley Erdman, *Staging the Jew: The Performance of an American Ethnicity, 1860–1920* (New Brunswick, N.J.: Rutgers University Press, 1997).

6. St. George, *Conversing by Signs*, 7.

7. Kertzer, *Ritual, Politics and Power*, 69. Kertzer discusses the ambiguity of symbols at length in Chapter 4, "The Virtues of Ambiguity," 57–76. Adrienne L. Kaeppler discusses the festival as a multifaceted communicative event specifically within the context of ethnic identity in *Time Out of Time: Essays on the Festival* (Albuquerque: University of New Mexico Press, 1967), 162–70.

8. James T. Lemon, *The Best Poor Man's Country: A Geographical Study of Early Southeastern Pennsylvania* (Baltimore: The Johns Hopkins University Press, 1972), 133.

9. Birdsboro, Robesonia, and Temple attracted immigrants because of the iron foundries there.

10. Raymond L. Ford Jr., "Germans and Other Foreign Stock: Their Part in the Evolution of Reading, Pennsylvania" (PhD diss., University of Pennsylvania, 1963), 1–5.

11. Eric Wolf in the preface to *Europe and the People without History* (Berkeley: University of California Press, 1982), x, uses the phrase "the people without history" in reference to the common people—peasants, laborers, immigrants, minorities—who were "as much agents in the historical process as they were its victims and silent witnesses." It is used here in a different sense, to indicate Italians who were cut off from their historical past through the process of emigration.

12. The largest concentration of regional identities were from towns in the Abruzzi; the town of Santo Stefano di Camastra on the north coast of Sicily; and from the town and province of Ascoli Piceno, in the Marches.

13. For references on the scholarly debate concerning the changes in the family system from Italy to the immigrant communities in the United States as well as how Sicilian immigrants in New York City expanded their network of support, see Donna Gabaccia, *From Sicily to Elizabeth Street: Housing and Social Change Among Italian Immigrants, 1880–1930* (Albany: SUNY Press, 1984), 100–16.

14. In 1920, the U.S. Census recorded 1,810 Italians in the city (1.7 percent of the population). In 1930, there were 2,282 Italians, comprising 2.1 percent of the population. U.S. Census 1860–1970.

15. See Micaela di Leonardo, *The Varieties of Ethnic Experience: Kinship, Class, and Gender Among California Italian-Americans* (Ithaca, N.Y.: Cornell University Press, 1984), 156, for comment on the role of ethnic brokers. In Reading, until 1900, working-class jobs available to Italians were primarily in the railroad yards, construction, and iron foundries, which required unskilled or semi-skilled labor. From 1900 to 1930, the economic situation shifted from one of heavy to light industry: primarily, textiles and garment manufacturers. These industries depended on semi-skilled and skilled workers and employed both sexes. By the 1920s, the Italian middle class consisted of one physician, clergy, and entrepreneurs engaged in artisan trades (baker, barber, tailor) or merchant/businessmen (construction and building trades or wholesale/retail businesses). Information on work patterns is based on qualitative research (primarily personal interviews) and some secondary-source material. Quantitative research still needs to be conducted.

16. John Higham defines the 100-percent Americanism campaign that took hold in the United States after World War I. Its aim was to stamp out any foreign influence in the United States, and its tactics favored

coercing immigrants to become citizens; adopt the English language; adhere without question to American institutions; and abandon the customs, beliefs, and any loyalties to their homeland. John Higham, *Strangers in the Land: Patterns of American Nativism, 1860–1925*, 2nd edition (New Brunswick, N.J.: Rutgers University Press, 1988), 247.

17. Columbus Day celebrations had not occurred in Reading since 1893. *Reading Times*, October 13, 1908, 1. No description of the 1893 events could be found in the local newspapers of that year.

18. Italians participated in other commemorative city-wide events orchestrated by the city fathers, such as the 175th Anniversary of the Founding of Reading held in 1923.

19. John Noble Wilford, *The Mysterious History of Columbus: An Exploration of the Man, the Myth, the Legacy* (New York: Alfred A. Knopf, 1991), 254–55.

20. Jackson Lears, *No Place of Grace: Antimodernism and the Transformation of American Culture, 1880–1920* (New York: Pantheon, 1981), 7. See "Roots of Antimodernism" for a fuller discussion of nineteenth-century American capitalist ideology, Chapter 1.

21. Carol Bradley, "Towards a Celebration, The Columbus Monument in New York," in *Italian Americans Celebrate Life: The Arts and Popular Culture*, ed. Paola A. Sensi-Isolani and Anthony Julian Tamburri (Staten Island, N.Y.: American Italian Historical Association, 1990), 93.

22. For a thorough discussion of this event, see the author's doctoral dissertation.

23. The squabbling was mentioned by people I interviewed who attributed it to "jealousy" and "suspiciousness" among the Italians (Joe Borelli, personal communication, August 13, 1992; Maria Battisti, personal communication, October 1, 1992; Charles Carabello, personal communication, July 10, 1992). Ruth B. DeFrancesco mentions the rivalry in conjunction with the plans to erect the Columbus monument in 1925 in the biography of her husband, Italo DeFrancesco, in *Journey to Another Hilltop: The Life of Dr. De* (Kutztown, Penn.: Kutztown Publishing, 1969), 63.

24. Although some Italians must have witnessed the Sesqui-Centennial Anniversary of Reading in 1898, which spanned an entire week in June, the first record of Italian participation in a city-wide occasion was the 175th Anniversary of the Founding of Reading. Several Polish societies marched in at least one of the parades during the Sesqui-Centennial in 1898: *Official Program Reading's Sesqui-Centennial Jubilee Week*. We can assume that Italian mutual aid societies would have marched in the Sesqui-Centennial, except that none were yet organized. The first to apply for a charter was Spartaco on May 20, 1899. Mary Ryan notes that anyone could apply for a permit to march in parades in nineteenth-century America. Ryan, *Women in Public: Between Banners and Ballots* (Baltimore: The Johns Hopkins University Press, 1990), 31. The official name of the 1923 event was the 175th Anniversary of the Founding of Reading, Pennsylvania. For brevity, it will be referred to as the 175th anniversary celebration.

25. David Glassberg, *American Historical Pageantry* (Chapel Hill: University of North Carolina Press, 1990), 21–23, addresses the participation of ethnic groups in public pageantry and how they often used the opportunity to express their own identities and traditions. For more about the 175th anniversary celebration, see Chapter 5, 252–97, of the author's dissertation.

26. DeFrancesco, *Journey to Another Hilltop*, 63.

27. Ibid., 62.

28. Also, it is worth commenting that the internal tensions persisted into the present day. In commemoration of the 500th anniversary of Columbus' landing, in 1992, Italian-American leaders organized the Columbus '92 Commission to plan events. One of the endeavors was to clean and refurbish the Columbus monument which was accomplished. In addition, a proposal was made to move the statue from its original location to the grounds of the Reading Museum, located in the Wyomissing neighborhood. Ultimately, the statue remained in City Park, but the reported disagreements within the group regarding the proposal indicated that many of the earlier tensions persisted.

29. DeFrancesco, *Journey to Another Hilltop*, 63.

30. Contract dated 17 August 1925 in file folder, "Unveiling and Dedication of the Columbus Monument," Historical Society of Berks County Library, Reading, Pennsylvania.

31. The men who signed the original contract on January 27, 1925, were only six: Ferdinando Colletti, M. G. Albert, Louis Vladi, Antonio DiStasio, Cologero Chiarelli, and Giovanni Viglione. In August, 1925, an additional contract was signed enlarging the dimensions of the statue. Three additional men signed this contract: Livio Sonsini, Michael D'Agostino, and Cologero Camilleri. (See copies of legal contracts in file folder "Unveiling and Dedication of Columbus Monument," Historical Society of Berks County Library.) The ten men who were listed as officers of the Columbus Monument Committee in the official pamphlet, *Unveiling and Dedication of the Columbus Monument*, 39, were Dr. F. Colletti, president; C. Chiarelli, vice president; G Penta,

vice president; L. Sonsini, vice president; L. Vladi, vice president; M. G. Alberti, treasurer; V. Ciofalo, corresponding secretary; G. Zaffiro, financial secretary; C. Gison, recording secretary; and Italo L. DeFrancesco, manager. Forty-seven other men are listed as members of the Monument Committee (see the official pamphlet, 38). Only the men who had signed the contract with the sculptor, however, were legally responsible for the debt. The cost of the statue was incorrectly given as $10,000 in the article by the author, "The Italians of Reading: Forging an Identity in the 1920s," 193.

32. Ann Chiarelli Winters, interview by author, April 23, 1991, Tape31.tra, 36, Historical Society of Berks County Library.

33. *Reading Times*, October 12, 1925, 1.

34. Jesse Mercer Gehman, a resident of New York City, was chosen by the sculptor to model for the statue because of his physique and because he was a former resident of Reading. From the pamphlet *Unveiling and Dedication of the Columbus Monument*, 22.

35. *Reading Times*, October 13, 1925, 1.

36. Oral interview accounts ranged from prejudicial comments made to Italians to social intimidation to systematic discriminatory practices in the workplace and housing. For instance, at the Berkshire Knitting Mills, few Italians were promoted to supervisory positions. Collaborators told me they knew these jobs were reserved for the Germans and the Pennsylvania Germans. See the author's dissertation, 80–81. Ruth B. DeFrancesco notes, "As laborers they were almost uniformly discriminated against, and the condescending attitude and sneering manner of more established groups had its subduing effect. *Journey to Another Hilltop*, 62.

37. See Marcel Mauss, *The Gift: Forms and Functions of Exchange in Archaic Societies* (New York: W. W. Norton, 1967), 10–12, 63, 71. Also see Virginia R. Dominguez, "The Marketing of Heritage." *American Ethnologist* 13 (1986): 553. She draws on the classical analysis of gift giving by anthropologists Marcel Mauss and Marshall Sahlins.

38. Annette Weiner, *Inalienable Possessions: The Paradox of Keeping-while Giving* (Austin: University of Texas Press, 1992), 43, quoted in Amy Shuman, "Food Gifts: Ritual Exchange and the Production of Excess Meaning." *Journal of American Folklore*, 113 (Fall 2000): 505.

39. Lewis Hyde, *The Gift: Imagination and the Erotic Life of Property* (New York: Vintage, 1983), 45.

40. Jane and Peter Schneider, *Cultural and Political Economy in Western Sicily* (New York: Academic Press, 1976), 86–87, 101.

41. The City Council approved the statue in May 1925. In compliance with state law, permission to erect a public monument was also obtained from the Pennsylvania State Art Commission. See Saverino, 1996, 274.

42. Ryan, *Women in Public*, 62, 78.

43. Italo L. DeFrancesco to C. R. Scholl, September 15, 1925, Historical Society of Berks County Library, Reading, Pennsylvania.

44. *Reading Times*, October 13, 1925, 1.

45. Philip Cannistraro, "Fascism and Italian Americans," in *Perspectives in Italian Immigration and Ethnicity: Proceedings of the Symposium Held at Casa Italiana, Columbia University, May 21–23, 1976*, ed. Silvano M. Tomasi (New York: Center for Migration Studies, 1977), 52.

46. Philip Cannistraro, *Blackshirts in Little Italy: Italian Americans and Fascism 1921–1929* (New York: Bordighera, 1999), 6.

47. Madeline Jane Goodman, "The Evolution of Ethnicity: Fascism and Anti-Fascism in the Italian-American Community, 1914–1945" (PhD diss., Carnegie-Mellon University, 1993).

48. Ann Chiarelli Winters, interview by author, April 23, 1991, Tape31.tra, 35, Historical Society of Berks County Library. Historian Warren Susman says that the more sophisticated uses of photographs, radio, and film during the 1930s created a "special community of all Americans (possibly an international one)." Warren Susman, *Culture as History: The Transformation of American Society in the Twentieth Century* (New York: Pantheon, 1973), 160. I suggest that ethnic communities were using these same resources to create a sense of ethnic identity in the United States as well.

49. Robert Orsi, "The Center out There, in Here, and Everywhere Else: The Nature of Pilgrimage to the Shrine of Saint Jude, 1929–1965." *Journal of Social History*, 25 (1991): 218.

50. The organization of the *fascio* in Reading by Brunicardi is noted in *Il Carroccio*, March 1923. The information on the conference in Rome with the accompanying photograph appeared in *Il Carroccio*, vol. X, November 1925. The listing of the "Fascio Nello Degli Innocenti" appeared in *Lega Fascista del Nord America*, 13. I am grateful to Philip V. Cannistraro for providing me with the above information.

51. For a full discussion of role of the YWCA in Reading and of folk dancing groups in particular, see the author's dissertation, Chapter 4 in particular.

52. Battisti scrapbook 2, 47, Historical Society of Berks County Library.

53. Gaetano Salvemini, *Italian Fascist Activities in the United States*, ed. and intro. Philip V. Cannistraro (New York: Center for Migration Studies, 1977), 92–93.

54. *Reading Times*, October 13, 1931, 17. In the 1933 newspaper coverage of Columbus Day, no mention was made of the event planned to take place in Rome. Apparently, the event never actually occurred, according to Madeline Goodman. Personal communication, February 1993.

55. The Italian translation of the telegram sent from Reading appears in Salvemini, 176–77. The original newspaper article about the Fascist party noting Brunicardi as the sender is from *Il Grido della Stirpe*, March 31, 1934 (incorrectly footnoted in Salvemini as May 31, 1934).

56. Information on the formation of the local *Amici dell'Italia* was from an unidentified newspaper clipping in file folder, "Battisti scrapbook 2," 47, Historical Society of Berks County Library. Although undated, from the text, it appears that the meeting was held sometime after Italy's invasion of Ethiopia on October 3, 1935. John P. Diggins, *Mussolini and Fascism: The View From America* (Princeton, N.J.: Princeton University Press, 1972), 304, mentions the Friends of Italy Committee as one organization that staged the letter-writing campaign to United States congressmen to protest Roosevelt's revision of the Neutrality Act regarding Italy and the Ethiopian War. The build-up of enthusiasm for Mussolini's take-over of Ethiopia on October 3, 1935, is described by Salvemini, 201–2. The Italian phrase is translated as "in order to give approval to their fraternal committee who come to swell the ranks and to expand the movement." Filippo Cipri Romano is described as "a Fascist of the old guard" by Salvemini (109). The Fascist stamps were probably printed locally, perhaps in Philadelphia; for information on the stamps, see Maria Battisti, interview by author, November 2 1990, Tape7.tra, 17–18, Historical Society of Berks County Library. For a picture of the stamp, see file folder "Battisti scrapbook 2," 47.

57. Battisti scrapbook 2, 47, Historical Society of Berks County Library. Socialist Park was the name of a public park reflecting the socialist leanings in the area. William C. Pratt, "The Reading Socialist Experience: A Study of Working Class Politics" (PhD diss., Emory University, 1969), found that the movement was the strongest among the Pennsylvania Germans. Although some success was attained among the Polish and Italians, generally they were anti-Socialist, 32–33.

58. Martorana scrapbook, 38–39, 41, Historical Society of Berks County Library.

59. The Italian General Consul was Ludovico Censi, and the judge from Philadelphia was Adrian Bonnelly. Battisti scrapbook 2, 84, 86–87, 90–91, Historical Society of Berks County Library. See pamphlet *Greater Italian Day of the Holy Rosary Church* in "Holy Rosary" file folder, Historical Society of Berks County Library for entertainment schedule.

60. *Greater Italian Day of the Holy Rosary Church* (pamphlet), in "Holy Rosary" file folder, Historical Society of Berks County Library.

61. Diggins, 343–44.

62. The original Italian text is "*In Voi, essa vede il Rappresentate del Sommo DUCE; che ha dato all'Italia Nuova Vita, Nuovo Entusiasmo, Nuovo Valore, Nuova Forza e che la porterà ai più alti destini. . . . La Vostra presenza in questa Patriottica Colonia è simbolo del legame spirituale che unisce gli italiani emigrati alla Grande e Forte Italia. A Voi, . . . il saluto più cordiale di tutti gli Italiani di Reading, e l'assicurazione della loro imperitura Riconoscenza e Fede.*" The above is only a portion of the original statement. Greater Italian Day of the Holy Rosary Church (pamphlet), in "Holy Rosary" file folder, Historical Society of Berks County Library.

63. *The Most Notable Facts Events Activities of Holy Rosary Church 1904–1944*. Historical Society of Berks County Library (1944).

64. *Reading Times*, August 14, 1939, in Battisti scrapbook 2, 103, Historical Society of Berks County Library. See *Reading Times*, August 14, 1939, for details on Tony Galento's arrival. Vincent Cianciosi remembers that the idea to bring in name celebrities such as Joe DiMaggio and several boxers (Primo Carnera, Tony Galento, and Jack Dempsey) was to attract large crowds.

65. Donna R. Gabaccia, *We Are What We Eat: Ethnic Food and the Making of Americans* (Cambridge, Mass.: Harvard University Press, 1998), 136, 150.

Changing St. Gerard's Clothes: An Exercise in Italian-American Catholic Devotion and Material Culture   PETER SAVASTANO

With the exception of public figures such as clergy and published scholars, or those persons already quoted in published texts, all persons appearing in this essay haven been given pseudonyms. In some cases the external circumstances of their lives have been altered in order to protect their privacy. The research conducted for this essay was made possible by a generous grant from the Ford Foundation given to the Newark Project of Drew University.

1. Charles Wesley Churchill, *The Italians of Newark, A Community Study* (New York: Arno Press, 1975 [1942]), 18–27; Michael Immerso, *Newark's Little Italy, The Vanished First Ward* (New Brunswick and Newark, N.J.: Rutgers University Press and the Newark Public Library, 1997), 88.

2. Based on the 1930 U.S. Census as well as estimates made by the leaders of the Italian community in Newark at the time, the number of Italians of all generations who immigrated to Newark during the years of the great migration was between 70,000 and 80,000. See Churchill, *The Italians of Newark*, 1.

3. Immerso, *Newark's Little Italy*, 81–98.

4. Although the saint's family name is Maiella, in the sacred biographies written about him in English his name has been anglicized and is thus spelled *Majella*.

5. Constance Petrucelli Ferrante, "A Walk Through Time: A Symbolic Analysis of the Devotion To St. Gerard Maiella" (PhD dissertation, Rutgers University, New Brunswick, New Jersey, 1993), 212. Participation in the changing of St. Gerard's clothes is by invitation only. There is no formal institutionalization of the practice by St. Lucy's Church itself, where the National Shrine of St. Gerard Maiella is located. Rather, a few prominent devotees of St. Gerard determine who is invited to attend. Many of these prominent devotees have family histories of either financially contributing to the purchase of new clothes for the saint's statue, or for the actual changing of the statue's clothes over the years. Some of these prominent devotees participate because they have made vows to change the clothes the saint's statue wears every year. Others are invited quite randomly. For example, by virtue of my research and fieldwork, I was invited for a number of years. Now that I am no longer "in the field," so to speak, I am no longer invited to the annual changing of St. Gerard's clothes, and this in spite of the fact that I still attend the *festa* and procession in honor of the saint every year.

6. Alphonsus de Liguori, *Alphonsus de Liguori, Selected Writings*, ed. Frederick M. Jones, C.S.S.R., The Classics of Western Spirituality Series (Mahwah, N.J.: Paulist Press, 1999), 25–28.

7. A reader of human hearts is a person who has the capacity to clairvoyantly read a person's deepest thoughts and emotions, which are often so unconscious (though not always) to the person into whose heart the clairvoyant peers.

8. St. Lucy's Church, *St. Lucy's Church, Newark, New Jersey, Centennial Celebration, 1891–1991* (Newark, N.J.: Privately published, 1991), 15.

9. A *Novena* is a devotional practice usually consisting in the recitation of formal prayers and perhaps some litanies (praises) contained in a booklet, which are directed toward Jesus, or the Virgin Mary in their various aspects, or toward any of the saints of the Roman Catholic Church. In the case of Jesus or the Virgin Mary, some of their aspects for which Novenas have been composed are The Sacred Heart of Jesus, The Divine Mercy, Our Lady of the Miraculous Medal, or Our Lady of Mt. Carmel. The prayers are called Novenas because they are said in sequences of nine, i.e., nine times, nine days, nine weeks, and nine months. The word Novena is derived from the Latin word for nine, *Novien*.

10. John Carr, C.S.S.R., *To Heaven Through a Window, St. Gerard Majella* (London: Sands & Co., Ltd., 1946), 107, 111, 327–28; St. Lucy's, *St. Lucy's Church*, 16.

11. Antonio Maria Tannoia [Tannoja], "The Life of Brother Gerard Majella," in *The Lives of the Companions of St. Alphonsus Liguori*, The Modern Saint Series, ed. Antonio Maria Tannoia et al. (London: Richardson & Son, 1849); Priest of the Same Congregation, *Blessed Gerard Majella, Lay-Brother of The Congregation of the Most Holy Redeemer, A Sketch of His Life and the Many Wonderful Favors Obtained Through His Intercession*, Translated from Italian (New York and Cincinnati: Fr. Pustet & Co, 1893); Rev. Edward Saint-Omer, C.S.S.R., *The Wonder-Worker of Our Days, Life, Virtues and Miracles of St. Gerard Majella* (Boston: Mission Church Press, 1907); Carr, *To Heaven Through a Window*; Rev. Joseph F.X. Cevetello, *Crucified with Christ: The Life of St. Gerard Majella, The Mothers' Saint* (Privately published, 1979).

12. I have written about gay men's devotion to St. Gerard in both my dissertation "Will the Real St. Gerard Please Stand Up?" and in the anthology *Gay Religion* (see endnotes 22 and 28 below).

13. Ferrante, "A Walk Through Time," 212.

14. Andrew J. Strathern, *Body Thoughts* (Ann Arbor: University of Michigan Press, 1999), 171–76.

15. Quoted in Harris M. Berger and Giovanna P. Del Negro, *Identity and Everyday Life* (Middletown, Conn.: Wesleyan University Press, 2004), 91.

16. Using physical exercise as a metaphor, by "work-out," I mean that devotees of the saint process their relationships to each other and to the institutional church through their bodies, and emotions, and not only through their minds, within the context of ritual. With respect to "perform," Deborah Kapchan writes: "Insofar as performances are based upon repetitions, whether lines learned, gestures imitated, or discourses reiterated,

they are generic means of tradition making. Indeed, performance genres play an essential (and often essentializing) role in mediation and creation of social communities, whether organized around bonds of nationalism, ethnicity, class status, or gender" in "Performance," 479. Although she doesn't mention it, the creation of social communities organized around "religion" is also relevant to Kapchan's point.

17. Deborah Kapchan, "Morroccan Female Performers Defining The Social Body." *Journal of American Folklore* (Winter 107 (423), 1994) 92–105.

18. M. M. Bakhtin, *The Dialogic Imagination, Four Essays* (Austin: University of Texas Press, 1981), 68–83.

19. My religious heritage is a bit more complicated than indicated in the body of the text. My paternal grandmother was Jewish and converted to Catholicism. My maternal grandfather was originally a Byzantine Rite Catholic (Greek Catholic), but when he came to Newark he attended a Greek Orthodox Church and eventually, even if unofficially as far as I know, was absorbed into the Eastern Orthodox Tradition, where he felt more comfortable.

20. And this is so despite the more complicated religious history and heritage of my family.

21. I have never been able to get a medical explanation for this life-threatening illness. The explanation offered by my mother is that she was very ill when she was born, she was not expected to live but a few days, and she had a hole in the top of her head into which doctors inserted various tubes. However, there were among Southern Italians a number of "folk" diseases, and this may have been one.

22. See Peter Savastano, "Will the Real St. Gerard Please Stand Up? An Ethnographic Study of Symbolic Polysemy, Devotional Practices, Material Culture, Marginality and Difference in the Cult of St. Gerard Maiella" (PhD dissertation, Drew University, 2002), 63–70.

23. Michael Atwood Mason, "I Bow My Head to the Ground: The Creation of Bodily Experience in Cuban American Santeria Initiation." *Journal of American Folklore* (Winter 107 (423), 1994, 23–29), 26.

24. Emilio, interview by Peter Savastano, July 29, 1999, transcription.

25. Tom, interview by Peter Savastano, August 24, 1999, transcription.

26. Donato, interview by Peter Savastano, March 16, 1996, transcription.

27. Peter Savastano, "Will the Real St. Gerard Stand Up?"

28. Peter Savastano, "St. Gerard Teaches Him That Love Cancels That Out: Devotion to St. Gerard Maiella Among Italian-American Catholic Gay Men in Newark, New Jersey," in *Gay Religion*, ed. Scott Thumma and Edward R. Gray (Walnut Creek, Calif., and New York City: AltaMira Press, 2005), 181–201.

29. Colleen McDannell, *Material Christianity, Religion and Popular Culture in America* (New Haven and London: Yale University Press, 1995), 176–86.

30. Peter Savastano, "Will the Real St. Gerard Please Stand Up?"; Peter Savastano, "St. Gerard Teaches Him That Love Cancels That Out."

31. Kapchan, "Moroccan Female Performers Defining the Social Body," 93.

32. Bakhtin, *The Dialogic Imagination*, 52–53, 59.

33. Bakhtin, *The Dialogic Imagination*, 59.

34. Bakhtin, *The Dialogic Imagination*, 58.

35. Michael P. Carroll, *Madonnas That Maim, Popular Catholicism in Italy Since the Fifteenth Century* (Baltimore and London: The Johns Hopkins University Press, 1992), 120–23.

36. Priest, *Blessed Gerard Majella*, 157, 165.

37. Priest, *Blessed Gerard Majella*, 175.

38. Personal conversation, February 11, 2000.

39. St. Lucy's Church, *St. Lucy's Church*, 31.

40. David Freedberg, *The Power of Images, Studies in the History and Theory of Response* (Chicago and London: University of Chicago Press, 1989), 74.

41. Henry Maguire, *The Icons of Their Bodies, Saints and Their Images in Byzantium* (Princteon, N.J.: Princeton University Press, 1996), 57.

42. In *Material Christianity*, Colleen McDannell notes, "religious artifacts act as windows onto a particular religious world," and, "objects become meaningful within specific patterns of relationships" (3–4).

43. Joseph Sciorra, "Yard Shrines and Sidewalk Altars of New York's Italian-Americans," in *Perspectives in Vernacular Architecture III*, ed. Thomas Carter and Bernard L. Herman (Columbia: University of Missouri Press, 1989), 185–98.

44. Deborah Kapchan, "Performance." *Journal of American Folklore* (Fall 108 (430), 1995, 479–508), 480.

45. This quotation is a composite of comments that many different devotees have made to me during personal conversations at different times over the years.

46. Emilio, Savastano interview, 1999.

47. Emilio, Savastano interview, 1999.

48. In the case of the small cup of what appeared to be bodily fluids, this was construed by some of St. Gerard's devotees as a contamination of the purity of their devotion by an ethnic or racial outsider using sorcery or "black magic" believed to be related to the practice of Vodou and/or Santeria.

49. "The implicit dynamic and 'end' of ritualization—that which it does not see itself doing—can be said to be the production of a 'ritualized body.' A ritualized body is a body invested with a 'sense' of ritual," in Bell, *Ritual Theory, Ritual Practice*, 98. (See note 50 for full citation.)

50. Catherine Bell, *Ritual Theory, Ritual Practice* (Oxford and New York: Oxford University Press, 1992), 19–54.

51. Robert A. Orsi, "Everyday Miracles: The Study of Lived Religion," in *Lived Religion in America, Toward A Theory of Practice*, ed. David D. Hall (Princeton, N.J.: Princeton University Press, 1997, 3–21), 8–9.

Cursed Flesh: Faith Healers, Black Magic, and (Re-Membering) Death in a Central Italian Town   LUISA DEL GIUDICE

I wish to acknowledge many who have assisted me in one way or another in this project. I thank foremost my sister, Franca Del Giudice Poldi, who generously opened her home and her heart and shared painful memories in order that we might begin to understand. I thank Giuseppe Poldi's family: Jolanda, Giancarlo, Aldo, Paola, Giuliana; and his friends: Bruno Di Giacomo, Rosario Marigliani, Ermanno Romagna, Fabio Polidori. I also thank the Di Fabio and Maniconi families, Ada, and Paola in particular, who most selflessly sustained my sister's family through harsh times, and continue to extend their warm friendship to me and mine. I must thank all those Terracinese women (on *this*—namely Toronto—and *that* side of the Atlantic) who agreed to be interviewed on such delicate issues as the local belief system: Ada, Paola, Vanda (deceased), Liberata (deceased), Salutina, Maria, Liliana, Rosaria, Rita. On the scholarly side, I thank Augusto Ferraiuolo, Sylvia Marcos, Lizette Larson-Miller, Michael Owen Jones, Mariella Pandolfi, the Rev. Frederick Erickson, Joseph Sciorra, Sabina Magliocco, and Claire Farrer.

1. On this metaphor, see my essay "Interpreting Treasure: Oral Tradition, Archaeology and Horace's Villa," in *The "Horace's Villa" Project: 1997–2003*, 2 vols., ed. Bernard Frischer, Monica De Simone, and Jane Crawford (Oxford, UK: Archaeopress, 2006), (Vol. 1, Ch. E.6) 345–64; Illustrations (Vol. 2), 951–56.

2. We expected, of course, that more advanced Western medicine would prevail over provincial Latina, Italy, and might provide the miracle cure to reverse Pep's disease. UCLA's findings however, confirmed the diagnosis and treatment of his Latina doctors. We sincerely thank Dr. Carter Newton, then-cardiologist at St. John's Hospital in Santa Monica, and friend, for arranging the UCLA examination (with Dr. Champlain, Hematology). The family is forever grateful to him for his kind efforts.

3. Augusto Ferraiuolo offers the tentative suggestion that by analogy, two cases come to mind in which blood plays a part. The first has to do with love spells, in which blood (especially menstrual blood) is used to "bind" the victim to the person on whose behalf the *filtro* (potion) has been concocted. The second, instead, perhaps has to do with an Italian folk medical system that considers the "blocking" of blood to cause a range of diseases—sciatica, among them. Michael Own Jones informs me that the particular case under consideration is a common practice in contagious magic: that is, the transferring of an illness to an animal that dies while the person lives.

4. This woman's illegitimate son died in a car accident shortly after Pep's death. In the Terracina cemetery, across a grassy corridor, their tombs now face each another. Several have commented on this strange twist of fate.

5. Accused of being a "witch doctor," Milingo was relieved of his African post where, in the healing of the body and souls of his community of faithful followers, he had for more than 25 years frequently communed with the spirits of the dead. He was later called to Rome for interrogations and remained there. In 1983, through the personal intervention of John Paul II, he was "rehabilitated" within the Church. Nonetheless, he continued to promote prayer meetings and to conduct mass healing rituals in Italy. In an interview conducted by Paolo Scarano, for the popular *Gente* magazine (on the occasion of Milingo's promotion of his book "*Guaritore d'anime*" ("Healer of Souls"), it was reported that the Italian authorities were considering transferring him to Segni, a small diocese 30 kilometers from Rome, where he could no longer perform mass healings. (Now-) Archbishop E. Milingo continued to be embroiled in controversy and conflict with the Vatican. His marriage to Maria Sung, a follower of Rev. Sun Myung Moon, captured international attention. He then renounced his marriage vows and returned to priestly life (cf. *The New York Times* articles, August 8–30, 2001), but thereafter became an anti-celibacy advocate on the behalf of priests who wish to marry.

Needless to say, I was surprised that the African bishop had traveled to Terracina, that he had come on a private house call in Pep's behalf, and I was fascinated by this cross-cultural, cross-continental contact between indigenous belief systems.

6. I read a version of this chapter at the meeting of the American Anthropological Association, Philadelphia, December 2, 1998.

7. I have recently completed a deeply personal reflection on these years of "wandering in the desert" in forthcoming "Ethnography as Spiritual Practice," which tentatively "resolves" some of the conflicted issues presented here. A preliminary essay based on this research was recently published as "Ethnography and Spiritual Direction: Varieties of Listening," in *Rethinking the Sacred*, Proceedings of the Ninth SIEF Conference in Derry 2008, ed. Ulrika Wolf-Knuts (Department of Comparative Religion, Åbo Akademi University, Religionsvetenskapliga skrifter, 2009), 9–23. See note 18.

8. As a child, in response to my frequent ear infections, I remember my grandmother Luisa performing this healing on me many times, as she did the cure for "worms" or stomach problems, about which I also frequently complained.

9. Although they somewhat shared a name, my paternal grandmother, Luisa (Palmacci) Del Giudice was related only through marriage to Luigina.

10. Another healer, Nazareno, from the hill town of Pico, a man whom Pep visited regularly, instead wanted nothing from Pep during the treatment and said, "When you're well, then you'll bring me something, oil, wine, or something."

11. In her mind, only evil could come of playing cards. Given the social plague of taverns and card playing in her mother's generation, one can understand this aversion. Husbands often came (or were carried) home, drunk from taverns, where they had squandered their meager incomes on wine and gambling. Often, they would then beat their wives and demand sex. Such had even been the case for at least one Del Giudice male.

12. The Marian matrix, indeed, cannot be ignored because it frames and informs traditional Italian womanhood generally, as cultural and religious historians have frequently noted. See, for example, Robert Orsi, *The Madonna of 115th Street* (New Haven: Yale University Press, 1985) and Michael P. Carroll, *Madonnas That Maim: Popular Catholicism in Italy Since the Fifteenth Century* (Baltimore: The Johns Hopkins University Press, 1992).

13. See my forthcoming "Ethnography as Spiritual Practice" for further exploration of the discernment of "call" in priestly and other vocational settings, through "spiritual direction." See note 18.

14. Some of this research was initiated during a writing course entitled "The Heroine's Journey," taught at UCLA by Maureen Murdock (author of *Spinning Inward: Using Guided Imagery With Children* [Boston: Shambhala Publications, 1987], and *The Hero's Daughter* [New York: Fawcett, 1994]), in which many of these issues were discussed. It was in the company of many empathetic women that I began investigating and writing on the women in my family—on Claudia, my oldest sister and somewhat a surrogate mother, as well as my paternal grandmother, among them.

15. These rosary beads drape my grandparents' portraits on my home altar (see photo on page 195) yet remain unused. Only in the early 2000s, however, while sitting by my father's (near) death-bed, it occurred to me that this might be the time to take up a rosary—as my grandmother had apparently wanted me to do. My oldest sister, Claudia, both purchased a rosary and inquired after instructions on its use so that we might pray together in the hospital waiting room while my father underwent open-heart surgery for a second time at the age of 75. In those prayers, I remember calling on my grandmother (his mother) Luisa, and on all his deceased brothers and sisters, for help. My father had a very slim probability for survival. That was in April of 1998, but he lived on. My father's explanation for his tenacity was found in his often-repeated saying: *la malerba non muore mai!* (weeds never die!). His health, however, sharply declined after about a decade. From January to April, 2007, I made three trips home to Toronto, always with the expectation of saying my last goodbyes. Alberto Del Giudice passed away on November 7, 2007.

16. It was my mother who chose this name, hoping to appease a difficult mother-in-law in Luisa (Palmacci) Del Giudice, and endear me to her. Indeed, I am known in my family not as *Luisa*, but as *Setta*, the diminutive of *Lisetta* (itself a diminutive of *Luisa*), by which name my grandmother was known.

17. I have since learned that Del Giudice may also be an Italian-Jewish surname (a modern translation of the Hebrew *Dayyan* (religious, political, and military leader of the ancient Israelites); cf. Emidio De Felice, *Dizionario dei cognomi italiani*, Milan: Mondadori, 1978, 139, s.v. "Giudice"). I asked family members about this possibility but turned up little except this: My father and other family members of his generation had repeatedly maintained the Spanish origins of the family. I had assumed that this may have been based on a confused understanding of our dialect's sharing certain lexical features with Spanish (e.g., *fuego* = fire, and

the like) and not on the possibility of the family actually having come to Italy as part of the 1492 Sephardic diaspora. Could it have been the hope of learning more about Italian Jews that prompted me to organize a symposium at UCLA, entitled *Italian Jews: Memory, Music, Celebration* (October 24–November 5, 2001)?

Nonetheless, I share Magliocco's caution in claiming a "family tradition" of magical inheritances (as have many Italian-American *streghe* [witches], for instance, in the Neo-Pagan movement). See Magliocco, *Witching Culture: Folklore and Neo-Paganism in America* (University Park, Pennsylvania: University of Pennsylvania Press, 2004), subsequently "Imagining the Strega: Folklore Reclamation and the Construction of Italian American Witchcraft," in *Performing Ecstasies: Music, Dance, and Ritual in the Mediterranean*, ed. Luisa Del Giudice and Nancy van Deusen (Ottawa, Canada: The Institute of Mediaeval Music, 2005), 277–301; and in "The Roots of Stregheria: Preliminary Observations on the History of a Reclaimed Tradition," in *Oral History, Oral Culture and Italian Americans*, ed. Luisa Del Giudice (New York: Palgrave Macmillan), 2009.

18. Since the first version of this paper was published in 2001, I have been engaged in various forms of spiritual exploration and further discernment of "callings." I completed an intensive six-month program, entitled "Psyche and the Sacred: A Depth Psychological Approach" at the (Jungian) Pacifica Graduate Institute in Santa Barbara, facilitated by Jungian analyst, Lionel Corbett. I became a "retreat junkie" attending all and any programmed retreats that seemed to answer questions about: discernment, women's spirituality, forgiveness, peace and justice, and other topics too many to recall here. I spent time in private retreat at Benedictine Monasteries. I enrolled in a three-year training program in spiritual direction ("an ancient ministry of listening to sacred stories and experiences of faith and accompanying persons along their spiritual path") with Still-point: The Center for Christian Spirituality, from which I graduated in June, 2007. I am in the process of sorting out and writing about this intensive spiritual journey of the past six years in "Ethnography as Spiritual Practice," which explores the intersections of ethnography and spiritual direction, and considers how both practices have been mutually sustaining. I delivered this paper at the October, 2007, joint annual meeting of the American Folklore Society/Folklore Studies Association of Canada in Quebec, at the Société Internationale d'Ethnologie et Folklore (SIEF) meeting in Derry/Londonderry, N. Ireland, in June of 2008, and at the AIHA annual meeting in New Haven, Connecticut, November, 2008. See note 7.

19. Recent involvement in the United Nations Commission on Status of Women congress in New York, 2008, has reenergized my passion for interfaith peace and justice around women's issues. For example, returning from New York, I presented, along with the Rev'd Joanne Leslie (and former professor of pubic health at UCLA), "Listening Globally, Acting Locally: The Beijing Circles Summit, New York, 2008," which explored ways of advancing the UN Millennium Development Goals, especially as they affected women *locally*. We established and coordinated the first Beijing Circle in Los Angeles (an interfaith group of women and men) at St. Alban's Episcopal Church, Westwood, from September 2008 to June 2009, now in its second year. Further, in the Spring of 2009, I began working with homeless women veterans (in a "New Directions" home), attempting to help these women *find, remember, and tell* their stories, as well as to listen for their own inner voice and life's calling, applying my training as a spiritual director in this most urgent setting.

Imagining the *Strega*: Folklore Reclamation and the Construction of Italian-American Witchcraft   SABINA MAGLIOCCO

1. Throughout the text, I use "Witchcraft" to indicate the revived religion, and "witchcraft" when I refer to the historical and anthropological meaning of the term. The same logic applies to my use of strega to mean a witch in the historical or ethnographic context, and Strega/Stregheria to refer to reclaimed practice.

2. As Wouter Hanegraaf suggests in his monumental study, the term "New Age," despite its popularity, is inherently vague and problematic. Many Witches and Neo-Pagans do not see themselves as part of this trend. For a thorough overview and explanation, see Hanegraaf, *New Age Religion and Western Thought* (Albany: SUNY Press, 1998).

3. See Benedict Anderson, *Imagined Communities* (London: Verso, 1983); Eric Hobsbawm and Terence Ranger, eds., *The Invention of Tradition* (Cambridge: Cambridge University Press, 1983); Werner Sollors, ed., *The Invention of Ethnicity* (New York: Oxford University Press, 1989).

4. Sollors, *Invention of Ethnicity*, xi.

5. Sollors, *Invention of Ethnicity*, xiv.

6. Sollors, *Invention of Ethnicity*, xiv; Regina Bendix, *In Search of Authenticity* (Madison: University of Wisconsin Press, 1997), 4.

7. Michael J. Fischer, "Ethnicity and the Post-Modern Arts of Memory," in *Writing Culture*, ed. James Clifford and George E. Marcus (Berkeley: University of California Press, 1986), 195.

8. Bendix, *Authenticity*; Richard Handler and Joycelyn Linnekin, "Tradition, Genuine or Spurious." *Journal of American Folklore* 97/385 (1984), 273–90.

9. Rudolph J. Vecoli, "Cult and Occult in Italian American Culture: the Persistence of a Religious Heritage," in *Immigrants and Religion in Urban America*, ed. Randall M. Miller and Thomas D. Marzik (Philadelphia: Temple University Press, 1977), 26.

10. Vecoli, "Cult and Occult," 28.

11. Ernesto DeMartino, *Sud e magia* (Milan: Feltrinelli, 1966, 1983), 71; cf. David Hufford, *The Terror that Comes in the Night* (Philadelphia: University of Pennsylvania Press, 1982).

12. Vecoli, "Cult and Occult," 25.

13. Rudolph J. Vecoli, "Peasants and Prelates: Italian Immigrants and the Catholic Church." *Journal of Social History* 2 (1969), 234; Luisa Del Giudice, "Introduction," in *Studies in Italian American Folklore*, ed. Luisa Del Giudice (Logan: Utah State University Press, 1993), 2.

14. Amy Bernardy, 1913, quoted in Vecoli, "Peasants and Prelates," 233.

15. Frances M. Malpezzi and William M. Clements, *Italian American Folklore* (Little Rock: August House, 1992), 131.

16. Peter Hartman and Karyl McIntosh, "Evil Eye Beliefs Collected in Utica, New York." *New York Folklore* 4, 1–4 (1978), 66.

17. Hartman and McIntosh, "Evil Eye Beliefs," 66.

18. Vecoli, "Cult and Occult," 40.

19. See Ronald Hutton, *Triumph of the Moon* (Oxford: Oxford University Press, 1999).

20. For an overview of the movement in North America, see Margot Adler, *Drawing Down the Moon* (Boston: Beacon Press, 1989); Loretta Orion, *Never Again the Burning Times* (Prospect Heights, Ill: Waveland Press, 1995); Helen Berger, *A Community of Witches* (Columbia: University of South Carolina Press, 1999); and Sarah Pike, *Earthly Bodies, Magical Selves* (Berkeley: University of California Press, 2001).

21. Robert Mathiesen, "Charles G. Leland and the Witches of Italy: The Origin of Aradia," in *Aradia, or the Gospel of the Witches*, ed. Charles G. Leland, trans. Mario and Dina Pazzaglini (Blaine, Wash.: Phoenix Publishing, 1998), 36.

22. Chas S. Clifton, "The Significance of Aradia," in *Aradia, or the Gospel of the Witches*, ed. Charles G. Leland, trans. Mario and Dina Pazzaglini (Blaine, Wash.: Phoenix Publishing, 1998), 61.

23. Mathiesen, "Leland and the Witches of Aradia," 168.

24. Clifton, "Significance," 61, 73–36.

25. Leo L. Martello, *Black Magic, Satanism and Voodoo* (Seacaucus, N.J.: Castle Books, 1973), 14.

26. Martello, *Magic*, 9.

27. Leo L. Martello, *Weird Ways of Witchcraft* (Seacaucus, N.J.: Castle Books, 1972), 71.

28. Leo M. Martello, *Witchcraft: The Old Religion* (Seacaucus, NJ, 1975), 150–56.

29. Martello, *Witchcraft*, 148.

30. Martello, *Witchcraft*, 71–72.

31. Martello, *Witchcraft*, 163.

32. Martello, *Black Magic*, 14.

33. Interview with Lori Bruno, August 26, 2000.

34. Interview with Lori Bruno, August 26, 2000.

35. Similar altered states of consciousness have been documented in Italian folk healers by Ernesto De-Martino in *Sud e magia* (Milano: Feltrinelli, 1966/87), 7; and Luisa Selis, "Prime ricerche sulla presenza delle streghe in Sardegna oggi," in *L'erba delle donne: maghe, strghe, guaritrici* (Rome: Roberto Napoleone Editore, 1978), 141.

36. Interview with Lori Bruno, August 26, 2000.

37. Raven Grimassi, *The Ways of the Strega* (St. Paul: Llewellyn Press, 1995), xiv.

38. Grimassi, *Strega*, xviii.

39. Recent DNA evidence suggests that the Etruscans were not indigenous to the Italian peninsula, but came from the Near East.

40. Grimassi has recently begun to collect family folklore, but has not published this material out of a desire to maintain his family's privacy and the secrecy of the tradition.

41. No such word appears in Nicola Zingarelli's *Vocabolario della lingua italiana* (Milano: Zanichelli, 1977), the most comprehensive dictionary of the Italian language. The closest is the adjective *grimo*, meaning "wrinkled, wizened" or "poor, wretched" (777).

42. Sabina Magliocco, "Playing with Food: the Negotiation of Identity in the Ethnic Display Event by Italian Americans in Clinton, Indiana," in *Studies in Italian American Folklore*, ed. Luisa Del Giudice (Logan: Utah State University Press, 1993), 107–26.

43. Grimassi, *Strega*, 200–1 and *Hereditary Witchcraft* (St. Paul: Llewellyn Press, 1999), 56–57.

44. Grimassi, *Strega*, 201 and *Hereditary Witchcraft*, 56.

45. Grimassi, *Strega*, 102–3.

46. Grimassi, *Hereditary Witchcraft*, 58.

47. Malpezzi and Clements, *Italian American Folklore*, 144.

48. Grimassi, *Strega*, xviii.

49. Interview with Raven Grimassi, August 23, 2000.

50. Grimassi and his partner closed the shop in 2004, and have since been doing business online. In 2009, they relocated to Massachusetts.

51. Wiccan ritual knife.

52. E-mail communication with Fabrisia, July 6, 2000.

53. That is, were practitioners of a pagan religion.

54. E-mail communication with Fabrisia, July 6, 2000.

55. This information is gleaned from Philip's website: http://members.tripod.com/~benandanti/.

56. Clifton, "Significance," 60.

Contributors

John Allan Cicala earned his doctorate in Folklore and American Studies at the Folklore Institute, Indiana University. He has published in material culture theory, urban folklore, and Italian folklife genres within the American experience. Currently, he is preparing a field-based study on Michigan's Italian folk traditions that will be published by Michigan State University Press.

Simone Cinotto holds a Ph.D. in American history and teaches twentieth-century history at the University of Gastronomic Sciences, Pollenzo (Italy), American history at the University of Turin, and Italian American studies at New York University. He is the author of *Una famiglia che mangia insieme: Cibo ed etnicità nella comunità italoamericana di New York, 1920–1940* (Otto, 2001) and *Soft Soil Black Grape: Labor, Social Capital, and Race in the Experience of Italian Winemakers in California*, which will be published by New York University Press.

Luisa Del Giudice, Ph.D., ethnographer and oral historian, was founder and director of the Italian Oral History Institute in Los Angeles (1994–2007) and professor of Italian folklore at UCLA (1995–2001). She has published widely, has produced many public events in Los Angeles, and is an honorary Fellow of the American Folklore Society and *Cavaliere* of the Italian Republic.

Joseph J. Inguanti has a Ph.D. in History of Art from Yale and is a professor of art history at Southern Connecticut State University. He maintains that the landscape—whether expressed in real space, in memory, in literature, or in material culture—plays a profound role in the construction of Italian-American identity. His research explores the meaning and history of the actual landscapes, imaginary landscapes, Italian-American grave-tending, and representations of landscapes in textiles and ephemeral art of Italian Americans.

Marion S. Jacobson earned her doctorate in music with a specialization in ethnomusicology from New York University. She has taught undergraduate courses in world music, Western music history, and world civilizations at New York University, SUNY New Paltz, and the Albany College of Pharmacy. She is currently working on a book entitled *Squeeze This! Accordion Culture in the United States in the Twentieth Century* (University of Illinois Press, 2011), which traces the piano accordion's popularity.

Sabina Magliocco is professor and chair of the Department of Anthropology at California State University, Northridge. A pioneering scholar of modern Paganisms, she is the author of *Witching Culture: Folklore and Neopaganism in America* (University of Pennsylvania Press, 2004) and numerous other books and articles. She has been awarded grants from the National Endowment for the Humanities and from the Guggenheim and Hewlett foundations. She is an honorary Fellow of the American Folklore Society.

Lara Pascali holds a B.A. in Italian studies and a M. Arch. in domestic environments from McGill University, and an M.A. in early American culture from the University of Delaware. Her training and research draw upon vernacular architecture, folklore, cultural landscape, and material culture studies to examine human relationships with the material world.

Peter Savastano holds a Ph.D. and M.Phil. in religion and society from Drew University. He is assistant professor in the Department of Sociology and Anthropology at Seton Hall University.

Dr. Savastano's research interests include religion and sexuality; lived religion within the African-based traditions of the Americas; Italian-American Roman Catholic devotional practices; and altered states of consciousness.

Joan L. Saverino is the Director of Education and Outreach at the Historical Society of Pennsylvania, where she created and directs PhilaPlace (www.philaplace.org), a collaborative neighborhood history and culture project. Saverino has a masters from the George Washington University and a doctorate from the University of Pennsylvania. Her work also appears in the edited volume *Global Philadelphia (Temple University Press, 2010)*.

Kenneth Scambray is professor of English at the University of La Verne. His poetry appears regularly in national reviews. His most recent two works are *Surface Roots: Stories* (Guernica, 2004) and *Queen Calafia's Paradise: California and the Italian American Novel* (Fairleigh Dickinson University Press, 2007).

Joseph Sciorra earned his doctorate in Folklore and Folklife at the University of Pennsylvania and is the associate director of Academic and Cultural Programs at Queens College's John D. Calandra Italian American Institute. He is editor of the social science journal *Italian American Review*, co-editor of poet Vincenzo Ancona's bilingual anthology *Malidittu la lingua/Damned Language* (Legas, 1990; republished 2010), and author of *R.I.P.: Memorial Wall Art* (Henry Holt & Co., 1994; Thames and Hudson, 2002). As the avatar "Joey Skee," Sciorra maintains the blog "Occhio contro occhio" at www.i-italy.org.

Index